THE PRESTIGE PR
A COMPARATIVE STUDY
OF POLITICAL SYMBOLS

by Ithiel de Sola Pool
with the collaboration of
Harold D. Lasswell, Daniel Lerner
Mary Chapman
Barbara Conner
Barbara Lamb
Barbara Marshall
Eva Meyer
Elena Schueller
Marina S. Tinkoff

THE M.I.T. PRESS
Cambridge, Massachusetts, and London, England

CONTENTS

v

Appendixes   281

FOREWORD

The RADIR* Project, a five-year pilot study (1947-52) sponsored by the Carnegie Corporation at Stanford's Hoover Institution, sought to devise and test systematic new ways of describing and interpreting major trends of contemporary history—what we called "the world revolution of our time." We focused our attention on an illuminating index of revolution proposed by Lasswell: "change in the composition and vocabulary of the ruling few."

This entailed a research emphasis on two types of studies: "Elites" and "Symbols." Our studies of the recruitment, composition, and behavior of "the ruling few" contrasted the relatively stable western elites over the period 1890-1950 with the revolutionary elites that convulsed much of Eurasia during the quarter-century between the world wars. These RADIR studies of the Bolsheviks, Nazis, Fascists, as well as the Kuomintang and Communist leadership of China have already reappeared in this M.I.T. Press series as *World Revolutionary Elites.* Books on the more stable western elites are planned for the future. Linkages with current work on the social backgrounds of elites in developing countries are exhibited in the studies of Turkey by Frey, Ceylon by Singer, Algeria by Quandt.

Our RADIR studies of changes in elite vocabulary took the form of a content analysis of the prestige press in the major world powers, here reprinted with a new Preface by its principal author. Together with its wartime predecessor, already reprinted as *Language of Politics,* the volume brings together in this series the two major world attention surveys from the early period of content analysis. Current work, applying the new computer technology stressed in Professor Pool's Preface, is represented in the series by *The General Inquirer* and *User's Manual* by Philip J. Stone and his associates.

For the new edition here presented, four main studies in content analysis produced by the RADIR Project have been selected and lightly adapted. The introductory chapter on "The Comparative Study of Symbols" was a joint product of Lasswell, Lerner, and Pool. Responsibility for the work

---

*RADIR is an acronym for Revolution And the Development of International Relations.

vii

reported in the next three chapters divided as follows: Lasswell was mainly responsible for the research design; Lerner (with a valuable assist from Bert F. Hoselitz in the summer of 1948) was mainly responsible for the data-processing and partially responsible for the data-analysis; Pool took over the completion of data-analysis and is the sole author of the three substantive chapters.

The present volume is a welcome addition to this series because it exemplifies with particular point our editorial interest in the continuity of empirical research on the historical context of current issues of public policy as they arise from the continuing "world revolution of our time."

Harold D. Lasswell
Daniel Lerner

INTRODUCTION
TO THE NEW EDITION

Every generation complains about the changes since its youth. The new generation is always being described as different from those who went before. A few years ago we were told that youth was disenchanted and detached, then that they were beat, and now that they are in rebellion. We are told that their mores are changing. But how do we know? Cynics may believe that it is all an illusion and that *plus ça change plus c'est la même chose.*

Recent research on sex practices provides an intriguing illustration of how hard it is to know if mores have changed. From all sides we are told that we are in a sexual revolution. Yet the few careful studies that have been made show no marked trend in the frequency of premarital sex relations over the past thirty years. When faced with such data, the interpreter says that perhaps young people are not behaving very differently, but they are talking quite differently. They are no longer hypocritical, ashamed, beset with feelings of guilt. Sex, it is asserted, has come out into the open. That assertion may be right, but how do we know? What kind of evidence can we produce about the flow of conversation to match the surprising evidence on practices? Could it not be that in the absence of evidence we are being fooled about the changes of attitudes just as we would have been about the changes in practice if we had not had data? That is a disturbing doubt, and one that can be matched when we talk about the history of thought and attitudes in any field.

There is little question that the period from 1890 to 1950 was a period of vast change not only in the condition of man, but also in his beliefs and values. Science, social relations, and politics were all in revolution. But can we solidly document these changes? How can we demonstrate the rise of democratic ideology or the shifts in national feelings? Traditional approaches to the history of ideas provide us with no truly satisfactory ways of providing evidence of asserted trends. The usual procedure used in histories of thought is simply to present striking quotations drawn from the works of leading thinkers; it is assumed that they somehow represent their societies.

Clearly, what is needed is what are currently being called social indicators.* We have economic indicators, such as price indexes or GNP to tell us how the economy is moving every year. We have indicators of demo-graphic trends in the census figures that we use to keep tabs on the population explosion. We need indicators of changes in men's thoughts, attitudes, moods, expectations, and values. There is no reason why opti-mism and pessimism, liberalism and conservatism, friendship and hostility should not be measured as they rise and fall, to give to the history of ideas some of the same solidity as is possessed by the history of actions. That was an objective of the RADIR project, which traced the flow of symbols in the newspapers of five countries during the period from 1890 to 1950,† a period that we called "the world revolution of our time."

Content analysis is a systematic and rigorous way of doing what human-ists have always done, namely, to note what symbols are used in available bodies of text and thereby to document the evolution of ideas. Such observation of the flow of symbols may be called content analysis if enough attention is paid to the procedures of observation to make the operation replicable. Other definitions of content analysis can be found in the literature. This, however, seems a useful definition. We can call a study a content analysis if the procedures used for processing the text are well enough defined so that a second person going through the same text would sort the same passages into the same interpretive boxes. Content analysis may be quantitative or it may deal with single unique statements. What makes it different from the usual procedures of intellectual history is that the rules for sampling the flow of text are made rigorous and explicit, and so are the rules for sorting the quotations as instances in support of one hypothesis or another.

As one of the more empirical and positivistic ways of producing intelli-gence about man's attitudes, expectations, and values, content analysis has been a particularly controversial manifestation of the scientific spirit. It has been controversial because its object of study, symbol flows, comes so close to the humanists' own domain of study. *Explication de texte* or the writings of commentaries on great books has been the life work of scholars through hundreds of years. Historians, Kremlinologists, lawyers, critics, all make their living by looking for the implications of men's choices of words.

The pretensions of social scientists to poach upon the humanists' exper-tise in interpreting ideologies, doctrines, and value systems seemed particu-larly intolerable and philistine to those who already disapproved of the social scientists' claims to have a better kind of magic. Content analysts

---

*Raymond A. Bauer, ed., *Social Indicators* (Cambridge, Mass.: M.I.T. Press, 1966).

†The present volume reprints (with some excisions) the reports of the RADIR project symbol studies that first appeared in 1951-1953.

have been repeatedly attacked on such grounds as that intellectual processes are too complex to be treated quantitatively, or the allegation that in counting manifest symbols the content analyst disregards the nuances of meaning that can only be ascertained from the context, or the claim that content analysts must naïvely count each symbol as having equal significance.

It is true that in the early days of content analysis when tabulations were made without the aid of a computer, the analyst often settled on a simplified criterion for counting which distorted the meaning but made the labor of counting more tolerable. Oversimplification was indeed one of the problems of content analysis in precomputer days. That need be less true today. The content analyst using a computer can often make his procedures of the degree of complexity that the job calls for. That was certainly not true at the time when the studies in this volume were done. Drastic simplification of categories had to be made to make the job feasible at all. At the same time we must insist, in reply to the critic, that some simplification is the essence of science. Holistic phenomenological description is neither good history, nor good philosophy, nor good science. Reduction of complexity to explanatory simplifications is exactly what we always strive to achieve. The issue is one of degree. Uniformity and rigorously defined procedures, if not too simple, are to be desired and not dismissed as an abuse.

We therefore believe that, because content analysis produces quantitative measures that are reasonably independent of the subjectivity of the observer, it is a convenient observational tool to use in the testing of hypotheses about changes in ideas.

Content analysis is only an observational device. It is not in itself science. An observational device that is useful for science may also be used in many other ways. Telescopes are used for recreation, for navigation, and for education, as well as for science. Content analysis, too, has many possible uses, including the scoring of psychological tests (e.g., for measuring need achievement), the prediction of political behavior (e.g., in wartime intelligence), and the comparison of propaganda from different sources.

One of the more significant uses of content analysis is its intelligence function. It provides a society with a mirror to itself and a way of observing the external environment in which it lives. It can be used as a tool for the measurement of trends in society—in short, as a social indicator. It was this notion of providing a set of measurements on the ideological trends that constituted the world revolution of our time that lay behind both of the major content analysis efforts of the 1940s: the Library of Congress wartime "World Attention Survey" and the RADIR studies at the Hoover Institute starting in 1948. These were both programs that made more than a passing effort at contributing to generalizing science, but they were also efforts to contribute to policy by recording and exposing developmental trends in values and in ideology in the modern world. The Library of Congress effort attempted to plot what changes were taking place in the mass media of the major nations during the then current war period. In media from different countries, it tracked awareness of and attitudes towards other nations and major political symbols. The basic categories used were favorable (plus) and unfavorable (minus) treatment of self and other. These are the fundamental set of political categories. They are the facts of which every diplomat, journalist, and politician intuitively keeps track. Nonetheless, as an intelligence operation on a current world crisis, the project had limited success. It was operating beyond the state of the art and, as a result, contributed far more to content analysis methodology that might at some future time contribute to intelligence than it contributed to substantive understanding of the enemy at that time. *The Language of Politics,* reprinted in the same series as the present volume,* summarizes the contributions of that project.

In a parallel effort at the same time in the Foreign Broadcast Intelligence Service, much more intuitive methods of content analysis were used with considerable success to anticipate German actions. These were complementary rather than competing efforts and we have learned much from both. The lessons of the FBIS effort have been thoroughly analyzed and evaluated for intelligence purposes by Alexander George in his book on *Propaganda Analysis.*† George demonstrates that at that time the efforts in the FBIS to use formal quantitative methods were fruitless. The technology then available for quantification did not permit flexibility either in the analysis in order to take account of considerations of propaganda strategy or in evaluating the varied importance of statements in different contexts. Quantification required rather mechanical simplifications that frustrated the intelligence objectives.

It should be noted that in 1968 that would no longer be true. The possibility of keypunching text into computer-readable form and of the analyst retrieving and regrouping textual material at the console in an interactive mode would lead to very different conclusions about the practical value of quantification than those that George reached regarding the effort in the 1940s. The quantification experiments of the Library of Congress effort laid a methodological basis for things that we can do only today.

---

*Harold D. Lasswell, Nathan Leites, et al., *The Language of Politics* (Cambridge, Mass.: M.I.T. Press, 1965).

†Alexander L. George, *Propaganda Analysis* (Evanston, Ill.: Row, Peterson, 1959). Cf. also Ernst Kris and Hans Speier, *German Radio Propaganda* (London: Oxford University Press, 1951).

The next major experiment with content analysis was the RADIR project, the symbol studies of which are reprinted here. The RADIR project was also a world attention survey, but this time for a sixty—year period. Newspaper editorials from prestige papers in five countries were examined to ascertain the rise and fall of major political concepts, particularly those pertaining to democracy and authoritarianism, violence and peace, and self and other (i.e., identity). A number of interesting, and for once documented, trends in the belief systems of our times emerged.

The rise in the currency of democratic ideology is abundantly documented. The word has become one of the sacred words of our time appropriated by every political movement to its own use. We show in Chapter 3 that its frequency in newspaper editorials rose from one editorial in every thirty-five before World War I to one in seven since World War II, a fivefold increase.

"For all to rule and be ruled in turn," was, according to Aristotle, a principle of liberty and the basis of democracy. To achieve this democracy in extreme form he suggested, among other things, election by lot, short terms of office, rotation of office, a weak bureaucracy, pay for public office, abolition of property qualifications and wide extension of citizenship, popular juries, conversion of private assocations into public ones, social welfare and security measures, redistribution of land or graduated taxes, avoidance of standing armies.

Thus, among the conflicting conceptions of democracy that existed in 1890 when our study starts, one can distinguish at least three: the rule of the masses, some procedures such as election by lot by which popular rule may be exercised, and, finally, a society with personal freedom. In the data that follow we note the rise and fall of these alternative concepts.

The rise in attention to democracy was more than just a fad in the use of a word. Along with increased use of the word "democracy" went increased reference to the class of objectives associated with it. At the same time, in the democratic states the conservative symbols of order and authority waned in use. Democracy, however, was everywhere less and less often interpreted in terms of the institutions of representative government and more often in terms of mass participation. Not only do we find the ratio of references to the masses to references to representative government rising in all five countries studied, but also we find that the proportion of favorable judgments of the masses rose. It is in Russia where the Marxist tradition provided the official interpretation of the word "democracy" that this trend was most marked.

The Communist movement was part and parcel of the democratic movement until after 1848. Marx was vice-president of the "Democratic Union" in Brussels in 1847. In the *Communist Manifesto* he describes the revolution and incidentally defines democracy as follows: "The first step in the revolution by the working class is to raise the proletariat to the position of ruling class, to establish democracy."

But the changing trend in the use of the word democracy, so marked in Soviet editorials (if not in Soviet practice), can be matched, even if less sharply, in the classic countries of liberal democracy, Britain and the United States. There, too, our study has revealed a reversal of the late nineteenth century trend by which the word democracy came to be adopted to refer to practices that earlier were called representative government or free government. The older mass conception of democracy has increasingly become the newer conception in the West, too. President Johnson's poverty program with "maximum feasible participation" of the poor came a decade and a half after the end of the period of our studies. The trend we measured foreshadowed the shape of things to come, for the trend toward an increasingly participatory conception of democracy seems to be with us still.

The most radical shifts in symbolism in the sixty years of our study are found, not surprisingly, in Russia and Germany. Revolutions produce great changes in language. It happened to French after 1789 and to Russian after 1917. But the sharpness of symbolic shifts in Russia and Germany, we find below, has another cause, too—the instability of totalitarian regimes. .Democratic systems have the inherent stability of any system governed by the law of large numbers. Pluralistic decisions result in gradual and limited change. Centralized control, often intended to stem the flow of change, results in a system that oscillates wildly when the dominant authorities change their minds. Our world attention survey shows this clearly. The censored presses zig and zag as the editorial writers over-conform to the demands of the prevailing line.

The Soviet press not only shifted markedly in its symbolic treatment of democracy and the people, but also dramatically in presenting the national self in relation to the outside world. There was a dominant trend of isolationism and nationalism, not only in comparison to the temporary internationalism of the years of the Revolution, but also in comparison to the Czarist era. This nationalist trend prevailed amid short-run fluctuations. The decline of Marxist ideology in favor of an ordinary plebian nationalist symbolism in the Soviet Union continued through the various zigs and zags of the Party line. More recent events, for example, the Sino-Soviet dispute and the classic sphere-of-influence approach by the Soviet Union towards Czechoslovakia, suggest once more that the trends noted up to 1950 were often predictive and are with us still. In a world in which the other countries we studied are generally paying increased attention to the outside world and to symbols of internationalism, the Soviet editorials are moving the other way. These and similar historical findings are to be found in the pages to follow.

Undoubtedly the reader would like to know which of the trends that were under way in 1950 have continued in the subsequent two decades. The author shares this curiosity. Unfortunately, the content analysis done in the RADIR studies has not been continued. It would be fascinating to know whether the Soviet press has continued the trend toward isolationist inattention to the outside world in an era when it is no longer able to shut out foreign shortwave radio and when receivers are available to perhaps 40 percent of the population. Has the Soviet press continued its extraordinarily chauvinistic set of symbols with a unique emphasis on FATHER-LAND and PATRIOTISM? We observed that hostile judgments of foreign countries waxed in situations of national frustration and waned as a nation gained power; has that pattern continued? For example, has the American press in this era of supreme power been temperate? Has *Izvestia* become more temperate as Soviet power has grown? Has the British press begun to denigrate foreign nations as British power declined? The closing sentence of this book identified bipolarity as the dominant trend in the closing years of the period covered. Has the bipolarity of the relations among the great powers continued to grow or even continued unabated at 1950 levels? Perhaps we were writing at the moment of the peak of polarization. Would an examination of the last twenty years reveal the French press drifting away from a solid Western alliance? More problematical is what has happened in the German press. Would a continuing analysis show a general weakening of Western solidarity in Germany as well as France or would it show the replacement of France by Germany as the close neighbor of the United States and Britain? How far does the graphic model of psychological distances among the four countries portrayed in the last chapter continue to describe the structure of relationships in the world today? We predicted an increasing emphasis on symbols of mass participation in the American symbolism of democracy. Has that happened? Is it demonstrated by the new symbols of community action? Has attention to the processes of representative government continued to wane, despite the debates about decentralization, community participation, and the electoral college? Has it continued to wane in France despite the Gaullist revolution and the passage from the Fourth Republic to the Fifth? Have FREEDOM and LIBERTY continued to be taboo subjects in the Soviet Union, or has the regime gained enough confidence to try to appropriate such terms for itself? We might also ask whether the prestige papers as an institution have remained unaffected by the media revolution that is now going on. Are they as distinct a type of paper, as easily identifed as in the past, as likely to be semiofficial mouthpieces of the government as they were in the past? For the moment these questions remain to intrigue us. Perhaps some time in the coming years a new content analysis will be undertaken to carry on the work done in the RADIR project and help us answer some of these questions. Perhaps, indeed, we are moving into an era in which there will be continuous auditing of symbolic trends to provide us with current social indicators rather than our having to wait for answers till decades later.

The studies presented were done in the precomputer era. They therefore suffer from a forced simplification of analysis. For example, the results of the RADIR project are not in sufficient detail to be truly policy relevant. Policy relevance was certainly one of our objectives. A byproduct of the RADIR project was a volume called *The Policy Sciences.** Yet it seems clear that, whatever the objectives of the RADIR content analyses, policy relevance in the sense of immediate utility was not achieved. A policy maker is not satisfied to be told that the total focus in American society on violence is growing, though he might find that fact, documented below, interesting and disturbing and thought-provoking. He wants to know such things as fluctuations in the mood in specific neighborhoods of thirteen cities during three hot months of the year. The technology available in 1953 precluded anything but a highly generalized broad sweep approach to a sixty-year content analysis.

In the decade and a half since these papers were first published, the systematic study of verbal material has undergone a revolution due to three technological developments: the computer, structural linguistics, and information retrieval. In the intervening period little large-scale content analysis was done; it was too tedious. But now content analysis has acquired a new lease on life.

Content analysis, as it was practiced in the years from 1935 to 1953 was a laborious business. Teams of coders went through the samples of text being analyzed and entered strings of symbols on coding sheets. That, however, was only the beginning. Then that mass of symbols had to be subjected to statistical analysis. But as the methodological paper in this volume explains, mere counts of single symbols could be misleading. Language has structure. Any kind of count that disregards the context of other symbols in which any given symbol appears is not likely to be very meaningful. Possible combinations of symbols are so numerous and complex that hand counts of relevant verbal structure are likely to prove beyond the capacity of the researcher and, therefore, he may be tempted to simplify what he counts beyond the point of usefulness.

In the summary of the RADIR project in 1953 we noted this difficulty and the prospect of a solution that was just appearing over the horizon, namely, the computer. That has turned out to be the case. Research using content analysis has revived in the last few years, thanks to machine computation.

The leading program for computerized content analysis is Philip Stone's

*Daniel Lerner and Harold D. Lasswell, eds., *The Policy Sciences* (Stanford, Calif.: Stanford University Press, 1951).

General Inquirer,* which has already been published, along with a *User's Manual,* in this series. In these volumes, Stone summarizes much of the work that has been done using his program, and also formulates the principles and procedures on which the program works. It is unlikely that anyone will again do the kind of voluminous content analysis represented by the RADIR project except by computer.

Other developments that are likely to change content analysis in the future are the progress in structural linguistics and in information retrieval, both of which also owe much to the computer. We now can store a large dictionary of words in computer memory and have the computer recognize the occurences (pretty much regardless of word form) of the dictionary items. We do not yet know, however, how to instruct the computer reliably to make sense out of grammatical combinations of these words. That lies somewhere in the future, though linguists have made substantial progress toward that goal. Work both on machine translation and on pure linguistics have established how hard the problem is, but have also succeeded in small part in devising systems to recognize sentences that have not been previously stored in computer memory and classify them according to meaning. It is not inconceivable, for example, that one could get fairly good computer recognition of sentences representing pro-administration and anti-administration views or representing liberal and conservative viewpoints. Of course, one cannot ask for complete correspondence between a computer and any one human judge, any more than there would be complete correspondence between any two judges, but we have made enormous progress in the application of linguistics if we can get a computer into nearly the same reliability league in classifying ordinary content material as a human judge. That now seems a future, but not impossible, goal.

That kind of capability is precisely what most information retrieval systems aim at. They, too, have to recognize what text is relevant to some category in which retrieval is being sought. That is done in various ways. Some systems require that tag words describing the subject matter be appended to the text, but other systems search directly in the text for key words.[†] To avoid retrieval of much irrelevant material, the text scanned may be limited to the most indicative areas, such as abstracts or topic sentences. The TIP system, for example, as one of its routines, selects articles which cite many of the same references as a criterion article. One feature which retrieval systems have in common with content analysis is the need to store large bodies of text and scan them quickly. The content

---

*Philip Stone, *General Inquirer: A Computer Approach to Content Analysis* (Cambridge, Mass.: M.I.T. Press, 1966).

[†]The Aspen Documentary Retrieval System used at the University of Pittsburgh searches the corpus of laws, for example, to retrieve any word that the searcher specifies.

analysis system *tabulates* instances of hits in the text, whereas a retrieval system *delivers* listings of these instances to the user. Otherwise their logic is very similar.

Clearly, in 1953 we were in no position to do any of these things efficiently. Today we have made much progress toward the realizable goal of efficient use of content analysis.

In the years since the initial publication of the RADIR symbol studies, a number of interesting analyses have appeared, though they each had a more restricted function than that of surveying world attention. They generally sought to provide parsimonious tests of hypotheses rather than serving the intelligence function of providing social indicators. Perhaps the most novel application of content analysis in that period was David McClelland's development of methods for scoring need for achievement in such bodies of text as children's primers. McClelland hypothesized that economic development takes place in a country when an appropriate personality syndrome is widely prevalent in the population, a syndrome that stresses achievement by the taking of modest risks to realize measurable goals. The presence of such a psychological orientation in a population is not open to easy direct observation, but it should appear as a recurrent theme in works of fantasy such as folktales or children's stories. McClelland devised a content analysis scheme which he applied to samples of stories from children's primers. Some decades after shifts toward achievement orientation appeared in the stories that a culture offered its young, its economy tended to show accelerated development.*

Other applications of content analysis in the decade after the RADIR studies that come somewhat closer in method and spirit to the tradition of the work represented in this volume are Richard Merritt's study of the newspapers of the era of the American Revolution[†] and Karin Dovring's analysis of land reform propaganda.[‡] Both these studies focus on political ideology and propaganda and examine trends in historical symbol flows. These excellent pieces of work attest to the continuing interest in the use of content analysis as an indicator of political trends.

Still more recently, as we noted above, the most significant work in content analysis has been that which uses the *General Inquirer*. Robert North, a member of the original RADIR project team, has done widely noted work at Stanford University on the flow of messages in the crisis that ended with the outbreak of World War I. He has also done some

---

*David C. McClelland, *The Achieving Society* (New York: The Free Press, paperback edition, 1967), pp. 70-79, 453-474.

[†]Richard L. Merritt, *Symbols of American Community, 1735-1775* (New Haven: Yale University Press, 1966).

[‡]Karin Dovring, "Land Reform As A Propaganda Theme," in Folke Dovring, *Land and Labor in Europe (1900-1950)* (The Hague: M. Nijhoff, 1956).

similar work with the *General Inquirer* on Chinese Communist and Soviet communications.*

One current study that can be described as a world attention survey is being conducted by the United Nations Institute for Training and Research UNITAR) under the direction of Dr. Alexander Szalai. For a six-week period in 1968, 1777 newspapers, 220 radio stations, and 96 TV stations in 49 countries were examined for references to the United Nations. A purpose of the study was to compare the UN's output of information with the output that ultimately comes through the media.

We shall not try to predict how long it will be before someone again picks up the challenge to provide society, by content analysis, with a continuous running measure of its interests and concerns. Most technical prerequisites for such an effort now exist. It is true that the *General Inquirer,* as so far developed, is efficient only for moderate-sized text bases, but by following out the basic conceptions of that program, it would be perfectly feasible to develop programs using more advanced machines that would be geared to rapid processing of larger bodies of text. There are numerous retrieval programs that lack the Inquirer's flexibility, but which scan great bodies of text rapidly. The main technological prerequisites for a large-scale content analysis system that reviews great bodies of text on a continuing basis are three: (1) One needs a computer system with large rapid-access bulk memory such as disk packs or other still more advanced devices for storing extensive bodies of text. (2) The programmer needs to have available to him list or string languages so that he can operate effectively on the complex relational data of language, and the user needs higher-order applications languages by which he can add new files and new items to files at will and find his way efficiently to items in them. (3) The user needs an on-line interactive computer system so that he can explore the stored text intelligently step by step instead of getting swamped in data. With these facilities a large-scale attention survey by content analysis could be effectively done.

What is feasible is, however, not necessarily useful. The standard answer of mountain climbers when asked why climb a high peak is that "it is there." That is not a good enough reason for engaging in content analysis. The fact that propaganda, editorials, speeches, political material of all sorts pour out in the public media does not per se make it useful to subject these materials to quantitative measurement of what is in them and how that changes.

Yet it would be useful. One of the greatest problems facing policy makers is the vast flow of unprocessed information that pours past them.

---

*Cf. Ole R. Holsti, "External Conflict and Internal Consensus: The Sino-Soviet Case," in Robert C. North et al., *Content Analysis* (Evanston, Ill.: Northwestern University Press, 1963).

Every day the Department of State receives about two thousand cables from abroad. Every day the Foreign Broadcast Intelligence Service records and transcribes the news and public affairs programs broadcast by hundreds of radio stations around the world. Every day, politicians, intelligence analysts, and public servants comb newspaper columns and editorials from places of interest looking for clues to reactions to events by various groups.

No doubt computerized processing and analysis of this flood of material is no panacea. Trivial and irrelevant material can be analyzed. Clumsy and irrelevant systems can easily be produced. Indeed, at this early stage of the development of the techniques of information processing, numerous examples of poorly designed systems exist. Yet the future expansion of computerized text processing systems is certain, for there is so much potential in them for doing what is useful.

Consider, for example, the present techniques of Kremlinologists and others who attempt to decipher Aesopian communication. They normally draw their conclusions from spotting sudden anomalies in the flow of statements. How much better off they would be if they had some way of verifying an impression that a formula spotted is new, or if not new, where else it had occurred before.

Whether the initial clue that the analyst wishes to check is provided by an anomaly in a systematic time series of a social indicator or by the subtle insight of an intelligent observer, it is undoubtedly true that the evaluation of the hunch requires subtle inference processes that are too varied and complex to be preplanned. Quantitative content analysis, however, no longer need have the rigid preplanned character that it did at the time that the essays in this book were written. On-line conversational computer systems permit the user to browse through samples of a set of data until he finds an interesting relation. He can then test it in sample after sample until he has satisfied himself that the relation holds up. He can also test it under varying conditions until he has established the limits of the environment under which it does so. He can also test for other or redefined variables which may better explain the finding. For example, a future content analyst looking at symbols of democracy between 1890 and 1950 would not, as we did, first count all of a fixed list of symbols, then tabulate them all, and then interpret without being able to make deeper cuts at the raw data where it proved interesting. His word list would change and grow as he found concepts that did shift under the impact of the world revolution of our time. He could go back and add, regroup, and redefine groupings at will. With these new technological resources content analysis as used to make broad intelligence surveys of the kind attempted in a primitive way in this volume is therefore likely to have a promising future. While world attention surveys will be done in quite new ways, what they will share with this early effort is the aspiration to help men, in a complex world, measure where they stand in the flux of social beliefs and ideologies.

Ithiel de Sola Pool

CHAPTER ONE
THE COMPARATIVE STUDY OF SYMBOLS:
AN INTRODUCTION*

I. Political Symbols

Plato and Ibn Kaldun

Plato's treatment of the myth in *The Republic* is the prototype of all discussions of the subject in the political and social theory of the West. Although the Arab historian and philosopher Ibn Kaldun did not influence the current of Western thought until comparatively recent times, he gave dimensions to the myth that at once enlarged and deepened the consideration of the role of ideas and sentiments in politics and society.

It should not be assumed that Plato saw in the myth a means by which a few ruling guardians could "put something over" on the rank and file of the community. He spoke of the desirability of having the guardians as well as the people accept the myth. We are, however, justified in suspecting that although Plato was in favor of binding the entire body politic with the thongs of common belief, he was willing, even in the ideal Republic, to acquiesce in some measure of impostorship on the part of rulers in dealing with the community at large. Plato said that the rulers ought to be able to accept the myth "if possible," clearly implying that they might be unable to do so. However, too much has been made of Plato's toleration of duplicity, and Cornford is right in protesting against the exaggerated impression that is conveyed by the custom of translating "a single bold flight of invention" as a "noble lie."[1]

It is more a question of "fiction" than of lying, and the difference is not trivial. The proper office of fictions is to provide metaphorical allusions to the common destiny, and by so doing to nourish the ties of cohesion between young and old. It is a mistake to think of myth only in terms of literal truth. Degrees of sophistication and innocence may exist side by

*Harold Lasswell, Daniel Lerner, and Ithiel de Sola Pool. Hoover Institute Studies, Series C: Symbols, No. 1 (Stanford, California: Stanford University Press, January 1952). Abridged and reprinted with permission.

side with no damage to enlightenment. Adults learn to treat many traditions as "just so" stories: It is not necessary to disabuse children of the idea that there is a Santa Claus, or that every founding father was a hero. Indeed, when the members of a ruling group or of the community become exercised over the literal truth or falsity of the myth, it is evidence that the older bonds of civic cohesion have frayed, perhaps beyond repair.

Plato tells us in so many words that he modeled his proposals upon the myths found among the primitive peoples known to the Athenians. Fictions about past and future are thematic material for the artist. Fictions also provide a vocabulary appropriate to the consideration of the common policies of the public politic. Since the specific meaning of the common inheritance varies with the maturity of the individual, key fictions possess some attributes of dreams, which are travels of the mind in the no-man's-land between the reality of the moment and complete unreality. Plato's idea was to convince all that the "nurture and education" which they had undergone was "something they seemed to experience as it were in a dream."

Ibn Kaldun's treatment of politics and society came many centuries after Plato, and was influenced by the wide experience of the Arab philosopher in different parts of the Islamic world. No writer before or since has excelled Ibn Kaldun in his clear perception of the interplay of power, solidarity, and belief. From his study of nomadic tribes, Ibn Kaldun seized upon the vital role of solidarity of sentiment and outlook as a formative factor in human affairs. The chief of the tribe depended upon acceptance by his fellows, not upon his physical power to coerce. Hence the leader was entirely dependent upon support freely forthcoming from the tribesmen. Whatever power he possessed was rooted in solidarity, or it had no existence whatsoever. Hence:

It is rare that a state can be securely established in lands inhabited by many tribes and bands . . . in such lands there will be a diversity of opinions and inclinations, each opinion or viewpoint being backed by a social solidarity to which it can appeal for protection. Defections and rebellions against the state then become frequent, even though the state itself be based on some solidarity, because each tribe feels itself secure and powerful.[2]

Ibn Kaldun points out that kingship and dynasties can be founded only on popular support and solidarity:

Victory, or even the mere avoidance of defeat, goes to the side which has most solidarity and whose members are readiest to fight and to die for each other.[3]

Further:

The end of social solidarity is sovereignty. . . . It is solidarity which makes men unite their efforts for common objects, defend themselves, and repulse or overcome their enemies. We have also seen that every human society requires a restraint, and a chief who can keep men from injuring each other. Such a chief must command a powerful support, else he will not be able to carry out his restraining function. The domination he exercises is Sovereignty, which exceeds the power of a tribal leader; for a tribal leader enjoys leadership [literally "mastery"] and is followed by his men whom he cannot compel. Sovereignty on the other hand is rule by compulsion, by means of the power at the disposal of the leader.[4]

With these fundamentals in mind, the role of religion is described as follows:

Vast and powerful Empires are founded on religion. . . . *A Religion reinforces the power which a state has already acquired from its solidarity and numbers* . . . religious fervour can efface the competitiveness and envy felt by the members of the group toward each other, and turn their faces towards the truth.[5]

In summing up, Ibn Kaldun remarks that "no religious movement can succeed unless based on solidarity," thus providing an important hypothesis for the study of the lines of diffusion of such beliefs.[6] Why do the masses acquiesce in "sovereignty" instead of insisting upon the fact of solidarity? He answers that the dependence of the dynasty upon solidarity is "usually unknown to, or forgotten by, the masses" after they have grown up generation after generation in a fixed spot under the rule of the dynasty.[7]

Once consolidated the state can dispense with social solidarity. The reason is that newly founded states can secure the obedience of their subjects only by much coercion and force. . . .
Once kingship has been established, however . . . the rulers do not need to rely on a great armed force, since their rule is accepted as the will of God, which does not admit of change or contradiction.[8]

When Ibn Kaldun developed his theory of cycles, the remarkable point was not the idea of a cycle, since this was present among the Greeks; nor was it even the specific hypotheses put forward about the processions of governmental forms. Ibn Kaldun saw that the grip of cycles on mankind *may* be broken by the use of human insight, no matter how remote or difficult this may be.

Nay, conflict may stop if every person is clearly aware, *by the light of his reason,* that he has no right to oppress his neighbour. . . . Oppression and strife might cease . . . if men undertook to restrain themselves.[9]

Ideology and Counterideology

So far as broad perspectives having to do with myth, solidarity, and power are concerned, it is safe to say that social and political theory have not gone much beyond Plato and Ibn Kaldun. Consider, for example, the following paragraph in which Gaetano Mosca, the Italian political scientist, summarizes the significance of myth in politics. Nothing in these lines would astonish Plato or Ibn Kaldun, given a little coaching on the historical details since their times:

... In fairly populous societies that have attained a certain level of civilization, ruling classes do not justify their power exclusively by de facto possession of it, but try to find a moral and legal basis for it, representing it as the logical and necessary consequence of doctrines and beliefs that are generally recognized and accepted. So if a society is deeply imbued with the Christian spirit the political class will govern by the will of the sovereign, who, in turn, will reign because he is God's anointed. So too in Mohammedan societies political authority is exercised directly in the name of the caliph, or vicar, of the Prophet, or in the name of someone who has received investiture, tacit or explicit, from the caliph. The Chinese mandarins ruled the state because they were supposed to be interpreters of the will of the Son of Heaven, who had received from heaven the mandate to govern paternally, and in accordance with the rules of the Confucian ethic, "the people of the hundred families." The complicated hierarchy of civil and military functions in the Roman Empire rested upon the emperor, who, at least down to Diocletian's time, was assumed by a legal fiction to have received from the people a mandate to rule the commonwealth.[10]

I shall suggest in the later parts of this discussion that modern scholars and investigators have invented means of linking broad interpretations of myth with concrete current situations. The categories and procedures devised by modern thinkers are adapted to the comparative study of politics from culture to culture and from epoch to epoch.

Modern thinking about symbols in politics dates from Marx and Engels, who elevated the concept of ideology to a dominant position among scholars and politicians. In the eighteenth century Voltaire and other writers of the Enlightenment undermined any simple faith in the prevailing religious myths of Europe, and Marx extended this corrosive attitude to the secular myths of politics. Later, Sorel subsumed the language of counterelites as well as elites under the concept of myth.[11] It is an exaggeration to speak of mere grumbling as "counterideology." We therefore reserve "counterideology" for oppositional viewpoints which are relatively well elaborated. (Karl Mannheim spoke of "utopia" in this connection.)[12]

In classifying political change it is useful to take myth as well as elite transformations into account. The two sets of criteria enable us to distinguish "revolutions" from "reform" movements and "political" from "social" upheavals. Revolutions may be classified as "parochial" or "world" revolutions. In the latter case a new myth is added to the prevailing pattern of world politics (or a myth of universal scope is more widely disseminated).[13]

Within any body politic the two principal questions about the political myth are: *Under what circumstances is one myth rejected and another accepted? Under what circumstances is an established myth successfully transmitted?*

On the postulate of value maximization we can formulate hypotheses about the myth. According to the postulate, choices are intended to maximize indulgence over deprivation, all values being taken into the reckoning. The term "value" is used to designate categories of preferred events, such as power, wealth, and respect. The act of choice is both conscious and unconscious.

Applying the postulate, we can put forward the following hypothesis: The probability of the rejection of a political myth is increased *if the adherents experience deprivation rather than indulgence; if attention is directed toward a new myth whose adherents are indulged;* and *if early adherence to the new myth is followed by relative indulgences.*

That the ruling myth tends to be discredited when a state meets military defeat is in harmony with the first condition just specified. The second proposition also appeals to common knowledge: Communism, for example, has often spread among the dissatisfied as a result of propaganda activity that brings the alleged benefits of communism to the notice of the masses. The third proposition appeals equally to common experience: When the adoption of a new belief is at once followed by victory and prosperity, the future of the new conviction is assured.

Another set of problems connected with myth has to do with the conditions under which a myth diffuses or fails to diffuse from one community to another. This is particularly important for world history and politics, where the prospects of a universal myth are one of the principal questions. Hypothesis: *The line of diffusion is from communities which are most indulged to the ones less indulged.* In terms of power, this implies that the strong will be copied by the weak.

The process of diffusion is complicated by the mechanism of "partial incorporation" which enables an existing pattern of power relations to be preserved at the same time that a foreign myth is largely accepted. Although the mechanism of partial incorporation operates in internal as well as external relations, it is particularly significant for the study of world revolutionary myths in international politics. Up to the present, such myths have not brought a united world state into being, even when a myth has been almost universally accepted.

An outstanding example is afforded by the French Revolution. When monarchical and feudal institutions were violently rejected, the rights of man were proclaimed by the new elite, and wars for the "liberation" of mankind were waged with some success. However, the scope of the elite of the "world revolutionary center"[14] was successfully curtailed by opposing elements in the world balance of power; and one factor in this curtailment was the borrowing of part of the new political myth by the ruling elites of the non-French world. Monarchs, for instance, learned to invoke the symbols of national patriotism, and even to proclaim the rights of man.

In our historic period a leading question is whether the world can be unified in the name of "communism" or "liberalism" (or some third ideology); and whether unification will take the form of a single state or a federation of states. There is not much dispute about classifying the Russian Revolution of 1917 (October) as a world revolution. Not only were the old elites superseded by elites based upon different social classes, but the doctrines proclaimed by the revolutionary leaders were comparatively new among great powers. Demands to unify the globe by means of uprisings supported by the Red Army came to little; and before long the balance of power circumscribed the scope of Moscow. As in the French case, the older elites adopted certain features of the new pattern as a means of consolidating their power. In Germany this process went to the point of creating a new center of political initiative in the name of a myth which, though incorporating some of the features of Soviet ideology, added new symbols of "race."[15]

Is it possible to state the conditions favorable to partial incorporation? Can we specify the features of a myth which are most likely to be incorporated? Such questions have been but little investigated in comparative history and social science, despite the many examples provided by recorded history and current affairs. We can, however, put forward the hypothesis that partial incorporation of practices occurs *when an elite expects to reduce the external threat to its power position by accepting a comparatively small reduction of power at home by means of the incorporation.* The symbols most eligible for partial incorporation are those which have *internal support, but are not the monopoly of counterelites connected with the external threat.* In the face of the Russian threat in the name of "Bolshevism," or "communism," many ruling groups played up such widely spread symbols as "socialism," "social security," or "worker," but fought shy of "communism." "National communism" versus "international communism" is the most striking example of restriction by partial incorporation, and this appears only as part of a secession movement against the Moscow elite. But once a state or system of states professing national, rather than international, communism comes into being, other elites have a wider range of choice for the partial incorporation of symbols which occupy key positions in communist patterns.

How Good Were We in 1900?

Our basic political task is that of achieving correct orientation of the self in the context including the future as well as the past of world politics. As a reminder of the problems connected with this enterprise, and as a partial guide to the most useful procedures of interpretation, suppose that we ask what would have been an outstanding intellectual performance at an earlier time. Imagine that we are transported by some mysterious method to the year 1900, carrying back with us our present knowledge. Could we have foreseen the main lines of ideological and counterideological development since then?

The term "foreseen" carries some ambiguities with it. In referring to future events we sometimes make "prophecies" in the sense of asserting that an event will occur on a definite date at a particular place. In 1900 a perfect prophecy would have foretold that Woodrow Wilson would have been reelected in 1916, and that he would have proclaimed the Fourteen Points on a definite date.

A "prediction" differs from a prophecy in several ways. It refers to a category of events rather than a unique occurrence, and puts the stress upon an estimate of probability (or randomness) rather than a claim of "inevitability." A prediction is made contingent upon the occurrence of conditions which, on the basis of past observations, have controlled the phenomenon being considered. Instead of naming Woodrow Wilson, the predictor in 1900 might have said that if the Democratic party wins the presidency, a governor (rather than a senator) is likely to head the ticket, and to come from an Eastern (rather than a Western or Southern) state. The forecaster might also predict that if the United States got involved in a European war, the war aims proclaimed during the struggle would include many of the policies which were actually listed at a later date among the Fourteen Points.

Predictions are projections into the future of two sets of relationships: trends and conditions. Recent trends in the distribution of myth, for instance, limit the scope of potential change in the immediate future. In 1900 we possessed enough knowledge of the distribution of socialist myths to have foretold that "socialism" had a significant place in the future of world politics. However, we might have overlooked the significant potentialities of "racial" myths. Perhaps we would have interpreted the Dreyfus affair in France in "religious" rather than "biological" (pseudobiological, of course) terms.

When inferences are based upon "conditions" rather than "trends," a scientific proposition is being deductively applied. In 1900 a predictor might have reasoned that since the extra-European world would increase in power, European nations would unite against non-Europeans. The erroneous inference would lie in assuming that Europeans were sufficiently identified with one another and sufficiently alert to social change to feel jointly threatened rather than individually advantaged by the growth of the Americas, Asia, and Africa. Very likely a crucial difficulty would have been the vagueness with which the proposition about unification might have been stated. It would not have been clear what conditions were to be assumed to hold before the proposition might have been supposed to apply.

It is evident that the task of prediction is more complicated than the simple act of extending (extrapolating) a trend line into the future or repeating the existing stock of scientific laws and hypotheses. When trends are extrapolated, it often appears that they will collide with one another. Then the problem is to estimate which factors are likely to resolve the conflict. Special procedures of thinking are needed in this connection. Such an instrument is the "developmental construct" (to employ the term introduced in 1935).[16]

The developmental construct is a provisional pattern of "from what—toward what" relationships. One set of terms refers to selected features of the past; another, to the future. In 1900 it was customary to assume "progress," and to interpret progress as a movement away from feudal institutions toward the establishment of a "free man's commonwealth" on a global scale. The terminal situation was understood by the liberals to signify the universalization of free markets, free governments, and free minds. Socialists, on the other hand, saw the picture as bringing to completion a transition from "capitalism" to "socialism." The socialists varied among one another, of course, in many particulars, notably regarding the "inevitability" of violent revolution or evolutionary gradualism.

In a strict sense of the term, the predictions made by liberals and socialists were not true developmental constructs, since it was usually assumed by the forecaster that he was making a deduction about the future from a valid scientific law. Clearly, developmental constructs are not scientific laws, or deductions from such laws, even when the construct proves to be confirmed by the future event. All that is essential is that the construct be formulated after consideration of trend information, and of all relevant scientific formulations available at the time. The "garrison state" construct, for example, is not put forward as a scientific hypothesis, or even as a simple deduction from an established proposition. Rather, the garrison-state idea is designed to aid the scholar in selecting topics worthy of investigation. If historians and social scientists admit that it is probable that continuing world crisis will culminate in a system of garrisons, research effort may be voluntarily directed to the historical cases where military states have come into being. In eighteenth-century Prussia, to take one famous example, what was the role of ideological factors? And what of Hitler's Reich? What was the relative role in a modern industrial despotism of the military and the police, especially the political police, in the struggle for power? Wherever "business" states or "civil bureaucratic" states have been undermined for the benefit of specialists on violence, such as the military and the police, what has been the part played by ideological tools? It may be, for instance, that the internal tensions of the business state reduced the intensity with which the prevailing ideology was sustained, and created the cleavages in which many alternative symbols could foment disunity. Hence political change may have been fostered less by the affirmative appeal of "communism" or "national socialism" than the negative effect of a cloud of dissatisfied feelings, complaints, protests, and proposals. Action in the name of the old ideology was in this way paralyzed to an extent enabling a determined minority to seize power. Generalizing for industrial societies, the following hypothesis may be looked into: *The principal role of ideological factors in political change is in spreading disaffection, confusion, and disunity, rather than in the propagation of faith in a new ideology.* In the sense of Ibn Kaldun, it is more the disintegration of solidarity and the undermining of established religion that produces political consequences than the embracing of a new symbol pattern. When the minority can seize the key posts of power, the propagation of the new ideology can greatly reduce the cost of holding power, since voluntary obedience is presently substituted for hostility or reluctance.[17]

The most sweeping developmental construct relating to our epoch suggests that the direction of history is changing from the *emergence of mobile societies toward the restoration of caste societies.* This is a sharp reversal of the trend toward progress which was affirmed with such confidence by most of the thinkers of the mid-nineteenth century, including Marx. The construct directs our attention to the conditions propitious for the formation of caste. Most of the historical studies of this question throw relatively little light on the factors which are most likely to influence the outcome under modern industrial conditions. The best-known historical examples of caste formation involve the invasion of settled peoples by conquering nomadic tribes. In the twentieth century the nomads will play presumably an insignificant role in the making of castes. It is far more probable that despotic rulers of industrial or industrializing states will take the lead in imposing compulsory labor conditions. We may therefore examine with special attention the rise of the ideologies of "duty," "obligation," or "responsibility" to work, often at the expense of doctrines which stress "individual rights."

If we are to keep the globe as a whole under observation we must develop "self-observatories" of properly trained historians and social scientists. The aim of such institutions is to describe significant trends, to analyze determining conditions, and to pretest on a small scale the innovations which may be introduced on a larger scale as a means of moving toward our basic goal values.[18]

The Meaning of Meaning[19]

Whenever we consider the significance of any political symbol in a critical spirit it is presently necessary to reflect upon the problem of meaning.

How much "meaning" is there in any given word, slogan, sentence? Suppose, for instance, that we are told by historians of the spread of "Christianity" during the past two thousand years. In what sense is this a meaningful statement in view of the enormous variety of interpretations which have been given to the Old and New Testaments? Does it make much sense to treat of Christianity or Mohammedanism as homogeneous when they are so variously understood?

No general answer can be given to such questions, since what is one man's sense is another man's foolishness. Perhaps the results will be more fruitful if we rephrase the issue. Instead of asking for an overall judgment of whether "Christianity" was in a significant sense a unit for two thousand years, we may ask how the key symbols of this religion were understood during various times and at various places. If such questions are to be answered, such detailed problems as these must be dealt with: What general or specific views are stated to be "Christian" or stigmatized as "unchristian"? To what extent did those who profess Christianity agree about these matters? To what extent did they conduct themselves according to these understandings?

No one will seriously dispute the statement that if we can answer such questions for a culture or social class at any given period, we are saying something relevant about the meaning of Christianity. When we ask about the meaning of secular rather than sacred ideologies, the same issues present themselves. We must admit that something meaningful is being said when contemporary historians say that "nationalistic ideologies" are significant factors in our historical period. We also agree that something is communicated when we are told about the "rise of democratic and socialist" ideologies, and the decline in various countries of the "feudal outlook" or even of "liberal" ideology. But we recall immediately that all sorts of claims are made in the name of "nationalism" or "democracy" or "socialism," and that all kinds of overt acts are performed in their name. The meaning of any given proposition must be found by research upon the interpretations which are accepted in specific circles, and the deeds which are done by those who profess the viewpoint in question. From the comparative study of ideologies, secular or sacred, our broadest hypothesis is this: *Any general symbol may be elaborated in support of any specific proposition; any general or specific symbol may be applied or nonapplied in action.*

The foregoing hypothesis is stated for all conceivable cultures and historical phases, and although it is probably true in this perspective, it is not likely to hold during any short period of time. The following hypothesis is the more probable: *During short periods of time for specific groups, the linking of general with specific symbols and of symbols with overt acts may be stable.*

Myth and Communication

As a means of bringing the discussion of myth into contact with modern methods of research, it may be useful to look at the phenomenon from the standpoint of the growing body of scientific work on communication. The major components of a political myth, as so regarded by political scientists, may be termed: *doctrine, formula, miranda*. These terms are roughly comparable to what is usually meant by such expressions as "prevailing political philosophy," "statutes and ordinances," and "folklore."[20] The literature devoted to the history of political theory usually deals with the doctrines current during a given period. The literature of international, comparative, and municipal law typically covers the formula. The miranda are described by historians who choose their material for the purpose of portraying the popular version of the commonwealth.

From the point of view of the communication process, a political myth is a recurring set of statements and key symbols appearing in the "content" of communication. The myth is "frozen meaning," a metaphor which is acceptable in the sense that it emphasizes the stability of the pattern.

A completed act of communication has often been described in these terms: *Someone says something somehow to someone with some effect.* The fundamental questions, therefore, are: *Who, says what, how, to whom, with what effect?* When studies are focused upon "who," we speak of control analysis; when they deal primarily with "what," it is content analysis; if the subject is "how," we call it media analysis; if "whom," it is audience analysis; and if "effect," it is, of course, effect analysis. As a preliminary mode of outlining the principal frame of reference of students of communication, this scheme has been useful, especially since it can be extended or condensed to fit many scientific and policy aims.

We identify the myth according to the source of the communication (the "who"). Political doctrines, for instance, are statements found in such fundamental documents as written constitutions, statutes, and special declarations of policy. If we are describing a nonliterate society, we treat the oral traditions which are authenticated by qualified spokesmen as the equivalent of documents.[21]

The following are some examples of the political doctrines of the United States:

1. The moral authority of our polity rests upon the consent of the governed.

[Governments derive] their just Powers from the Consent of the Governed.

—Declaration of Independence, 1776

2. In terms of rights, all men are created free and equal.

... all Men are created equal ... they are endowed by their Creator with certain unalienable Rights ... among these are Life, Liberty, and the Pursuit of Happiness.

—Declaration of Independence, 1776

3. The function of government is to secure these rights.

... to secure these rights, Governments are instituted among Men. ...

—Declaration of Independence, 1776

4. The proper method of government is the balancing of functions among various agencies of the state and society.

[We hold] ... that the legislative and executive powers of the state should be separate and distinct from the judiciary; and that the members of the two first may be restrained from oppression, by feeling and participating the burdens of the people, they should, at fixed periods, be reduced to a private station, return into that body from which they were originally akin, and the vacancies be supplied by frequent, certain, and regular elections, in which all, or any part of the former members be again eligible or ineligible, as the laws shall direct.

—Virginia Bill of Rights, 1776

5. Our ideas are self-evident.

We hold these truths to be self-evident. ...

—Declaration of Independence, 1776

When we describe the political formula, it is also necessary to pay strict attention to the source of the statement. The source must be locally understood to be the authorized maker of binding prescriptions for the conduct of the community. In a word, it must be "law." (Political doctrines may be declared without necessarily having the significance of law.) In the United States we turn to the codes of the federal, state, or local government, depending upon the detail appropriate to a given investigation. There are also collections of court decisions and opinions which must be taken into consideration when we summarize the sense of the sentences found in the statutes.

The problems involved in the selection of source are simplified, in some respects, when we turn from the survey of doctrine and formula to miranda. We are no longer plagued by the question, "Is this individual (agency or document) authoritative?" Instead, the task is to determine whether an individual is, or is not, a member of the community. If so, his political statements do concern us, and we proceed to locate the individual according to his place in the social structure. However, detailed information about the position of a given "source" is often missing; and we may be compelled, in the beginning at least, to treat what is said as representative of the community as a whole. Later, when more information is gathered, we can reclassify according to the currency of the miranda among upper-class, middle-class, or lower-class groups in the population. Louie M. Miner, for instance, collected American political poetry published between the end of the Revolutionary War and the adoption of the Constitution. He did not provide systematic information about the author of each poem, and we are therefore compelled to treat the following specimens of the miranda of that day as part of the whole American pattern, without making any further specification.

This is the universal goal of a poet of 1785:

Give laws to the world, to improve on each plan,
And by Liberty ev'rywhere, dignify man.[22]

There were many more specific demands, as in foreign affairs:

In peace let your stripes round the globe be display'd,
From nation to nation establish your trade;
In the language of freemen enforce your decrees,
Make the ocean your empire, and sail where you please.[23]

Glorious expectations were entertained about the future of the country:

From Europe's proud, despotic shores
  Hither the stranger takes his way,
And in our new found world explores
  A happier soil, a milder sway,
    Where no proud despot holds him down,
    No slaves insult him with a crown.[24]

But the presentation of the self was not uniformly favorable:

Equality's the cry, and just the sound,
For equal all in poverty are found,
Equal in fraud, injustice, and deceit
Is church, is law, is physic and is state.[25]

When we examine the globe as a whole, the most concentrated bodies of symbol material pertinent to the myth are the constitutions, the programs of political parties, and the official declarations made by heads of states. The miranda are by their nature widely dispersed; and it is often essential to conduct field studies of living communities before the popular interpretations of political doctrine and formula are intelligible.[26]

Key Symbols and Clichés

As a means of surveying the significant features of a vast body of symbol material, it is convenient to focus upon key symbols occurring in the flow of political statements. The role of key symbols in political life is deeply woven into the texture of the body politic, since symbols enter into the experience of everyone, irrespective of status. Key symbols are focal points for the crystallization of sentiment, uniting child with adult, layman with expert, philosopher with lawyer, the speculative man with the man of action. The common denominator of doctrine, formula, and miranda is the key symbol.

The unifying role of the symbol is not restricted to the institutions of power. The key words in the vocabulary of any specialized group may disseminate beyond the limited circle of the technically proficient and enter into the lives of laymen. There is an ever contemporary ring about the following comment:

> Just as today people talk glibly about Freudianism who have never read Freud, and apply the language of relativity-theory to fields where it has no applicability, so in the eighteenth century people talked about mechanism or general utility who had no more than heard of Newton or Bentham.[27]

Key symbols can be classified into those referring to persons and groups (symbols of identification), to preferences and volitions (symbols of demand), and to the assumptions of fact (symbols of expectation). The sequence of movements in history can be conveniently read by scanning the dominant symbols of successive epochs. When religious passions began to subside in modern Europe, the most influential focal points of identification became secular and national. Later identifications were made with symbols of "economic class," for instance, the "proletariat," and of "race," such as "Aryan." Demand symbols rose and fell, registering the currents of the age, and also contributing to their fate. Shifting panoramas of hope and despair are signalized in the symbols of expectation, such as "progress" and "the inevitable triumph of world revolution."

A given ideology can be conveniently summarized according to the key terms receiving positive or negative treatment (or frequent mention of any kind). In Communist ideology, for example, the following are among the symbols which receive almost uniformly negative treatment in doctrinal pronouncements: *bourgeoisie; capitalism* (capitalist, capital); *imperialism;* God (religion, church); *plutocracy; idealism* (subjectivism); *anarchism.* Among positive terms are: *communism* (Communist party, Communist International, Cominform); *world revolution; dialectical materialism; dictatorship of the proletariat; collectivism* (collective ownership); *classless society* (of the future); *class struggle.*

The political cliché occupies an intermediate position between the simplicity of the key symbol and the elaborateness of creeds and codes. Many clichés are sentences in the creeds or codes; they are statements which are brief and widely quoted. Many clichés are "persuasive definitions" in the sense of C. L. Stevenson,[28] such as Proudhon's "property is

theft." Innumerable changes have been rung on the following epigram-
matic cliché of 1831:

What is a communist? One who has yearnings
For equal division of unequal earnings.

—Ebenezer Elliott

Among the clichés are the *slogans* of politics, which may be defined as
brief statements addressed to the masses for their guidance.[29] The tremendous role of slogans is an old story in politics. Victory has often been
aided by skill in appropriating the best slogans of a rival. In the summer
and autumn of 1917, for instance, the Bolsheviks adopted one of the most
successful slogans of the Social Revolutionaries, "The Land for the
Peasants."[30]

Neither key symbols nor clichés are confined to words. Such emblems as
flags, monuments, and edifices are symbols of identification. Hans Speier
has shown how "magic geography" can be used to communicate the cliché
of "encirclement."[31]

The physical media used in communication themselves perform a
symbolizing function when an audience attaches special significance to
them. This is the "ikon" role of "signs." The silhouette of the White
House and of the Washington skyline are ikons identifying the American
nation in innumerable films, cartoons, and floats.[32]

The extraordinary economy with which meanings can be communicated
by key symbols and clichés is well known intuitively to every creative
artist. An explicit indication of how the counting of such items can reveal
the character of an individual is given by Marcel Proust in *Swann's Way:*

Had anyone subjected Mme. de Gallardon's conversation to that form of
analysis which by noting the relative frequency of its several terms would
furnish him with the key to a ciphered message, he would at once have
remarked that no expression, not even the commonest forms of speech,
occurred in it nearly so often as "at my cousin's the Guermantes," "Elzear
de Guermantes's health," "my cousin Guermantes' box."[33]

World Symbol Surveys

When it is desired to survey politically significant communication for
any historical period on a global scale, the most practicable method is that
of counting the occurrence of key symbols and clichés. Only in this way
can the overwhelming mass of material be reliably and briefly summarized.
By charting the distributions in space and through time it is possible to
show the principal contours of the political history of doctrine, formula,
and miranda.

Since authoritative sources of the most important doctrines and formulas can be found in relatively concentrated form, such an inquiry can

begin with these sources, subjecting them to preliminary analysis for the purpose of selecting a list of the important terms and propositions. This step was taken by one of the present writers in preparing the survey of politically significant symbols in World War II.[34] This list of symbols was also the basis for the Stanford University study of the world revolution of our time.

After the most important symbols and clichés are selected, the next problem is to choose the most representative and accessible channels of communication in the various countries to be described. One possibility is to choose the *major public pronouncements* uttered by the heads of states and of the most important parties of the state. Another alternative is to concentrate upon *party platforms* or upon the *programs of pressure groups* (and of voluntary associations making political pronouncements). A further possibility is to examine the *debates of deliberative bodies,* such as the Congress *(Congressional Record)* or Parliament *(Hansard).*

Undoubtedly these sources are important in most modern states during the twentieth century, and all would be included in a comprehensive survey of the myth-practices of the world. However, these sources vary more in relative importance from country to country than do the *newspapers.* In many countries the head of the state makes few public statements, and these may be almost purely ceremonial. Party platforms often go unrevised year after year. So far as pressure groups are concerned, there are great differences in importance from state to state, and the task of gathering such fugitive material is a vast research project. The published proceedings of legislative bodies are often scanty, or altogether lacking. All states are modern enough to publish newspapers, however, so that comparable channels can be used for comparative purposes. Further, we can be relatively sure of who controls and who reads the news. In nearly all states some papers are understood to be leading organs of the party in office and of the government. Where the party system is competitive, the principal organs of parties and factions can be identified. Even with the coming of radio and television, the daily paper continues to occupy an important position in the media (and newspaper content is more accessible to study than are broadcasts).

There are other considerations of feasibility favoring use of the press rather than other media. The flow of symbols in film and radio has less regularity in sequence. Newspapers appear regularly and frequently, in uniform formats. Also, they have a more or less explicit point of view. The press is mainly an information medium rather than an entertainment medium; and the most significant category on which the press regularly presents news and views is the political, including the ideological. As compared with such verbal flows as after-dinner speeches, golf-club stories, psychiatric interviews—all of which provide data symbols of great value—

the press is both accessible and rich in the vocabulary of political ideology current among the elite of any given time. For these reasons the RADIR symbol studies concentrated on the press.

In nearly all newspapers it is possible to distinguish news from editorials. Usually, news headlines, or the most conspicuous news items, reach a larger audience than editorials. But editorials are read by the "self-selected elite" who are most concerned with politics. News columns are more responsive than editorials to political and social change, since editorials perform a stabilizing, assimilative, and anticipatory role. The distinguishing function of editorials is to apply the prevailing ideology to recent developments and to emerging problems of policy. If the editorial disappears from the press of a state, it reflects either the desire of the controlling elite to exclude the reading audience from political participation or a desire on the part of the community to be "apolitical." By studying newspapers, and most readily by studying editorials in them, we can describe the frequency with which political doctrines are emphasized.

Style and the Unconscious

Besides establishing scientific relationships, research is important when it goes no further than to describe trends and distributions. When we estimate the future, our projections call for data about world trend, which summarizes the existing state of predisposition. Such investigating would provide information about the diffusion (and restriction) of all major ideologies.

So far, we have had little to say about the style in which communications are made. But in the study of trend, as indeed of every aspect of the process of communication, style is particularly interesting since, for the most part, it lies beyond conscious control. The manifest content (purport) of what is said can be subordinated to deliberate management. The subtle *unconscious* patterning of speech, handwriting, posture, and involuntary movements is generally recognized, and has given rise to testing procedures invented by psychologists and psychiatrists. The legal historian Rudolf Sohm was speaking more truly than he knew when he noted in his introduction to *The Institutes* that "The greatest and most far-reaching revolutions in history are not consciously observed at the time of their occurrence." It is by the investigation of style that we may gain more insight into the currents of history which are usually below the threshold of consciousness.

Perhaps it ought to be made explicit that we do not use "style" in the sense of "beautiful writing." Our aim is more commonplace. We need a word to designate the patterning which is displayed by the elements employed in transmitting messages. The elements themselves are "signs" and "symbols." It is a matter of style when we describe the vocabulary, enunciation, or gestures of a speaker; or when we describe the grammatical forms, word choice, and sentence length of a writer. In fact, the range of stylistic analysis is inexhaustible, since the context in reference to which a pattern may be construed is infinite.

As an example of the potentialities of style analysis, consider the characteristics of democratic and despotic style. Not enough work has been done to speak with confidence of final results, but a large number of indications point to comparatively clear differences in the language of politics under the two systems. If we approach the problem from a fundamental point of view, and think of the postulate of maximization, a number of hypotheses suggest themselves, some of which have been at least partially confirmed by observation. Since the demand to share power (as well as other values) characterizes democratic society, we expect that the language of politics will adapt to the dominant demands of democracy. Similarly, we anticipate that the demand to exercise power over others will produce characteristic patterns of culture. Where democratic audiences are the target, the communicator will adapt himself to what he conceives to be the audience's conception of what it is to be addressed with full recognition of basic equality. Opposite expectations will guide the nondemocratic communicator who addresses the lower orders. He will be concerned with eliciting evidences of submission from the audience.

We shall first consider the peculiarities of the nondemocratic style. We are familiar with the history of many societies where power is unshared, and can, therefore, subject our hypotheses to preliminary test. If we establish the pattern of style prevailing in conscious nondemocracies, we can interpret the appearances of features corresponding to this pattern as an indication of unconscious nondemocratic drift in a consciously democratic society. As an aid in making hypotheses, we have the benefit of psychiatric observations of the subtler responses of patients falling in the paranoid category. The paranoids express the demand to be infinitely superior to others, and to have this supremacy acknowledged. The patterning of political discourse in nondemocracies will presumably reflect the tendency to withdraw from neighborly contact and also to ascend above the rank and file.

One fundamental hypothesis about nondemocratic language style is that discourse between strong and weak excels in *effect contrasts* rather than *effect modeling*. By an effect contrast is meant the use of symbols and signs in ways which are unlike the expected replies. Effect modeling, on the contrary, employs symbols and signs as they are expected to be used in reply. Consider, for a moment, the way in which a powerful primitive potentate may communicate with his people. He may stand or sit proudly upright while the audience grovels in the dust. The posture of the body is a physical instrument for conveying the message, and it is modulated to emphasize effect contrasts.[35]

The symbolic pattern of antidemocratic discourse may be characterized as *adulation of the powerful and depreciation of the nonpowerful.* Adulation is carried on by employing symbols to affirm or imply an exalted position in all values, such as strength of body and mind (well-being), riches (wealth), power, skill, knowledge, and wisdom (enlightenment), loving kindness (affection), and goodness (rectitude). The literature of sycophancy through the ages provides a library of such effusions. Adulatory statements may be made by both the strong and the weak; but the situation remains one of effect contrast, since the powerful do not return the compliment to the weak.

The powerful and the weak join in depreciation of the weak; but the relation remains one-sided, since the powerful are never the target. Depreciation, of course, portrays the individual or the group as severely deprived, not indulged.

The following relates to a more subtle matter: *denial of equality and acceptance of the denial in a communication contact.* For example, the powerful are exceedingly difficult of access; when access is obtained, the one desiring to communicate may be ignored; the superior may not deign to reply; he may make his meaning excessively difficult to comprehend by using an alien tongue, by talking cryptically, or by making his speech obscure in other ways; may neglect to speak loud enough or slowly enough; may disregard the subject matter and divert attention continually to other matters; may interfere by interruptions and by rude and upsetting aggressions. The acceptance of inequality is indicated by approaching with great diffidence; by communicating with evident embarrassment; and by patient endurance of all aberrations of the powerful.

The style peculiarities of democratic communication include *free play of praise and adverse criticism of the self or other.* Thus we do not accept the maxim that the "people can do no wrong" as an example of fully democratic communication. However, we classify the flattery of the "people" as *more* democratic than, for example, the flattery of an absolute ruler.

Further, democratic language style emphasizes the *acceptance of equality in the communication contact and nonacceptance of inequality.* Observers of democratic societies have usually been impressed by the informal manners and the "folksy" vocabulary of democracies. During the transition phases of a social movement toward democracy, rudeness of manner and the abruptness in reacting against any seeming violation of equality are prominent in the response of the "common man." Anything "high-toned," for instance, is a reminder of denials of respect to the common man which were made by the "upper class" intonations and the rituals of etiquette. The conversational tone of the late Franklin D. Roosevelt successfully counterbalanced the traces of "upper-class" and "Eastern" accent that clung to many words. Roosevelt's radio chats appeared to respect the claim of the listener to be treated as an equal who might talk back at any moment, and who, in any case, was entitled to be told in clear and simple words what was important for him to understand when making up his mind. Hitler, too, spoke over the radio to the rank and file. But his ranting style was no invitation to reply, or to consider opposing facts and interpretations, or to make private judgments.

The demand for superiority in a nondemocratic society involves the demand to exclude the community as a whole from having controversial matters brought to their notice. Political news and comment are resented, and, if possible, all communication contacts between the rulers and the ruled are reduced to rites on ceremonial occasions. In Czarist Russia, for example, *the* czar almost never addressed a public gathering of his subjects. Speeches were few and far between and were both brief and cliché-ridden.

A newly installed elite in a power-concentrated state is more expressive, since it wants to stimulate action against nonconformers and to develop, partly by trial and error, the elements of its future ritual of communication. Even old elites step up the volume, variety, and diversity of content in their communications during times of crisis. Leaders of an autocratic state may increase effect modeling by multiplying common religious services. If the monarch bows at the shrine, even as the lowliest worshiper, he is accepting, in some degree, equality before the gods.

The insistence upon ritual on the part of nondemocratic rulers springs largely from the fear of disobedience. Evidences of contrary opinion are readily exaggerated into harbingers of revolt. Conformity is reassuring, and the style of discourse becomes highly stereotyped. More specifically, *the tendency is to elaborate the ornamental features of discourse relatively more than the symbols which convey the purport of the message.* Hence the signs used in writing, the parchment utilized in official documents, the implements employed in affixing of signatures—all accessories above the bare minimum needed for comprehension—are inflated and embellished. The excess of *accessory* over *pure* signs indicates the strength and even the character of the values sought in the act of communication beyond the efficient transmission of a "manifest" message. By elaborating the trappings of an oracle, the ocular message becomes a pronouncement that takes on an authoritative nimbus of mystery and weight. The signs are transmuted into ikons which are interpreted as saying, in effect: "What I say is even wiser and more powerful than you think. Disregard it at your peril."

By observing trends in matters of style we may become sensitive to the currents in democracies that are moving away from democracy, and we may detect drifts toward democracy in despotisms. We may also gauge the level of crisis, whether in the relations of elite and nonelite or in external affairs. We can throw light on the degree of civic cohesion among men of action, intellectuals, and the rank and file, since the stream of communication from one elite to another, and from upper to middle to lower classes, can show whether tensions are rising or falling.

This brings us to the problem: Under what circumstances can the adaptation of the ideology to a changing context be carried on without revolutionary uprisings or reactionary rigidity? The strategy of humane politics calls for continuous search for better general answers to this question and especially for more efficient methods of relating answers to the unfolding processes of human history.

II. Scope and Methods of the RADIR Project

The search for better answers to questions like the last—how to adapt ideology to changing contexts—has motivated the emergence of social sciences. They rest on faith; a faith that better answers exist and may be found by way of empirical and objective research. That our understanding of myth and its relation to power has not advanced much beyond Plato and Ibn Kaldun does not prove further insights impossible. New lines of research may open new vistas. Perhaps the new technique of counting key symbols may reveal truths not heretofore established. That, at least, is a provisional hope of the social scientist. That is the hope which led social scientists concerned with problems of myth and communications to experiment with the type of content analysis exemplified in the RADIR Project.

In recent years social scientists have grown more aware of style as a clue to the unconscious. They have increasingly noted the role of communication. They have sought for means to systematize the study of doctrines. The counting of key symbols offered a practical road of advance. For the political scientist and historian concerned with those doctrines which have shaped world history, the world symbol survey offered a way to summarize reliably an overwhelming mass of data. Thus the interest in mass communications, which had emerged in the twenties and thirties, led in the forties to a number of quantitative symbol studies and to two systematic world symbol surveys.

The first such survey began during World War II, at the Library of Congress in Washington, D.C. There, the Experimental Division for the Study of Wartime Communication completed a number of studies oriented both toward developing new research tools and toward offering effective aid on war problems. The results of this research are largely reported in *The Language of Politics.*[36]

After the war a more extended survey was made at the Hoover Institute and Library on War, Revolution, and Peace at Stanford University. In January 1948 the Carnegie Corporation of New York made a grant to the Hoover Institute for a study of present-day revolutionary developments and their effects on the relations among nations. This project, the RADIR Project, studies the "world revolution of our time." Our belief is that the circumstances and consequences of social change now operate on a world scale. Our purpose is to discover the similarities and differences in the way this global process of change has worked itself out in different societies within the contemporary world. This accounts for our interest in the "world community" as the unit of historical study.

A few words may be useful in clarifying at the outset, what we mean by the term "revolution." We do *not* mean simply a violent episode which transfers power from any one set of power holders to any other. We *do* mean a process, under which such episodes are likely to occur more frequently than otherwise. The period covered by the RADIR Project, 1890-1950, does, indeed, include several such violent transfers of power, but we study them in the context of a world revolutionary process. Our interest in these particular episodes is focused on how they conform to, and deviate from, this process.

We postulate that the common consequences of revolutionary change—in whatever society it occurs and from whatever sequence of events it results—is "rapid and extensive change. in the composition and the vocabulary of the ruling few."[37] This postulate makes comparative analysis of "the world revolution of our time" manageable, as well as important.[38] Composition and vocabulary are two characteristics of the ruling group in any society which are amenable to direct observation. Whether changes in these characteristics are "rapid and extensive" at any time can be determined by a variety of feasible and objective comparative measures.

The research efforts of the RADIR Project have been directed largely to describing and analyzing changes in the composition and vocabulary of the ruling few in various societies within the world community. The data accumulated by these studies are presented in two main series of research reports: (1) the elite series, which reports on changes in the composition of the ruling group; (2) the symbol series, which this study introduces and which reports on changes in their vocabulary.

Why Symbol Analysis?

What most students who speak of "symbols" (as a technical term for words) have in common is an interest in a flow of words as an expression of *attitude*. Words are "symbols" because they stand for (symbolize) the attitudes of those who use them, as distinguished, for example, from "signs," which are words that point to (signalize) objects external to their user. The symbol analyst works with words by selecting those which best stand for the attitudes whose presence or absence he wishes to detect and describe. Symbols, thus conceived, serve as his "operational indices" of attitude.

Since there are other, apparently more direct, ways of indexing atti-tudes, the question may fairly be raised: Why symbol analysis? As between words and deeds, for example, what a man does would seem to be a simpler and more dependable guide to his "real" attitudes than what he says. It is clear that what a man says may be a misexpression of his attitude—that is, he may deliberately conceal his attitude by asserting opinions which he does not in fact believe; or he may misrepresent his "real" attitude through unconscious repression of thoughts (and words) which he is unable to acknowledge explicitly. Although these statements are true, two points may be mentioned to show that they do not invalidate symbol analysis, but, instead, only emphasize that it must be used with caution—as must every inquiry whose conclusions are formed by means of an inference from observed data to nonobserved continua.

First, the same objections which apply to words as indices apply equally to deeds as indices. A man may *act* in such a way as to misrepresent his "real" attitude—either by deliberate concealment or by unconscious re-pression. Second, if the good sense of these objections to words as data is taken into account in designing a symbol analysis, they may enrich, rather than invalidate, the conclusions reached. As we shall show in more detail later, if we remain aware of these points in forming our symbolic indices, we may be able to discover the regularities of verbal behavior associated with various types of deliberate concealment or unconscious distortion of "real" attitudes. Thus, words are not necessarily less valid than deeds as data on attitudes, but may, indeed, provide certain valuable clues to account for deeds otherwise inexplicable.

The questions which next arise are: Which words? How analyze them? No general answer to these questions will be offered here, save that the choice of words and techniques depends on what one wishes to find out. For a study of style, modest words may be chosen, but for a survey of doctrinal trends political key symbols provide the most relevant concise indices. These key symbols shed light on what the RADIR Project desires to study. We have already stated what the RADIR Project wishes to learn, and we shall confine our remarks here to clarifying how symbol analysis has been used to contribute to this purpose. The purpose is to determine whether "changes in the vocabulary of the ruling few" have been "rapid and extensive" in any common direction among the elites of various soci-eties in the contemporary world community. Symbol analysis has been used to provide us with a variety of measures that would produce reliable answers to this question.

Since our focus is on changes in the vocabulary of contemporary elites, we chose as our data symbols those key words most directly associated with elite stability in the world today—the competing vocabularies of political ideology. The general framework of the RADIR Project calls for comparative analysis of world trends with respect to five goal values—democracy, security, fraternity, abundance, and enlightenment. Since these have been more fully described elsewhere in the RADIR Studies,[39] we need mention here only two points about them. First, it was recognized that these were only five goal values in a list that could be extended almost indefinitely; since choices had to be made, these five were selected as central goal values in the sense that their fluctuations would provide reliable clues to trends affecting most of the others. Second, it was recognized that these symbols—like all words of doctrinal intent—were loaded with a heavy freight of ambiguities in use. Accordingly, for purposes of the RADIR analysis, they were provided with uniform operational meanings, so that each of these resonant symbols was taken to signify practices affecting the widespread sharing of power (democracy), safety (security), respect (fraternity), income (abundance), and information (enlightenment). These terms, too, were further analyzed into operational equivalents current in the various societies being investigated—as indicated by the symbol list used for the studies in this series, which is reprinted as Appendix A. This list and the parallel list for the wartime World Attention Survey were based upon a preliminary examination of authoritative doctrinal pronouncements. The direct relevance of it to the vocabulary of political ideology is clear from a glance at this symbol list, and from a reading of the subsequent analyses of data accumulated with it.

The foregoing discussion answers the question "which words?" with respect to the symbol studies of the RADIR Project, and states the reasons for the choice of words that was made. We turn, in the next section, to answer the question "how analyze them?"

Why Content Analysis?

We have already mentioned various types of analysis—logical, aesthetic, propagandic—which can fruitfully be applied to a flow of words. The general method involved we have been calling symbol analysis, and the special technique used in the RADIR Project is known as content analysis (or quantitative semantics).

The exposition of what content analysis is becomes somewhat easier if one deals first with its more technical name, quantitative semantics. The usual method of semantics is qualitative—that is, the flow of words in *single* situations is tested according to the criteria of meaning and truth which have been established. Quantitative semantics analyzes the flow of symbols in a *series* of situations. Since a class of more than one member is involved, the method must account for the *distribution* as well as the *references* of the symbols selected for study. To describe distributions, the analytic categories must be used according to certain statistical conventions. This is what is meant by quantification.

The question "Why content analysis?" thus includes, as its leading element, the question "Why quantify?" An important reason is the unsatisfactory character of symbol analyses which do not quantify their observations. One of the present authors has recorded some of the questions which typically are raised but not answered by qualitative symbol studies, however excellent these may be in other respects, as follows:

Can we assume that a scholar read his sources with the same degree of care throughout his research? Did he allow his eye to travel over the thousands upon thousands of pages of parliamentary debates, newspapers, magazines and other sources listed in his bibliography or notes? Or did he use a sampling system scanning some pages superficially, though concentrating upon certain periods? Was the sampling system for the *Frankfurter Zeitung,* if one was employed, comparable with the one for the *Manchester Guardian?* Were the leaflets chosen simply because they were conveniently available to the scholar, or were they genuinely representative of the most widely circulated propaganda leaflets?[40]

The handling of symbolic data in quantitative form is designed to provide readers of content analyses with the answers to these, and other, questions. Through the use of statistical methods, content analysis aims at achieving objectivity, precision, and generality.

Objectivity is commonly regarded as a prerequisite of scientific research, but one that is difficult to achieve in research on human behavior—and particularly in research on the verbal behavior of men. Words are often treated with anthropomorphic reverence for inherent qualities they are supposed to possess; and even when not so treated, they are used more often for the analysis of data than as data for analysis. This coy approach to the human vocabulary shows among scholars in such habits as "reading *between* the lines" of verbal texts used as data. Such habits, when used by a skilled person, produce insights which are often brilliant but usually unverifiable. Content analysis is, in the first place, a method for "reading *on* the lines" and for reporting the results which can be verified. Some of the results may be surprising and reveal things about the text whose presence we did not expect. But these results are obtained by looking at the words that are there, rather than by guessing at meanings that were not recorded. Thus content analysis, by making prerequisite an explicit statement of criteria and procedures used to describe the content of any communication, minimizes the characteristic uncertainties with which "impressionistic" analysis leaves its audience; and in so doing it fulfills the main condition of objectivity: to provide sufficient information to enable other observers to replicate the observations made on the given body of data.

Precision is gained through describing observations in numerical terms. It is always more precise—though not always necessary or possible—to describe observations dealing with large-small, many-few, more-less in numbers than in words. Numbers are the special language of size and quantity: thus, the statement "49 percent of the class specified" is always more precise than "a little less than half of the class specified," regardless of whether the class specified is the number of apples in a bushel or of symbols in an editorial. Neither the apples nor the symbols are affected by the terms we use to describe them—a point which is neglected by the anthropomorphic view that things change as we change our style of talking about them. All that changes, in fact, is the state of our information. When we use numbers, this change is always in the direction of increased precision.

Generality is another aim which content analysis shares with all scientific inquiry that is not interested in merely precisioning the trivial. Description through simple enumeration is precise, but on most important phenomena one cannot simply "count up" all the possible observations. Content analysis therefore works toward generality through hypothesis and sampling. We shall describe both of these operations more fully in the chapters which follow. Here we wish only to emphasize that generality in content analysis is obtained by using suitably designed samples of determinate universes, whose limits have been determined either empirically or theoretically. Generality through sampling is important because, without it, one's findings are applicable only to *unique* situations and therefore possess merely historical interest. Since we are interested in the *regularities* of symbolic behavior in the past, and in the prediction of such behavior under specified conditions in the future, content analysis aims at results which are sufficiently general to validate inferences beyond the specific situation analyzed.

III. How Content Analysis Works

We have seen that content analysis operates on the view that verbal behavior is a form of human behavior, that the flow of symbols is a part of the flow of events, and that the communication process is an aspect of the historical process. What is *said* in the communication channels of any country at any time is, therefore, part of what is *done* in that country. Content analysis is a technique which aims at describing, with optimum objectivity, precision, and generality, what is said on a given subject in a given place at a given time.[41]

How Content-Analysis Research Is Designed

The unit of study in content analysis is the space-time distribution of any symbol or symbol cluster (e.g., theme, concept, idea). The class of units to be observed, and the limits of the space-time continua within which the observations are to be made, must be specified in advance of actual research operations. Such specifications constitute the first step in content analysis—the step which makes the universe of discourse determinate and enables us to take the second step of constructing an appropriate sample.

After a determinate universe of discourse has been defined, the second step is to formulate the rules by which the actual coding, recording, and periodizing will be done. This is the step which we call, for brevity, sampling. It requires the following decisions: which symbols are to be observed (i.e., the class of units or symbol list); which sequence of symbols is to be observed (i.e., the space continuum, such as the editorials of one paper or the front page of another); which order and limits are to be used in taking observations on these symbol sequences (i.e., the time continuum, such as every eighth day for the five-year period 1945-50). The construction of the sample is completed, after the foregoing decisions have been made, by the construction of a rulebook which codifies the procedures to be followed in recording the observations.

These decisions are not easy to make, and many different decisions have been made which proved to be relevant and feasible for different research purposes. Thus, one content analysis described the fluctuations in the occurrence of key symbols used in the annual May Day slogans of the U.S.S.R. over a period of twenty-five years.[42] Another described the distribution (by column inches) of all topics treated in two hundred forty newspapers on the same day.[43] Between such extreme variations of technique are other variants less drastic but equally important in regard to differences in the data they produce. For the research which is reported in the next several studies of this series, the editorials of one newspaper (the leading one) in each of five countries were read on the first and fifteenth days of each month for the sixty-year period 1890-1950.

The third main step in designing a content analysis study is *pretesting*. In the first two steps a determinate universe is chosen and an adequate sample is constructed. Whether the sample will actually represent the universe with optimum relevance and feasibility, however, can only be decided by trying it out. By pretesting one's research design one can secure better "coverage" in the symbol list (e.g., by dropping those symbols which are used in irrelevant ways or not at all, and by adding those symbols which are relevant but were not thought of before pretesting); one can test the validity of the sample (e.g., the first and fifteenth days of each month may be strongly biased by the fact that budgetary news and discussion regularly occupies the space designated for study on these days and on no others, and hence that the fifth and twentieth days—with two "budgetary days" picked at random each year—would provide a more representative sample of the symbol flow in this place during the five-year period); one can also test the reliability of the analysts (e.g., their agreement in applying the procedures specified in the rulebook). An adequate pretesting thus should obviate most of the "bugs" which are bound to occur in any a priori research design, however well conceived.

Once the pretesting has been completed, the actual research operations begin. These include the reading of the texts selected and the recording, in the prescribed manner, of data they contain. After the data have been recorded, the final step—their analysis—can be commenced. This analysis, involving as it does the testing of the hypotheses and the fitting of data to postulated models, is inevitably the longest and most expensive step in content analysis, but the labors of recording and evaluating the symbol data can be considerably economized if the first three steps have been performed with a lively sense of the practical uses and limits of content-analytic technique.

How Content-Analysis Data Are Analyzed

That which is under observation in content analysis is the *space-time distribution* of symbols. To this observed unit, three measures can be applied. The simplest measure disregards the distribution of symbols along the continua and reports simply the *amount* (or number of total occurrences) of any symbol in a certain place within a certain interval of time. Secondly, attention to the amounts in more than one segment of the space or of the time continua gives a *distribution*. The third measure is *prominence*. These three measures—amount, distribution, and prominence of occurrence—are the chief tools for analysis of the data recorded by content-analytic methods.[44]

These measures are used, severally and jointly, to analyze three classes of characteristics of any symbol sequence: attention, direction, intensity. The word *attention* refers to the characteristic of occurrence or nonoccurrence. The amount and distribution of occurrence are regarded as a measure of the attention paid to individual symbols (or symbol clusters). Occurrence, as an index of attention, is often expressed as a ratio (or percentage) of actual to possible occurrences in the given sample. Other ways of handling attention have been used, however, of which the following may be mentioned here:

1. Actual occurrences of one symbol as a percentage of actual occurrences of the whole class of symbols to which it belongs in the sample
2. Actual occurrences of one symbol as a percentage of actual occurrences of all symbols studied in the sample (i.e., the total amount of occurrences of the entire symbol list)
3. Comparison of actual occurrences, in percentages or whole numbers, of different symbols in the same time period
4. Comparison of actual occurrences of the same symbol in different time periods (e.g., index numbers).

Each of these methods is useful for producing different sorts of conclusions.[45] Each of these methods, too, is used to reach conclusions about direction and intensity. These, as we saw above, are also characteristics of symbol sequences and therefore subject to the same measures as those of attention.

The word *direction* in content analysis refers to the attitude expressed toward any symbol by its user. Such expressions of attitude are usually categorized as favorable, unfavorable, or neutral. Various or related polarities—e.g., positive-negative, friendly-hostile—are sometimes used. The actual recording operations usually use the symbols + (plus), − (minus), and 0 (zero) for the three categories. It is important that the rules for classifying individual observations into these three categories should be very clear and explicit in order to maximize reliability in recording the data and validity in the inferences from data to conclusions.

The same methods, and cautions, are useful for taking measures of the characteristic called *intensity*. Here the problem is to supplement frequency and amount by other criteria which can be applied metrically to symbolic behavior. One such criterion we have described as prominence, i.e., the formulation of position and style factors as indicators which can be measured. Although the procedures available for measuring intensity require improvement, it is now possible, by the methods discussed above, to reach some valid conclusions concerning the intensity of attitudes expressed on symbols.

We turn next to the three main ways which have been used to organize data on symbolic behavior. Although time-space units, in principle, can be organized by holding either the time or the space dimension constant, most content analyses (including the RADIR studies) in fact have been based on time series. These studies have used three main methods which, respectively, permit us to reach conclusions (i.e., make statements) about trend, covariance, and interaction.

Trend. This is the simplest form of organizing content-analysis data. It involves the presentation of attention (and direction) data on the occurrence of selected symbols in a selected medium according to a predetermined time series. The results enable one to say whether the trend has been toward more, less, or constant attention throughout the whole period or any part of it; and whether these fluctuations of attention have been accompanied by more, less, or constant approval of the selected symbols.

Covariance. This involves the matching of trends with respect to two or more symbols, or symbol clusters, in the same or different media. The results enable one to say whether, for example, increasing attention to, and approval of, the symbols of democracy in a given medium varies directly or inversely: with increasing attention to, and approval of, the United States; with decreasing attention to, and approval of, the Soviet

Union; or with constant attention to, and approval of, the symbols of national security, international cooperation, war and peace. Similar conclusions can be reached about symbolic behavior in two or more different media. As in the treatment of single trends, the analysis of covariance data can be expressed statistically by the use of correlation coefficients and similar measures. Illustrations of covariance analysis are provided by the several cases in which content-analysis data were accepted as legal evidence by courts of law to prove "collusion" between domestic propagandists and foreign powers. A particularly relevant content-analysis technique was used in preparing the case against William Dudley Pelley.[46]

Interaction. This is the most difficult use of content analysis. The aim of interaction analysis is to associate the flow of symbols directly with the flow of events. In the ideal case, fluctuations with respect to a single type of event (e.g., voting behavior in a parliamentary chamber) could be correlated with fluctuations in treatment of a single type of symbol (e.g., symbolic behavior toward the symbol "voting" in the same chamber). In such a situation, a numerical correlation could be expressed, showing, in the foregoing example, the regularity of the sequences (presumably causal) between the typical voting behavior of any member and his typical attitudes toward voting. Alternatively, one of the variables may not be graduated but may involve merely the presence or absence of a given trait, or both variables may be of this kind. However, some "interaction" situations which one wishes to explore contain too many "variables" of different kinds to be treated easily in numerical fashion. That is, more than one type of event is capable of influencing the fluctuation of the selected symbols, and several influencing events of the various types intervene between occurrences of symbols. To correlate the interaction of symbols and events in such a situation requires an especially careful research design, in which the variables selected are both empirically relevant and amenable to statistical treatment. The choice usually lies between greater inclusiveness and greater precision. Content analysis should be used mainly in situations where precision is desired, since less precise, but more inclusive, interaction sequences can be obtained by simpler methods of observation. Wherever possible, the situation should be defined so as to gain optimum precision and inclusiveness simultaneously. An example of such definition is the study of how the propaganda omissions of the Communist International (a symbol sequence) interacted with (were made responsive to) successive specific defeats in electoral and strike situations suffered by that body (an event sequence).[47]

A well-designed content-analysis project may produce results of all three types described above. Trends are the basic way of organizing the data, as always when we are dealing with observations in a time series. (As we have pointed out before, even when such data are combined and presented as a single total, it is useful in reaching conclusions to remain aware that such totals are a summation of the frequency distribution of qualitative variates even though they may look like quantitative variables.) Covariance data are derived from comparison of two or more trends, if the period, code, and recording units have been planned so as to make systematic comparison possible. The interaction of symbol trends and event sequences can be obtained from the foregoing data, if the situation has been defined so that the inferences which establish causal sequences between words and deeds can be made with confidence.

What Purposes Does Content Analysis Serve?

In the preceding section we discussed the ways in which content analysis has been used to describe, with objectivity, precision, and generality, the frequency, amount, and prominence of any symbols in a given symbol sequence. The exposition referred to the use of such data in forming conclusions concerning the attitudes of their users. The context throughout this discussion was that symbols operate as a stimuli.

This contextualization can, and for many important research purposes should, be inverted. There are many cases when it is valuable to apply content analysis to a sequence of symbols which are a *response* to some stimulus external to the sequence. Interaction studies of the type described above may apply content-analytic techniques to situations where the symbols to be analyzed interact, either as stimulus or response, with other words or with deeds. Three main types of situation are as follows:

Stimulus	Response
Symbols	Symbols
Symbols	Deeds
Deeds	Symbols

Content analysis thus takes on a more general character as a technique of analysis than may have been apparent from the preceding discussion. It should be plain, before we conclude our summary of purposes for which content analysis actually has been used, that potentially the technique can be applied to any situation which includes a sequence of symbols.

Content analysis has been applied to psychiatric symbols recorded in clinical interviews, to value symbols embodied in popular fiction, to doctrinal symbols in interrogation surveys, and to the flow of attention in casual conversation.[48] Such studies have revealed no limits, in principle, to the applicability of content-analysis technique. So long as a flow of symbols occurs, content analysis can be used to detect the characteristic attitudes of their user for or against selected ideas and policies, individuals and groups, parties and nations. It can be used also to study the diffusion of attitudes and beliefs through space and time by comparative analysis of trends among several users of selected symbols, and to study the consequences of certain attitudes upon the formation of other attitudes and beliefs, policies and practices. It can even detect causal sequences leading to changes—as in the study of the effects of defeats upon Soviet propaganda—whenever either cause or consequence receives symbolic expression, i.e., is discussed in public.

Since practically all important matters are discussed in public, this gives content analysis a very wide field of applicability. The fact that most extant content-analysis procedures have been conventionalized with respect to the mass media of communication, and particularly the press, is accounted for by the brief history of the technique, by the pressure of events during this brief history, and by considerations of convenience. Content analysis, as practiced today, is a development of the 1940s. Although some important thinking in this direction was done earlier,[49] the elaboration of the technique was not accomplished until the Experimental Division for the Study of Wartime Communications was established at the Library of Congress during World War II. Since the emphasis at this time was on the analysis of propaganda, the Experimental Division concentrated its attention on the medium which produced the symbol sequences most directly relevant and accessible for this purpose—the public press.

We have mentioned many dimensions of attitude which can be studied by content analysis of the media of public communication. In summary: The *distribution of attention* in a given medium to various threats and promises can be determined with a high degree of precision by analyzing content of an appropriate sample of that medium. The *values attacked or defended* can be investigated by the analysis of attributes, i.e., by an analysis in which the symbols studied are attributed values (e.g., unity, equality, etc.). The *bias toward or against certain nations, leaders, or classes* can be determined by the analysis of designations, i.e., an analysis in which the symbols studied are generally names of persons, groups, and so on. *Diffusion of attitudes or beliefs* can be investigated by comparing the output of a wide range of diverse symbol producers. *Intensity of attitudes* can be measured by various techniques, of which the simplest is counting the frequency (repetition), amount (space), and prominence (position and style) devoted to symbols bearing on these attitudes. *Changes* can be detected by use of trend graphs, chi squares, and similar procedures. *Causes of these changes* can be established if we have sufficient information to detect preceding covariants.

The foregoing discussion of content-analysis research in the past decade may be summarized concisely in schematic form, as follows:

I. TREND
   A. Attention
      1. High-low

         2.   More-less
         3.   Increasing-decreasing
    B. Direction
         1.   Favorable
         2.   Unfavorable
         3.   Neutral
    C. Intensity
         1.   Extreme
         2.   Moderate
         3.   Low

II. COVARIANCE
    A. Through time
         1.   Several sequences in one space
         2.   One sequence in several spaces
         3.   Several sequences in several spaces
    B. Through space
         1.   Several sequences at one time
         2.   One sequence in several spaces
         3.   Several sequences in several spaces

III. INTERACTION
    A. Symbol-to-symbol
    B. Symbol-to-event
    C. Event-to-symbol

IV. The RADIR Symbol Studies

The prestige paper has become an institution in all modern major powers. In each there is one paper, and usually only one, easily identified as being addressed to an elite audience and providing statements of public policy which are not available to readers of the ordinary papers. This paper is often, although not always, a great paper in the sense of having widespread news coverage. It is often, though again not always, an official or semiofficial organ of the state. It always maintains intimate relations with the government, especially the foreign office. It is widely read abroad by those seeking clues as to the dominant attitudes in the countries in which these papers are published.

The existence of such papers is a testimonial to the importance of public opinion in the modern world. They provide the elite with large amounts of information relevant to policy and provide a public medium for the expression of elite attitudes. This important institution, surprisingly, has not been given adequate recognition by students of society. (Some elementary information about this institution and how it operates is given in Chapter Two: "The Prestige Papers.") The prestige papers included in our sample were the following:

Country	Paper	Years Covered
Great Britain	*The Times*	1890-1949
Russia	*Novoe Vremia*	1892-1917
	Izvestia	1918-1949
United States	*The New York Times*	1900-1949
France	*Le Temps*	1900-1942
	Le Monde	1945-1949
Germany	*Norddeutsche allgemeine Zeitung* *	1910-1920
	Frankfurter Zeitung	1920-1932
	Völkischer Beobachter	1933-1945

*This paper is usually referred to by its more recent title, *Deutsche allgemeine Zeitung* (D.A.Z.). At the time of our use of it, however, it had not yet dropped "Nord" from its name.

In most cases the choice of paper was not difficult. Reasons for the choice, in the few cases where there was some question, are given in Chapter Two. Where the full sixty-year period is not covered, the reason is that missing issues were not available, either because no issues appeared or because copies could not be obtained.

The sample consisted of the editorials in these papers on the first and the fifteenth of every month. When no paper appeared on either of those days, the nearest possible day was chosen. Thus we normally had five series of twenty-four papers for each year of the roughly one-half century. This sample was obviously designed to measure long-range trends in editorial content.

In each editorial in the sample, the coders noted (according to prescribed rules) the presence of any of 416 symbols which constituted our symbol list. Of these, 206 were the names of national or similar units (countries, national minorities, continents, etc.) and 210 were key symbols of the major ideologies which have been contending in world politics during the past half-century. These included, to cite the "N's" as an example, Nationalism, Nazism, Neutrality, and Nonintervention. The full list is given in Appendix A. Each time one of these symbols appeared in an editorial it was recorded (1) as being present, and (2) as being either approved, disapproved, or neutrally judged.

Even if a symbol appeared in an editorial more than once, it was recorded only once: that is to say, our recording unit was the number of editorials in which a symbol appeared, not the number of appearances. If an editorial used a symbol more than once, with variant judgments, then either approval or disapproval was recorded once according to which judgment was more frequent. Each of the few editorials in which variant judgments were exactly equal was recorded as giving one neutral judgment.

The list of symbols was drawn up by Harold D. Lasswell, who also drew up the basic instructions for the readers. In the early stages of the reading a few symbols were added and a few removed, but the basic list stood the test of experience.

The reading was done by a team of coders. They worked under the supervision of Daniel Lerner. Each reader kept a notebook in which the symbols were recorded in a preliminary fashion, together with any problems which arose. These problems were taken up either individually with the director or in a staff meeting. Thus a measure of agreement among coders was assured. Each coder worked from a symbol list translated into the language of the paper being read.

When the reading was completed, time-series graphs and frequency tables were drawn up for each symbol on a year-by-year basis. The statistical analysis of the results after this point was done by Ithiel Pool.

The main results reported concern attention to, or judgment of, individual symbols or symbol clusters (symbols added together to form an index). Attention is reported either as a percentage of the editorials in a given period or as a percentage of the total symbol count for a given period. Thus a given symbol may be said to appear in 13 percent of the editorials and to account for 1.5 percent of the symbol count for that period. Judgments are also reported in two ways, for differing purposes. In most cases the number of favorable judgments was divided by the sum of the favorable and unfavorable judgments, or $f / (f + u)$. In other cases the equation used was one suggested by the Janis-Fadner coefficient of imbalance.[50] The difference between the number of favorable and the number of unfavorable judgments was divided by the total number of symbols, favorable, unfavorable, and neutral, or $f - u / t, t = f + u + n$.

In interpreting these results it is often important to distinguish a symbol from the idea to which it refers. These two things, though obviously related, are not the same. Sometimes fluctuations in a word may indicate fluctuations in a given idea; sometimes not. The increase in the use of the symbol DISARMAMENT during the interbellum probably reflects an actual increase in *concern* with the problem, but it certainly does not reflect an increase in the *act* of disarming. In other cases, fluctuations in the symbol may not even indicate *concern* with its referent, but may only reflect other "extraneous" considerations, such as censorship. The fact that the Vichy press did not talk about the NAZIS or about the ALLIES reflects no decline in interest. The possible relationships between the use of a word and feelings toward its referent are many and complex. It would be fallacious to confuse the two.

In order to make the distinction clear, we refer to the symbols themselves in capital letters throughout these studies. Whenever a word appears in capitals, like ALLIES above, the passage refers to the symbol. When a word appears in lower case it refers to its referent. Thus the statement,

"Concern with PEACE increased as the war progressed" means that the word PEACE was increasingly used during a real war. "TERRORISM disappears as terrorism increased" is also a perfectly possible statement containing no contradiction. It simply means that the word was less used in public communications when the practice became more widespread—a quite probable sequence of events in the twentieth century.

V. Lessons of RADIR Experience

It is no doubt premature to attempt to lay down rules for using content analysis. The technique is too new, the experience too limited, for anyone to say with certainty for what purposes content analysis can best be used, when it should be used, what its units should be, and how its results should be reported. Someday there may be a handbook which will specify standardized types of investigations that may be undertaken with confidence by moderately skilled personnel. Although any trained social scientist today can produce useful results with a poll or attitude scale if he follows the prescriptions of the handbooks, he cannot yet do so with content analysis. We do not undertake here to write a handbook; nonetheless, it may be useful to formulate some tentative conclusions that have grown out of several years of work. From this experience, we have learned some lessons about questions which any content analyst must face: whether to count, when to count, what to count, and how to count.

Whether to Count

Quantification.   There is clearly no reason for content analysis unless the question one wants answered is quantitative. Content analysis will not tell us whether a given work is good literature; it *will* tell us whether the style is varied. It will not tell us whether a paper is subversive; it *will* tell us if its contents change with the party line. It will not tell us how to convince the Russians; it *will* tell us what are the most frequent themes of Soviet propaganda.

Many questions about communications are asked nonquantitatively but require answers that are, in part, quantitative. For example, the question is frequently asked whether textbooks deal *fairly* with x, y, or z—say labor, Negroes, or capitalism. This question always involves, in the first place, some standard of what constitutes a fair attitude. Should the textbooks be favorable, unfavorable, or balanced? This is a question of values to be answered by citizens and not by content analysts. But once it is answered, questions of fact arise which are amenable to content analysis: What is the actual *distribution* of favorable, unfavorable, and neutral items in the current body of textbooks? The original question, although asked nonquantitatively, actually involves another question which is a quantitative one. There is a statistic, knowledge of which would help in answering whether textbooks deal *fairly* (as defined by the enquirer) with *x, y,* or *z.*

That is the test of whether to count. The researcher should ask himself: "Is there any statistic on the contents of this communication which, if obtainable, will help solve my research problem?" Perhaps the researcher begins by wondering what elements of the current French ideology make France susceptible to Russian or American propaganda. Perhaps he begins by wondering how fully the press covers international affairs, or what the comic books do to the reading habits of children, or whether a given document is a forgery.

Before he undertakes a content analysis, he must think through these questions until he has arrived at one or more statistics, knowledge of which would be part of the answer; e.g., which of the themes that are most *frequent* in Russian and American propaganda are also most *frequent* in traditional French material? How *many* column inches are devoted to international events of certain kinds? How does the vocabulary of comic books *correlate* with that of other media? How does the vocabulary of the suspect document *correlate* with that of known works by the author?

None of these strictly quantitative questions gives a full answer to the broader initial question, but each has some bearing on it. If the statistic answering one of these limited questions is wanted, then content analysis may be called for; otherwise not. Too often public officials or other consumers of content analysis leave the analyst with the broad initial question and then are dissatisfied when the analyst's magic produces only a limited statistic which, while relevant, does not resolve the original problem.

Having decided that there is a statistic which is wanted, we are still not sure that content analysis will give us what we want. There are many statistics we should like to know but, for practical reasons, cannot discover. For example, which are the most common reasons for favoring candidate X? We can analyze the newspapers, but newspaper attitudes are not what we want to know. We want to analyze the flow of citizen conversation. To get a sample of that is both difficult and expensive.

Another example: We want to know whether newspaper alarmism is a good index of international crisis. The intensity of international crisis is a quantity, but not one for which we have a good measure. How, then, are we to make a correlation with it? The fact that our question is quantitative does not automatically make counting feasible, but it does justify exploring the possibility. If the question about symbols is quantitative, and if it can be answered at all, content analysis will make the answer more accurate and more reliable than it would otherwise be.

The costs of this accuracy are high, for content analysis is not a cheap technique. But the advance of science has always been expensive. Our advantage over Plato and Ibn Kaldun is certainly not that we have more insight. We cannot expect to go far beyond their results without introducing tools which they did not have. These tools may be cheap compared with the cost of a cyclotron, but compared with the costs of an intelligent scholar in a library they are high. For the consumer of content analysis, then, there is always the question whether the limited statistic he will get is worth the price. If, however, he decides to go ahead with his content analysis, a by-product of his purchase will be another experiment to advance the young science. For the ultimate development of a satisfactory theory of symbolic behavior, the cost of quantification is probably well worth while if the problem to which it is applied has any scientific interest.

Precisioning the obvious.   Sometimes content analysis has no value even in answering a quantitative question, because the answer is obvious without it. Its use on such questions is sometimes justified on the grounds that it yields more precise answers than impressionistic techniques. Under this statement lies an important truth, but taken at face value it may also be specious. It is specious both when used to justify a precision that is not needed and also when used to justify precision that is unusable. Since we sometimes must report our results on continua whose dimensions are not clear, we often find ourselves just as uncertain about the meaning of our data after content analysis as before. Quantification of symbols must not be allowed to become a branch of numerology.

An illustration is the proposal to use content analysis to measure the recent relationships of Russia and the United States. It takes neither content analysis nor genius to predict the findings of research: the relationships are bad and getting worse. It may be argued, however, that it would be desirable to have a more precise scale. That is true, but we need to be clear about what, exactly, is meant by precision. If we had a thermometer of crisis with a standardized scale on which 50 is normal and war breaks out at 100, it would be highly useful to know whether tension is at 73 or 98. But that is not the kind of result that content analysis will give us. From content analysis we may find that the proportion of unfavorable statements about Russia in the American press rose (to use imaginary figures) from 60 percent in 1946 to 80 percent in 1950; and that anti-American statements in the Russian press rose from 70 percent to 90 percent in these years. These would be useful facts for some purposes, but if one hoped to come out with an immediately usable overall index of Russo-American tensions, he would surely be disappointed. The scale is too unfamiliar to permit ready interpretation. What is normal? How closely do events correlate with press sentiments?—the questions are innumerable. For a commonsense problem, like the degree of Russo-American tension, the content-analysis thermometer may initially be no better than none.

In this it does not differ from an ordinary mercury thermometer. One can well imagine a similar sequence of events in the early days of the thermometer. People had long talked of temperature. They were perfectly aware that it was a matter of degree (i.e., quantitative). Yet estimating temperature was so difficult and inaccurate that whether to wear an overcoat was about as complex a problem as could well be imagined.

The thermometer would initially be no help at all in solving this one practical problem. It took time and experience to learn how one feels at 50, 60, 70, and 80 degrees on a particular scale, and to gain confidence in its psychic reliability. Yet no one would argue that the thermometer has been useless. Its precision has enabled us to answer questions that no one thought of asking before, since people ask only those questions to which the answers are at least conceivable. We now write equations for the acceleration of a chemical reaction with each additional degree of temperature. We measure the mean diurnal and seasonal variation in temperature for a given climatic zone. We distinguish degrees and calories. The thermometer has proved its importance, not merely in giving more precise answers to the old questions but in opening up new ones. We now know that temperature is only one of several variables determining the need for an overcoat. At precisely the same air temperature, comfort varies with wind, humidity, and the amount of food in one's stomach. Our vista now includes unsuspected complexities that underlay the old questions.

The same sequence may be expected from content analysis. The questions we ask today are those we can at least begin to answer by ordinary reading techniques. Where we are dissatisfied with the answers thus obtained, our dissatisfaction probably reflects the fact that there are unsuspected complexities to the problem. Content analysis may reveal some of these complexities. It may answer questions whose existence we now suspect only vaguely or not at all.

Specifically, on the question of Russian-American relations, content analysis may someday make it possible to talk about the symbol modes in which hostility is expressed, the relative frequency of these, and their relationship to the intensity of this hostility. But we shall probably not find a simple relationship. Starting out to measure tension, we may end up with but few scientifically worth-while results on quantity of tension, although we may have several on the rate at which a change of tension is reflected in different types of media.

The conclusion from this is that content analysis is most likely to be fruitful where there is an open-minded desire to investigate the mechanisms of certain kinds of symbolic behavior. As a method for documenting conclusions which can be established by traditional techniques with all the precision required, it is too expensive in research time and money.

There are exceptions to this advice. An outstanding instance has been the use of content analysis in the law courts. That a given newspaper followed a Nazi line may have been fairly obvious to sophisticated readers. However, to meet the requirements of legal evidence it was necessary to document the obvious. In this situation, the value of content analysis was that it did explicitly and on the record what the intelligent reader did intuitively.

This explicitness may, indeed, turn out to be the first step toward opening new problems. If so, however, content analysis must then go beyond the first step and become more than an elaborate verification of what was already known and more incisively expressed.

When to Count

Having decided to explore the possibility of counting, we are ready to enter upon the research program. We are tempted at this point to start counting at once and to budget most of our time for this purpose. Our experience is that this is a trap. Not more than about a third of the man-hours allowed for should go to coding the texts of the sample. The final analysis of the data takes as long as the reading; and the preliminary explorations may also take as long.

There is the temptation to proceed immediately with counting because language seems deceptively simple. Like Molière's M. Jourdain, we have been talking prose all our lives. We think we understand it. We easily think of the most direct ways of expressing the ideas whose presence we wish to study, and we are apt to see no obstacle simply to counting the expressions. For example, the scholar who wishes to find out how the press is treating a given legislative proposal may think he can merely count all statements for or against it. He is likely to find, however, that one paper smothers the bill in silence; that another runs a series of articles exposing the evils the bill is designed to cure, but never indulges in the heavy-handed technique of explicit judgment on the bill; and that a third paper, which is really most neutral, makes explicit editorial judgment more often than the other two.

It does not follow from this that counting is futile or impossible. Rather, the conclusion, in this instance, would be that one must first try to discover the major modes *actually* used for revealing a given attitude, and that one may then set up a scheme to count all of them. This is difficult because there is as yet no good theory of symbolic communication by which to predict how given values, attitudes, or ideologies will be expressed in manifest symbols. The extant theories tend to deal with values, attitudes, and ideologies as the ultimate units, not with the symbolic atoms of which they are composed. There is almost no theory of language which predicts the specific words one will emit in the course of expressing the contents of his thoughts. Theories in philosophy or in the sociology of knowledge sometimes enable us to predict ideas that will be expressed by persons with certain other ideas or social characteristics. But little thought has been given to predicting the specific words in which these ideas will be cloaked. The content analyst, therefore, does not know what to expect.

This difficulty can be illustrated by the history of our own RADIR Project. Some of the mistakes we made might have been avoided by prudence, but others were the inevitable missteps of any new line of research. Now, out of hindsight, we can see that many of our original expectations about the results were based on an inadequate concept of the language of the editorials.

The RADIR Project set out with the proposition that certain symbols, such as DEMOCRACY, FRATERNITY, SECURITY, and ABUNDANCE, stood for the common aspirations of people in the modern world. We hoped that these symbols would directly index trends in formal allegiance to the values to which they refer. We had, in the end, a far more complicated series of hypotheses.

Take the symbol DEMOCRACY, for example. We found increasing emphasis on this symbol. Could this be treated as a simple function of increasing concern with democracy? Close inspection of the figures revealed that, actually, complex factors were involved. Use of the symbol DEMOCRACY increased but little more than could be accounted for by increased attention to the subject matters to which it is most relevant. In other words, modern editorial writers are not much more prone to relate their discussions of current issues to this term than would have been their predecessors. What has happened is that subject matters which would have been related to DEMOCRACY at any point in the past fifty years have increased in frequency of attention. Concern with relevant contexts has increased, but emphasis on democracy within these contexts has increased perhaps little, if at all. If we call the frequency of the symbol DEMOCRACY y and the frequency of these related symbols x, then we find that y is a function of x. That finding itself was more complex than our a priori analysis. But the function for a given symbol may be more complicated than $y = bx$. The equation may be of the form $y = a + bx$, with a and b being different in different papers, or the equation may not even be linear.

Though we suspected before we started that in order to discuss trends in attention to DEMOCRACY we should have to consider it not as an independent case but as a "joint product," no procedures were available to show us how to work this hypothesis into our research design. Had we understood these things to begin with, we might have chosen our symbols differently and might also have constructed our sample differently. We should then have tested our list of symbols related to DEMOCRACY with a view to checking whether they represented in a full and rounded fashion the *context* in which the general concept DEMOCRACY might appear, and we should probably, as a result, have expanded our list of terms referring to the mechanics of representative government.

We should also have increased the number of periods we were using and should have constructed the sample in such a way as to have a larger selection of the relevant symbols in a few of the smaller subsamples. We had, however, no way of estimating in advance the likely order of magnitude of key political symbols, since previous relevant studies scarcely existed. As it stands now, the above conclusions about DEMOCRACY, although probably correct, rest on somewhat thin data. Fortunately, in this instance, our final hypotheses, though more complex than our original ones, could still be verified, although not so securely as could have been done if these final hypotheses had been incorporated into our initial design.

Another illustration is provided by our study of peace symbols: The general endorsement of world peace as a value seems to be a fairly obvious fact, but what of the symbols which express this value? Which are they, and have they shown any trend in use? The most obvious indices are WAR and PEACE. But WAR and PEACE refer more often to specific acts than to the abstract concepts. In editorials, for instance, one finds such expressions as "the WAR powers of the President," or "before the WAR" or "while we are at WAR" or "PEACE conference." They are more often so mentioned than as the concepts WAR and PEACE. As a result, the use of these symbols correlates most highly with the fact of war. They are most often used during war or when war is imminent. Their occurrence, as such, does not measure concern with the goal value, peace.

This difficulty could have been solved by appropriate rules for coding. Had we spotted the trouble in advance, we could have had our coders count only references to the abstract nouns WAR and PEACE, not references to concrete ones. Here, again, the need for specific hypotheses, pretested on the communication content to be analyzed, is made clear by the difficulties which confront the analyst when they are absent.

With respect to the value fraternity, another difficulty appeared: inadequate frequency of relevant symbols. Our data on judgments of fraternity symbols is weak because of insufficient frequencies. We made the mistake of assuming that in editorials, unlike news stories, judgments would be numerous. Consequently, we defined judgments narrowly, requiring that they be quite explicit. In fact, however, explicit judgments proved to be fairly rare. The sophisticated editorial writer makes his point of view clear without wasting words to say "this is a good thing" or "that is a bad thing." The reader, having inferred the judgment, does not even realize that it has not been stated—only implied.

Thus the lessons on when to count can be summarized under two heads: (1) hypothesis, and (2) pretesting. Our discussion, in the preceding section, of whether to count stressed the role of hypothesis in making this decision. The researcher should undertake content analysis only if he reaches an affirmative answer to the question: "Is there any statistic about the contents of this communication which will solve my research problem?"

Having decided to use counting, the decision *when* to start counting should depend upon pretesting. Pretesting is the technique which will indicate whether the prescribed symbol list, coding rules, and recording procedures *actually* will produce the statistic wanted. If not, pretesting (which includes, initially, "impressionistic" immersion in the material to be analyzed) will indicate what alterations should, and can, be made to produce the desired statistic. For some general clues to these operations, we turn next to the question "what to count?"

What to Count

The complexity of the language with which we deal does not imply that the data we accumulate should also be complex. On the contrary, the purpose of mastering the complexities of the text is to simplify the data collected. There is a strong temptation to solve every new problem by complicating the data being collected. That, however, only defers the problem till later. If one yields to the temptation, one may, in the end, need to conduct a content analysis of one's collected content-analysis data.

Let us ullustrate: Suppose one wishes to measure the treatment of Russia in the American press. Immediately one will discover that there are whole categories of statements that cannot be classified as simply for or against Russia. For instance, there are statements saying Russia is strong and statements saying she is weak. These may cut both ways. The Communist *Daily Worker* and the anti-Communist *New Leader* both make capital out of the size of the Red Army. One is, therefore, apt to add categories other than plus or minus to take care of these cases. Besides allegations of strength and weakness, such cases might include ambiguous stories, or stories on changes of personnel, or a Kremlin denial of rumored aggressive intentions, etc., none of which lends itself to simple plus or minus classification. Finding many such cases, we might elaborate our study, recasting our categories to provide a complete typology of things said about the Russians.

Having done that, we should further find that it makes a difference which Russians are referred to. There is Stalin, and there are the Russian people; there are also those who chose freedom, and those who work in the salt mines. We, therefore, might add a subscript to each statement about Russia to indicate its subject. Then we discover that time subscripts would also be useful. Statements about Czarist Russia, Russia today, and Russia after Stalin's death are apt to be different. The statement that Russia was once strong and the statement that Russia will be stronger in the future carry almost opposite emotional implications.

So far, the analytic scheme here sketched in outline continues to be manageable, but the consequences of the tendency toward complication are becoming clear. In attempting to reproduce all the possible complexities of language, we are returning to a body of data that cannot be handled except by a second series of simplifications. The most complete analytic scheme possible would be one which assigned every word in the dictionary a code number and recorded these code numbers in the sequence in which they occurred. By so doing, none of the richness of the original language would be lost, but it would, consequently, be worthless.

It should be frankly recognized that content analysis is a procedure of deliberate simplification. Such deliberate simplification is painful. Coders are pained at losing some of the richness of the meaning of the text. Invariably a conscientious reader will bring to his supervisor some passage full of innuendo, metaphor, or *double entendre* and protest that the scheme being used distorts its real meaning. Toward such difficulties the analyst may well be ruthless. When the questionable passage has become but one of fifty-seven checks in category *xyz,* the analyst will have neither time nor cause to consider its individuality. Content analysis is a statistical procedure, and, like any statistical procedure, it disregards the individuality of the particular case for the sake of discovering the uniformities in the mass.

Categories should, therefore, be added only when they bear upon the hypotheses being tested. The purpose of elaborate preliminary examination of every possible complication is not to incorporate all of them in the schemes, but rather to find the simplest schemes which will yield the data wanted.

Let us review the RADIR experience in these regards. In our studies, we tried two different types of content-analysis schemes. One was just about as simple as possible; the other was fairly complex. For our newspaper analysis we had a list of symbols, against which we checked merely whether the symbols occurred and, if so, whether approved, disapproved, or neither. For a speech analysis we used a scheme in which we recorded for any statement the "designation" or person to which it referred, the "attribute" or quality of the person, whether he acted for or against that quality, whom or what he affected by so doing, and several other things. Perhaps the optimum scheme would have been somewhere between the two in complexity, but if one had to choose one or the other scheme, a strong case could be made for the simpler one.

Our actual newspaper scheme used 8 periods, 5 subsamples, 416 symbols. Had all the cells been filled, we could have had 49,920 results to work with. Our total number of symbols counted was 105,004. The latter is quite a sizable number—certainly a larger number than most research projects can hope to attain. Yet when compared with the number of cells into which these items might fit, it is clear that the average frequency of any symbol judged in a given way in any paper during any one period was only two. This explains why it was necessary to combine symbols and why, even when this was done, we sometimes ran out of usable data at key points. It also partly explains why it took over a year to analyze the data. It was wise that this "simple" scheme was not allowed to become much more complex. One may wonder whether just one further subdivision, multiplying the possible number of combinations by two, might not have made the whole scheme unmanageable.

The speech analysis which was so much more complicated was manageable because it was tabulated on IBM punch cards; but, obviously, most of the complexities which the scheme allowed for could not be used. There were 14,574 cards or coded statements. The number of possible combinations the scheme allowed for was 8,382,009,600. Clearly, we should have been just as well off with a simpler scheme, since, in tabulating the results, it was necessary to do a great deal of consolidating.

Consolidation after coding, rather than before, has certain advantages. Often a special subcategory makes possible the testing of an additional hypothesis. Furthermore, unsuspected discoveries sometimes arise from the data which would not arise if the scheme were trimmed down to the extent that it was capable of testing only the initial hypothesis. Provided the analytic scheme is set up so that the subcategories can be easily combined afterward into the major categories which one believes will prove relevant, there is no loss, except that of some time and expense, in classifying one's data initially into numerous detailed categories.

The proviso that consolidation afterward be possible is important, nonetheless. The mere presence of a very refined breakdown does not necessarily make possible the grosser combinations that one wants. For example, it occurred to us that the count of country names might give some interesting results as to trends in the areal distribution of political attention, and this turned out to be so. When, however, we tried to summarize the results, by continents, certain difficulties arose. References to RUSSIA, for example, were ambiguous as between Europe and Asia. References to the BRITISH or FRENCH EMPIRES were also ambiguous. This difficulty was not very important, because the proposal to summarize the results by continents was merely one possible convenient device for presenting the data. If, however, one of our major original objectives had been to map the areal distribution of attention by large regions, it would then have been necessary to make our subcategories quite differently. We should have had to define the subcategories quite differently. We should have had to define the subcategories so that each was a distinct part of one, and only one, of the larger categories we should ultimately be interested in. This may seem obvious, but when one is setting up a content-analysis study, it is not always obvious that one must have mapped out in advance the equivalence between groups of subcategories and the major categories that one knows one needs.[51]

The units. The goal of simplicity is easily approached by a word count, but other considerations may often indicate a theme count or other procedure. The possible units of content analysis are separate symbols, statements, or collections of statements, such as paragraphs or whole articles.

If the statement is taken as the unit, one may code by complete thoughts (theme analysis) or by some characteristic of the statement, such as the persons or things referred to (designation analysis) or the traits attributed to them (attribute analysis). Larger units may also be classified by their main theme, by their main subject, or by the main attributes dealt with or other such characteristics. Since designations, attributes, etc., are parts of statements, it is also possible to make a count of each of the parts, keeping them in their constellation in the statement. This technique gains in flexibility but loses by complexity.

A single list of words, statements, attributes, or designations provides a very simple system and is therefore to be preferred if it will give the necessary results. Whether any of these will give the results wanted, and which one will, depends, of course, upon the goals of the research. No general preference can be expressed for one type of unit as against another. The choice is entirely a function of the goals at hand.

One important advantage of a word count should, however, be mentioned. We stated above that no general theory of symbolic behavior exists to enable us to predict the pattern of symbols. This is less true for a straight word count than for a count of statements or other combinations of words. We know something about the normal pattern of words in the language. We know roughly how many there are. We know something of their individual frequencies in various media. We know something of the shape of their frequency distribution. We have a grammatical classification for them, and we know that words of certain classes are likely to come before, or after, or in other set relationships to words of other classes. No one of these propositions could be asserted of statements. We have no idea what is the normal relative frequency of certain types of statements. We lack, therefore, a base from which to measure deviations. With statements we have, therefore, far less basis for allowing for the operation of chance and also far less basis for arriving at parameters of a model than we do with individual words.

Since our own study used a word list, the comments to follow will be couched in terms of such a list. Many of them apply, *mutatis mutandis,* to a theme list or to any other list.

Validity. The list itself might, in some cases, conceivably contain all the possible relevant words. An interesting study has been made of the frequency of the first person singular in the speeches of leading statesmen. Studies of the frequencies of parts of speech can list the relevant symbols by classification rather than enumeration and can thus be exhaustive. Most often, however, a coding list contains a purportedly representative selection of words of a given kind. Words are usually chosen to provide an index to some form of behavior to which they are relevant.

Thus the RADIR study needed a list of symbols representative of discussions of five selected values: democracy, fraternity, security, abundance, enlightenment. It was obviously impossible to enumerate all the words, synonyms, or senses of homonyms, which are relevant to any one of these values. It was, however, not difficult to draw up a list which was sufficiently representative of these values, so that the words on the list formed a good index to the extent and tendency of discussions of these values. A list of words including ORDER, SECURITY, INSECURITY, WAR, PEACE, REVOLUTION, COUP D'ETAT, ARMAMENTS, etc., covered the range of political discussions of safety sufficiently well so that fluctuations in the index might be taken as a measurement of fluctuations in the total flow of symbols respecting the subject matter.

These general principles were understood by us before we designed our newspaper study. In retrospect, however, certain specific injunctions and problems appear relevant to the construction of such lists. These are mainly problems of sampling, since a desirable list would be one that is a good sample of the relevant universe. The problems bear either on the composition of the sample or its size.

The number and variety of words needed on the list is a function, first of all, of the complexity of the concept being indexed. To index the concept of safety required symbols referring to both domestic and foreign violence, since these two variants, discussed with quite different words, are both comprehended by the one value. Democracy we found to involve three fairly independent constellations of symbols: one referring to freedom, one to the people, and one to the institutions of parliamentary government.

Seeing the problem in this way opens up two possible lines of approach, both of which were used at some points in our study. It is possible to subject a concept to logical analysis, to determine how many different subconcepts it consists of and what their relative importance is, and thus to draw up a list with an adequate and balanced representation of symbols of each subconcept. This procedure involves an a priori analysis of the ideological factors making up a concept. The other approach involves an a posteriori grouping of symbols. If the list of symbols is sufficiently extensive, it will be found that groups of symbols follow common patterns. It will be possible, in other words, to apply a sort of factorial analysis to the list, by which one will find that the large number of symbols occurring do not each represent an independent variable, but that groups of symbols form constellations, certain words appearing together. The independent factor is an idea to which the group of symbols refers and whose fluctuations it indexes. It was by the latter method, rather than by any theoretical analysis, that we found the three components into which discussion of democracy in the editorials fell.

The ideal procedure is one that uses both approaches. As in constructing a psychological test, one first draws up an a priori scheme. Then one modifies it and validates it by empirical analysis of a trial run. Only then does one have a list that forms a pretested and satisfactory measuring device. Alternatively, and to the same effect, one may use an untested a priori list if one evaluates and ranks the items after counting but before use of the list as an index. But, in either case, one validates a modified version of one's original list before accepting it as an index.

This systematic validation of a content-analysis scheme has not yet been tried. Content analysts have been much concerned with problems of reliability of coding, but problems of validity have seemed so inaccessible to solution that they have not been dealt with. Up to now, an impression of reasonableness, sometimes based on trial runs, has been the only test of validity used. If the categories listed seemed to include the main ideas at issue, this was all that could be asked.

This was all that we asked of our own scheme. It was an a priori list, drawn up by a qualified political scientist and modified as we read the papers. It was in many ways a very satisfactory list, but when we came to analyze the data we found inevitable holes. To illustrate from the symbols of democracy, one of the three elements, the institutions of parliamentary government, was represented by too few symbols to give a fully reliable index. It was on the basis of this experience that it became clear to us how an experimental validation of a list could be organized.

It is important to realize, however, that the test of a common factor is not simple covariation over time. The possible relationships are more complex than that. Let us assume for a moment that the idea of freedom is an independent variable, to which a number of symbols are relevant. We can measure increases or decreases of attention to that idea by fluctuations in attention to the list of symbols. But it would be fallacious to assume that, therefore, all of these symbols will move up and down together, although most of them will. On the contrary, precisely because the symbols are so close in meaning, some of them may be negatively correlated. For example, FREEDOM and LIBERTY are alternative terms. A fad in the use of one may be at the expense of the other. On the other hand, an increase in discussion of CENSORSHIP or TYRANNY will lead to an increase in reference both to FREEDOM and to LIBERTY. The relationship of terms relevant to a single variable may be complementary or supplementary, although most often they will be supplementary.

Criteria for the validity of a list may now be stated more formally, although the statistical working out of the procedure remains to be done. Suppose we start with a list of n words, $w_1 \ldots w_n$, which are suspected on the basis of careful analysis to be related to some idea or group of ideas, each of which may be independent factors in the thinking of the symbol emitters. One is apt to find several groups of items which seem to appear in clusters. An obvious cluster, labeled factor x, may consist of w_1, w_2, w_3, w_4, w_5. The test of whether any given item, w_6, is appropriate to the index for factor x, is whether it is more likely to appear in the presence of that cluster than in its absence in the same medium and at about the same time. Few terms will appear with one factor only; that is, few terms are unidimensional. A good index, however, will consist of those terms which are most nearly so, the others being discarded.

For a time-series study, terms should be selected which appear with the same clusters throughout, although the relative frequency of the word in the cluster may vary over time. Thus, for example, AUTOCRACY appears more often in all cases where FREEDOM and LIBERTY appear, both in 1890 and today. The same may be said of DICTATORSHIP. But DICTATORSHIP is today used where AUTOCRACY would have been used in 1890. They will usefully complement each other in a good index, since both are fairly unidimensional to the cluster of freedom terms if time is held constant and the cluster is looked at for each moment separately.

It should be noted that, for certain studies, an a priori list remains most appropriate. Here, as always, purpose is the controlling consideration. For a study of attitude toward a nation, the country name is so much the most obvious symbol to use that further exploration may be unnecessary. In a study of the gradual popularization of a new word, one starts with the word given. The word is not here an index, and there is no problem of validity. For most studies, however, the problem of validity is important.

The number of symbols.   Having found symbols which validly index each factor to be measured, one wonders how many such symbols are needed on each list. One or two, even three or four, usually do not make a satisfactory index, although, if one selects the right symbol or symbols, they conceivably may. The reason that more are needed is that, as noted above, the relationships between any one word and the other words dealing with a given subject matter are complex. They are partly complementary, partly supplementary. Also, any one word is likely to be used in discussing only certain phases of a subject matter. "Brooklyn Dodgers" would not be a good index of attention to baseball, nor "revolution" a good index of attention to violence. They both meet the test that they are more likely to occur when the general subject is under discussion than when it is not, but they do not meet the test of generality. Other aspects of the subject than those referred to by the indicatory word may be under discussion, e.g., the American League or War.

A single word or a few words may be a valid index only when they are highly general key terms which appear in any discussion of the subject matter. The name of the subject matter itself most often fits this test. Thus the term "baseball" would probably be a valid index to discussions of that subject, but there is probably no one word which would serve the purpose for attention to violence. Whether there is one symbol which always occurs in the appropriate contexts is an empirical matter subject to test.

If there is no such term, then one must use a list of terms large enough to cover the different phases of the subject matter. The number of terms needed is partly a function of the likely frequencies of each. We shall note, in a subsequent chapter, that a very few words are used often, while many terms are used seldom. As a result, a short list is apt to be dominated by one or two symbols and reflect nothing more than their fluctuations. This happened to some extent to our list of symbols of safety. The symbols WAR and PEACE were so much more numerous than any of the others, and so numerous as compared with all the others combined, that our results reflected military history more than anything else. To avoid this we had to treat these two words and the rest of the list separately. It is often possible to avoid such difficulties by consulting the standard tables of word frequencies or by pretesting.

Parts of speech.   We saw above that some subjects were easily indexed by a few words, others not. A general hunch is that when a subject is defined by a rather concrete noun it is easiest to index. Attention to baseball or England is easily indexed by the names. Attention to safety from violence or to antiauthoritarianism is not. In general, where alternatives exist in speech or in writing, it is easier to use the concrete nouns. When the subject they refer to is discussed at all, such concrete nouns are likely to be used and therefore they form good indices. Other more abstract words, even if equally adequate in defining the subject matter, are likely to be replaced occasionally by concrete nouns referring to special aspects. Thus, WAR plus REVOLUTION index violence better than any generic term such as VIOLENCE itself. Either one of them, however, may be misleading in that it does not fully cover the subject matter of violence.

Although concrete nouns thus have some obvious advantages as indicators, there are many purposes which are better served with other types of words. Abstract nouns, verbs, adjectives, adverbs, even pronouns or particles, may be most appropriate for some purposes. The only thing to be avoided is an indiscriminate mixture which does not take into account differences in the frequency distributions of different parts of speech.

Verbs are fewer and more frequently used individually than nouns. They are less distinctive according to authors or subject matter. There is no noun so universal to all communication content as the verbs to *do,* or to *be,* or to *have.* Nouns are, therefore, better for detection of authorship and similar purposes. For these and similar reasons, content analyses have not yet been done on word lists of verbs. Although, such lists might prove a better indication of attention to violence than the more flagrant and obvious nouns, verbs, such as to *attack,* to *force,* to *hurt* etc., are used in many contexts where violence is only metaphorical (e.g., "The speaker attacked the law as likely to hurt the economy"). It is this kind of use that makes verbs unsatisfactory for overt subject matters; but for many psychological investigations the prevalence of this covert type of violence reference would be far more relevant than any overt direction of attention.

Our own symbol list, like those of previous studies, was limited to nouns, and for our purposes this was probably wise. But as we went along it became clear that for many questions a different approach would be better. Vast unexplored territories remain, for future content analysis, in the nonsubstantive parts of speech.

Translation.   The influence of grammar depends in part on the language being analyzed. No symbol list is perfectly translatable between languages. The difficulties of translation are great and obvious. VOLK, with its heavily nationalist and mystical overtones, is not quite the same word as PEOPLE, and they are both different from NAROD. Translation difficulties of this sort are often cited in objection to comparative content analyses. We do not wish to minimize them. What stands out from our experience, however, is not the difficulties (since we understood those before we started) but the fact that they are not insuperable.

We drew up our original list in English. We then translated it into French, German, and Russian. Sometimes two words took the place of one. Sometimes the meanings of a foreign word had to be restricted by a rule as to when to count it. The result was four lists as comparable as the languages permitted. How comparable were the resulting indices?

There is no precise answer to that question, for we have no measurement of comparability. We came up with some results that seemed to be independent of language, but that does not prove the absence of linguistic distortions. Two statistical considerations, however, lead us to put less emphasis on the distortions. The critic who worries about translation is thinking in the conventional mode of interpretation which puts emphasis on the individual word and context. If, once in ten times, the word SOCIALISM is used in France or Germany to mean not a system of nationalized ownership of the means of production but, instead, a cooperative or social approach in contrast to INDIVIDUALISM, this makes it significantly different from the English word for the translator, philologist, or political theorist. His awareness of the difference makes him forget the 90 percent overlap which is the important fact for statistical analysis.

Second, when one combines lists of such words into indices, the statistical difference becomes still smaller. VATERLAND and PATRIE may be somewhat different; so, too, may REICH and STATE. But, by the time all of these and other symbols have been lumped into national self-references, the particular mode of expression assumes little statistical importance. A Frenchman, a German, or an American faced with communicating an idea about his country is going to use some word of national self-reference. The choice of word will depend partly on the differences in the overtones of the individual words in the various languages, but the concept encompassed by the whole group is not substantially very different.

For other projects, with other purposes, linguistic difficulties may be greater than they were for us. There is no reason to assume, however, that they are insoluble.

Samples. Our sample, the editorials of every fifteenth day over a sixty-year period, is designed according to the indications given by Alexander Mintz.[52] The form of the sample proved altogether satisfactory. The one thing we learned from experience was to give more careful advance consideration to sample size.

We did not take full enough account, in our plans, of the very great concentration that exists on a few symbols. These few symbols (WAR, PEACE, PEOPLE, SOCIALISM, etc.) occurred thousands of times in our sample. Of these we had more than enough instances for any purpose at hand. We implicitly assumed, however, that any well-known and standard political symbol would appear often enough in the sample to make possible measurements of trends. In that assumption we were wrong. BALANCE OF POWER or FREEDOM OF ASSEMBLY are not esoteric concepts, yet the former occurred 31 times and the latter 17 times in 19,553 editorials. Such frequencies, scattered over five papers and sixty years, are not likely to be useful.

These two symbols were not extreme cases; they are typical of many symbols whose frequency we tended to overestimate because they were altogether familiar. We failed to take full account of the human storage capacity for symbols. A word that appears only once in every thousand editorials may still be a reasonably well known word, associated with a very well-known idea. The lesson from this is that, unless one is interested in the most common symbol or group of symbols, a rather extensive sample is necessary. The reading necessary to cover such an extensive sample, however, places strict limits on how intensive the analysis can be.

If one set out with the specific goal of making a content analysis on FREEDOM OF ASSEMBLY or the BALANCE OF POWER, one either would have to adopt a scheme to allow for very rapid reading or else would have to limit the sample to media where these are extensively discussed (e.g., books known to deal with the subject). Of course, headlines or other aids to scanning may make it possible to skip quickly to the relevant passages and then analyze them intensively. But any scheme which attempts to make a more or less comprehensive analysis of a large body of material will come up with considerable data on only a few symbols.

Because we had, in the end, so many symbols whose frequencies were too small for individual analysis, and because we had so much data in the bulk, it was clear when we came to statistical analysis of the results that little could be done with individual symbols. The 416 symbols had to be treated almost entirely as ingredients for a few indices. This did no harm, for these indices were, after all, the things we were most interested in. At this point a serious mistake was made.

The original scheme had been set up with full awareness that the independent event for statistical analysis would have to be the editorial, not the symbol. An editorial on the tariff will contain the word TARIFF several times, because the subject has come up. These word occurrences are not independent events within the editorial. On the other hand, just because there is an editorial on the tariff on the first of the month, there is little reason to expect one on the fifteenth. If the subject does come up both times, it is probably because an external cause (say a new bill) is operating throughout the period. Editorials, in other words, are *relatively* independent of each other. We therefore counted the number of editorials in which a given symbol appeared.

To combine symbols in such a scheme is a problem in combining binomial distributions. Symbol w_1 appears in p_1 of the editorials in a given period and does not appear in q_1. Editorial w_2 appears in p_2 and not in q_2. The problems are: what is the probability of (a) both, and (b) either w_1 or w_2 appearing in a given editorial? This can then be compared with the actual proportion of editorials in which one or both symbols appear. The difference between the expected and actual frequencies can be subjected to tests of significance. From this data we can say which symbols tend to appear together more often than expected, thus forming a constellation. We can give the proportion of editorials in which symbols belonging to a given index appear, and can give their mean frequency within those editorials in which they do appear.

This procedure for combining binomials was not used, for two reasons. First, it would have added a year to our work. Second, and really more to the point, we did not see the problem with the same clarity at the beginning as now. It took the author who did the statistical analysis a year to see the problem in the terms stated above. What we did, instead, was to construct indices by pooling the data for the individual symbols. We were perfectly aware that this made impossible the application of these significance tests which could be applied to individual symbols (and which we now see could be applied to correctly constructed indices), but there seemed no practical alternative.

What was done was to add together the frequency f_1 of editorials containing symbol w_1 with the frequency f_2 of editorials containing symbol w_2 to get a frequency, $F = f_1 + f_2$, for the index of a given period. It was thus impossible to say in what proportion of editorials these F items occurred.

It is these figures which constitute the bulk of our attention data below. There is no reason to doubt their approximate validity as indicators of political trends, but they do not have the elegance or the susceptibility to exact measures of significance which they might have had. In some of our later computations for this series, some of the procedures are revised so as to avoid the earlier error. But it was not possible to recompute all the data, and it would hardly have been worth while. One might, by recomputation, add to the conclusions, but it is doubtful that by so doing one would change them.

How to Count

We have already alluded to many of the difficulties that arose after the analytic scheme was set up and the counting was under way. We have mentioned the tendency to multiply categories and we have mentioned the problem of reliability.

Reliability, one of the recurrent headaches of content analysis, is a *sine qua non* of any scheme. Reliability is usually measured by the percentage of all entries identically coded by different coders. This may be an overly strict measure, since often there are degrees of error: a theme about war may often verge on both "self is strong" and "other is weak." This is a less serious discrepancy than would be a divergence between "self is strong" and "self is weak" or a divergence as to whether strength or morality is involved.

Our word count, fortunately, presented few such problems, since we were coding by explicit symbol rather than by more interpretive categories. There remained, nonetheless, several sources of error: oversight, synonyms, homonyms, grammatical variants, translation between languages. The errors arising from these sources, however, seldom involved a choice of symbol. They took the form of either erroneous inclusion or erroneous exclusion. In addition, there might be disagreement on judgment of an included symbol. The disagreement was generally between 0 and classification +, or between 0 and −, almost never between + and −.

Unfortunately, only one reliability test was run on this project. We took three readers who had been reading various languages and put them all on editorials in the one language they all knew: English (*New York Times* editorials). They were familiar with the special rules only for the language in which they had been working, not for English. Their reliability would undoubtedly have been higher in the language in which they had been working or after some special training. The codings of each of these three readers were compared with those of a regular *New York Times* reader. On inclusion and exclusion, reliability ran 66, 68, and 70 percent, respectively; on judgments of the included symbols, 91, 87, and 93 percent. The first set of figures is disappointing, the second set surprisingly good. Reliabilities in content analysis seldom run over 90 percent. Reliabilities between 70 and 80 percent are quite usable where the error is not systematic on the topic in question. Realizing the adverse conditions of the test, we may consider our results as falling into the usable, though by no means optimum, category.

Reliability could undoubtedly have been increased by training. Even more valuable, however, are simplicity and arbitrariness of the coding rules. Our coders probably were too deeply aware of the aims and interests of the study to let themselves forget the sense and context of what they read. As we noted above, such considerations of sense and context often get lost in the end, regardless, since content analysis is a method of structuring and simplifying a body of communications. Even greater literal mindedness than our scheme provided for would probably have gained more by reliability than would have been lost by distortion.

The results of our newspaper analysis were tabulated by hand—a process that proved to be time-wasting. The use of IBM (or possibly Keysort) cards would probably have been wiser.

Our own rather elementary hand technique was to code each symbol on a separate sheet. Each sheet had sixty columns (for the sixty years) and twenty-four lines to a column. The occurrence of a given symbol in a given issue simply required a check mark (or rather 0, +, or −). From these sheets, time-series tables were made up for each symbol on a year-by-year basis. These were consolidated into periods, and then several symbols were consolidated into indices.

The advantage of a sufficiently flexible mechanical system would have been that we could have gone back to the original data at will. With the system actually used, tabulation was so laborious that, once the summary tables by periods were made up, it was almost never possible to go back for another look at them.

VI. Typical Problems

The disciplines which study symbol flow include most of the humanities and social sciences. To any of these, content analysis can, on occasion, be useful. For example, a recurrent problem in both humanities and social studies is to identify the authorship of documents. Yule has shown that the shape of the word-frequency distribution may be used for this purpose.[53] So may the choice of particular words, parts of speech, sentence forms, and so on. The work of Ritter[54] suggests that the age of an author can be guessed from the characteristics of his language. Perhaps the same is true of his personality or of his state of mind at the time of writing. We do not now know which linguistic traits, if any, indicate such author traits, but by content analysis we could seek to find out. If successful, the results would be of value for literary, psychological, and intelligence research.

Literary criticism can use content analysis in other ways. The work of Edith Rickert[55] and that of Josephine Miles[56] suggest that the quality of an author's style may be examined in part by determining the distribution of such elements as images, metaphors, sounds, parts of speech, rhythm, and grammatical forms.

A field less fully explored is the quantitative analysis of action in literary works. More or less quantitative studies have been made of stereotyped characters or situations. The race or the occupation of heroes, heroines, and villains has been counted.[57] The frequency of such events as accidental meetings of the lovers instead of formal introduction has been noted.[58] But there is room for much more intensive quantitative types of analysis. On a single page of the text of a short story or novel there will typically appear from two to six personal interactions. For example, *Silence,* by L. N. Andreyev, deals with a conflict between daughter and parents. In one paragraph the mother begs the father to relent; he remains silent. In the next two paragraphs the wife turns accusatory; the husband then laughs and agrees. The father then goes to the daughter to patch up the quarrel; she remains silent. The tone of the story thus set is one of disproportion between affect-stimulus and response. At no point does the affect produce an equivalent reply. The distribution of such types of interaction determines the flow of the story. A content analysis might count, for example, the frequency of acts of aggression responded to by counteraggression, or by withdrawal, or by indulgence; and of acts of indulgence responded to by affection, or by withdrawal, or by aggression. One might find different frequencies depending on whether the interactions were between males or females, older or younger persons, aristocrats or plebeians. The patterns found in any work or author or literature would perhaps reveal, in part, its conception of the world.

Intellectual history may also be illuminated by content analyses. Ideas, like pottery or recipes, diffuse through culture areas and their distribution can be counted. The rise of operational formulations and the decline of statements about essences might be a fruitful index of the shift from medieval to scientific forms of thought. Similarly, one might study the diffusion of certain conceptions of democracy.

The idea that in democracy the mass stifles individuality, leveling all to dull mediocrity, spread rapidly in the first half of the nineteenth century, popularized particularly by Tocqueville. The traditional investigation of the history of such an idea seeks to identify an originator—as though any idea is ever fully new—and then traces its spread by citing examples. Content analysis could make the investigation accurate by substituting the notion of accelerated incidence for origin and by making precise assertions about spread.

Such investigations could also be used to trace intellectual influences in the current political scene. The allegation that Russia may strike a hard bargain, but once it gives its written word it keeps it, had wide circulation a few years ago. It was, of course, a notion possibly initiated and certainly propagated by crypto-Communist sources, but it was heard and repeated by many non-Communists and anti-Communists. The spread of such an idea could be studied by content analysis. The use of quantitative methods in such studies of intellectual influences would involve more work than current methods of assertion and example, but it would probably prove of significant worth in the validity of conclusions.

Although literary and historical research may, in the end, use content analysis as much as the social sciences, the greatest immediate interest in content analysis seems to be among sociologists, political scientists, and psychologists. Undirected or "deep" interview materials are often quantified. This kind of content analysis has proved rather fruitful in connection with a number of kinds of interrogations including thematic apperception tests, questioning of war prisoners, and political opinion studies. In such instances the feasibility of quantification has been repeatedly demonstrated. What is needed is a refinement of categories that may come with the development of general theories of symbolic behavior. The development of sufficiently relevant, reliable, and rapid procedures might make it possible to gain simultaneously some of the advantages of the poll and of the free-answer interview. Coded free answers could have the arithmetical convenience of poll results.

The greatest advantage of content analysis, however, is its adaptability to the analysis of unstructured flows of communication. What people talk about on the telephone or on the streets, what they write in their letters or diaries is often a better index of attitudes than any formal interview. Such informal materials are, of course, usually too diverse to be subjected, in any successful fashion, to a structured analysis by impressionistic methods, but appropriate methods of content analysis may eventually be devised.

On the other hand, such procedures are often more difficult than asking a respondent the precise question to which one wishes the answer. Where interviews can be used they are often preferable, but there are situations where a direct question is impossible. One of these situations is typical in intelligence work. The enemy will not usually answer questions. The intelligence value of content analysis arises largely from its applicability to situations where direct questioning is impossible. If we wish to detect internal conflicts among the elite of a totalitarian enemy, we cannot detect them by asking questions of the elite members. Perhaps we can detect them by a careful analysis of their speeches.

In much the same way content analysis can be used to test homogeneity and heterogeneity of attitudes and interests between media or over a given period of time. Are two papers following the same line?[59] Is the range of editorial opinion in the public press growing smaller? Are the lines between parties growing sharper or less sharp? Such questions can be dealt with by modifications of some of the content-analysis techniques described in Chapter Two.

Analysis of a symbol flow by other than conventional reading is particularly worth while when the item investigated is one of which the writer or reader is not ordinarily conscious. The psychoanalytic approach, for example, deals with motivations quite different from those made explicit. A researcher with this approach might take two political speeches both defending an identical policy, say the Marshall Plan. One might contain a symbolism abounding with metaphors of, or allusions to, resistance to tyranny and the defense of freedom. The other might stress order, economy, and straightening up the mess left by the war. The reader or writer absorbed in the political point is not likely to suspect what he might find were he to approach the text in another mental set. Quantification can prove the presence in a text of psychological or social traits which our habits of impressionistic reading cause us to overlook. Such psychological analysis of written materials is one promising and largely untouched area for content analysis.

We have omitted, in the above examples, a major use of content analysis: the measurement of political trends in the mass media of communications. We have omitted it here because it has been the central subject of this chapter. The study of political trends has been among the most widespread uses of content analysis, and current methods of content analysis have largely been developed for this purpose. Our own researches, reported in the subsequent chapters, further illustrate some of the possible uses of content analysis in this field.

NOTES

1. "This phrase is commonly rendered by 'noble lie,' a self-contradictory expression no more applicable to Plato's harmless allegory than to a New Testament parable or the Pilgrim's Progress, and liable to suggest that he would countenance the lies, for the most part ignoble, now called propaganda." (*The Re-*

public of Plato, trans. F. M. Cornford [New York: Oxford University Press, 1945], p. 106n.)

2. Ibn Kaldun, *An Arab Philosophy of History,* trans. Charles Issawi (London: John Murray, 1950), p. 111.

3. Ibid., p. 108.

4. Ibid.

5. Ibid., pp. 131-32.

6. Ibid., p. 133.

7. Ibid., p. 108.

8. Ibid., p. 110.

9. Ibid., p. 103.

10. Gaetano Mosca, *The Ruling Class,* trans. H. D. Kahn (New York: McGraw-Hill Book Company, Inc., 1939), p. 70.

11. See *Reflections on Violence,* trans. T. E. Hulme and J. Roth (Glencoe, Ill.: The Free Press, 1950).

12. Karl Mannheim, *Ideology and Utopia,* trans. Louis Wirth and E. A. Shils (New York: Harcourt, Brace and Company, 1936).

13. Systematic distinctions are in chap. x of *Power and Society: A Framework for Political Inquiry,* by Harold D. Lasswell and Abraham Kaplan (New Haven, Conn.: Yale University Press, 1950).

14. The center of a given pattern of world revolution is distinguished from the center of an *epoch.*

15. The problems of myth diffusion and restriction have been dealt with by Harold D. Lasswell in several connections. For example: *World Politics and Personal Insecurity* (New York: McGraw-Hill Book Company, Inc., 1935). This was reprinted by the Free Press of Glencoe, Ill., under the title *A Study of Power* jointly with volumes by C. E. Merriam and T. V. Smith. See also, *World Revolutionary Propaganda: A Chicago Study,* with Dorothy Blumenstock (New York: Alfred A. Knopf, 1939).

16. Lasswell, *World Politics and Personal Insecurity,* chap. i.

17. Ibn Kaldun has this to say about the imitation of the strong by the weak: "The vanquished always seek to imitate their victors in their dress, insignia, belief, and other customs and usages. This is because men are always inclined to attribute perfection to those who have defeated or subjugated them. Men do this either because the reverence they feel for their conquerors makes them see perfection in them or because they refuse to admit that their defeat could have been brought about by ordinary causes, and hence they suppose that it is due to the perfection of the conquerors." Ibn Kaldun's *Arab Philosophy,* p. 53.

18. Harold D. Lasswell, *Power and Personality* (New York: W. W. Norton and Company, Inc., 1948), chap. vii.

19. To borrow once more the famous title of C. K. Ogden and I. A. Richards, whose book, *The Meaning of Meaning,* 8th ed. (New York: Harcourt, Brace and Company, 1946), did so much to focus scholarly interest in this area.

20. Lasswell and Kaplan, *Power and Society,* chap. vi. The categories are adapted mainly from Gaetano Mosca and Charles E. Merriam.

21. K. N. Llewelyn and E. A. Hoebel, *The Cheyenne Way: Conflict and Case Law in Primitive Jurisprudence* (Norman, Okla.: University of Oklahoma Press, 1941).

22. Louie M. Miner, *Our Rude Forefathers: American Political Verse, 1783-1788* (Cedar Rapids, Iowa: The Torch Press, 1937), p. 1.

23. Ibid., p. 26.

24. Ibid., p. 32.

25. Ibid., p. 157.

60   COMPARATIVE STUDY OF SYMBOLS: INTRODUCTION

26. Modern social anthropologists have undertaken to cover in detail the basic features of the local myth, and to show how it enters into the lives of the people as a whole. Among the outstanding contemporary analysts are Malinowski, Radcliffe-Brown, Evans-Pritchard, and Fortas.
27. Lois Whitney, *Primitivism and the Idea of Progress* (Baltimore: The Johns Hopkins Press, 1934), p. 334.
28. C. L. Stevenson, *Ethics and Language* (New Haven, Conn.: Yale University Press, 1944).
29. See Lasswell and Blumenstock, *World Revolutionary Propaganda*, chap. vii.
30. Discussed in relation to revolutionary strategy by Katherine Chorley, *Armies and the Art of Revolution* (London: Faber and Faber, 1943), p. 31. Concerning "socialism in one country," see I. Deutscher, *Stalin: A Political Biography* (New York: Oxford University Press, 1949), pp. 289 ff.
31. Hans Speier, "Magic Geography," *Social Research* VIII (1941): 310-30. Reprinted in Daniel Lerner, ed., *Propaganda in War and Crisis: Materials for American Policy* (New York: George W. Stewart, 1951).
32. Charles W. Morris discussed the ikon function of the physical elements in communication.
33. Marcel Proust, *Swann's Way* (New York: Random House, Inc., 1934), p. 253.
34. The War Communications Research Project was financed by the Rockefeller Foundation and housed at the Library of Congress in Washington, D.C. See Harold D. Lasswell, Nathan Leites, et al., *Language of Politics: Studies in Quantitative Semantics* (New York: George W. Stewart, 1949).
35. Ibid., chap. ii.
36. Ibid.
37. Lasswell, *World Politics and Personal Insecurity*, p. 4. This postulate is elaborated in the Hoover Institute Studies, Series A, Monograph No. 1.
38. This advantage often is minimized in the social sciences. The story is told that I. I. Rabi, Nobel Prize physicist, once engaged a prominent social scientist in earnest inquiry about the typical problems and methods of his own and neighboring disciplines of social research. For some time, as the social scientist expounded, Rabi found the situation getting worse and worse. Finally illumination came: "Ah," he said, "now I see the difference. You deal with questions that are important, and we deal with questions that we can answer."
39. Series A, Monograph No. 1, Hoover Institute Studies by Harold D. Lasswell entitled *The World Revolution of Our Time: A Framework for Basic Policy Research*.
40. Lasswell, Leites, et al., *Language of Politics*, pp. 42-43. This chapter, entitled "Why Be Quantitative?" should be read by those interested in a fuller statement of the advantages gained by quantifying observations in symbol analysis.
41. A full exposition, though by no means a definite statement, of content analysis is that by Lasswell, Leites, et al., in the volume mentioned above. Separate chapters of this book are cited at appropriate places in this chapter. Also useful are: B. Berelson and P. F. Lazarsfeld, *The Analysis of Communication Content* (Columbia University, Bureau of Applied Social Research, 1948); A. L. George, *Propaganda Analysis* (New York: Harper & Row, 1959); N. Leites and I. Pool, *On Content Analysis* (Library of Congress, Experimental Division for Study of Wartime Communications, Document No. 26, 1942).
42. S. Yakobson and H. D. Lasswell, "May Day Slogans in Soviet Russia, 1918-1943," in *Language of Politics*, chap. x.
43. Lasswell, Leites, et al., *Language of Politics*, p. 46.

44. These points are discussed in greater detail in Harold D. Lasswell's "Describing the Contents of Communications," in B. L. Smith et al., *Propaganda, Communication, and Public Opinion* (Princeton, N.J.: Princeton University Press, 1946).

45. For a discussion of alternative indexes and index ambiguity, see Paul F. Lazarsfeld and Allen H. Barton, "Qualitative Measurement in the Social Sciences: Classification, Typologies, and Indices," in Daniel Lerner and Harold D. Lasswell, eds., *The Policy Sciences: Recent Developments in Scope and Method* (Stanford, Calif.: Stanford University Press, 1951), pp. 180-88.

46. See Lasswell, "Propaganda Detection and the Courts," *Language of Politics,* chap. ix.

47. See N. Leites and I. Pool, "The Response of Communist Propaganda to Frustration," *Language of Politics,* chap. xii. In using this essay it should be noted that by a typographical error the points in the final diagram were misplaced.

48. Respectively, Harold D. Lasswell, "A Provisional Classification of Symbol Data," *Psychiatry* I (1938): 197-204; Bernard Berelson, "The Quantitative Analysis of Case Records: An Experimental Study," *Psychiatry* X (1947): 395-403; Bernard Berelson and Patricia Salter, "Majority and Minority Americans: An Analysis of Magazine Fiction," *Public Opinion Quarterly* X (1946): 168-90; Leo Lowenthal, *Prophets of Deceit* (New York: Harper and Brothers, 1949); Uma Bose, "A Psychological Approach to the Development of Religion and the Origin of the Concepts of God and Ghost in Children," *Samiksa* (Calcutta) II (1948): 25-64; and T. W. Adorno et al., *The Authoritarian Personality* (New York: Harper and Brothers, 1950).

49. See H. D. Lasswell, *Psychopathology and Politics* (Chicago: University of Chicago Press, 1930); also "A Provisional Classification of Symbol Data."

50. Lasswell, Leites, et al., *Language of Politics,* pp. 153-72.

51. On these points see Lazarsfeld and Barton, "Qualitative Measurement in the Social Sciences," in Lerner and Lasswell, eds., *Policy Sciences,* pp. 155-59.

52. See A. Mintz, "The Feasibility of the Use of Samples in Content Analysis," *Language of Politics,* chap. vii.

53. G. Udny Yule, *The Statistical Study of Literary Vocabulary* (Cambridge: The University Press, 1944).

54. Constantin Ritter, *Platon* (Munich: C. H. Beck, 1910).

55. Edith Rickert, *New Methods for the Study of Literature* (Chicago: University of Chicago Press, 1927).

56. Josephine Miles, *Pathetic Fallacy in the Nineteenth Century* (Berkeley, Calif.: University of California Press, 1942); *Wordsworth and the Vocabulary of Emotion* (Berkeley, Calif.: University of California Press, 1942).

57. Bernard Berelson and Patricia Salter, "Majority and Minority Americans: An Analysis of Magazine Fiction," *Public Opinion Quarterly* X (1946): 168-90.

58. Nathan Leites and Martha Wolfenstein, *Movies: A Psychological Study* (Glencoe, Ill.: The Free Press, 1950).

59. Harold D. Lasswell, "Propaganda Detection and the Courts," *Language of Politics,* chap. ix.

CHAPTER TWO
THE "PRESTIGE PAPERS"*

I. Problem and Method

The Papers

In each major power one newspaper stands out as an organ of elite opinion. Usually semiofficial, always intimate with the government, these "prestige papers" are read by public officials, journalists, scholars, and business leaders. They seldom have large circulations, yet they have enormous influence. They are read not only in their own countries, but also abroad by those whose business it is to keep track of world affairs. They differ among themselves, but, despite national and temporal differences, they are a distinct species. It is generally possible to name with fair confidence one paper in any given country which plays the role of prestige paper at any given time.

This, of itself, is a curious fact. There is no inherent reason why such a paper should exist. That it does is a tribute to the role of public opinion in modern culture. The elite has everywhere found it important to make full and responsible statements of policy available to wide circles, both of its own members and others.

Whose policy it is that has thus been stated is a fairly good index of who wields power. The prestige papers have fallen into three groups. In Communist Russia and Nazi Germany, where the dominant elite was a state elite, they have been official organs. In Great Britain, France, Imperial Germany, and czarist Russia they have been semiofficial. In the United States, where the elite has been but little identified with the state, the *New York Times* has often followed a line quite different from that of the administration in power. Yet even in as pluralistic a culture as our own, the *New York Times* retains some of the traits of the semiofficial papers in more politicized countries. Its reporters have special entree to key political figures, and its columns are often used for covert propaganda or for trial balloons in statements commonly attributed to "an official source," or "usually reliable sources."

*I. Pool, Hoover Institute Studies, Series C: Symbols, No. 2 (Stanford, California, Stanford University Press, January 1952). Abridged and reprinted with permission.

In the modern world the pattern of the prestige paper is sufficiently uniform for us to describe it as an institution. "Not a paper, but an institution," is indeed the way the London *Times*[1] has described itself. This social institution, the prestige paper, is, however, still a relatively unformalized one. Unlike the state or the church, whose institutional existence no one doubts despite the manifold forms in which the institution happens to appear, the prestige paper has not yet received full recognition as an entity, nor has it received a body of doctrine justifying it. Indeed, it has not even been christened although it has been present for some time.

What papers are we including under the heading of prestige paper? In the RADIR studies we compared trends in the major world centers over a sixty-year time span. Our selection of papers was determined by this program. We considered as major powers Great Britain, Russia, France, Germany, and the United States. As regimes changed there were changes in the top papers. In some instances, files of these papers were unavailable for the full period since 1890. The list of periodicals actually studied will be found on page 34.

Papers of the various countries were included or excluded from our study for the following reasons:

Russia.—For Communist Russia there existed the alternative of using *Pravda* or *Izvestia*. The current positions of the two papers would make it difficult to justify any choice but *Pravda*. But for the full span since 1918 the choice is much more even. *Izvestia's* circulation in 1947 was 800,000 copies, compared with Pravda's 2,500,000. But "before the war (1939) *Izvestia's* circulation was 1,600,000, second only to *Pravda.*"[2] *Pravda,* the organ of the Central Committee of the Communist party, was always a more important and more influential paper than *Izvestia,* the organ of the government, even though, in the 1920's and early 1930's, *Izvestia's* comments on foreign policy were regarded as more authoritative. The advantage of *Izvestia* from our point of view is that it is more directly comparable than *Pravda* to the other papers in our sample. As a governmental organ its tone has been slightly more subdued than *Pravda's,* thus bringing it a little nearer the stuffiness of the typical prestige paper. It gives more emphasis than *Pravda* to governmental matters, laws, ordinances, and appointments. As a result, it, as well as *Pravda,* is read by those limited circles of persons actively concerned with public affairs. To have used *Pravda* for our Russian sample would probably have enlarged the statistical differences between the Russian paper and others, but it would have made these differences more difficult to interpret because of the lesser degree of comparability. Yet *Pravda's* position is so pre-eminent that there obviously would be considerable value in a comparative analysis of its record.

United States.—Our file of the *New York Times* began with 1900.

Great Britain.—Our file of the London *Times* is complete for the full period covered by the RADIR studies, from 1890 on.

France.—Papers for the years before 1900, and for 1943 and 1944, were not available. Under the Vichy regime, *Le Temps* appeared in southern France until November 30, 1942, when it was suppressed. After liberation, *Le Monde* took its place journalistically and in our sample.

Germany.—Our German sample is the least adequate. Our file of the *Norddeutsche allgemeine Zeitung* began only with 1910 and is incomplete through 1914. Our usual sample consisted of twenty-four issues a year. For the first years of our German series, however, we had to be content with samples, as follows: 1910, four issues; 1911, four issues; 1912, six issues; 1913, two issues; 1914, fifteen issues. Our file of the *Frankfurter Zeitung* was complete. The Nazi regime, and with it the *Völkischer Beobachter,* came to an end in the first half of 1945. Since then, there has been no clearly definable independent German elite, and certainly no newspaper representing any such independent elite opinion.

Of these papers only the *New York Times,* the *Völkischer Beobachter* and *Izvestia* have succeeded in obtaining a mass circulation. The circulation of the *New York Times,* which has for some time been pushing toward the half-million mark, was already over a quarter of a million during World War I. The circulation of *Izvestia* in the middle 1930's was about 1,600,000; now it is 800,000. The *Völkischer Beobachter* in its various editions had a circulation of about 310,000 in 1934.

Probably the lowest circulation of any of the papers in our sample was that of the *Norddeutsche allgemeine Zeitung,* which in 1917 sold about 6,000 copies. It had once been a more successful paper, but from the time of Von Bülow it was subjected to such bureaucratic control that it gradually became uninteresting. This paper was more an official house organ than any of the others except the *Völkischer Beobachter* and *Izvestia,* but unlike those it was not pushed forward by a propaganda-conscious government. It represented the old rather than the new type of autocracy. The *Norddeutsche allgemeine Zeitung* is accurately, though critically, described by a publication of the French Ministries of War and Foreign Affairs of 1918:

> The articles published in the first column under the title Politischer Tagesbericht are official communiques of the Wilhelmstrasse, whenever the Chancellory wants to make the point of view of the government on any particular question publicly known. The rest of the paper, which, moreover, is in large part made up of extracts from German and foreign papers, does not include anything which censures the government. . . . It sells little outside of its official circulation.[3]

With the Weimar regime this highly autocratic type of prestige paper gave way to one more typical of a Western democratic state. The *Frankfurter Zeitung und Handelsblatt* (to cite its full name), like the London *Times*, *Le Temps*, and the *New York Times*, was a paper for the intellegentsia and the business community. It was bought partly for its excellent business statistics, for full coverage of which it published a section of the paper in the morning, another in midmorning, and a third in the evening. Its business circulation and its sale at home and abroad among those concerned with public affairs provided the bulk of its 50,000 circulation.

The dependence of papers of this type on the business community is abundantly attested to by the profit-and-loss statement of the London *Times*, which closely paralleled the status of the financial markets. This is explained by Viscount Camrose, one of the magnates of the British press:

So large a proportion of the revenue of *The Times* is derived from the insertion of Company Meeting Reports, Financial Prospectuses and other City announcements that its prosperity depends considerably on whether the world of finance is active or not.[4]

The London *Times's* circulation was only 40,000 when Lord Northcliffe bought it in 1908. He managed to push it up to a peak of 160,000 by 1914. Then, under the new regime of Lord Astor, it climbed in 1947 to over a quarter of a million. But these figures should be compared with the circulation of the *Daily Express*, 3,850,000; the *Daily Mirror*, 3,600,000; and the *Daily Mail*, 2,078,000. Clearly, the position of the London *Times* rests on the character—not the size—of its circulation.

Although all the privately owned prestige papers adhered to the conservative business point of view, *Le Temps* was probably most militant in this respect. This is clearly reflected in some of our findings below, but it was also generally recognized in impressionistic journalistic discussions. Ordinarily, *Le Temps* has been characterized as vigorously liberal in the older laissez-faire sense of the word. It was republican, though not anticlerical, and it vehemently opposed all varieties of socialism or *étatisme*. It is charged that, in 1931, *Le Temps* came under the control of the ultrareactionary Comité de Forges, the trade association of the iron and steel industry. Even before this, however, it was very conservative. All the chief editors of *Le Temps* during the period of our sample show evidences of having had some wealth, although only eight or ten out of thirty-one editors of other prestige papers seem to have been rich.

Despite the fact that it represented effectively the point of view of the economic elite, *Le Temps* was unable to make a mass appeal. Its circulation was about 30,000 in 1917, when *Le Petit Parisien* sold 2,500,000 copies; it was 70,000 in the middle 1930's, when *Paris Soir* sold almost

1,500,000 copies. *Le Monde* now has a circulation of about 170,000.

In foreign affairs all of these papers tended to support their own governments. This goes without saying for *Izvestia* and the *Völkischer Beobachter,* which were nothing but official propaganda organs. It also goes without saying for such completely controlled, although private, papers as the *Norddeutsche allgemeine Zeitung* and *Novoe Vremia.* To a large extent, however, it was also true of the more independent papers. It was generally taken for granted that a foreign-policy editorial in *Le Temps* was either a feeler or a statement of policy by the Quai d'Orsay.

The London *Times* was a little more free. It followed a consistently imperialist policy which sometimes brought pressure on the government, but, on the whole, it maintained intimate relations with the Foreign Office and expressed the latter's point of view. The Library of Congress survey, *The European Press Today,* could still say in 1949 that, despite the Labour government, *The Times* "usually reflects government views, particularly on foreign affairs, and thus assumes semiofficial character which it maintains despite change of government."[5]

The New York Times was most independent, having favored tariff reductions all through the 1920's and having advocated international cooperation even when the administrations, under pressure, had to give allegience to isolationism. In these respects it was probably closer to the views of our career diplomats than was official policy, and with the former it has always maintained close relations.

How a prestige paper is tied to the government may be understood if we look at the situation for the most independent of them, the *New York Times.* The closeness of these ties is illustrated by the story of H. H. Kohlsaat:

> As it happened, President Harding and Mr. Miller [the editor of the *Times*] never met but they had a cheery intermediary in H. H. Kohlsaat. ... He had known Mr. Ochs and Mr. Miller for years, and nothing more natural than for him to become an almost daily luncheon guest of *The Times* while he stayed in New York. His genial charm and genuinely sweet nature were open sesame everywhere and leading men of all parties made him their confidant. From President McKinley's day on, the latch string of the White House had always been out to him, and President Harding followed his predecessors in welcoming "H. H." as an advisor and friend.
>
> Mr. Kohlsaat delighted to visit between New York and Washington and from this penchant of his there came into being an informal "ambassadorship." Official circles in Washington knew Mr. Kohlsaat to have friendly associations with *The Times; The Times* realized the extent of his entrée at Washington. Almost spontaneously the idea occurred to both parties to utilize for mutual benefit Mr. Kohlsaat's good offices. Accordingly, and with the consent of everyone, he would repeat at *The Times* office con-

versations he had had at the White House and State Department, and, returning to Washington, he would bring to President Harding and Secretary Hughes the comments which Mr. Miller and his associates had made on the disclosures. . . .

During this period Mr. Kohlsaat received a regular retainer from *The Times*. . ."[6]

On the other hand, the independence of which the *New York Times* was capable was illustrated by the reply of Mr. Miller to a senatorial investigating committee. In a situation in which few men have had the courage to answer back and many have felt helpless, Charles Ransom Miller spoke as follows:

I can see no ethical, moral or legal right that you have to put many of the questions you put to me today. Inquisitorial proceedings of this kind would have a very marked tendency, if continued and adopted as a policy, to reduce the press of the United States to the level of the press in some of the Central European countries, the press that has been known as the reptile press that crawls on its belly every day to the foreign office of the Government officials and Ministers to know what it may say or shall say—to receive its orders.[7]

This subservience is, of course, the behavior which has since become characteristic of the totalitarian papers; but most of the papers in our sample fall somewhere between the *New York Times* and those papers in degree of independence. As noted already, the social structure of the prestige newspapers reflected the nature of the elite in the country in which the paper appeared. The editors of these papers were, indeed, a part of the elite and in their own life histories shared the traits of the elite. The editors of the London *Times* for seventy-one of the past seventy-three years have been public school men and for sixty years have been Oxford men. Three of them have been related to nobility, and five out of six have come from prominent English families. In America, on the other hand, the editors have generally been Main Street boys who made good. They all came from towns with a population of under 25,000.

Similarly, the relationships between the editors and the government reflect both the structure of the society and the position of the prestige paper in it. In the United States—the most pluralistic society under discussion—only one of the editors had an extensive governmental career, and that was in state, not national, government. Just as the typical member of the American elite is a private individual, so is the typical editor of the prestige paper. In England and France, where the elite is more governmentalized, the editors were, also. In each country four of the editors were lawyers; in England two had governmental careers, and in France three were elected to the Senate or Chamber. The editor of the *Norddeutsche allgemeine Zeitung* also had a governmental career before entering journalism. When we turn to the totalitarian papers, we find that their editors are, above all, politicians. They devoted their lives to being "professional revolutionaries." A model of this type was Alfred Rosenberg, the top Nazi theoretician who joined the party even before Hitler and ended his career on the gallows after the Nuremberg trial. Of the five *Izvestia* editors on whom there is information, all joined the revolutionary movement at ages between fifteen and twenty-one. Only one records no czarist arrests in his biography. Three were sent to Siberia and two were exiles abroad. Three sat on the Communist party Central Committee, one on the Central Control Commission, and one on the Politburo. These men were politicians first and journalists by party assignment.

As the editors are in some way typical of the elite they represent, so, too, the papers they publish represent, in some sense, elite opinion. It is an oversimplification to say, as muckrakers often do, that these papers are pawns moved by conspiratorial masterminds in the halls of the mighty. Where the elite is organized under a recognized leadership which uses totalitarian controls, this may be almost true. But where the elite is pluralistic and has a wide variety of opinions within itself, a prestige paper has much leeway for individuality. In a democratic country, where the members of the elite openly debate issues, the prestige paper can have a distinctive policy of its own. Yet even in such a situation, the prestige paper is in some respects a good index of elite behavior. It is read by the elite and influences them. In addition, it is produced by men who have themselves become part of the elite and share the typical life pattern of the elite. (For additional information on the careers of the editors, see Appendix C.)

On the whole, the papers tended to be conservative, and some of them had party affiliations. The *New York Times* is an independent Democratic paper, although probably more independent than Democratic. The London *Times* started as a Liberal paper, but by the beginning of the period of our study it had already swung to the Conservatives and it became increasingly Conservative. Yet none of these papers has permitted itself to swing too sharply against government policy. They have never become leaders of the opposition. They may criticize this measure or that, and they may favor the opposition in an election, but they have also swayed with the election returns. For some of the papers this has been facilitated by a strong tendency toward moderation. The independent prestige papers have been slow to criticize and willing to consider, even when government policies have conflicted with their predispositions. Most of the time, however, they have not been subjected to such strains, since more often than not the government in power has reflected the same elite as the paper.

When the prestige papers have had a policy different from that of the government, it has generally been a traditional and institutional policy rather than the individual policy of the editor. Great editors may have built the institutions and collected the staffs out of which these policies came. They have thus left their imprint on editorial policy. But we shall find in the results of our study that there is seldom much of the individuality of the editorial writer in the contents of his editorial. This is partly because of the collegial system of editorial writing. On the *New York Times,* the London *Times,* and the *Frankfurter Zeitung,* at least, the editorials are an outcome of an editorial conference. Suggestions are made from all sides and a policy is arrived at, which one or often more members of the staff is then asked to write up.

In the totalitarian papers the party line takes the role of the editorial conference in suppressing individuality. Only in the French papers is the mode of editorial writing individual enough that one might suspect a content-analysis result of showing characteristics of the writer rather than of an institution or social stratum. Our results, however, do not support such a supposition. Throughout the study we find that when one editor in chief replaces another there will be a change in the frequencies of, at most, one or two symbols. A particular editor may have a hobby. One American editor, for example, made a fetish of the tariff and was interested in Greek affairs, while a certain British editor was even more strongly imperialist than typical for his government and party. But except for the riding of one or two such hobbies, the symbol structures of the papers seem to be little affected by the changes in the individuals who fill the top editorial chairs.

We find, then, that despite local and individual variations, the prestige paper has come to be an important and respected institution. Governments, politicians, and businessmen depend upon it. One might ask what would happen in Washington if the *New York Times* stopped publication and no other paper took its place. There would certainly be a deterioration in American political intelligence. The owners of the London *Times* have given concrete expression to their realization of the importance of the institution of which they are the current guardians. They have written into their statutes a provision that *The Times* may not be sold to new owners without the approval of a group of trustees who are: the Lord Chief Justice of England; the warden of All Souls College, Oxford; the president of the Royal Society; the president of the Institute of Chartered Accountants; and the governor of the Bank of England.

The Editorials

The subject of our study is trends in newspaper attitudes. Attitudes can be treated as vectors. They may be *for* or *against,* as well as *neutral.* Their dimensions are not exhausted by measurements of column inches devoted to different topics. The problem is to find some simple way of gauging the direction and intensity of newspaper feelings regarding the topics attended to.

Some device could probably be worked out for measuring newspaper attitudes from the news columns. Biases can be detected even in the most objective reporting. The characteristics by which we detect bias could be enumerated and then observed. To state such a proposal, however, is enough to reveal its difficulty. It is obviously wise at the present primitive stage of the development of content-analysis technique to turn directly to those pages where the paper explicitly avows its attitude: namely, the editorial pages. We do this without for a moment forgetting the limitations of editorials. We know that in some countries they are less fully read than the news columns, although in others they are probably read more. We also know that not all attitudes are regarded as appropriate to editorial statement. We know that the biases of the editorial writers are sometimes different from those of the news reporters. But it is not possible to measure everything at once, and the editorials provide us with the best first approximation of the attitudes of the newspapers.

"Editorial," however, is a concept of considerable ambiguity. In the *New York Times,* the London *Times,* and *Le Temps,* editorials can be identified readily enough, for they appear with a fixed format on a page set aside for them. Every day the third from the last page of the first section of the *New York Times* contains six or seven unsigned editorials, to the left of the letters to the editor and just below the masthead. The London *Times* has a similar format, though with fewer editorials. *Le Temps* places its editorials on the front page, but they are no harder to identify. In all these papers, especially the *New York Times,* expression of attitude in the rest of the paper is kept to a minimum. In such a situation the editorial is an obvious unit of analysis.

Editorials are less easily distinguished in most of the other papers. Editorialized articles in various places in the paper, signed or unsigned, make it hard to draw a clear-cut line between editorials and news stories. In fact, if the subject of our research were journalistic technique or format, we would probably have to conclude that the category "editorial" is not usable. But for us the editorial is a convenient source because it is rich in attitudes. If editorials, strictly speaking, are absent, editorialized articles will do equally well. Hence, in the *Völkischer Beobachter,* we used those general evaluative articles which served the purposes of editorials. When we talk of editorials, therefore, the reader should understand that the term refers to the material of this sample, although probably not all of the material fully meets the criteria that a journalist might wish to set up for the term.

It might be well to summarize, then—particularly for the papers presenting difficulties—the type of article which we included in our sample under the general heading of "editorial."

Norddeutsche allgemeine Zeitung.—Editorials were unsystematically placed; some unsigned or initialed articles appeared without dateline on the first or second page and were devoted to expression of opinion rather than reporting of news. These ran about one to four items per issue.

Frankfurter Zeitung.—There was generally only one editorial a day. It appeared in the most prominent position—the upper left of the front page—usually of the evening section. It generally filled most of two columns.

Völkischer Beobachter.—Although the entire paper was very highly editorialized, the articles most comparable to standard editorials were the signed articles by important Nazi figures. These were usually placed in the left- or right-hand column of one of the prominent pages, often the first. Such articles, which we treated as editorials, averaged a little over one an issue.

Novoe Vremia.—Editorials were usually on the left-hand side of the front page and were distinguished by being set in larger type than the rest of the paper.

Izvestia.—As in *Novoe Vremia,* the front page left was the usual location of editorials. They generally ran in a wider column than was standard, and were often set off by rules. The headline usually had a general rather than a newsy character. The later editorials were anonymous, but in earlier years they were often signed and sometimes difficult to distinguish from noneditorial articles.

Le Monde.—As in *Le Temps,* the editorials were generally on the front page. The left-hand column was generally devoted to an article headed "Bulletin de l'Etranger." There was generally one other item that might be called an editorial although it was not as regular in format. The small number of editorials as compared with *Le Temps* was in part due to the fact that *Le Monde* is a much smaller paper with less space to devote. The nature of the sample from *Le Monde* obviously results in an emphasis on foreign policy.

The differences in format between papers have some effect upon the contents of the editorials. A paper that runs only one editorial an issue will naturally touch on the highlights, all other considerations being constant. At the other extreme, the *New York Times,* with abundant newsprint and many thousands of editorial words daily, can afford to editorialize on the coming of spring and similar subjects. Almost any issue picked at random will have some such editorial as "The Christmas Glow," or "Good Will Visit," which dealt with an exchange of visits by baseball teams of the

New York Police Athletic League and the Montreal Police Juvenile Club. One can imagine such an editorial in the *Völkischer Beobachter* or in *Izvestia*, but only if that sporting event fitted into a major propaganda campaign. Clearly, the number of editorials must be kept in mind in interpreting the results that follow. The average number of editorials per issue is indicated in Table 1. It reveals that the *New York Times* had by far the most, followed by the London *Times* and *Le Temps*.

The editorials in the *New York Times* were short, however, and in comparing editorials, one must also take into account their length. Although the *New York Times* and London *Times* undoubtedly led in the number of editorial words just as they did in the number of editorials, their lead was by no means so great as it might seem. Editorials in the *Völkischer Beobachter* or *Izvestia* generally ran two, three, or even four times the length of *New York Times* editorials. Unfortunately, we kept no record of the wordage of our sample, but a glance at these papers will leave little doubt about these generalizations. The editorials in the *New York Times* and the *Norddeutsche allgemeine Zeitung* were shortest; those in *Izvestia* were longest.

It is hard to say just what is the net effect of editorial length and editorial frequency on editorial content. We have already noted the fact that, where editorials are fewer, the possible variety of central subjects is less. On the other hand, if these editorials are longer they may incorporate a greater variety of subsidiary topics in the more elaborate treatment of the central subject matter. A three-hundred-word editorial on the Russian invasion of Poland in 1939 is not likely to go into such background topics as the *cordon sanitaire,* the cooperation of the Russian and German general staffs in the 1920's, the grain and consumers' goods shortage in Russia, the authoritarian character of Russian society, and the parallelism of Soviet and czarist foreign policy. A thousand-word editorial might deal with a number of these topics. Table 2 compares the papers as to the number of different counted symbols appearing in a typical editorial.

Table 1
Average Number of Editorials Per Issue in Prestige Papers

New York Times	6.6
London *Times*	3.7
Le Temps	3.1
Le Monde	1.9
Novoe Vremia	2.1
Izvestia	1.3
Norddeutsche allgemeine Zeitung	1.7
Frankfurter Zeitung	1.1
Völkischer Beobachter	1.1

Table 2
Average Number of Different Counted Symbols Per Editorial in Prestige Papers

New York Times	3.6
London *Times*	5.1
Le Temps	7.4
Le Monde	9.6
Novoe Vremia	6.5
Izvestia	11.1
Norddeutsche allgemeine Zeitung	3.9
Frankfurter Zeitung	7.7
Völkischer Beobachter	6.5

Such considerations of format are important in the design of content-analysis researches. If, in a sample of articles, one is to make a count of the main subjects only, one would expect samples with more articles in a given time period to cover a greater variety of topics. In this study, however, we are counting not main subjects, but symbols. It is not at all clear how their distribution is affected by format. Let us suppose there were 10,000 words in each of two samples. Suppose, further, that in one sample the 10,000 words were in ten articles and in the other in thirty. How would the distribution of symbols be expected to differ? Unfortunately, we do not know, and the data from this study, which was not designed to answer such questions, does not provide an answer. All we can say from this study is that there was no discernible regular relationship between editorial format and our findings about the distribution of symbols in our samples. This fact makes it possible to use these samples with some measure of confidence in studying other variables. Still, the reader is invited to keep in mind the data of Tables 1 and 2 and the presence of these unanswered questions. It is to be hoped that future research will answer some of them.

Even with all the differences that we have pointed out, and others that we may have missed, the newspaper editorial is probably as good a unit for international comparisons of attitudes as exists at the moment. As we noted above, the prestige paper and the editorial have become extensively institutionalized in Western society. Both in totalitarian and liberal states, the elite has accepted the obligation and desirability of stating its policies through this medium. The reading of such statements is an accepted function of governmental and private intelligence personnel throughout the world. What goes into these editorials is written and read with great care, even when it is not necessarily regarded as the truth. International comparisons are difficult because each item in a culture must be seen as part of an overall cultural pattern. For all the differences, however, there is something distinctly similar in the picture of a congressman reading the editorials of the *New York Times* over his breakfast coffee and that of a commissar reading the editorial in *Izvestia* over his morning tea. Of course the contents of the two editorial columns will be very different. It is that difference which is the subject of our study.

The Sample

The newspapers included in our study have contained many thousands of editorials during the past half-century—far too many for complete coverage. To get a representative sample of them we read the editorials on the first and fifteenth of each month. (If no paper was published on that day, the nearest possible day was selected.) This sample was obviously designed to measure long-term trends. Since any given subject is dealt with editorially only on occasion, it may be just chance that a given symbol turned up or did not turn up on the first or fifteenth of a given month or months. The sample for a year, twenty-four papers, might begin to provide a minimum basis for estimating the frequency of a common symbol—say, a symbol which occurred in one out of five editorials—but it would still be completely inadequate for many symbols. For most purposes we have to be satisfied with estimates of frequencies for periods of two or three or more years.

Our total time period might have been arbitrarily divided into a series of equal subperiods such as decades or half-decades. Against the statistical convenience of such a procedure must be set the fact that it obliterates the politically significant turning points. The sample for the decade 1911-20 in Russia, for example, includes editorials in *Novoe Vremia* and *Izvestia* during periods of war and peace, czarism and Bolshevism. Frequencies of symbols in such a subsample would mean little. We therefore decided to divide our time period into natural subperiods, defined by the flow of events.

The decisions as to where to draw the line were necessarily arbitrary. No two scholars would fully agree. The divisions represent our prediction as to when significant symbolic changes would be found. In some of our predictions we were right, in others wrong, but, on the whole, the divisions seem to have been reasonable.

Two limiting factors made periodization difficult. First, our data were transcribed from records covering calendar years. This was unfortunate, since some turning points occurred in the middle of years. Thus the two wars broke out and ended at definite dates other than January 1. Nevertheless, it was necessary to assign each year to one period and thus to include in our data for that period some editorials which properly belonged elsewhere. Were this not so, a number of the differences we found between continuous periods would be greater than in the data that follow.

Second, we wanted not only to make intercountry comparisons possible, but, at the same time, to make the periods for any given country correspond to the historical development of that particular country. Between these two objectives compromise was necessary. Two turning points were the same for all countries: 1913 and 1938, which represented the end of peacetime in all five subsamples.

In other cases the date of a turning point might be a year farther back or a year farther forward in one country than in another. Thus 1918, the last war year for all countries except Russia, was an obvious turning point. In Russia, however, the obvious dividing line was the Revolution of 1917. Similarly, the Five-Year Plan and other developments made it logical to start the next Russian period one year early, that is, with 1929. In each country World War II broke into two phases, but the two phases were separated at different points. For the United States, Pearl Harbor marked the dividing line, while for Germany the dividing line occurred with the beginning of reverses in 1942. For France and England, however, the date when the war news changed was the date of the fall of France—1940. For Russia, the crucial date was obviously the invasion. The end of the war for all countries was 1945. But for 1945 our French sample consisted of issues of the Free French paper, *Le Monde,* and it would have been absurd to include that paper with the Vichyite *Le Temps* of 1941 and 1942. We therefore added these few wartime issues of *Le Monde* to the postwar sample. All of these modifications still leave considerable comparability between countries, since they involve shifts of only one year in the dividing lines.

In one instance, comparability was sacrificed to domestic history. The 1930s in each subsample were represented by the period 1930-38 (Russia 1929-38). But this broad period was divided into two periods. In Germany and the United States, new regimes came into power in 1933. For the other three countries, 1935-36 seemed to be a better dividing line. The two halves of the 1930s, therefore, do not lend themselves well to international comparison.

Table 3 shows the subperiods used and the number of editorials in the sample from each.

In retrospect, it is easy to see that the design of the sample could have been improved. Some of the subsamples were of more than adequate size, but some were not. The data could have been recorded according to the desired turning points instead of year by year, and the sample itself could have been concentrated on the specific critical periods with which we are now most concerned. But this is hindsight acquired when it was no longer practical to go back to the original data. We shall therefore use the above subsamples throughout. All references to a given period refer to the years

Table 3
The Sample Periods: Length and Number of Editorials in Each

Country	Pre-World War I	World War I	1920s	Early 1930s	Late 1930s
United States	1900-1913 2047	1914-18 720	1919-29 1949	1930-32 545	1933-38 896
Great Britain	1890-1913 1869	1914-18 334	1919-29 1053	1930-35 606	1936-38 305
France	1900-1913 1020	1914-18 378	1919-29 912	1930-35 460	1936-38 169
Germany	1910-13 53	1914-18 124	1919-29 251	1930-32 90	1933-38 177
Russia	1892-1904 745	1914-17 171	1918-28 440	1929-35 208	1936-38 75
	1905-13 321				

Country	World War II		Post-World War II	Entire Sample
	Phase 1	Phase 2		
United States	1939-41 477	1942-45 615	1946-49 616	1900-1949 7865
Great Britain	1939-40 207	1941-45 501	1946-49 413	1890-1949 5288
France	1939-40 71	1941-42 88	1945-49 222	1890-1942 3320
Germany	1939-41 81	1942-45 75	–	1910-45 851
Russia	1939-40 48	1941-45 125	1946-49 96	1892-1949 2229
Total				19,553

and number of editorials indicated in Table 3 unless there is a statement to the contrary.

The Symbols

The procedure of this study was to look for instances of any of 416 selected symbols in each of the editorials in the sample. The independent event which became the unit of statistical treatment was the editorial. The frequency of a given symbol within an editorial was not recorded. A symbol was simply recorded as present or absent, so that in any given subsample (i.e., a given paper during a given period of years) there would be n editorials containing symbols s_1 through s_{416}, each of which would have occurred in $p_1 \ldots p_{416}$ percent of the editorials.

The list of 416 symbols contained two separate types of symbols. Names of national units accounted for 206 of the symbols, while 210 were key symbols of the major ideologies which have been contending in the world political arena during the past half-century. (The symbol list is reproduced as Appendix A.) These two groups of symbols will be analyzed separately. The state names are dealt with in the third chapter, *Symbols of Internationalism*. A logical line between these two groups of symbols would be hard to draw. Where, for example, should one put the symbols ZIONISM and SOVIET? Consequently, our reasons for separating these two groups of symbols were not semantic or philosophical; we separated them because different rules were followed in their classification. Each count of one of the ideological symbols means that the phoneme was present in explicit form in an editorial. In a few cases, explicitly enumerated synonyms were admitted, as, for example, FREEDOM and LIBERTY, or LABOR and WORKING CLASS. But with that one qualification, the count of the ideological symbols was a count of *specific words*.[8] The count of mentions of national units, on the other hand, was a *subject-matter count,* since various forms of mentions of the nation were recognized. Thus the symbol FRANCE referred not merely to a geographic entity, but also to a nation-state. The state, France, could be referred to not only by name but also by reference to its official spokesmen. Thus editorial mentions of the head of state or other top officials were coded as mentions of FRANCE. So also were references to French armies fighting abroad. This set of rules obviously makes the distribution of symbol frequencies different from that which would be found in a word count. It is therefore necessary to keep these heterogeneous populations separate.

The list of symbols was arbitrarily selected. The validity of the selection is the largest unresolved question of procedure in this study: how does one validate the index value of a list of symbols? This list of symbols was supposed to reflect trends in world politics with particular reference to changing attitudes toward the values of democracy, fraternity, security, and well-being.[9] The problem of validity of the word list arises as it does for any behavior indexed by the use or nonuse of words on a selected list.

Our own procedure in attempting to draw up a relatively valid list was to draw upon the best knowledge available and to use a long enough list so that the arbitrary decisions about inclusion or exclusion would affect the relatively infrequent terms in the tails of the word usage distribution, rather than more common words. To draw up the list we called upon Harold D. Lasswell, for thirty years one of the leading students of political movements and propaganda. The list he drew up consisted of nouns, although the listed words were also counted when they appeared in other forms.[10] The list was then subjected to the test of use. Any expert, by pure oversight, might omit some symbols of obvious importance. Our readers were, therefore, instructed to note and report any additional symbols that seemed appropriate to the list. It is reassuring that only a relatively small number of symbols were added in this way. Perhaps one reason for the completeness and representativeness of Lasswell's list was that it was based upon the experience of the World Attention Survey which he directed during World War II.

One test of the presumptive adequacy of any such list is whether it produces a distribution of frequencies of occurrence which is reasonably probable. All studies of word frequencies have shown that relatively few different words account for the bulk of all words used. The frequency of appearance of successive words in the array rapidly tapers off until many words appear very few times each. A relatively smooth curve describes the whole array. A list of words that did not have these characteristics might be suspected of omitting words or including an unrepresentative number at some levels of the distribution. Later on in this chapter, we shall present data for our own distributions. They are, in the main, remarkably regular, and they correspond to the expected norms. The few somewhat irregular curves seem to be concentrated in wartimes. Although our list contained such leading war words as WAR, PEACE, ALLIES, NEUTRALS, and ARMAMENTS, it may be that it was drawn up with the peacetime political situation in the center of consciousness and consequently lacks a representative selection of middle-frequency war words. On the other hand, the author cannot think of any omitted symbols directly relevant to the values here being studied and likely to fall in this middle-frequency category. It therefore seems more plausible that, in time of war, ideological discussion of the issues with which this study is concerned had to share the center of the editorial stage with quite separate military discussions. Hence, the few irregularities could be due to the frequencies of those symbols that were parts of two different distributions.

A survey of the results leads to one other qualification of the validity of the list used. There seems to be a distinct upward trend in the frequency of counted symbols (see Table 4). There are two plausible explanations of such a trend. It might be that there has been an increase in all countries in attention to the whole complex of values with which we are concerned. Again it might be that the list included a more representative selection of recent political terms than of older words. There is no sure way to decide between these explanations. All that we can do is to offer some considerations bearing on the plausibility of each.

We can by no means exclude the possibility that there may have been a universal increase in attention to the values of democracy, security, fraternity, and well-being, but it is not self-evident. That there have been

Table 4
Average Number of Counted Symbols Per Editorial by Time Periods

Paper	Period	Names of National Units	Ideo-logical Symbols	All Symbols
New York Times	1900-1913	1.3	1.0	2.3
	1914-18	2.5	1.9	4.4
	1919-29	2.1	1.8	3.9
	1930-32	1.7	1.3	3.0
	1933-38	1.7	1.4	3.1
	1939-41	3.0	2.1	5.1
	1942-45	3.3	2.0	5.3
	1946-49	2.6	2.1	4.7
London *Times*	1890-1913	3.0	2.0	5.0
	1914-18	3.6	2.2	5.8
	1919-29	2.5	2.0	4.5
	1930-35	2.3	1.9	4.2
	1936-38	2.5	2.5	5.0
	1939-40	3.7	3.0	6.7
	1941-45	2.9	2.6	5.5
	1946-49	2.9	2.6	5.5
Le Temps	1900-1913	2.4	3.1	5.5
	1914-18	4.4	3.3	7.7
	1919-29	3.0	5.1	8.1
	1930-35	2.6	5.5	8.1
	1936-38	4.2	7.3	11.5
	1939-40	5.4	6.5	11.9
	1941-42	4.4	3.5	7.9
Le Monde	1945-49	4.7	4.9	9.6
Norddeutsche allgemeine Zeitung	1910-13	.8	1.8	2.6
	1914-18	3.3	1.2	4.5
Frankfurter Zeitung	1919-29	3.2	4.7	7.9
	1930-32	2.1	4.9	7.0
Völkischer Beobachter	1933-38	2.3	3.2	5.5
	1939-41	4.9	3.1	8.0
	1942-45	4.0	3.4	7.4
Novoe Vremia	1892-1904	3.3	1.9	5.2
	1905-13	4.8	3.0	7.8
	1914-17	5.3	4.2	9.5
Izvestia	1918-28	4.0	7.9	11.9
	1929-35	1.9	7.2	9.1
	1936-38	1.8	9.4	11.2
	1939-40	1.8	9.5	11.3
	1941-45	3.1	8.7	11.8
	1946-49	1.7	9.3	11.0

changes is clear. We should be very much surprised to find the same attention to this list of symbols in totalitarian as in democratic papers, in communist as in fascist papers, in papers with much editorial space as in papers with little, and in war as in peace. But it is by no means clear that we should find an increase in attention to these symbols in *all* papers since the beginning of this century.

There is at least one piece of evidence, however, to support the supposition that there has been a general increase in attention to political symbols. In three of the five countries there has been an increase in the incidence of names of national units parallel to that for the general political symbols. The list of names of national units is complete—not an arbitrary selection—and it is highly objective. Hence, it is not subject to personal biasing factors as is the list of general political symbols. The results for three countries, then, lead us to believe that there may have been a real increase in attention to political issues, an increase which is reflected both in the list of names of national units and in the list of ideological symbols.

This conclusion, however, does not rule out the possibility that personal bias tended to load the list of ideological symbols with modern terms. In the first place we find the increase of country names in only three out of five countries—not a very conclusive showing. In the second place, both factors may be operating: some genuine increase in attention to political symbols does not rule out an overestimate of it as a result of the tendency to look for the terms that have been prominent in recent years.

There are good reasons to anticipate such a tendency. Even a scholar with exceptionally good grounding in history is apt to think more easily of those slogans and expressions which are part of his own political experience. We do not know whether this tendency actually weighted our list with terms of a vintage since World War I, but it can do no harm to be cautious and assume that it did. If we make this assumption, we interpret our list not as an index of attention to the major areas of politics in general, but as an index of attention to what have become the major areas of politics since World War I. An increase or decrease in frequencies at any earlier period may be interpreted as an increase or decrease in attention to those things which were emerging as the key issues of a few years later. For example, an increase in attention to symbols of national security around 1900 would be interpreted not as indicating, necessarily, that national security as then conceived was less thought of a few years earlier, but perhaps as indicating that national security as we have now come to conceive it was coming into the focus of attention. In other words, what we are studying is the development of certain modern political ideas, not necessarily the leading political ideas of each period. In attention to these contemporary ideas there certainly has been an upward trend.

One other bias that one would expect, parallel to the bias in favor of recent terms, is a bias in favor of symbols familiar in the language and country of those framing the list. For the men engaged in this study, the *New York Times* has been almost daily fare for years. Even a scholar who is expert in international affairs might less fully recollect the terminology of the other papers. The data, however, do not indicate any bias of this kind. On the contrary, Table 5 shows that the less familiar papers show a greater richness in enumerated symbols. If there is a bias in favor of American or English political symbols, it is not important enough to show up against the more ideological character of the editorials in the Continental papers. The greatest use of listed ideological symbols was in *Izvestia*, followed by the French papers and the *Frankfurter Zeitung*. The least use of these symbols was in the *Norddeutsche allgemeine Zeitung* and the *New York Times*.

The Variables

In examining the editorials in the prestige papers we recorded both the presence or absence of listed symbols, and also the attitude expressed toward them. Each symbol recorded as occurring was also recorded as being favored, opposed, or neutrally mentioned; favorable and unfavorable judgments were recorded only when the editorial judgment was explicit. We thus have two basic types of data on the symbols: attention data and judgment data.

Table 5
Number of Counted Symbols Per Editorial by Paper

Paper	Names of National Units	Ideological Symbols	All Symbols
New York Times	2.0	1.6	3.6
London *Times*	2.9	2.2	5.1
Le Temps	3.0	4.4	7.4
Le Monde	4.7	4.9	9.6
France, whole sample	3.2	4.4	7.6
Norddeutsche allgemeine Zeitung	2.5	1.4	3.9
Frankfurter Zeitung	3.0	4.7	7.7
Völkischer Beobachter	3.3	3.2	6.5
Germany, whole sample	2.9	3.5	6.4
Novoe Vremia	4.0	2.5	6.5
Izvestia	2.9	8.2	11.1
Russia, whole sample	3.6	5.0	8.6

In subsequent monographs we shall examine the attention and judgment data for selected groups of symbols having common subject matters. In this preliminary monograph we are concerned with certain characteristics of the total political content of the editorials. The characteristics on which we have significant data are five in number:

1. *Amount of attention to the key symbols of recent political controversy.* Some data on this have already been given in Table 5, which compared the different papers in our sample, and in Table 4, which dealt with attention trends.

2. *Variety in the symbols used.* When and under what circumstances do the editorials hammer away on a few key symbols, and when do they use a rich and varied vocabulary of political concepts?

3. *Change in the symbols used.* Change in the symbols used would be one very important index of social change. When and where have there been big changes in symbolism?

4. *Direction of judgment.* An important index of satisfactions might be derived from the tendency of editorials to praise or to deplore. When and under what circumstances were editorials more positive or more negative?

5. *Uniformity of judgment.* Where and when were the attitudes toward different matters sharply stereotyped, and where and when were the attitudes expressed in the editorials varied?

Each of these variables in political communications is apt to be affected by circumstances of both political and journalistic nature. Editorial writing is apt to be different in quiet times from what it is in turbulent times; to be different in war and in peace, in a free press and in a totalitarian press. Also there may be long-term trends. We shall attempt to assess the impact of events upon the general character of the prestige press.

II. Variety and Repetition in Political Language

General Propositions

In language, as in many kinds of behavior, a few common items account for the vast bulk of all events, while a large variety of items occur only rarely. Of the 500,000 to 700,000 words in the English language, thirty words account for half the words *spoken* in English and sixty-nine account for half the words *written* in English. In other words, a foreigner knowing the right sixty-nine English words could translate roughly every second word in an English text.[11] A number of different counts have supported the conclusion that the bulk of symbol uses involves few different symbols. Table 6 summarizes a number of those studies.

Table 6
Variety of Vocabulary in Different Universes of Discourse[12] (Number of different words)

Universe of Discourse	Percentage of All Words Accounted for by Given Number of Different Words		
	50%	64%	80%
Spoken English	30	65	155
Popular Songs	41	100	250
Written English	69	250	640
Romantic Poems	86	210	530

Of course, the commonest of all symbols are such colorless ones as THE, OF, AND, TO, A, IN, THAT, IT, IS, I. To the philologist these may be important. To the student of politics the interesting symbols are such relatively rare ones as FREEDOM, PEACE, and DEMOCRACY. The most common among them constitutes but one or two tenths of one percent of either spoken or written English. Only two of the symbols on our symbol list (PEOPLE and STATE) appear among the 737 words used in one percent or more of telephone conversations, and these two should probably be excluded because of homonyms. On the telephone PEOPLE is usually not a political symbol but a synonym for "persons." STATE, the noun, may refer to an address, health, or the progress of a business deal, at least as often as to the government.[13] It seems fair to conclude that discussion of things political entered less than one percent of the analyzed conversations.

It would be easy to use this data to deplore people's apathy toward public affairs. It would also be foolish. Telephone conversations normally deal with the most immediate practical problems facing a person, not with ideological matters.[14] The reader of these pages, almost certainly a socially conscious individual, may ask himself in what percentage of his telephone calls he talks about political principles. Telephone English is not a very useful sample for measuring the incidence of the symbols on our list.

Written English or the English of leisure-time oral discussions might be expected to contain more political symbols. Indeed, though still rare, we do find more of our symbols in lists of the most common written words. In 1918 Godfrey Dewey listed each word that constituted more than one one-hundredth of one percent of a sample of general writing including newspaper and magazine stories, editorials, advertisements, books, and letters. He found, in all, 1131 such words. They included the political symbols shown in Table 7, all of which, except when noted, are on our list.[15]

Even if we make the most generous allowances for the political components of the homonyms above it seems likely that well under half of one

Table 7
Political Symbols in Dewey Count

	Rank Among Symbols in Dewey List	Frequency per 100,000 Words
Symbols which are generally political		
WAR	59	217
PEACE	195	62
PATRIOT	493	27
ALLIES	696	15
FREEDOM	930	11
Symbols which are often political, but may also be nonpolitical		
LABOR	244	52
LIBERTY	706	19
NEUTRAL	841	15
Symbols which are probably less often political than not		
PEOPLE	70	180
STATE	135	92
PROGRESS	640	21
Political symbols on the Dewey list not included in our study*		
COUNTRY	116	111
GOVERN	155	78

*GOVERN is a verb and therefore not appropriate to our list. COUNTRY in a phrase like "my country" would have been coded under the name of the nation-state. Most editorial instances of the word where it did not mean rural would have been taken care of in our study. Thus our list seems to stand up fairly well against the test of the leading actually used political symbols.

percent of written English consists of politically relevant terms. In any case, the bulk of our political language consists of terms which appear less often than once in ten thousand words.

The mere infrequency of the terms on our list does not derogate from their importance. The human mind is such an extraordinary filing device that it can use thousands of items stored for rare occasions. The word TARIFF or the word ANARCHISM may not cross a person's lips for months or even years at a time, but any person of moderate education can call either of them forth instantaneously when needed. It is the thousands of words in the tail of the frequency distribution of language, not the THE's, THAT's, WHICH's, and A's, which make language a tool of fabulous potency.

In the telephone study, 1655 different words, or 74 percent of the total, each constituted only between .00001 and .0001 (inclusive) of all words used (one through eight occurrences). In the Dewey study, 9134 different words, or 90 percent of the total, each constituted only between .00001 and .0001 of all words used (one through ten occurrences). These may be considered the rare words. The difference in their frequency is due to the difference in the medium, and perhaps to a difference in the basis of counting. In any case, the conclusion is that much of what is said involves use of some of the many relatively rare terms. About one in twenty words spoken over the telephone and one in seven written words is a rare word by the above standard.

When we turn from these earlier studies to our own study of political language, we find most of the same conclusions repeated. This is true despite the fact that we are dealing with a selected list of symbols largely drawn from the tail of the general word distribution.[16] The distribution of enumerated symbols in our study is reported in Table 8 and Figure 1. The symbols are summarized separately for each country (i.e., language) for the entire half-century studied. We find that in each case 13 to 19 of the 210 symbols accounted for half of all instances of use. Also 58 to 79 of the symbols accounted for 90 percent of all symbol uses.

Thus we find in political discussions, as in most areas of symbolic behavior, a great concentration on a relatively limited number of symbols. At the same time there are a large number of reserve symbols available for occasional use. These rarely used symbols may, of course, be the salt that makes the product palatable, but it is nonetheless striking how few are the central themes which editorial writers manipulate in the bulk of their writing. These few central symbols are, of course, symbols of considerable

Table 8
Cumulative Frequency of Symbols in Editorials

Cumulative Percentage of Symbol uses	Number of Words				
	United States	Great Britain	France	Germany	Russia
10	1	1	2	2	2
20	2	3	5	4	4
30	5	6	8	7	6
40	8	11	13	11	9
50	13	16	19	15	13
60	19	22	28	21	17
70	29	31	40	29	25
80	44	46	56	38	40
90	70	69	79	58	64
100	165	166	143	130	155

Percentage of Occurrences

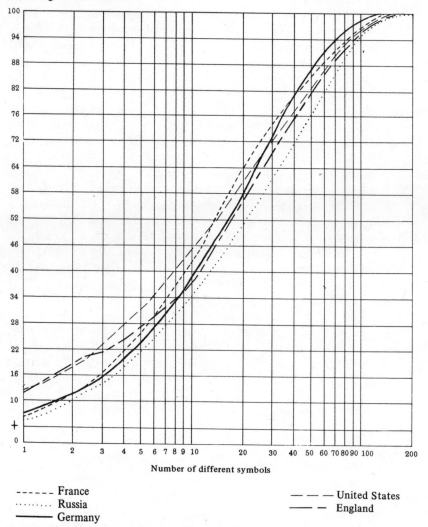

Number of different symbols

------ France   — — — United States
.... Russia   —— — England
——— Germany

Figure 1. Ogives of Frequency Distribution of General Symbols

ambiguity which lend themselves to a variety of meanings and produce an impression of rich and meaningful language. Because of this ambiguity of the common symbols, plus the occasional use of rare symbols, one is slow to realize that, in fact, the variety of political symbolism is small.

Although this is always true in some degree, there is not always an equal poverty in the political content of editorials. The variety of themes expressed varies with the circumstances and with the paper. These variations in the variety of political language, which we are about to consider, are perhaps more important than the fact that all the editorials concentrate heavily on a few symbols.

Yule's K

One of the hypotheses which we sought to test was that there would be less variety of symbols in periods of tension. This hypothesis proved to be too simple a summary of the situation, but the data do suggest the validity of Lasswell's more qualified guess:

> When the crisis is recognized as serious, and as one in which energy must be conserved, the tendency is for what is communicated to be terse, repetitious, and effect-contrasted. In crises in which it is assumed that the outcome can be affected by communication, and more energy can be devoted to it, the style grows more prolix, varied, and effect-modelled.[17]

While a simple correlation of repetition with crisis did not hold up, we did find four variables which in our sample were related to symbolic variety. These were:

1. War. During wars, more than in peacetime, editorials concentrate intensively on four to six main symbols.

2. Totalitarianism. The contents of a controlled totalitarian press are impoverished as compared with those of a free press. Totalitarian editorials tend to concentrate heavily on fifteen to twenty key symbols.

3. Style. In this political research project, we have not attempted to discern just which elements of style are relevant. Still it seems clear that languages and types of writing vary in diversity of symbols.

4. Time. As times change, the words used change, too. The shorter the time span from which a sample of symbols is drawn the more uniform it tends to be; the longer the time span the greater the variety we should expect.

Of these four variables two are clearly related to crisis, and it is these first two which interest us here. War and totalitarianism both coincide with heightened tension. The increased poverty of symbols under these circumstances fits our original hypotheses. What is missing in our results is evidence that a parallel constriction of symbols takes place in peacetime crises in democratic countries, e.g., in depressions. For our present data, therefore, we must seek more specific explanations than a simple general hypothesis correlating crisis and poverty of symbols.

The two hypotheses concerning style and time are not of central interest in a political investigation such as this one. In an experimental situation these are things we should hold constant so as to be able to measure the relationship of war and totalitarianism to political vocabulary. However, we are not working in a laboratory situation. The only way we can hold these nonpolitical variables constant is to measure them. If we find style sufficiently stable over time, then we can correlate the shorter fluctuations with political events. But we dare not assume style to be constant without investigating. We must measure the effects of the major nonpolitical variables before we can fairly estimate the effects of the political ones.

To test *any* of our hypotheses, we therefore need an accurate measure of dispersion in the distribution of symbols. Without some such measure we cannot state that the degree of concentration on a few symbols was greater or less at one time than at another; with it we can make such comparisons. The best measure that exists for this purpose is G. Udny Yule's K. As we shall see, it does not answer all relevant questions, but it is the first step that has been taken toward a sound statistical basis for content analysis. We shall use it to provide a first approximation of the shape of the distributions of the enumerated symbols.

Yule's K was first reported in 1944,[18] and to the best of the author's knowledge it has not been applied since Yule's own pioneer investigation. Since it is so little known, it would be well to review its origin and characteristics before using it. The late G. Udny Yule was one of the world's leading statisticians, and a scholar in the best British humanistic tradition. Upon retiring from Cambridge, he devoted himself to the old debate whether Thomas a Kempis or someone else wrote *De Imitatione Christi.* Yule soon discovered that each writer or form of writing has his or its own characteristic degree of concentration or dispersion in vocabulary. He also realized that no statistical measure had yet been devised for describing such linguistic distributions. He set himself the task of devising one.

To Yule's statistically trained mind the problem seemed similar to that of accident rates. Just as some people are more prone to accidents than others, so are some words more likely to occur than others. In a population of n persons, each one has an individual probability, $p,$ of having an accident in a fixed time period. The risk of an accident (i.e., p) is, however, a function not only of the individual but also of time. The longer the time span, the more likely anyone is to have an accident.

By analogy, the "risk" that a certain word will appear varies not only with the word but also with the length of text read. Most studies of vocabulary before Yule had been unsound because they failed to allow for the vital effect of sample size on the results. For example, if one read 5,000 words one might find 250 different words among them. The word AND might be 3 percent of the total, whereas 100 different rare words might each occur only once. Suppose that one then doubled the sample. In 10,000 words one might find 350 different words and 150 might each occur only once, but presumably the incidence of the word AND would still be 3 percent of 10,000 words, just as it had been of 5,000. In other words, the shape of the distribution at this point has entirely changed, since it varied at one end but not at the other as the size of the sample grew. To meet this difficulty Yule needed a characteristic that would be independent of sample size. He got it, devising one involving only the first and second moments of the distribution. This characteristic was, therefore, little affected by the tail of the distribution.

The formula for Yule's K is as follows:

$$K = 10,000 \ \frac{S_2 - S_1}{S_1{}^2}$$

S_1 equals the sum of the symbols occurring in the sample (e.g., 5,000 or 10,000 in the above example), and S_2 equals the sum of squares of the incidences of the individual symbols in the sample.

We have computed K for each period in our sample. The results appear in Table 9. They enable us to begin to test our hypotheses. The higher the value of K the greater the concentration on a limited number of symbols. The lower the value of K the greater the diversity.

War.   Let us start with the first of our four hypotheses: that the variety of symbols decreases during wars. It will be noted that the nine highest K values, all those over 510, occurred during either World War I or World War II. Furthermore, under all the nontotalitarian regimes the lowest wartime value of K was considerably higher (at least 45 points higher) than the highest peacetime value for that country. No significance tests for K have yet been worked out, but no reasonable doubt can exist that the first hypothesis holds up well in this data. It is important, however, to note that by "wartime," in this context, we mean whenever a major war was going on, irrespective of whether the country itself was involved. In wartime, K values are high even in temporarily neutral countries. The World Wars dominated the political scene in all the major powers, when they were formally neutral as well as when they were actual belligerents. In both circumstances, wartime editorials are of less varied contents than their peacetime counterparts.

Table 9
Yule's K by Time Periods

	Pre-World War I	World War I	1920s	Early 1930s	Late 1930s
United States	358	543	334	424	287
Great Britain	288	878	330	284	267
France	221	307	218	204	212
Germany	—*	577	239	196	509
Russia	257‡	400	306	408†	454
	261§				

	World War II		Post-World War II	Entire Sample
	Phase 1	Phase 2		
United States	696	837	379	328
Great Britain	536	654	383	299
France	268	287	263	189
Germany	493	562	–	235
Russia	493	530	487	261

* Sample too small for stable distribution.
† Figures for totalitarian situations are double underlined.
‡ 1892-1904.
§ 1905-1913.

Totalitarianism.   Totalitarianism has an effect on the editorials similar to that of war. In Germany the coming of Hitler raised K by double or more, up to the 500 level. In Russia the evolution was more gradual. From 1918 through 1928, the Soviet press was hardly free, yet it did not have the dismally banal and repetitious tone of the typical totalitarian paper. Within the limits of Communist doctrine the press was full of controversy and debate. The writers took pride in individuality. In such circumstances K for *Izvestia,* although higher than in *Novoe Vremia,* was at a level characteristic of a nontotalitarian paper. With the Stalin era, however, K jumped at once and proceeded to rise steadily throughout World War II. Since the war it has dropped somewhat, but it is still higher than in the last peacetime period. The repetitiousness of *Izvestia* is of an extent found elsewhere only in Nazi and wartime editorials.

At least two hypotheses may be suggested to explain the repetitiousness and lack of variety of totalitarian papers. It may be the direct effect of censorship and a "line," or it may be the indirect effect of these and other forces in stifling thought, creativity, and individuality. The low K values in Russia before 1928, when censorship and a party line already existed, and the low K values in France during World War II and under the Vichy regime, when strict censorship also existed, lend support to the conviction that the second and more slowly acting of these causes was the more important one. In time, totalitarian regimes seem to lose the power of inventing varied and original self-justifications. If so, there is an important chink in the totalitarian armor. Is totalitarianism bound to undercut its own propaganda effectiveness by creating a dull orthodoxy incapable of fully utilizing the range of human sophistication? This thesis has often been maintained, and our data tend to confirm it.

A further hypothesis to explain the repetitiousness of totalitarian propaganda is that it was a result of a deliberate propaganda policy based on a low estimation of human intelligence. The Nazis certainly held to such a doctrine of propaganda technique. Their writings on propaganda drew heavily on the beliefs of American advertising experts that the way to sell the public is to say the same thing over and over again. Adolf Hitler summed up this doctrine in *Mein Kampf*:

The great masses' receptive ability is only very limited, their understanding is small, but their forgetfulness is great. As a consequence of these facts, all effective propaganda has to limit itself only to a very few points and to use them like slogans until even the very last man is able to imagine what is intended by such a word.

Equally bald statements cannot be found in Soviet propaganda doctrine, but, stated somewhat differently, Soviet theorists reach a similar conclusion. Directives from the party to the intellectuals who produce Soviet communications place great emphasis upon talking the language of the proletariat and being understood by them. Esoteric forms of art, music, and literature have been subjected to sharp criticism. This is an attitude not limited to Russia, but in Russia it has become official policy. The best-known example of this policy is the demand made on Shostakovich that he write symphonies with themes that the workers can whistle.

This emphasis on simplicity and directness is not uniform throughout Soviet communications. On the contrary, as Alex Inkeles points out, a considerable portion of the Soviet press is devoted to imbuing the party members and nonparty intelligentsia with Marxist-Leninist theory. He adds:

It is not possible to say whether or not these materials directed toward the party and Soviet cadres are also read by the average reader. The evidence at hand suggests that a large proportion of the ordinary readers find this material rather deep.[19]

The presence of two antithetical standards for writing is explained by a sharp differentiation made by Soviet theorists between "agitation" and "propaganda." Plekhanov defined these terms, "A propagandist presents many ideas to one or a few persons; an agitator presents only one or a few ideas, but he presents them to a mass of people."[20] The Soviet press, contrasted with the pre-Soviet press, is explicitly regarded as, above all, an instrument for propaganda and agitation. Its deliberate assumption of the role of leading agitator for Soviet goals may help to explain its propensity to hammer away at a limited number of themes.

This explanation of the repetitiousness of Soviet editorial symbolism would be more convincing if we knew that there had been a deliberate shift around 1928 from stress on "propaganda" to stress on "agitation." That there has been such a shift in practice, whether conscious or unconscious, our data seem to indicate. But was there a calculated change of emphasis? Inkeles indicates such a change in at least one respect:

In the early years of the Soviet regime it was stated that one of the three chief tasks of the Soviet press was "to spread knowledge among the masses of workers and peasants, and to raise their cultural and political level." A considerable amount of newspaper space was indeed devoted to straightforward adult education in the first Soviet decade, but with fuller development of regular formal education, decreasing emphasis was placed on such material.[21]

On the other hand, as with so many Soviet policies, there have been sharp zigs and zags throughout:

The utilization of the press for propaganda purposes was given fresh impetus in 1938, when the Central Committee called for liquidation of what it termed the tendency to undervalue the significance of the press as the most important instrument of Marxist-Leninist training.[22]

Whether the criticized tendency really existed, whether the fresh emphasis on stressing propaganda amounted to anything, whether there has been any general trend toward *deliberately* simplifying the content of the Soviet press, the present author is unqualified to say. Russian specialists might well devote themselves to this question, which has important implications for counterpropaganda. All our study shows is that *in practice* there has been a decrease in variety of symbols, a trend more appropriate to agitation than to propaganda.

Style. In addition to war and totalitarianism, a third variable related to K is style. Style, as we use the word here, is something of a catchall for otherwise unexplained differences between papers. The French papers, for example, generally have K values much lower than those in any other country. The wartime values barely reach 300 (which would be low in peacetime in the United States). The peacetime values are in the low 200's. The K values of *Novoe Vremia* and the *Frankfurter Zeitung* are also low. Those for the London *Times* are fairly high and for the *New York Times* fairly high by democratic standards.

These differences could be due to differences in the languages in which the papers are written and to differences in traditions of editorial writing. They could also be a function of the literary pretensions of the writers and literary demands of the readers, as well as a function of the degree of emphasis on ideology in each paper.

Yule's own work showed clearly the effect of literary style on K. He analyzed samples from the works of Thomas a Kempis, Gerson, Macaulay, Bunyan, and the Gospel according to St. John (A.V.) Table 10 summarizes his findings.[23]

Table 10
Summary of Yule's Findings

	K
Macaulay	20.1
Bunyan	51.3
Gerson	35.9
a Kempis	59.7
St. John	161.5

It will at once be noted that these values are considerably lower than those found in our study, even though our study de-emphasized repeated symbols by counting them only once per editorial. That is not surprising. We may presume that the vocabulary of a high-grade literary author would normally be more varied than the daily outpourings of even the best editorial writers. Furthermore, Yule's count is based on total vocabulary, ours on a select list. In selecting, one omits the rarer symbols, partly deliberately, partly by inadvertence. Thus one shortens the tail of the distribution. This, as noted above, has little effect on K, yet its effect might conceivably be measurable. No research has yet been done to estimate the adequacy of lists constructed from remembered information. In any event, the difference in the literary level of the writing—and perhaps also the differences between a count of unselected and selected symbols—easily account for the differences between Yule's findings and our own.

Within Yule's own results there are compared materials in two different languages, Medieval Latin and English. Latin is a highly inflected language which does without many of the small and most frequent words in English, but this does not greatly affect K values for nouns.

Within English texts we find great variations, depending on the style of the author and the type of material read. Yule picked Macaulay and Bunyan because one is a writer with a very elaborate style and the other is a very plain stylist. The K values faithfully reflect this.

What role similar literary factors play in explaining the differences among the editorials is a question which we shall leave to specialists in such matters. It seems likely that the cultural emphasis on quality of literary style is a factor of some importance. The French educational system places considerable emphasis on literary values; so to some extent do all the European educational systems. The ranking of the K values for the French papers, *Novoe Vremia,* the *Frankfurter Zeitung,* the London *Times,* and the *New York Times* is certainly not incompatible with a hypothesis that the K value varies with the extent to which the editorial writers and readers care about quality of writing.

This ranking may also be explained by variations in the conception of public opinion. An elite which wishes to include the whole class of middle-income skill groups within its opinion orbit is not likely to trust its chief editorial exposition to a writer whose style appeals to the literati, but not to the lawyers, engineers, and corporation executives. A society with aristocratic attitudes, which uses literary skill as a symbol of status, is more likely to have well-written prestige papers than one with a broad elite including less sophisticatedly intellectual elements. The papers with low K values tend to come from the former type of society whereas the democratic papers with high K values come from the latter type.

This same ranking is, however, equally compatible with the hypothesis that K values depend upon the emphasis on ideological matters. (Our list is, of course, loaded with words with heavy ideological overtones.) Among the democratic papers, the *New York Times,* which is the paper least prone to dogmatic positions, makes least extensive use of the symbols on our list, and the French press, which we find over and over to be most prone to emphasize doctrinal abstractions, has the greatest variety of symbols. By reference to Table 5 it will be noted that the frequency of the listed symbols follows an order not greatly different from that for variety of symbols. We are perhaps justified, therefore, in concluding that the *New York Times* and the London *Times* were the least strongly ideological papers, showing this both in the infrequent use of such symbols and in the use of a small number of different ones. The French papers and the *Frankfurter Zeitung,* on the other hand, acquired a heavily doctrinal tone by using such symbols frequently and in great variety.

Time. This is the last variable of the four listed at the beginning of this section which remains to be related to K. It will be noted that the periods into which we grouped our data are of very uneven lengths. They are intended to be natural periods, defined by the flow of events. They are divided by wars, revolutions, changes of regime, and changes of the business cycle. They were grouped in this way so that the editorials within any period would be as homogeneous as possible, and the differences between periods would be as large as possible. This method of division results in a variation in periods of from two years to twenty-four years.

Furthermore, the periods of crisis are apt to be short and the periods of stability long. A war, a revolution, or other event of great intensity will produce distinctive editorials as well as great changes, but it will usually burn itself out in a few years. Note, too, that the longest periods in our breakdown are the farthest back and the shortest periods are the most recent—perhaps as a result of the almost universal tendency of historians to foreshorten the past, a tendency to which the author may easily have succumbed in periodizing the data. Geologists or historians have given definitions to past epochs such that each one is several times as long as the succeeding one, and we may have done the same. Perhaps, on the contrary, it is not just the tendency to simplify what is farther away that has resulted in the shortening of the more recent periods. It may be the result of the more violent and dynamic character of the past few decades. Perhaps it is true that changes occurred more slowly before World War I and in the 1920s than they have since. In any case, it is important to note that our periods are of very uneven length, and it is important to see how this affects the K values.

In a world of evenly flowing events, one would expect K to be a simple inverse function of time. Some verbal changes arise from the impact of events upon the language, but some change in the language would take place even if we could hold all external influences constant. It is obvious that a sample including Elizabethan English, eighteenth-century English, Victorian English, and Modern English would have a considerably greater variety of words than a sample drawn from 1951 only. In this respect it is necessary to qualify one of Yule's conclusions. He argued that the formulas for the risk of appearance of symbols differed from those for the risk of accidents in one respect only, i.e., time. This factor he considered of negligible importance in the study of symbols and he was right in respect to his own problem, which concerned individual literary works. For other problems, however, techniques are needed to measure the effect of time. Although one may usually disregard the length of time it took to write a single literary work; in studying a series of works, as we are doing here, the effects of time on the language should be held constant along with sample size. Lacking satisfactory techniques as yet, the best we can do here is to estimate the rough order of magnitude of the effect of passage of time on our results.

Having done so, we are pleased to find that the duration of a subsample makes far less difference in the results than one might expect. Despite the changes which we shall study below, the dominant political symbols have persisted in the center of attention over all or most of the half-century. Because the rate of change in the language has been slow, the chief variations in K have been the result of the other three variables, war, totalitarianism, and style, rather than of time. This is most easily seen by comparing the K values for the entire half-century with the K values for individual periods. In each case, the K value for the entire period of thirty-five to sixty years is, as expected, distinctly lower than the average K values for the individual periods. In other words, the variety in the symbols used during the entire half-century was distinctly greater than the variety within a typical subperiod. Yet the order of difference was not great. In every country except France, there was at least one subperiod which had a greater variety of symbols within itself than did the entire half-century sample. Some of these subperiods were very short; in fact, the lowest value of K in our study is that for the *Frankfurter Zeitung* during the three-year period 1930-32. The lowest British K was also found in a three-year period, 1936-38. Comparable periods of uneven length generally had very comparable K values. Thus the fact that we divided World War II into two uneven halves does not seem to have had any appreciable effect on the K's in them. All in all, it seems clear that the effects of time were small compared with the effects of events; they were insufficient to modify seriously our previous results.

On the other hand, as we have just noted, the effects of time were discernible. We computed the average K for each country, weighting the K's for the different periods by the number of years in that period. In Table 11 these average K's are compared with the K's for the entire half-century. It will be noted that, except in Germany, the difference in each case is under 100 points. In France it is under 50 points. In Germany it is about 175 points. This, in a rough way, measures certain changes over the half-century. These facts do not give us any very satisfactory method for equalizing periods, but they do provide us with a rule of thumb which can prevent gross misinterpretations. If, in comparing one period with another of unequal length, one adds or subtracts two for each year of the difference in length, one will avoid stretching the data too far in explaining small differences. (For France or Germany adjustments by a lower or higher number might be preferable.) For example, if a period of three years has a K value ten points higher than a period of eleven years, we should have no right to draw conclusions about a difference, because the eight years' difference in length of period could easily account for the difference in K. For that reason alone we should expect K for the short period to be perhaps sixteen points higher than for the long period. If this allowance is made, variety of symbolism in the short illustrative period is no less than in the long. In our actual results, however, the allowances that had to be made for time turn out to be fairly small compared with the actual differences in K's. Thus, findings about other variables continue to hold up.

In the last paragraph, we noted that a comparison of K's for an entire sample with those of its subsamples gives us a rough measure of certain kinds of change. Perhaps statisticians can develop the proper use of this

Table 11
Effect of Time Upon K

	K Value for Entire Sample	Weighted Mean of K for Subperiods	Difference	Years in Entire Sample
United States	328	427	99	50
Great Britain	299	385	86	60
France	189	236	47	48
Germany	235	409	174	32
Russia	261	353	92	58

measure, but as it now stands, it is more seductive than safe. We shall develop later a more satisfactory approach to the study of symbolic change. For the moment, let us simply indicate the very broad conclusions which the present data permit. What, for example, is the significance of the very peculiar German data? In Germany we have a series of periods, in each of which, on the average, there is a high degree of concentration on a few symbols, but among which the degree of concentration on a few symbols is low. This is the situation which one should expect to find when there has been drastic change between symbol patterns, each of which was relatively cohesive within itself. This is what one expects to happen with a revolution. One expects to find a prerevolutionary and postrevolutionary symbol pattern, each fairly cohesive itself, but very different from the other. The two German revolutions within our period apparently produced this effect. Did not the Russian revolution also? That is a question we must leave for later.

As it has been worked out to date, K does not permit us to carry this analysis further.[24] For measurements of change we need a somewhat different approach. With the aid of Yule's K, we have, however, been able to measure the effects of war and totalitarianism on the variety in communications at any given period, and we have found this variety to be a significant social variable.

War and Totalitarianism

So far, our data have shown a striking similarity between wartime and totalitarian propaganda. As measured by Yule's K, they both share a tendency to use restricted political symbolism. Both beat the drums on a few central themes. Both are more intense and at a lower level of intellectual sophistication than peacetime, democratic propaganda. War and totalitarian propaganda are not the same, however. Our findings do not conform to the familiar thesis that the controls and hysteria of wartime necessarily produce the same intellectual conditions at home which we are fighting abroad. In symbolic flexibility, at least, there is an important difference.

The difference between the wartime press of the democracies and the totalitarian press is in the range of ideas subjected to regulation and uniformity. Wartime propaganda brings a single overwhelming aid to the forefront. The symbols which express that aim are hammered home repetitiously and incessantly. The distribution of other symbols, however, is affected relatively little, and variety continues in the expression of other ideas. Totalitarianism, on the other hand, impoverishes the whole range of political discussion. On all political topics repetitiousness to the point of banality becomes characteristic.

These conclusions about the difference between totalitarian and war propaganda do not show up with the summary characteristic K, since that rests only upon the first two moments and therefore does not fully describe the shape of the distribution. They do show up when we measure the degree of concentration on the few most used symbols: for example, the first five or the first eighteen, listed symbols.

Table 12 indicates the percentage of total attention received by the five most common words. In each paper, wartime material shows greater symbolic concentration than does peacetime material. In Russia, it is true, Soviet peacetime material shows even greater concentration than the wartime material from *Novoe Vremia*. But separating *Novoe Vremia* from *Izvestia*, we find that in each paper the wartime material is less varied than the peacetime material from the same paper. The effect of a war on the editorials appears strikingly in the first five symbols, because the key symbols for any war (e.g., WAR, ALLIES, NEUTRALS) are, during hostilities, the most numerous of all political symbols.

The effects of totalitarianism are seen in a larger range of vocabulary. Totalitarian papers stress, of course, the four or five key words referring to the immediate situation; in addition, the limitations of totalitarian vocabulary can be seen in our data right through the first fifteen or twenty words. We chose the first eighteen words as a good measure of concentration, because, depending on the period, between 52 and 86 percent of all symbols are encompassed by the first eighteen. Beyond eighteen words, the frequency ogives for the least varied periods enter their unstable tails. Table 13 shows for each period the proportion of all words comprised by the first eighteen.

The effects of totalitarianism do not stand out from the data quite so obviously as the effects of war, since the degree of concentration on the first eighteen words is partly a function of the degree of concentration on the first five. In other words, a democratic paper during a war will, because of its heavy concentration on the first five symbols, also show heavy concentration on the first eighteen symbols. If 50 percent of attention is devoted to the first five symbols, clearly well over 50 percent of attention must be devoted to the first eighteen. To distinguish the effect of totalitar-

Table 12
First Five Symbols as Percentage of All Symbols

Wartime Periods		Peacetime Periods	
United States			
World War I	40	1900-13	33
World War II, 1939-41	45	1919-29	33
World War II, 1942-45	50	1930-32	39
		1933-38	30
		1946-49	37
Great Britain			
World War I	51	1890-1913	30
World War II, 1939-40	50	1919-29	30
World War II, 1941-45	42	1929-35	28
		1936-38	29
		1946-49	35
France			
World War I	33	1900-13	23
World War II, 1939-40	28	1919-29	23
World War II, 1941-42	29	1930-35	22
		1936-38	22
		1945-49*	28
Germany			
World War I	47	1910-13	−†
World War II, 1939-41	43	1919-29	24
World War II, 1942-45	45	1930-32	29
		1933-38	39
Russia			
World War I	36	1892-1904	26
World War II, 1939-41	42	1905-13	28
World War II, 1942-45	40	1918-28	28
		1929-35	34
		1936-38	39
		1946-49	38

*To avoid lumping postliberation papers with Vichy papers, 1945 was added to the French postwar sample. This period is, therefore, part war part peace. Exclusion of 1945 would lower the percent.
†Too few cases for stable distribution.

Table 13
First Eighteen Symbols as Percentage of All Symbols

Paper	Period	First 18 Words	Sixth Through 18th Word	First 18 Words Other Than WAR, PEACE, and ALLIES
New York Times	1900-1913	70	37	64
	1914-18	70	30	44
	1919-29	62	29	49
	1930-32	66	28	56
	1933-38	59	29	48
	1939-41	75	30	50
	1942-45	75	25	40
	1946-49	67	31	51
London *Times*	1890-1913	61	31	51
	1914-18	79	28	39
	1919-29	63	33	45
	1930-35	60	31	48
	1936-38	56	27	43
	1939-40	70	20	46
	1941-45	71	29	44
	1946-49	66	31	49
Le Temps	1900-1913	53	30	48
	1914-18	55	23	47
	1919-29	53	30	45
	1930-35	52	30	48
	1936-38	53	32	48
	1939-40	61	33	49
	1941-42	63	33	51
Le Monde	1945-49	59	32	50
Norddeutsche allgemeine Zeitung	1910-13	*	*	*
	1914-18	70	23	47
Frankfurter Zeitung	1919-29	57	33	48
	1930-32	52	23	47
Völkischer Beobachter	1933-38	77	38	71
	1939-41	83	41	70
	1942-45	83	39	78
Novoe Vremia	1892-1904	60	34	50
	1905-13	57	29	47
	1914-17	63	27	45
Izvestia	1918-28	67	39	64
	1929-35	77	43	76
	1936-38	78	41	78
	1939-40	82	41	80
	1941-45	86	46	78
	1946-49	84	46	80

*Too few judgments for stable distribution.

ianism, therefore, we want to eliminate the already measured effect of war on the first few symbols. This can be most easily done by measuring the concentration of attention on the sixth through the eighteenth symbols. This is done in the second column of Table 13, which begins to separate the totalitarian papers fairly distinctly.

The same objective can be even better achieved by eliminating from the first eighteen terms a few of the characteristic wartime symbols. Specifically, we eliminated WAR, PEACE, and ALLIES whenever these symbols were among the first eighteen. The resultant figures for the first eighteen words other than these three are presented in the third column of Table 13. These figures make the effects of totalitarianism very clear. In the nontotalitarian papers, roughly half of all symbols are encompassed by the first eighteen other than WAR, PEACE, and ALLIES. In the totalitarian papers (i.e., *Völkischer Beobachter* and *Izvestia* for the years boxed in Table 13) these make up about three-quarters of the symbols.

Again, as above, we find that it is full-fledged and effective totalitarianism which constricts the scope of the editorials. Such constriction is not found in the incipient totalitarianism of Russia before 1928 nor in editorials in independent papers operating under censorship. The mere presence of controls need not constrict variety of expression. For such constriction, the controls must be effective. These additional data also help us to see the striking difference between war and totalitarianism in the degree to which originality and individualism are suppressed in editorial contents; neither during wars nor during incipient totalitarianism does political symbolism become as generally impoverished as it does under full totalitarianism.

III. Editorial Judgment

Three aspects of editorial judgment are measured by our data: the amount of judgment, the direction of judgment, and the uniformity of judgment. The amount of judgment is indicated by the percentage of symbols on which judgment is passed. The direction of judgment is indicated by the balance between approval and disapproval. The uniformity of judgment is indicated by the frequency, or, rather, infrequency, of judgments contrary to the ordinary stereotyped attitude toward a symbol.

Amount of Judgment

In one sense, the editorial columns of a paper are entirely devoted to judgment, but it does not follow that all important symbols are assigned an explicit evaluation. On the contrary, the majority of the symbols we counted were recorded as neutral or unjudged. This was due in part, to the coding rules adopted in this study. In part, it was the result of the fact that

Table 14
Judged Symbols as Percentage of All Symbols

Paper	Period	Ideological Symbols	The Self	Outside World
New York Times	1900-1913	24	26	13
	1914-18	20	18	15
	1919-29	04	00	01
	1930-32	01	02	00
	1933-38	03	02	01
	1939-41	04	01	02
	1942-45	07	23	09
	1946-49	11	12	09
	1900-1949	10	10	07
London *Times*	1890-1913	18	46	21
	1914-18	11	16	10
	1919-29	09	10	03
	1930-35	07	07	01
	1936-38	07	03	00
	1939-40	10	18	11
	1941-45	11	24	14
	1946-49	06	22	06
	1890-1949	12	25	12
Le Temps	1900-1913	26	22	17
	1914-18	53	46	31
	1919-29	27	22	14
	1930-35	43	38	16
	1936-38	39	33	14
	1939-40	35	39	22
	1941-42	27	56	03
Le Monde	1945-49	28	32	25
	1900-1949	33	29	19
Norddeutsche	1910-13	27	15	20
allgemeine Zeitung	1914-18	41	73	52
Frenkfurter Zeitung	1919-29	21	20	25
	1930-32	17	17	08
Völkischer Beobachter	1933-38	52	66	28
	1939-41	37	56	22
	1942-45	35	55	30
	1910-45	30	43	29
Novoe Vremia	1892-1904	41	51	35
	1905-13	35	48	24
	1914-17	37	53	37
Izvestia	1918-28	38	45	26
	1929-35	30	47	17
	1936-38	28	36	15
	1939-40	31	46	69
	1941-45	63	43	52
	1946-49	54	46	37
	1892-1949	40	48	30

an editorial designed to support a single judgment on political policy will also include many factual statements and many incidental symbols used without judgment. And, finally, it was partially the result of the very detached and objective tone affected on the editorial page of many prestige papers.

The coding rules which guided the readers permitted the recording of explicit judgments only. It has been generally found that coders will agree better in categorizing explicit meanings than implicit ones, so the rule against including implicit judgments was adopted primarily to increase reliability, which purpose it undoubtedly served. At the same time, it sharply reduced the number of judgments recorded. An editorial describing conditions in slave-labor camps and using the symbol COMMUNISM would not be coded as COMMUNISM (minus), unless it explicitly said something like "These are the horrible consequences of communism." Clearly, many judgments made by allowing facts to speak for themselves were omitted.

Thus, although reliability was increased by counting only explicit judgments, the procedure cut down on the number of judgments more than expected. We had not taken sufficient account of the propensity of some prestige papers to let the facts stand alone and to understate. Consequently, our sample of judged symbols from the New York Times and the London Times was reduced to the point where for many periods it could not be used. It will be noted that some of the comparisons we should like to have made, and some of the tests we should like to have applied, could not be made or applied because frequencies were too low to support statistically valid conclusions. Our judgment data and conclusions are, therefore, generally less adequate than those bearing on attention. In retrospect, it seems probable that we should have done better to include some implicit judgments, even at the cost of somewhat reduced reliability.

Table 14 reports the judged symbols as a percentage of all symbols judged and unjudged. It includes, for purposes of comparison, not only the ideological symbols, which we treat here, but also the names of national units. These national symbols are, of course, important and may cause us to qualify some of the conclusions we might otherwise draw, but, for the moment, we shall concentrate on the ideological symbols.

Judgments were assigned to the manifest symbol between 63 percent of the time—in Izvestia during World War II—and one percent of the time—in the New York Times between 1930 and 1932. These extremes well characterize the papers from which they come. It is not only in these periods that Izvestia ranks highest in judgments and the New York Times lowest; yet, within each paper, there are also considerable variations between periods.

At the end of World War I, the New York Times, and, to a smaller degree, the London Times, suddenly adopted an extremely sober tone.

Even before World War I, these two papers contained fewer judgmenf's than any of the Continental papers in our sample, but the difference then was not great. After the war, however, the Anglo-American papers cut out judgments almost entirely. This was true not only of the treatment of ideological symbols but also of the treatment of the self and the outside world. These papers continued to be highly restrained until World War II. Then the London *Times* (in 1939) and the *New York Times* (in 1942) began to express their attitudes in less covert forms. To some extent both papers have continued to express judgments since World War II. The London *Times* has gone back to its prewar pattern of detachment, except in its references to Great Britain. Perhaps its reaction to the objective deterioration of Britain's position has been to continue repeatedly affirming national values. The *New York Times* has not gone back to the prewar pattern of almost total abstinence from judgment. Yet both papers remain far below any of the others in number of judgments.

It is tempting to suggest that the recent increase in judgments in the British and American prestige papers may be a response to growing insecurity. It may be that the code of detachment is giving way in a situation which makes it difficult to deny emotional involvement, but one wonders if such an explanation is adequate. Certainly the great depression and the international crisis preliminary to World War II were periods of enormous insecurity. Yet the *New York Times* managed to discuss such topics as WAR, NAZISM, DICTATORSHIP, FREEDOM, and LABOR without explicitly judging any one of these symbols in the issues of our sample from 1933 through 1938. Needless to say, the *New York Times* had a strong attitude on all these topics and one it made clear to its readers. But it did not abandon the techniques of factualism and indirect expression of attitude.

When we turn to our German sample, we find that the *Frankfurter Zeitung* tended, although to a lesser extent, to approximate the detached tone of the Anglo-American papers. The *Norddeutsche allgemeine Zeitung* and the *Völkischer Beobachter,* however, were quite open in expressing judgments. The latter was exceeded in this respect only by *Izvestia,* which in recent years has contained the most judgments.

The pattern of judgments in *Izvestia* is extremely interesting, but a full explanation of it will have to await a subsequent chapter. For the moment let us simply note that, in the 1920s, judgments in *Izvestia* were higher than in any of the other papers, although no higher than they had been in *Novoe Vremia,* which also contained many explicit judgments. Then, in the 1930s, the number of judgments in *Izvestia* fell off markedly, but temporarily. With World War II, *Izvestia* started judging the majority of symbols used, and it has continued to do so since. Only in the *Völkischer Beobachter* from 1933 through 1938 and in *Le Temps* during World War I

has there been a comparably didactic tone in the editorials. It will come as
no surprise to students of Russian affairs that *Izvestia* has spelled out for
its readers what is "good" and what is "bad" in no uncertain terms. What
is more peculiar is that there was a temporary avoidance of explicit judgments in the 1930s; to that fact we shall return.

Direction of Judgment

In making any judgment it is possible to use either a positive or negative
form: it is possible to be *against* WAR or *for* PEACE; to condemn
DICTATORSHIP or praise DEMOCRACY; to demand SECURITY or to
protest INSECURITY. The choice may seem at first glance a purely
stylistic one, and, indeed, stylistic considerations of no political significance enter into the selection of statement form. Yet a consistent
tendency toward one or the other form of expression might be an important political or psychological index.

It is not an index which sheds any light on the substance of attitudes. A
general tendency to be *for,* or a general tendency to be *against,* does not
determine what one is for or against. A democratic paper may choose to
stress that it is *for* DEMOCRACY, or it may choose to stress that it is
against COMMUNISM and FASCISM. A fascist paper may choose to stress
that it is *for* FASCISM, or it may choose to stress that it is *against*
DEMOCRACY and COMMUNISM. A Communist paper may choose to
stress that it is *for* COMMUNISM, or it may choose to stress that it is
against FASCISM and BOURGEOIS DEMOCRACY. Any of them may
show either a positive or negative approach. The prevalent direction of
judgment may be of significance, but it is not to be confused with the
contents of attitudes. Probably the prevalent direction of judgment is
related not to ideology, but to the patterns of control over the press, and
to the basic psychological mechanisms which the editor wishes to mobilize
on behalf of his cause. Table 15 reports the distribution of judgments for
or against the symbols on our list.

On the whole, negative judgments are more common than positive ones.
There seems to be a prevalent sixty-forty ratio between unfavorable and
favorable judgments. It would be tempting to interpret this ratio as a fair
measure of the balance of attitudes on the editorial page, for it may
perhaps be that the nature of the editorial page as a place for expressing
opinions on controversial matters may invite a predominance of criticisms
over praise. There is, however, a second possible explanation of this
phenomenon in terms of the structure of our symbol list. The most striking political symbols are perhaps those which are most controversial, i.e.,
those which are under attack. Perhaps, therefore, it is these symbols which
are most heavily represented on our list.

Table 15
Favorable Judgments as Percentage of All Judgments

Paper	Period	Ideological Symbols	The Self	Outside World
New York Times	1900-1913	38	60	42
	1914-18	45	72	27
	1919-29	27	*	11
	1930-32	*	*	*
	1933-38	38	*	*
	1939-41	43	*	30
	1942-45	41	69	63
	1946-49	45	61	36
	1900-1949	40	63	40
London *Times*	1890-1913	46	66	52
	1914-18	35	21	24
	1919-29	36	44	23
	1930-35	40	45	0
	1936-38	53	*	*
	1939-40	48	100	52
	1941-45	44	87	58
	1946-49	43	71	44
	1890-1949	44	65	49
Le Temps	1900-1913	32	61	47
	1914-18	57	83	42
	1919-29	37	82	27
	1930-35	43	93	45
	1936-38	42	79	52
	1939-40	49	100	37
	1941-42	55	100	*
Le Monde	1945-49	34	52	24
	1900-1949	39	78	36
Norddeutsche	1910-13	27	*	20
allgemeine Zeitung	1914-18	56	78	23
Frankfurter Zeitung	1919-29	36	74	28
	1930-32	31	*	*
Völkischer Beobachter	1933-38	47	79	25
	1939-41	26	97	15
	1942-45	30	100	12
	1910-45	38	82	22
Novoe Vremia	1892-1904	34	45	31
	1905-13	38	46	28
	1914-17	32	38	19
Izvestia	1918-28	26	28	09
	1929-35	59	80	02
	1936-38	58	60	20
	1939-40	73	92	*
	1941-45	73	90	30
	1946-49	82	97	19
	1892-1949	48	49	23

*Insufficient judgments for reliable result.

In view of this possibility, it seems best to interpret the ratio of plus and minus judgments not as an absolute measure but as a relative measure, variations in which are significant. To determine the absolute balance of glorification and vilification, the familiar technique of the column-inch space count is more appropriate than a symbol count of the kind used here. With the present measure we can, however, record changes in the amount of praise and blame accorded the specific ideas represented by our listed symbols.

The sharpest deviations from a rough forty-sixty ratio between favorable and unfavorable judgments occur in five situations: (1) in the *Norddeutsche allgemeine Zeitung* before World War I; (2) in the *New York Times* in the 1920s; (3) during wars in France and Germany; (4) in the *Völkischer Beobachter;* (5) in *Izvestia.* The first of these cases, the *Norddeutsche allgemeine Zeitung* before World War I, need not be explained since the results are based on so few judgments that the deviation may be no more than chance. There were only twenty-six judgments in that sub-sample.

The critical character of the judgments in the *New York Times* during the 1920s probably had something to do with the fact that in this period the *Times* began making a very small number of judgments. For reasons that are not clear (and that do not apply as fully to the London *Times*), those symbols about which explicit judgments continued occasionally to be made were symbols which were disapproved. The adoption of a factual editorial tone free of expressions of subjective attitude was apparently easier where no great hostility or indignation existed.

A highly laudatory treatment of ideological symbols appeared in the *Norddeutsche allgemeine Zeitung* and *Le Temps* during World War I and in *Le Temps* under Vichy. If this were accompanied by a similar treatment of the self we might conclude that emphasis on national unity and the suspension of criticism resulted in a Pollyanna-like tone. Only under Vichy, however, was there consistently high praise of both these sets of symbols. This tone was approached in *Le Temps* during the first phase of World War II, before the fall of France, and in the London *Times* during the same period. The proportion of favorable judgments of the ideological symbols was not quite so high as in the three periods just listed, but judgments of the self were entirely favorable.

It is curious to note that the two totalitarian papers in our sample showed completely different tendencies in the use of glorification and vilification. They shared only a tendency to swing to the extremes and to present a polarized picture of a world divided between a good self and a wicked and hostile remainder. In the German and Russian papers, even before the totalitarian regimes, references to the outside world had been notably hostile. The *Völkischer Beobachter* continued this pattern, not much intensified, until World War II. Then it started increasingly to praise the self and to condemn the outside world until, at the end, all references to the self were favorable whereas (despite allies) only 12 percent of references to other national entities were favorable.

In *Izvestia*, similarly, there has been a growing contrast between the presentation of the self as good and the outside world as evil. In the early years of the Bolshevik regime, both the self and the outside world were overwhelmingly condemned. This was in line with the negative revolutionary character of Bolshevik attitudes toward all existing institutions and practices. Then, around 1928, there was a sharp reversal of attitudes toward the self. These became overwhelmingly favorable until, by the postwar period, 97 percent of all references to the national self were favorable—this despite the much-publicized Soviet practice of "self-criticism." Self-criticism, if addressed to anyone high enough to rank as a spokesman or member of the government, would show up under our coding rules as criticism of the self. This, indeed, is why the proportion of favorable judgments of the self went down from 1936 through 1938, the years of the great purges. But by now, whatever self-criticism remains is limited to relatively minor individuals, seldom to the leaders of the state. (Subordinate officials were not coded as "self.") Thus recorded judgments of the self have become almost wholly favorable.

At the same time, there has been a slight increase in favorable judgments of the outside world, reflecting only the decrease in the real isolation of the Soviet Union. From 1918 through 1935, Russia had no allies worth mentioning. Then came the period of cooperation with the democracies against Nazism, followed by a short period of cooperation with Nazism against the democracies, followed in turn by war on the side of the democracies against Nazism. Since the war, Russia has had satellites to which she refers favorably. Hence, the occasional favorable references to the outside world are easily accounted for. What is more striking is the growing spread between the continuing hostile attitude toward the outside world and the uniformly favorable attitude toward the self.

So far we have noted the parallelism between the judgment pattern in *Izvestia* and that in the *Völkischer Beobachter;* both have increasingly portrayed the world as divided between a good self and evil enemies. What is strikingly different between these papers is the way in which the ideological symbols were fitted into this picture. Starting with World War II, the Nazi press became violently vituperative. The ideological symbols it used were subjected to the same kind of adverse judgment as the outside world. They were, in other words, "devil" symbols: words like DEMOCRACY, PLUTOCRACY, JEWS, and BOLSHEVISM. In Russia, on the other hand, the trend has been just the other way. Back in the 1920s, when *Izvestia* generally condemned not only the outside world but also the self, the ideological symbols were just as negative as in the more recent Nazi press. BOURGEOISIE, IMPERIALISM, MONARCHY, CAPI-

TALISM, and similar terms of abuse were freely employed, but even such terms as SOVIET, WORKING CLASS, and PEOPLE were more often criticized than praised. This situation changed abruptly around 1928. Since then, the bulk of judgments of ideological symbols has been favorable—and increasingly so. Indeed, since the war, 82 percent of all judgments of these symbols have been favorable. The *Izvestia* editorials are not heavily weighted with political devil symbols. On the contrary, they are all sweetness and light.

This may seem incredible to those whose conception of Russian propaganda is based on the U.N. speeches of Malik or Vishinski, or on the cartoons in *Krokodil.* Yet it is not altogether surprising, if one examines the implications of our figures with some care. In the first place, it should be observed that foreign affairs have played a smaller and smaller role in *Izvestia* editorials. (This point will be developed in a later chapter.) Foreign readers are too apt to look only at the foreign policy statements of Soviet propagandists and to take these as representative of the whole. Actually, they are a small portion of the total volume of Soviet attention. In Soviet propaganda, we find the emergence of a complete dichotomy in the mode of presentation of the two sides of the world. The Soviet side, which has received an increasing portion of the total attention, has been drawn in increasingly idealized colors; while the capitalist side, which has received a decreasing portion of the total attention, has been increasingly diabolized. (This point is illustrated in Figure 2 below.) Aside from a very few ideological terms, such as IMPERIALIST, which continue to be used in negative fashion, the devils in the *Izvestia* editorials are the foreign nations. These, when discussed, are portrayed as almost wholly black, but they are discussed only to a limited extent. Except for this external threat, the editorials present a picture of a happy life in the best of all possible worlds, Russia.

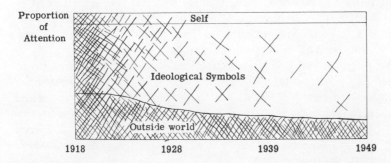

Figure 2. Simplified Model of Changing Structure of *Izvestia* Editorial Symbolism

The darker the shade the greater the hostility or vituperation; the lighter the shade the greater the praise or glorification.

It is noteworthy that internal enemies are no longer dignified by treatment with any degree of concreteness. TROTSKYISM, for example, has ceased to be an important symbol. Internal enemies are still referred to in demands for vigilance against unnamed traitors and saboteurs, and, if they are given concrete characterization, it is usually in terms of the foreign power of which they are purported agents. This is not to deny that the Soviet press continues to carry very significant articles attacking specific persons of moderate importance as "cosmopolitan" or inefficient. But the more general material of the editorial column has been reduced to a very simple world picture in which the only quantitatively important elements are a small amount of attack on foreign states and a large amount of self-glorification, to which the bulk of the ideological symbols are devoted.

Uniformity of Judgment

Most words of importance carry a favorable or unfavorable connotation which partly determines their use, in spite of empirical identities in meaning. The man who changes from Party A to Party B, or Religion A to Religion B, or Country A to Country B, is called a convert or a traitor, depending on whether one approves or disapproves the specific change. The use of one or the other of these words implies no difference in the facts, yet one can hardly imagine an editorial welcoming "the traitor, John Doe" to his new side. Another illustration of a term with stereotyped judgment is LIBERTY. Men argue whether a given practice is LIBERTY or LICENSE, as though these two words meant different facts, not just opposite judgments of the same thing.

The extent to which any given word is stereotyped as favorable or unfavorable of course varies. It is perfectly practicable for a propagandist to pronounce himself as either for WAR or against WAR. It is far less practicable for him to pronounce himself either for PEACE or against PEACE. The word PEACE is so highly sentimentalized that only under rare circumstances is it rhetorically effective to state that one is against it. Even propaganda for WAR seldom attacks PEACE.

Our judgment data provide us with a means of measuring the extent to which any particular term, or the language of any particular subsample, has been stereotyped in this way. A word that is sometimes approved and sometimes disapproved is free of automatic connotations and subject to varying judgment from the facts of the case. On the other hand, a word that is judged as almost always approved or almost always disapproved is a stereotyped political concept.

The complete absence of stereotyping would be no more normal than rigid stereotyping. To use words without any regular judgment would imply absence of principles and would involve deciding each question *de novo* from its own facts, an obviously impractical procedure, especially in mass communication. The point can be illustrated with reference to the symbol DEMOCRACY. At one extreme would be a use of the word DEMOCRACY that automatically meant something good. If, like LIBERTY, the word had invariably favorable connotations, one could not well say that the long ballot represented exaggerated or misapplied DEMOCRACY. One would have to find another word or phrase, such as mob rule, for this. At the other extreme would be a use of the word DEMOCRACY without any normal preference. To lack a general attitude toward such a key concept would show, not rationality, but only political confusion and absence of a coherent point of view. The normal situation would be one with reasonable consistency in the judgments of such a concept.

Hence, in any normal body of communications, we should expect to find some tendency toward the stereotyping of the judgments of symbols, but also a number of judgments contradicting the stereotypes. Besides such normal bodies of communications, there are also atypical ones marked by great rigidity in stereotypes and other atypical ones marked by ideological flexibility (instability of judgment patterns). We can characterize the degree of stereotyping in our samples of editorials by measuring the degree of uniformity of judgments within them.

To measure the uniformity of judgments seems at first glance rather easy, but actually it involves a number of problems. It is necessary, first, to find the normal sentimentalization of each symbol. This can be done a priori on the basis of general political knowledge, but to characterize words this way is harder and less reliable than one might think. What, for example, should we assume to be the normal direction of judgment of AUTHORITY in *Le Temps* or in the *New York Times,* of DISCIPLINE in the *New York Times,* of JEWS in the *Norddeutsche allgemeine Zeitung,* or of HINDUS in the London *Times?* All of these are obviously ambivalent symbols. They are symbols regarding which we were unable to predict the dominant explicit judgments with any reliability.

The alternative to arbitrary ratings was to use our sample data to estimate the prevailing direction of judgment in the universe. If a symbol was judged favorably thirteen times and unfavorably seven times it was listed as a positively sentimentalized symbol. Obviously, such a system requires that the symbols be judged often enough to be characterized. (Here was one respect in which our data suffered from the sharp restriction on the number of judgments which our coding rules produced.) We characterized all symbols judged ten or more times; the others are not included in the following tabulations. Ten events are, of course, a very low number for statistical purposes: a sample with four judgments one way and six the other does not give us a very reliable estimate of the universe. But to get enough symbols to work with effectively, we needed to set the figure fairly low. Ten seemed the best compromise figure between a higher one, which would have reduced the number of symbols used to characterize the body of communications, and a lower one, which would have made our estimates for some particular symbols utterly unreliable.[25]

Also complicating the problem is the fact that sentimentalizations of words change. SOCIALISM was a negative word in *Novoe Vremia,* but a positive one recently in *Izvestia.* ARMAMENT and DISARMAMENT change their connotations with changes in the world scene. It seemed clearly necessary to characterize the symbols separately for each period. To do this meant having in any given period an adequate number of words judged a minimum of ten times each. Such frequencies were obtained in some cases by combining periods. Thus, the following data are not reported for all the periods most frequently used in this study. Some of the periods used below cover a longer time span, as, for example, the interbellum rather than the 1920s and 1930s separately. Even this did not save some subsamples from being discarded because of inadequate data. We cannot report results for those periods where judgments were least frequent.

Having once obtained for each period a list of symbols characterized as to normal sentimentalization, we simply added up the number of judgments in the normal direction and the number against it.[26] This gave us a percentage of judgments which conformed to the stereotype or, conversely, a percentage which did not. The percentage of judgments which conformed to the stereotype are reported for the various subsamples in the first column of Table 16.

These percentages give a rough indication of the degree of stereotyping in various papers at various times. It is only a rough one, since allowance has not been made for the percentages which would result by chance.

How far the figures in the first column of Table 16 might exceed 50 percent by chance, in the absence of stereotyping, is difficult to ascertain. It depends, in part, on how even the tone is which the paper assumes as between praise or blame, or, conversely, on how much it tends toward a persistent tone one way or the other. Figures on the latter point are given in the second and third columns of Table 16. If there were no stereotyping at all, the figures in the first column would approach those in the second column, though they would always be a little larger. The difference is a measure of stereotyping, but it is a measure whose interpretation depends also on the overall tone (second column, Table 16) and on sample size. The discussion of these complexities which follows in the next six paragraphs may well be skipped by those not interested in the details of statistical technique.

The problem viewed statistically is one of predicting the distribution of majorities and minorities. It is a problem of widespread applications, but

Table 16
Percentage of Judgments on Majority Side and Related Data

Paper	Percentage of Majority Judgments	Favorable Judgments as Percentage of All Judgments or Unfavorable Judgments as Percentage of All Judgments, Whichever is Larger	
	(Based only on symbols judged 10 or more times)	(Based only on symbols judged 10 or more times)	(Based on all symbols)
New York Times			
1900-1913	86	71	62
1930-49	98	65	58
London Times			
1890-1913	81	50	54
1919-35	90	82	63
1936-49	92	54	54
Le Temps			
1900-1913	89	79	68
1914-18	86	52	57
1919-29	96	72	63
1930-35	94	59	57
1936-40	98	65	73
1945-49	78	67	66
Frankfurter Zeitung			
1919-32	86	72	66
(1919-29)	85	65	64
Völkischer Beobachter			
1933-45	94	60	52
(1933-38)	95	54	54
Novoe Vremia			
1892-1913	68	62	64
1914-17	71	51	68
Izvestia			
1918-28	79	74	74
1929-35	96	63	59
1936-40	99	55	64
1941-45	94	75	73
1946-49	98	89	82
(1929-49)	96	73	65

one which has been discussed in the literature but little, if at all. It may be visualized in an example involving election returns instead of language. If a club has no political parties, then it is impossible to identify a vote for Candidate A in Election Number One with a vote for any of the alternative candidates in Election Number Two. In both elections, however, there would be a majority and a minority. Voters may be identified as majority or minority voters.

Any given voter may have been a majority voter in both elections, a minority voter in both, or a majority voter in one and a minority voter in the other. It would be interesting to know how voters in real situations distribute themselves in these respects: what types tend to go with the majority; what types tend to be persistently in the opposition; also to what extent certain voters consistently line up with the majority or with the minority. To answer such questions, we should have to compare the actual distribution with that which might occur by chance, since chance alone would lead some voters to be in the majority (or minority) more often than others. We should, therefore, need to determine the likely distribution of majorities and minorities for a club of n members holding s elections without political parties.

The problem of word stereotyping is exactly the same. One word, such as DEMOCRACY, may have mostly plus judgments; another, such as DICTATORSHIP, mostly minus judgments. But the direction of judgment does not bear on the amount of stereotyping. The measure of stereotyping is the one-sidedness of judgments, whatever the judgments may be. Another way of saying this is to say that the measure of stereotyping is the size of the majorities given to the prevailing judgment. Here again we must estimate the majorities that would occur by chance and compare the actual distribution with that figure.

We have a number of variables to deal with in estimating the most probable size of majority. One of these is sample size. Another, that we can now consider, is the overall balance of favorable and unfavorable judgments in the medium. Let us assume a language in which there was no stereotyping of individual words. Every word has the same probability, p, of being favorably judged and, q, of being unfavorably judged. Still, p and q need not be .5. If they are actually .5 in the universe, then a sample of words from that language would still reveal small majorities one way or the other owing to sample variation. But the modal majority will be a bare majority of one, with larger majorities decreasingly frequent. (We assume an odd number in the population.) If, for example, p is .7 then majorities will tend to cluster around 70 percent. Thus, although all words in this language, too, are used in a uniform way and there is no stereotyping, expected majorities are, nevertheless, much larger. The expected majority will vary with the size of p until, at $p = 1.0$, the expected majority will approach 100 percent.

Let us now consider the equation for the likely size of the majority, assuming p and q are uniform for each symbol or election, i.e., that there is no stereotyping.[27] Let EL stand for the most likely proportion of votes or judgments on the majority side. Let n stand for the number of judgments or votes. Let $n = 2k + 1$; thus, we disregard the no majority case that occurs where there is an even number. Let d stand for the difference between the total majority and total minority judgments or votes. Let $m = n - 1$. Then:

$$EL = \sum_{d=0}^{k} (n-d)\, \frac{n!}{d!\,(n-d)!}\, p^d q^{n-d} + \sum_{d=k+1}^{n} d\frac{n!}{d!\,(n-d)!}\, p^d q^{n-d}$$

This works out to:

$$EL = nq \sum_{d=0}^{k} \frac{m!}{d!\,(m-d)!}\, p^d q^{m-d} + np \sum_{d=0}^{k} \frac{m!}{d!\,(m-d)!}\, p^{m-d} q^{d}$$

From this we see that the range of EL is $n/2$ to n. Having established EL for the appropriate value of p and n, the difference between that and the actually observed proportion of majority judgments or votes would be a measure of the amount of stereotyping. If a standard deviation were worked out for EL, the significance of the hypothesis of stereotyping could also be tested. Perhaps qualified scholars will carry further the investigation of some of these problems.

For the particular data at hand, further refinement would be irrelevant. The design of our investigation bars use of strict tests of significance, since data were pooled. (This is explained in the first chapter.) It will suffice for us now to have a general idea of the likely proportion of majority judgments at various levels of n (sample size) and p. As the sample size grows large, EL approaches p or q, whichever is larger; but it approaches it more quickly at extreme values of p. Thus we find that when $p = .5$, EL varies as follows: $k = 3$, $EL = .75$; $k = 5$, $EL = .69$; $k = 7$, $EL = .66$; $k = 13$, $EL = .61$; $k = 30$, $EL = .57$. When $p = .75$, EL varies as follows: $k = 3$, $EL = .82$; $k = 5$, $EL = .78$; $k = 7$, $EL = .76$. When $p = .9$, EL varies as follows: $k = 3$, $EL = .91$; $k = 5$, $EL = .902$. Thus we see that, for data as crude as that at hand, and for frequencies of the order at hand, p or q as presented in Table 16 provides an adequate standard for comparison with the percentage of judgments on the majority side.

In Table 16 we listed the proportion of symbols in the majority in various papers and periods. The lowest such proportion, representing the least stereotyped pattern of judgments, was found in *Novoe Vremia* before World War I. Sixty-eight percent of the symbol judgments in this paper were majority judgments. Thirty-two percent of the judgments went against the usual sentimentalization of the symbol.

Since this is the least stereotyped of our subsamples, let us hold it up, so far as may be, against our model of a language in which individual words have no stereotypes and see whether or not this observed sample can be explained as a product of chance variations of judgments. Our best estimates for p and q from this universe are p and q from the sample. The best n for us to use is the mean frequency of the twenty-four words in this subsample, which turns out to be 29.

Here, q, the unfavorable judgment proportion, is 0.62, and the proportion of judgments in the majority is 0.68. Taking n as 29, we should expect 63 percent of judgments in the majority where q is 0.62. The 5 percent difference between the expected and actual majorities might prove significant if we could apply significance tests. We should probably conclude that the hypothesis of an absence of stereotyping of word judgments in the prewar *Novoe Vremia* cannot be maintained.

Moreover, the lack of any more clear-cut stereotyping in *Novoe Vremia* is indeed a surprising result, since one normally expects each of the key symbols of politics to have a rather strong and definite sentimentalization. In no other period is anything like this degree of ambivalence toward the various symbols approached. Indeed, in the Russian press more recently, the situation has been completely reversed. Each word has a definite and almost invariable sentimentalization. COMMUNISM is "good," almost without exception, whereas IMPERIALISM is "bad." The FATHERLAND is almost always "good"; FASCISM, "bad." In fact, since World War II, 98 percent of recorded judgments have been on the majority or stereotyped side. Obviously, in this respect a great change separates the style of *Izvestia* from that of its Czarist counterpart. Perhaps this difference represents more than a simple change; possibly it indexes a causal relationship between the state of mind of the Czarist elite and that of the Soviet elite.

The most obvious interpretation of the ambivalence in the style of *Novoe Vremia* would be that it reflects a disturbed and unsettled system of values on the part of those who produced the paper. Torn between the traditional values of Czarist autocracy and the challenging values of Western liberalism, the spokesmen of the elite expressed themselves in contradictory and uncertain tones. Whether the concept was LIBERALISM, REFORM, FREEDOM, PEOPLE, ORDER, FATHERLAND, or MONARCHY, judgments were divided. The elite was not sure what it was for or what it was against. It was undermined by ambivalence between self-esteem and self-scorn and paralyzed by Hamlet-like indecision. This was a problem that troubled many Russian thinkers, Turgenev, for example. They admired the resolute man of action. They felt that from activists would come the salvation of Russia. But this admiration of certainty and action sprang from a consciousness that they themselves were really more like the critical and speculative Hamlet. Turgenev was himself one of the "repentant noblemen" he so often portrayed—liberal noblemen anxious to be modern and half-ashamed to be part of a system they disapproved.

That this state of mind prevailed in Russia has been suggested by more than one historical observer. This historical thesis, now further confirmed by our observations of the press, goes further and asserts that this loss of self-confidence by the elite was one of the essential conditions of the Russian Revolution. The Russian Revolution was in this respect typical. A general proposition of the theory of revolutions asserts that only when the old elite has lost faith in its own myths and its own right to rule does it stand in danger of being overthrown. When it does lose faith it not only becomes indecisive; it even produces much of the leadership for the challenging classes. This proposition has often been asserted; but how does one measure the ideological disintegration that forewarns of revolution? To date, there has been no index beyond the judgments of intelligent observers. Perhaps our new technique for measuring uniformity of judgment provides the clue. Operating with one case, as we are here, we cannot be sure. But this case suggests that it would be interesting to test judgment trends in other revolutions. Would all of them be preceded by the disappearance of an integrated system of values?

A situation in which the majority judgments are less than 80 percent of the total seems generally to be an unstable one. The only subsample, aside from those from Russia, in which we have recorded such a low value for uniformity of judgments is *Le Monde* since World War II. Our small sample of postwar French material shows 78 percent of judgments on the majority side. This is about 10 percent more than is most probable in an unstereotyped language, clearly a significant amount of stereotyping. Yet it is a markedly lower figure than the figures from the period before the fall of France. In the periods since World War I, between 94 and 96 percent of the judgments in *Le Temps* have been on the majority side. The change from these high figures to the low one for the period since World War II reflects the disintegration of the French myth under the impact of defeat. The myth of *Le Temps* was, of course, not that of the traditional French Left, nor of *Le Monde*. Yet it was a consistent and clear-cut variant of the French myth. *Le Monde* has no such consistency. Only the symbols of communism are unambiguously rejected. Neither symbols of the Left, such as DEMOCRACY, nor symbols of the Right, such as SECURITY, are consistently judged. The choice of political values has not seemed simple to the editors of this paper in the era since liberation. In foreign policy, they have seized on an uneasy and half-hearted "neutralism" instead of firmly accepting their Western affiliation, and in domestic policy they have been equally indecisive.

The Russian and French instances of unusually low uniformity in evaluation of symbols are both instances of the disintegration of an established myth. The one other instance of comparable lack of uniformity is somewhat different. *Izvestia* from 1918 through 1928 had 79 percent of judgments which conformed to the stereotypes and 21 percent contrary.[28] In a sense, this period, too, was one in which an old set of values was giving way before a new, but that may not be an adequate explanation. We expect prerevolutionary regimes to be ambivalent toward major political symbols, but not revolutionary regimes. Further research may prove that revolutionary regimes do generally show this ambivalence, although more likely this is a peculiar feature of Marxist-Leninist thought. In part, it grows out of the peculiar manner in which Marxism simultaneously both accepts and attacks such concepts as DEMOCRACY and the STATE. Even more, it grows out of the extremely critical character of Marxist doctrine. The distinctive feature of early Bolshevik judgments was that there were almost no purely positive symbols. There were purely negative ones like MILITARISM, but the Bolsheviks made such a fetish of blunt self-criticism that even such symbols as SOCIALISM, COMMUNISM, RED, and REVOLUTION were often disapproved; and, strange as it may seem, disapproval was more common than approval for BOLSHEVISM, SOVIET, LABOR, PROLETARIAT, PEOPLE, MASSES, DEMOCRACY, and PEACE. For obvious reasons, these symbols were often positive in *Izvestia*, but because of the Soviet tendency toward public self-flagellation they were also often negative. As a result majority and minority judgments are fairly even.

Normal stereotyping seems to place between 80 and 95 percent of the judgments of the enumerated key symbols on the majority side—such, at least, is the amount of stereotyping that we find in our samples of the free papers. Percentages lower than this seem to indicate instability of values; percentages higher than this seem to indicate doctrinal rigidity. This rigidity arises in conflict situations when the sides become polarized, each with its own orthodoxy, deviations from which are suspect. On the whole, the higher values—over 90 percent—have occurred in recent years, while uniformity at the 80 to 89 percentile level marked the more stable earlier decades of our study. The trend toward increasing uniformity of judgments is perhaps an index of the polarization of political life in recent years.

The hypothesis that, in times of crisis, political lines tend to polarize has often been confirmed from voting data or historical studies. In revolutions, in depressions, or in other crises, the third force in the middle tends to be ground between the upper and the nether millstones. In Weimar Germany, the votes of the Communist and Nazi extremists grew at the expense of the middle groups. In the civil wars in Spain and China, many men of good will who wanted a moderate liberal regime felt forced to line up with the "lesser evil" of the reactionaries or the Communists. In the world politics of today, it has become more and more difficult to steer a middle course of compromise between the dominant policies of the Kremlin, on the one hand, and those of the American government, on the other. Many people are forced to choose sides. Small powers which would much prefer to remain detached from the struggle find it increasingly difficult to do so. A multipolar world gives way to a bipolar world.

As lines become rigid, judgments become rigid, too. In place of an atmosphere in which one could say of a given country or party that some of what it did was good and some was bad, there comes an atmosphere in which it verges on treason to speak well of the enemy or poorly of one's allies. It is this change that is reflected in the increasing polarization of judgments in the press.

That this change occurred in the Russian press we have already noted. It occurred also in the London *Times* during World War I. Before the war, majority judgments were 80 percent; after the war, they were 90 percent. Since 1936, they have been 92 percent, and if we take only the period since 1939, they have been 94 percent. Apparently the growing crisis in Great Britain has produced increasingly sharp ideological lines.

In the *New York Times* we find the same thing, although we can compute indices only for the years before World War I and the years since 1932. Judgments in between were too scarce. In the first of these periods, 86 percent of the judgments conformed to stereotype; in the second, 98 percent. This latter, very high figure should be interpreted with an eye to the very small number of judgments involved. It was necessary to include a span of 18 years in order to find 11 symbols judged more than 10 times each. Since the *New York Times* judged so few symbols, the ones it did judge were obviously the ones to which most heat was attached. It is to be expected that symbols such as STRIKES, RACIAL PREJUDICE, NAZISM, ISOLATION, FREEDOM, FASCISM, COMMUNISM, and DEMOCRACY should be more one-sidedly judged than symbols of a less often judged character. It is to be expected, in other words, that, where other factors are constant, explicit judgments will be more one-sided when they are reserved for occasions in which feelings are strong than when they are freely stated on a large variety of occasions, including emotionally peripheral cases. Nevertheless, the *New York Times* data clearly confirm the hypothesis of a trend toward more polarized judgments. Since in both the early and late periods the amount of judgment is small and the lists are short, restriction of judgment alone will not account for the increased polarization. The trends that explain it are most probably related to the intensification of political conflicts in the modern world.

The German press also shows this polarization. The majority judgments in the *Frankfurter Zeitung* were 86 percent. In the *Völkischer Beobachter* they were 94 percent. Judgments in the *Norddeutsche allgemeine Zeitung* were too infrequent to permit a comparison. Judgments are also inadequate to make a comparison between the more stable middle Weimar years and the more critical years at the beginning and end. We might, however, note that including the years 1930-32 raises the Weimar judgment-uniformity figure by one percentage point rather than lowering it, as might be expected from the mere fact of a longer time span. With judgments, as with attention, one should expect changes to increase with time. Therefore, the uniformity of judgments toward particular symbols would normally be lower for a longer period. This we find in the *Völkischer Beobachter,* for example. From 1933 through 1938, a total of 95.4 percent of the judgments were majority ones, but if we add 1939 through 1945, this figure goes down to 93.6. On the other hand, adding 1930-32 to the period from 1919 through 1929 raises the percentage of stereotyped judgments from 85.0 to 86.4. Thus, the sample editorials from those crisis years just before Hitler came to power were more uniform in judgment than those in the other Weimar years. Significance is, of course, doubtful; the direction of our result is the same as in the other cases. Again we find polarization of judgments with growing political tension.

Except for the period since World War II (discussed above), the French press shows the same growing polarization of judgments. Before World War I, 89 percent of the judgments were on the majority side. In the 1920s, this proportion went up to 96 percent. In the shorter period from 1930 through 1935, it was 94 percent, and from 1936 through 1940, it was 96 percent. Again our index shows a definite association with political crisis.

On the whole, uniformity of judgments seems to be a highly sensitive index of polarization of attitudes in the face of crisis. The correlation seems too clear-cut to be accidental. Yet, at first glance, a contradiction appears between this statement and the earlier observation that consistent judgment breaks down in some crisis situations. A political conflict is sharpened when one party aggressively challenges another for dominant power. The challenging party may be a new elite, or it may be the old elite trying to augment its power. It may be communist; it may be fascist; it may be democratic. Whatever the nature of the challenge, it threatens rival groups having conflicting ideologies or interests. At this point, the threatened parties react, and they may react in a number of different ways. Sophisticated reactions are conceivable in which the challenged group deliberately refuses to be disturbed or in which it accepts the challenge but refuses to modify its ideology. This kind of reaction is advocated by those for example, who wish to fight a war without hating or maligning the enemy, or by those who at the present time are against both communism and anticommunist hysteria. Whether such sophisticated reactions can ever be mass reactions we need not here consider. Certainly the more common reactions to a threat are either counteraggression or demoralization.

These two alternative responses are the ones we have found in crisis editorials. Suppose the challenged party reacts with confidence and determination. In such an instance it will begin to express greater hostility than before to the ideas and organs of the threatening aggressor. The aggressor will also sharpen his language, so that in the communications of both we shall find an increasing uniformity of judgment, although on opposite sides. This is polarization, strictly speaking. On the other hand, the threatened parties may lose their nerve and their belief in themselves. They may become ideologically divided with respect to the challenging force. In so doing, they are apt to assure the transition of power to the challenger. The growing conflict will be expressed in a one-sided and determined fashion only by the parties who are firm in their points of view. The demoralized or uncertain parties will express a more mixed distribution of judgments.

There is, therefore, no contradiction in the fact that in time of crisis we find increasing uniformity of judgment in some papers and decreasing uniformity in others. Each deviation from a normal balance reflects its own type of response to the crisis. Both types of response do actually occur.

The interpretation of such data in terms of morale raises one further problem. In a free press, it might provide a valid index, though additional research would obviously be needed to test it. In a totalitarian press, however, it seems unlikely that uniformity of judgment growing out of genuine feelings could be distinguished from uniformity imposed by fiat. It is noteworthy that the totalitarian papers generally show great uniformity of judgment. Not too much can be made of this, because democratic papers also exceed 95 percent stereotyped judgment of the symbols on our list in some periods of crisis, and totalitarianism has existed only in the recent crisis era. Yet it is probably no accident that Nazi judgments were 94 percent stereotyped and that the most stereotyped judgments of all were found in certain periods in the Russian press.

The most stereotyped judgments that we have been able to measure occur in *Izvestia* in recent periods, in the *New York Times* in recent periods, and from 1936 through 1940 in *Le Temps*. We noted that the high uniformity of judgments in the *New York Times* could, in part, be accounted for by the low number of explicit judgments. This explanation does not apply to the other two papers, both of which had many judgments. In both these papers, therefore, there was a highly rigid attitude toward the key political symbols, the mere mention of which evoked an almost invariant response. In *Izvestia* 96 percent of all judgments have been in conformity to stereotype from 1929 through 1949, inclusive. The peak of uniformity was reached from 1936 through 1940, during which years only 1 percent of the symbols in our sample were judged contrarily to their stereotype.

The war produced a significant change in the uniformity of *Izvestia* judgments, indicating that even totalitarian papers may profitably be analyzed for stereotyping. Favorable judgments of allies appeared. Also, occasional counterstereotype judgment of such terms as SOVIET, BOLSHEVISM, COLLECTIVISM, FATHERLAND, PEOPLE, RED, REVOLUTION, and SOCIALISM indicate that, under the threat of defeat, dissatisfaction with the self made itself felt despite the almost complete suppression since 1929 of such high-level self-criticism. During the war, only 94 percent of judgments conformed to stereotype, in contrast to the 99 percent before and 98 percent since.

In interpreting these cases of extreme stereotyping of judgment, it should be recalled again that allowance must be made for the majorities that would occur by chance. In the recent Russian material, and in one or two other cases, all judgments, regardless of symbol, are so strongly in one direction (in the Russian case, favorable) that counterstereotype judgments are necessarily few, although not so few as actually occur. Another way of stating this would be to say that there are two ways in which judgments may be straitjacketed. The paper may assume a generally positive or generally negative tone, excluding from the editorials anything that does not conform. Alternatively, the paper may use words of both positive and negative character, but assign to each term its own invariant judgment. Either of these procedures will result in few minority judgments. In the former case, almost all judgments are the same way. In the latter case, judgments for different words go in different directions, but judgments for any one word almost always go the same way. In the former case, the tone of the paper is stereotyped; in the latter case, the individual word.

In making allowance for the case in which the whole tone of the editorials is positive or negative, it will be remembered that where favorable and unfavorable judgments *(p* and *q)* are very unbalanced, the expected number of majority judgments is quite close to p or q, whichever is larger. Highly unbalanced judgments among the words judged ten times or more are found in three situations: in the London *Times* from 1919 to 1935, in *Le Temps* before World War I, and in *Izvestia.* In all but one case, the percentage in the majority is at least eight points greater than p or q, indicating that there was still considerable stereotyping of individual words. In the first of these cases, the London *Times,* the number of judgments is low. The strongly negative tone of the symbols is probably a chance variation. The negative tone of *Le Temps* before World War I probably accounts for the fact that this paper had fewer minority judgments than any other at that time. Allowing for this factor would make the French, British, and American prewar samples appear very similar in degree of stereotyping.

It is *Izvestia* in which the overall direction of judgments is most significant. We have already noted above that, up to 1928, there was remarkably little stereotyping of individual words in *Izvestia*. The paper then had a generally negative tone (74 percent), but words judged on the majority side were only 5 percentage points more (79 percent). Then in 1929 came both a reversal of tone and a marked increase in the stereotyping of individual symbols. Since World War II, 89 percent of the symbols were favorably judged whereas 9 percentage points more (98 percent) were judged according to stereotype. It is obvious that when 89 percent of all judgments are in one direction there is little room for distinctive stereotyping of individual words. But that the 11 percent of negative judgments were concentrated on their own particular words is indicated by the fact that counterstereotype judgments were but two in a hundred. The strength of the stereotypes in the modern Russian political vocabulary is most clearly shown by what happened in the period from 1936 through 1940, when the great purges and the struggle against fascism resulted in a considerable number of negative judgments. In this period favorable and unfavorable judgments were fairly evenly balanced, but, nevertheless, 99 percent of judgments were on the majority side for each particular word. In addition to the adoption of a general tone of glorification, the Soviet press has rigid stereotypes for all its main symbols.

IV. Change

Amount of Change

Social change is a concept which has largely eluded quantification. Yet change is clearly a quantitative notion. Discussion of change in any science invites its measurement, but in the study of society the challenge has not been successfully met.

True, sociologists have tried to measure social change. They have created indices of the rate of invention, the rate of mobility, and rates of change in other social variables. Nevertheless, one or both of two objections may be raised against each such measurement:

1. Most indices refer to only a small segment of the total process of social change.

2. The index is not stable; that is, the units and measurements are of such indeterminate size that they do not give a consistent index.

One can quantify the growth of armaments, the growth of cities, the change in subjects of books published, or the replacement of the horse by the auto, but neither singly nor collectively do these approach the ideal of a clear, comprehensive, and determinate measure of social change. Individually, of course, they do not. Collectively, they may give a good general picture if sufficient examples are cited, but a picture composed of a series of examples is not a measure.

In the absence of a single summary measure, one must discuss the indices seriatim, since each index measures a single partial aspect of the whole process. These partial indices being in incommensurable units, they cannot be combined in any easily justifiable fashion. What is needed—and does not exist—is an index somehow so pervasive of all kinds of social change that it will measure changes in a multitude of fields at once.

Inventions would make an index of this kind. If inventions of all kinds could somehow be reduced to equatable units, we should have an excellent index of social change; but inventions are not all of a piece. Both the internal-combustion engine and the cheese slicer are inventions, but their effects on society cannot be equated.

Are these problems insoluble? Is there no way of constructing a stable index of social change? Perhaps not, but here we suggest an approach which may ultimately help to solve the problem. Our results on editorial changes in the elite press suggest one conceivable and quantifiable model of social change. These results also provide the first tentative and inconclusive trial of the mechanics of the proposed procedure. The proposed model involves the use of changes in verbal flow as a stable index of social change.

There is one social phenomenon which permeates almost every social event: namely, words. No matter what change is occurring, it will be indicated in the statements of men. Whether the change is between war and peace, prosperity and depression, winter and summer, a fad for hot jazz or sweet, or between optimism and pessimism, the fact of change will be recorded in a change in the things people say.

Furthermore, a word is a sufficiently precise unit so that en masse the quantity of change in the words expressed may prove a reasonably reliable index of the quantity of social change. The words men use are the best index we have of the things on their minds. An individual in a particular situation may hide his thoughts, but it seems plausible that a change in the overall content of the thoughts of society would show up in changes in the words expressed. If so, there may be a stable way to measure the amount of change in men's thoughts, provided we can measure the amount of change in the contents of the flow of symbols.

Via this index of changes in things thought about, we may measure social change. Impact on the minds of the men provides a common dimension in otherwise different changes, as, for example, the introduction of the automatic gearshift and an off-year Republican swing. It is the common dimension of subjective response by human beings which, after all, makes these events both social changes and equatable. An index of changing ideas, therefore, would probably be a good index of social change.

A second index, which also meets the criteria of pervasiveness, stability, and susceptibility to being segmentalized into convenient units, is mobility or change in the personal composition of social groups, classes, and strata. Our elite studies use this measure. In the overall RADIR model of the revolution of our time, the two measures complement each other.

These general comments about social change are suggested, rather than tested, by the results of the RADIR Project. In our project, we were not seeking an overall index of social change but rather an index covering the political values of the ruling elite. Even if the procedures worked out below for measuring such change are valid, or can be made valid by appropriate statistical advances, the procedures would still have to be extended to a sample representative of the total symbol flow of a society before one would be justified in treating the resulting indices as general measures of social change. Here we are testing the procedures while we are working with a sample of a restricted kind of social change. We have tried to measure changes in elite attitudes toward major political concepts.

Specifically, we wish to discover whether there has been any significant change in editorial symbolism between selected time points in the past sixty years and, if so, to establish how great the change was. To establish *presence* of a significant change the chi-square test is most appropriate and was, therefore, computed. The chi-square test indicates whether a distribution of frequencies deviates significantly from a hypothesis about the distribution. The hypothesis may be derived from a theoretical model, as in the case of the expected Mendelian frequencies of dominants and recessives, or it may be actuarially derived.

Our hypothesis was of the latter type. It was the hypothesis of no change from an earlier period. Using the frequencies found in the earlier period as an estimate of the actual earlier distribution, we asked ourselves whether the observed changes in frequency from then until the later period could be accounted for by chance, or whether the change was too great to be so explained. In other words, what we asked was whether the hypothesis of no change was plausible.

Such a hypothesis can be tested by the use of chi square. If an event can occur in one of two ways, we need the following data to compute chi square:

1. The number of events of which the sample consists
   a) The number of these which turned out one way
   b) The number of these which turned out the other way
2. A hypothesis which predicts the proportion of events turning out in each of the two ways. This enables us to predict for the given size sample:

   a) The number of events likely to turn out one way
   b) The number of events likely to turn out the other way

In our study, we have such data on symbol changes. The hypothesis of no change in the frequency of a single symbol can be supported or dis-proved with the following data:

1. The number of editorials in the sample from the later period
   a) The number which turned out to contain the symbol
   b) The number which turned out not to contain the symbol
2. The proportion *(p)* of editorials in the earlier period containing the symbol and the proportion *(q)* not containing the symbol. Multi-plying these by the number of editorials in the later period, we get a prediction of:
   a) The number of editorials likely to contain the symbol
   b) The number of editorials likely not to contain the symbol if there had been no change

We can therefore use the chi square to test whether there has been change in the use of a symbol in a sample.

If chi square could be applied to only one symbol at a time, it would not solve our problem of testing change in the total symbol flow. Chi square, however, has a very extraordinary property which makes it ideal for our purpose. Chi squares from several samples may be added together to give a single chi square for the whole series of samples. Thus if we took ten, twenty, or fifty different symbols appearing in two periods and computed chi square for each, the sum of chi squares for the individual words would be a chi square for the whole list.[29] Thus, to test whether there has been change in the total symbol flow, we need have only a representative sample of words in that flow to which to apply the chi square test.

In our study of newspaper editorials, we had a sample of one particular flow: a kind of elite political communication. We applied the chi-square test to determine whether there had been change:
   a) Between successive periods
   b) Between the period before World War I and all subsequent periods
   c) Between the period before and the period after each World War
(There were a few exceptions where frequencies were inadequate, and a few additional exceptions to be referred to.) In every case, there was found to be a significant change. The smallest change between two periods was found in the *New York Times* in the 1930s, but the least significant change (owing to a smaller sample size) was in *Izvestia* between the period 1936-38 and the period 1939-40. Chi square in this case was 109 with 20 degrees of freedom. With this number of degrees of freedom, a chi square of 45 would occur by chance in the sample only one in a thousand times. The odds against a change as great as the one we found occurring in the

sample, if there were no change in the universe, are millions to one. Real changes in political language were clearly taking place all the time. Since changes in editorial contents have been so rapid and sharp, they were easily demonstrable even in that paper and period where change was slowest and even in the smallest usable sample. The hypothesis of no change is a completely unapplicable one.

Hence, it was of no great importance to demonstrate the significance of change between any two periods. What was needed was an estimate of how much change there was. Before we can discuss this, however, we must say a little more about our procedure in computing chi square.

The first problem was to get a representative list of words to be used in measuring change. We decided to draw up a list of twenty words for each change between two periods. There were two reasons for using just twenty words. Reference to Figure 1 and Tables 12 and 13 indicates that if these twenty are the twenty most frequently used symbols from our list, they will encompass the great bulk of the total symbol uses. It will be recalled, from our discussion above, that when we wished to exclude the tail of the distribution but to estimate the concentration on some of the most-used words, we found eighteen words to be the most convenient number to use. These eighteen symbols gave us an adequate picture of the major symbolic attention in any one period. Since in each measurement of change we should be dealing with two periods, and thus with a somewhat greater variety of symbols, it seemed desirable to push the number of symbols up slightly. Twenty symbols, it seemed, would give a good representation of the change between any two periods.

The second reason for deciding on twenty is that the chi-square test should not be applied when the frequencies expected or observed are less than five. The size of our subsamples was such that this requirement made impossible the inclusion of more than twenty words in many periods. In many cases the twenty-first or twenty-second word appeared only four or three times. In a number of cases, as we shall see, even the twentieth or nineteenth word did not appear often enough. But aside from a few subsamples which needed special treatment, twenty words appeared, each of which occurred often enough.

To select twenty words representative of the two periods at either end of the change, we proceeded as follows. We listed first the most frequent word in the earlier period. Then we listed the most frequent word in the later period. If it happened to be the same word, we listed the second most frequent word in the later period. Next, we listed the second most frequent word in the earlier period, if it was not yet included on the list. Then we listed the second most frequent word in the later period, if it was not yet on the list. We proceeded in this manner until we had twenty words. Of these, ten were chosen from each period, but since the most common words are apt to be most common in both periods, we had on the list not ten but perhaps about fifteen out of the first twenty words from each period.

One other modification had to be made. Sometimes a brand-new word would appear, e.g., BOLSHEVISM after 1917. Sometimes an old word would disappear. Most often a word which was neither new nor completely dead was so infrequent in one of the periods that, in subsamples of the very limited size of some of ours, it would not appear five times, although in the other period it was one of the major words, e.g., LEAGUE OF NATIONS after World War II. Because the chi-square table is not reliable for items with such low frequencies, initially we had to cross off our list all words appearing fewer than five times in either period. For these we substituted another word, proceeding as indicated in the last paragraph to pick the next most frequent word from the period which had contributed the deleted word. This procedure meant that we deleted the words which had changed the most—the ones which were newborn or long dead. Since the fact of change was established in every case anyhow, this did not matter for the significance test, but, in estimating the amount of change, it had to be allowed for, as we shall see later.

From the lists of words so constructed, we had the following data: chi square for each of twenty words representing the symbol flow during two periods being compared; and the sum of these chi squares, which is the chi square for the whole list.

As already noted, chi square is a test of a finding in a sample. It is a function of two things: (a) the amount of difference between the actual and the expected values, (b) the size of the sample. It is the first of these things which we are now interested in measuring. We want to know the amount of change, not the reliability of our estimate as affected by sample size. Since chi square is a simple inverse function of sample size, we shall, by dividing the value of chi square by the number of events in the sample, get a figure which represents the amount of change.

This measure has certain clear advantages over some alternative ones and it was also easily computed from already available data, but it cannot be regarded as either the only or demonstrably the best metric for the purpose; in fact, it is far from satisfactory. The problem of metrics for comparing proportions is indeed a thorny one. Which is a bigger change: a change from one percent to 10 percent, or from 51 percent to 60 percent, or from 91 percent to 100 percent? Which is a bigger change: a change from 10 percent to 20 percent or a change from 30 percent to 59 percent?[30]

For the purposes at hand, various alternative indices might be suggested, such as the root mean square of the differences in frequency between the two periods of the twenty indicatorial words. That index and some others, however, would make a change from one percent to 10 percent no larger than a change from 51 to 60 percent, whereas common sense tells us the former change is much more significant than the latter. The chi-square index seems more reasonable in this case. It should, however, be stressed that the results indicate that the latter metric, too, is far from satisfactory. It will become clear as we look at the data that there is a need for a metric based upon a more adequate theory of the problem.

Our samples from different periods were of varying sizes, ranging from periods in which we had read fewer than a hundred editorials to ones in which we had read more than a thousand. To get a number representing the amount of change from any earlier period to any later period, we simply divided the chi squares for the later period by the number of editorials in that period. We then had a scale which applied in the same way to all periods. If, in one country, postwar material deviated from the hypothesis of no change since before the war with a chi square of 200 and the number of postwar editorials was 200, then the index of change would be 1.0 (multiplied by 1000 for convenience). If, in another country, the chi square for the same span of change were 400 and the number of editorials were 500, then the index of change would be 0.8 (multiplied by 1000 for convenience). Thus, although the chi square is greater in the latter case (indicating that, because of the larger sample, we are more sure that there really was a change), the change itself seems to be smaller.

The index of change was computed for each word on the list being used, which made it possible to compute both a mean and median index for each period. The median had two rather significant advantages deriving from the fact that it is less affected by extreme cases. In the first place, it often happened that one or two words had such an enormous index of change that they largely determined the mean. In the second place, it was possible to use newly born or newly dead words in computing the median. Although the precise chi-square figure for words which appear fewer than five times in one period but are frequent in the other is unreliable, it is clear that these are words which have undergone very great change. If, in computing the median, these are assumed to be the words with the largest indices of change, we can compute the median for the first twenty words without deleting these, as we did earlier. The median is the value halfway between the values of the tenth and eleventh highest indices of change. The precise numerical value of the index of change for any other word on the list does not matter, provided we can rank them, and the newly born or the newly dead words can be ranked right at the head of the list.

The mean and the median differed most sharply in changes from war-time to peacetime periods or vice versa. As we noted previously, the war-time periods are marked by a very sharp increase of a few central symbols, with the rest of the symbols remaining relatively unaffected. It is in this situation, where a few extreme cases greatly affect the mean, that the mean and median will differ most.[31]

If, however, we compare the mean and median as indices of change between peacetime periods, we find that the two indices give similar measures of the amount of change. The rank correlation between the median and the mean for changes between successive peacetime periods is .81 (the correlation being based on eighteen changes). In other words, both the median and the mean give fairly similar estimates of the amount of change between peacetime periods.

The median indices of change are reported in Table 17. (The corresponding mean indices are given in Appendix B.)

Table 17 brings out a number of suggestive results, but it also reveals some of the problems that remain to be solved before this measure of symbol change will be completely satisfactory. Let us consider some of these difficulties before proceeding to the interpretation of the results. In the first place, the statistical properties of the scale obviously call for work by qualified statisticians. In what sense, if any, do the units represent equal distances? If they do not, what corrections are needed to make them do so? A glance at the "successive" and "cumulative" columns makes clear that the index as it stands is not additive.

In the second place, the sample most appropriate for use with this measure would be somewhat different from the sample actually used. It should be large enough to allow every word in the list to appear well above five times in both periods. Barring this, the sample should, at least, be relatively uniform in size from period to period, so that the number of indeterminately large indices for individual symbols would not be a function of sample size. Furthermore, the list of words should be of such length and homogeneity that the median or mean will be a relatively stable value. In our results, in many instances only a word or two may excessively influence the index for the period as a whole. We must, therefore, treat the figures in Table 17 with a certain amount of caution. They point the way for future research. They demonstrate the feasibility of measurements of symbol change, but they are not sufficiently reliable as they now stand for us to base any very firm conclusion on any single figure.

At the same time, some general trends in the figures are suggestive. There are noteworthy differences between papers in the general rate of change. The greatest changes have been in *Izvestia*. The most drastic change in the period which we are studying was clearly the Russian Revolution. It is marked by an index of editorial change at least four times as great as that for any other change in our sample. Russian changes since then have also been large. At the other extreme, the least drastic changes have been in the *New York Times* and London *Times*. These points may be documented by the index of changes between successive periods. These indices are lowest in the *New York Times* and London *Times*. They are higher in the French and German papers. They are still higher, at least until World War II, in *Izvestia*.

The same thing can be documented, perhaps even better, if we look at

Table 17

Change in Editorial Content Between Successive Periods and Cumulative Change Before World War I

Period	United States			Great Britain			France			Russia			Germany
	Succes-sive	Skip-Wars	Cumu-lative	Succes-sive	Skip-Wars	Cumu-lative	Succes-sive	Skip-Wars	Cumu-lative	Succes-sive	Skip-Wars	Cumu-lative	Succes-sive
Pre-War I to World War I	10		10	49		49	35		35	202		202	*
World War I to 1920	18			13			126			638			*
Pre-War I to 1920s		40	40		40	40		63	63		2306	2306	*
1920s to early 1930s	9		57	10		44	12		80	70		4872	29
Early to late 1930s	6		43	14		102	56		302	116			110
Late 1930s to World War II, phase 1	54			19			136			89			68
World War II, phases 1-2	26			19			153			113			66
World War II, phase 2 to post-World War II	60			58			110			79			†
Late 1930s to post-World War II		111	131		65	71		139	85		160	6950	‡

* Insufficient data.

† Indeterminately large because 10 words were either new or disappeared. The 11th word had an index of change of 10,273. The median would be halfway between that and an indeterminately large figure.

‡ No data.

the index of cumulative change since the period before World War I. This index may seem puzzling at first glance. Why do we find a change of 139 in the decade between the late 1930s and the late 1940s in France, but a change of only 85 in the inclusive period from before World War I until after World War II? The answer is manifestly the surprising one that, in the last decade, there was a sharp change back toward the kind of symbolism that appeared before World War I. Specifically, the disappearance of Nazism as a major topic of discussion resulted in a large change during the last decade, a change that brought back a somewhat more familiar symbolism. Other factors also were operating in the same direction. Each successive change does not necessarily lead farther from the starting point; some lead back toward it. There is no reason to assume that the magnitude of the cumulative change will be a direct function of the changes between successive periods. Whether it is or not depends upon whether the changes taking place are all in the same direction, or whether they are cyclical, the cycle eventually returning to its point of origin.

The extent to which social changes are cumulative rather than cyclical has been one of the questions most discussed by historians and sociologists. It has been discussed at the macrocosmic level by writers like Spengler, Toynbee, and Sorokin. It has also been discussed at more microcosmic levels in connection with the national policies of various states. It has been much discussed by those dealing with Russian developments. Is Russian symbolism new or old? Was the Revolution merely a wave on the surface of eternal Russia or was it the start of a dynamic new trend? We note that the great change, the Revolution, has been followed by further changes, not of cataclysmic proportions, but still large by Western standards. We can check whether these changes brought each successive Russian subsample farther from the contents of the pre-World War I Czarist sample and toward some new socialist symbolism, or whether the changes after the 1920s were changes backward, away from the high tide of the Revolution. Similar questions may be asked about the symbolic trends in each of the papers we have studied. The answer may be found by an index of cumulative change from a base period to each subsequent period.

Figures 3 and 4 suggest the answers for four of the countries in our sample. These show us what we might expect: a general trend of cumulative change over time on which are superimposed short-term fluctuations of such magnitude that they sometimes obscure the trend. The base line in these figures represents the symbolism of the pre-World War I editorials. As a curve swings higher on the x axis, it represents an increasingly different symbolism; as it swings back toward the base line, it represents growing similarity to the prewar symbolism. The trends of these curves are estimated from just four points over the half-century. Obviously, any pro-

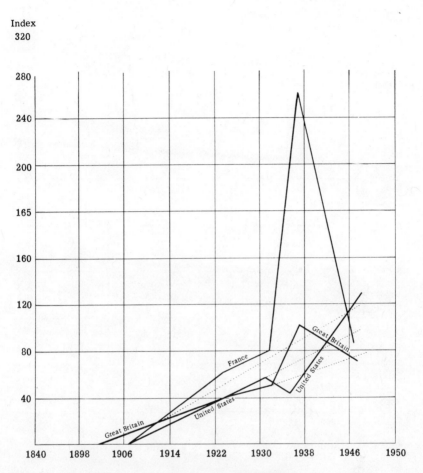

Figure 3. Cumulative change since before World War I.

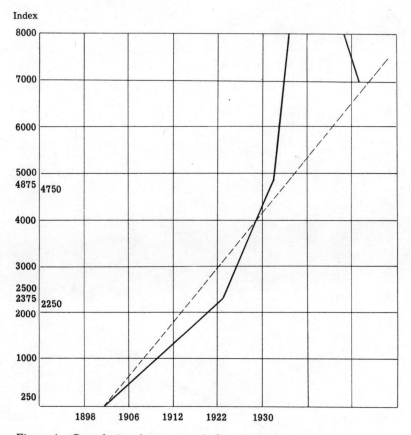

Figure 4.   Cumulative change since before World War I; Russia.

jection based on such a trend is a mere suggestion and not a statistically significant conclusion. Since these trends represent historical facts, however, they are of interest, even though their interpretation as psychocultural generalizations can be, at best, only suggestions.

A glance at Figure 3 reveals that, as a historical fact, the pace of change in the London *Times* has been slower than that in any of the other prestige papers. It seems that the conservatism of British character and public life has been here recorded in a verifiable measurement. Both World War I and the world crisis of the late 1930s brought rather sharp changes in the editorial contents of *The Times,* but in the end there was always reversion to a pattern not unlike that of the early 1900s.

The pace of change in the *New York Times* has been a little more rapid. The outbreak of World War I had a less profound effect on the thinking of the *New York Times* than it had on that of the London *Times* and, similarly, the world crisis of the late 1930s was less fully felt; but, with the coming of World War II in Europe, the *New York Times* underwent a fairly considerable change in editorial contents. In the long run, it seems to be less conservative than the London *Times.*

The cumulative trend of change has been less regular in the French press than in the *New York Times* or the London *Times.* That is to say, the short-term fluctuations from period to period have been more marked. The impact of the revolution of our time was felt somewhat earlier in France than in the two English-speaking powers. World War I had a more drastic impact on France than it had on her two main allies, and so we find a greater change in French editorial symbolism from before the war to the 1920s than we do in that of the other two Allied Powers. In the same way, the world crisis of the late 1930s threatened France more severely than it did England or America, and French opinion was more polarized by it. Despite all this, the basic conservatism of French political attitudes stands out from our cumulative results. When all is said and done, the main themes of the French editorials have not changed more over the past half-century than have those in the *New York Times. Le Monde's* responses to the world are, if anything, less different from those of *Le Temps* at the turn of the century than are the responses of the *New York Times* today and then. If we are justified in projecting a linear trend of cumulative change from the data we have, it might be somewhat more rapid than that found in the *New York Times,* but not much more so. We have no standard for juding what is "normal" in amount of change. We have no basis for saying that symbolic changes in the half-century have been "much" or "little." All we can do is to compare the papers among themselves. On this basis, we can say of the French editorials (as of the French cabinets) that, although they were more changeable from period to period, their basic pattern was not correspondingly more unstable. Short-term instability can be, as demonstrated here, superimposed on a basic inflexibility.

The Russian changes, because they are the greatest, are perhaps the most interesting. The rate of change in the Russian editorials was rather low until World War I. It will be recalled that we divided our prewar *Novoe Vremia* sample into two subsamples: 1892-1904 and 1905-13. The median index of change between these two periods was only 13. World War I, however, produced a bigger change in the symbolism of *Novoe Vremia* editorials than it did in the symbolism of any other contemporaneous prestige paper. The index of change from the later prewar subperiod, 1905-13, to World War I was 113, and the index of change from the whole prewar period to World War I was 202. Whether these large changes in some way foreshadowed the even more drastic changes to come is a question we may leave to students of Russian history.

In any case, the Revolution itself produced an entirely new symbolism. The rejection of such old words as MONARCHY and REFORM and emphasis on such new words as COMMUNISM, BOLSHEVISM, REVOLUTION, PROLETARIAT, and SOVIET made the new editorials quite unlike the old in political language. Furthermore, as time went on, the *Izvestia* editorials moved further and further from the Czarist pattern. As totalitarianism impoverished the vocabulary of the editorials, the old words disappeared one after another and concentration on the new Bolshevik terminology became greater and greater. Thus, until the most recent period, *Izvestia* terminology moved further and further from that of *Novoe Vremia*. In part, this is simply a reflection of the above-noted fact that the variety of symbols used has grown constantly smaller. Repetitiousness of style, especially in recent issues, is one of the main respects in which *Izvestia* departs from *Novoe Vremia*. But, until very recently, the words chosen for repetition were increasingly those that were safely orthodox by Bolshevik standards. Whatever may have been happening in other respects, *Izvestia* has been careful to talk a strictly Bolshevik language. In fact, so stylized was it in this respect that the old symbols became difficult to find. As has been pointed out before, there was a tremendous concentration on a number of very positive symbols like REVOLUTION, COMMUNISM, etc. These provided the bulk of the content. There was a heavy concentration on a small number of negative words such as FASCISM. There was a very restricted attention to words which could not be simply pigeonholed, words with mixed evaluations or words referring to unpleasant objects other than the one main enemy.

The reintroduction, in the later periods, of such old but rehabilitated words as FATHERLAND, PATRIOTISM, and STATE did not, as one might expect, bring the postwar Soviet editorials into line with those in *Novoe Vremia*. Changes in a nationalist direction do account for the fact that relatively large indices of change between periods are found even in the later 1930s and since. But far from producing a revival of an old pattern, the new Soviet editorial patriotism is so much more intense than that in *Novoe Vremia* that *Izvestia* editorials today are as different from the pre-Soviet ones as were the more Marxist editorials of a somewhat earlier period. Our index of change records not merely presence or absence of words but also their frequency. In frequency of nationalist words, *Izvestia* is almost as far ahead of *Novoe Vremia* as in the Marxist ones. The word that has increased most in frequency from before World War I to after World War II is SOCIALISM.[32] The next largest increase is in the symbol WORKING CLASS. The third largest increase is in FATHER-LAND.

It was in the 1930s, not the 1940s, that the nationalist symbols were at a level close to that of the *Novoe Vremia* editorials. The hypothesis of no change between *Novoe Vremia* and *Izvestia* of the period 1929-35 is tenable for the symbols FATHERLAND and STATE. Between *Novoe Vremia* and *Izvestia* of the period 1936-38, it is tenable for PATRIOTISM. The chi squares are, respectively, .07, 1.17, and 1.94; a chi square of 3.84 is usually taken as constituting significant deviation from the hypothesis. Since the 1930s these words have risen to unprecedented levels.

Thus our results show that either assumption—of a simple reversion to the pre-Soviet symbolism or of a straight-line evolution in a Bolshevik direction—is too simple. There has, in recent years, been reversion in limited respects toward older patterns, and there certainly has been a marked change from the Bolshevik pattern of the 1920s. At the same time, however, the new totalitarian Soviet symbolism is really quite unlike anything that has gone before. It is unlike both the symbolism of the 1920s and that of *Novoe Vremia*. Its distinctive feature, as noted above, is its extremely limited and very repetitious character.

As a final check on the assertion that there has been a rather large change away from the symbolism of the 1920s, as well as away from that of earlier periods, we computed the index of change in *Izvestia* between 1918-28 and each of the subsequent peacetime periods. The results, demonstrating the large changes within *Izvestia*, are presented in Table 18.

Table 18
Change in *Izvestia*

From 1919-28 to:	Median index	Mean index
1929-35	70	356
1936-38	424	1055
1946-49	410	1179

The words that have increased most in attention from the 1920s to the most recent period are, in order, FATHERLAND, COLLECTIVISM, and PATRIOTISM.

So much for the general picture of the amount of change in the political contents of the editorials of the prestige papers. Before we leave the topic of change, however, it would be well briefly to record the areas of discussion in which the changes took place.

Areas of Change

In Appendix B full tables of changes in the major symbols are given, with the change index and chi square for each change. The summary historical survey that follows is based on these tables, which should be consulted by those wishing precise data. In the subsequent discussion of the major changes, only those are referred to which are not simply the symbolic reflection of well-known events. It is obvious that in the 1930s the LEAGUE OF NATIONS was referred to, and in the 1940s the U.N. Similarly, during wartime, military symbols emerge. Other changes are somewhat less obvious, and we shall concentrate on these.

Russia. The Russian editorials changed little from 1892 until the Revolution. Within *Novoe Vremia* there were few anticipations of the storm that was brewing. The symbol REVOLUTION increased moderately from 1892-1904 to 1904-13, but during the war years it showed no significant change from the prewar period. ORDER increased moderately during the prewar years, then disappeared completely during the war. SOCIALISM showed no significant increase until the war, whereupon it increased by only a small amount. References to the czar (coded under MONARCHY) also increased moderately during the war. But, aside from these small changes, there was no indication in *Novoe Vremia* of the issues on which the Bolsheviks and *Izvestia* were soon to turn the spotlight.

The Revolution and the shift from *Novoe Vremia* to *Izvestia* brought a whole new vocabulary to the fore. Words that were once part of the specialized jargon of small left-wing sects mushroomed—like the movements that spawned them—into part of the daily vocabulary, SOVIET, BOURGEOISIE, PROLETARIAT, COMMUNISM, BOLSHEVISM, RED, and COUNTERREVOLUTION were all words new to the editorial columns. IMPERIALISM, MASSES, WORKING CLASS, REVOLUTION, CAPITALISM, SOCIALISM, and REACTIONARY were all words that appeared with greatly increased frequency.

For the most part, this new vocabulary has persisted, but with some changes in the years since 1928. Especially at first, the Stalinist editorials strove to demonstrate their orthodoxy by repeating ad nauseum the key words of the revolutionary period. Such words as BOLSHEVISM,

SOCIALISM, SOVIET, and COMMUNISM are used more now than in 1918-28. MASSES and WORKING CLASS are used just as much as before 1928. BOURGEOISIE, PROLETARIAT, and CAPITALISM have recently declined, but until World War II they were also used just as much as in the early years. Their decline has been more than offset by the rise in the majority of Bolshevik words.

The persistence, even intensification, of the Bolshevik character of *Izvestia's* vocabulary is, in part, an effect of the successive impoverishment of its editorial language, as we noted earlier. Fewer and fewer words have been used more and more often. The key revolutionary words are part of the core of increasingly repeated symbols.

Some new words have been added to the select list of oft-repeated symbols. Collectivization (coded as COLLECTIVISM) became a major Soviet term around 1929 and has remained such.

A group of nationalist terms has been restored to favor. PATRIOTISM changed little in frequency between the *Novoe Vremia* and the *Izvestia* editorials of the early revolutionary years. It was not played down, as one might suspect, but neither was it played up. In the period of the Stalin-Hitler pact, however, it began to be used somewhat more. With the coming of World War II, it was used still more, and it has continued to be frequent since. FATHERLAND declined somewhat in the early years of the Bolshevik regime, but starting with the late 1930s, it was used more. It increased in use in the early 1940s, and since then it has remained a common word. STATE and FAMILY also increased in frequency with World War II.

Other symbols had a temporary vogue at one time or another. DEMOCRACY had a fad in the late 1930s. TROTSKYISM also had a vogue during the great purges, but it has not been a leading word since. Like other allusions to the enemy, it did not become a stable major part of Soviet symbolism. The image of the enemy has changed from time to time. During the early 1930s, the class struggle was stressed with the rise in prominence of the symbols CLASS ENEMY and DICTATORSHIP OF THE PROLETARIAT (both of which later gradually faded). During the later 1930s, TROTSKYISM and FASCISM rose. But these terms, as also BOURGEOISIE, REACTIONARY, and COUNTERREVOLUTION, have declined in prominence in recent years. The tendency of *Izvestia* editorials has been to play down hostile and uncongenial symbols, with the exception of the one central foe of the moment, who is abundantly referred to. In effect, *Izvestia* says all is well with the world—or would be were it not for one devil who threatens to ruin everything.

France. In France, the striking fact is the emphasis placed on security and insecurity during the interwar period. Among the words showing considerable increase from 1900-13 to 1919-29 are PEACE, SECURITY, and

CRISIS; a moderate increase is also shown by ORDER. In addition, words referring specifically to threats of international or domestic conflict and protective agencies against them make up all the rest of the list of words which markedly increased in incidence. Among the threats were BOLSHEVISM, COMMUNISM, WAR, and LEFT. The replies to these threats were ALLIES, LEAGUE OF NATIONS, VERSAILLES, DISARMAMENT, and STATE.

The same trend of increasing stress on security continues on into the 1930s. CRISIS, SECURITY, and ORDER increase in frequency again between 1919-29 and 1930-35. From 1930-35 to 1936-38, ORDER once more increases in frequency, and CRISIS and SECURITY stay at the same high level. Meanwhile, some other symbols referring to international and domestic conflicts are rising, though several decline in importance with the changing situation. Specifically, references to the ALLIES decrease as World War I receded into history. Similarly, references to WAR reach a low point in the early 1930s, after which they start increasing in the face of a new threat. But while these two symbols of security or insecurity were receding or fluctuating in frequency, NAZISM and MARXISM were both becoming more frequent in *Le Temps* in the early 1930s and INTERVENTION, LEFT, and TRADE UNIONS in the late 1930s.

Since the fall of France and the replacement of *Le Temps* with *Le Monde,* this tendency to stress security symbols has been partly reversed. CRISIS and ORDER are less used and SECURITY somewhat less. LEFT, REVOLUTION, and MARXISM also appear less often. Of the international symbols, some have gone up and some have gone down in incidence. For obvious reasons, MILITARY OCCUPATION and ALLIES are more referred to than before the war, but PEACE is spoken of less often.

This decline in security symbols could be a sign of a significant trend in French thought, or it could be a mere reflection of the fact that *Le Monde* is a less conservative paper than *Le Temps.* In a subsequent study of security symbols, we shall note some reasons for believing that the former hypothesis has some merit, although the latter is also true. For the moment, we can only note briefly the possible reversal of what was the dominant twenty-year trend in the French editorials studied.

This trend toward security consciousness has been often noted and is not hard to explain. France came out of World War I technically a victor, but actually a leading victim. She no longer had the manpower or the industrial strength to protect her own borders, much less her pretensions to be a great power. Bolshevism posed a new threat to the French elite, and inflation hit the French middle class, for whom security had always been a major economic goal. Psychocultural predispositions to demand security were thus reinforced by real threats, and the French response was to stress security symbols. French foreign policy aimed at collective security against a renascent Germany, while French domestic policy aimed at financial stability. *Le Temps,* a conservative and semiofficial paper, reflected this foreign policy and became obsessed with the domestic threat of disorderly leftist proletarian movements.

Great Britain. Changes in the British and American editorials were less dramatic than those in the Russian and French papers. Not only were they smaller, as already noted, but they were more often reflexes of events rather than projections of changing attitudes. Symbols rose or declined under the impact of changing external factors, rather than under the impact of internal changes in the goals or strategies of the editors. In a nutshell, both the London *Times* and the *New York Times* were more objective.

There were, however, some changes in the London *Times* that reflected the changing ideology of the day. After World War I, attention to some of the classical symbols of nineteenth-century liberalism went down. REFORM, RADICALS, LIBERALISM, PROGRESS, and, to some extent, FREEDOM declined from the prewar period to 1919-29. At the same time, attention to the LABOUR PARTY and the TRADE UNIONS was coming up.

In the subsequent period, the early 1930s, SOCIALISM received increased attention, along with such transitory topical symbols as NAZISM and TARIFFS. Since World War II, NATIONALIZATION has risen to the center of attention, along with such other currently topical symbols as U.N., COMMUNISM, and SOVIET; also increasingly popular recently is PATRIOTISM.

If we look at the full span of change from before World War I to after World War II, we get a good picture of the general tenor of change in the editorials of the London *Times.* The symbols which have declined drastically or disappeared in the last half-century are: RADICALS, REFORM, and LIBERALS. The symbols that have newly appeared, or appear much more, are: COMMUNISM, SOVIET, STATE OWNERSHIP (NATIONALIZATION), LABOUR PARTY, LABOR, U.N., WAR, SECURITY, and CRISIS.

In part, the change has been a change in party strength. Although references to the CONSERVATIVES have remained substantially constant in number, references to the RADICALS and LIBERALS have given way to references to the LABOUR PARTY.

In part, the change has been a change in the ideologies associated with the leading parties. References to REFORM have given way to references to STATE OWNERSHIP and LABOR.

In part, the change has been a reflection of the growing difficulties of Great Britain's position, both internal and external. COMMUNISM,

SECURITY, and CRISIS are words used to discuss the dangers of our times.

In part, finally, the change reflects the nationalist and military reaction which Great Britain, like all countries, has had to adopt toward the growing dominance of war over the lives of everyone. WAR is increasingly used in Great Britain, as in every country in our sample, and so is PATRIO-TISM.

United States. The impact of a warlike world upon the United States is clearly visible. The four old symbols which rose most from before World War I to after World War II were PEACE, WAR, ARMAMENTS, and SECURITY. CRISIS also rose considerably, as did DISARMAMENT. Among the new symbols that appeared were: U.N., COMMUNISM, SOVIETS, NAZISM, and ATOMIC POWER. On the other hand, TARIFFS and FREE TRADE, symbols of peaceful world intercourse that once were important, disappeared from the editorials.

Aside from these war-related symbols, few symbols have shown marked changes in frequency. REFORM and TRUSTS, key symbols of the muck-raking era, declined, while FREEDOM and DEMOCRACY rose somewhat to become key symbols of today. A number of symbols of domestic political relevance that one should expect to have assumed greater prominence since the New Deal did not do so. No significant long-run change has taken place in the incidence of SOCIALISM, PROGRESS, REVOLUTION, TRADE UNIONS (perhaps LABOR too), FREE ENTER-PRISE, or NEGROES.

The long-run changes we noted commenced with World War I. After that war, REFORM disappeared, and the following new words entered the editorial vocabulary: LEAGUE OF NATIONS, COMMUNISM, ALLIES, VERSAILLES TREATY, BOLSHEVISM, and SOVIETS. In addition, WAR and PEACE, ARMAMENTS and DISARMAMENT rose considerably, and WORLD COURT and NATIONALISM somewhat less. TRUSTS and TARIFFS began their decline.

In the New Deal period, ARMAMENTS came up even more while TARIFFS continued to decline. In the *New York Times,* at least, the social ferment of the era was not reflected in an increased use of socially significant jargon. The only symbol of "social significance" which in these years rose enough to merit notice was DEMOCRACY, and the increase in its incidence was moderate.

In the post-World War II period, the trends that commenced with World War I continued. The new words included U.N., ATOMIC POWER, and ALLIES. SOVIETS, PEACE, WAR, SECURITY, and COMMUNISM increased markedly in incidence. In addition, DEMOCRACY and FREE-DOM showed some increase, and PROGRESS made a comeback from a previous decline. Out of the two wars, America has become involved in the world arena, and this is reflected in the *New York Times* editorials. This and a moderate change in the symbols of liberalism are what we find.

Germany. For Germany our data are too sketchy to be of much value. We can, however, take note of the impact of the Nazi seizure of power. Most of the changes in vocabulary between the *Frankfurter Zeitung* and the *Völkischer Beobachter* were so gross that they are obvious. The overall median index of change, 110, is large, but not extraordinary, because, while some gross changes were taking place, much of the other vocabulary of the editorials was unaffected by the *Machtergreifung*. But those symbols that did change in frequency changed drastically. JEWS, COMMUNISM, FUEHRER, and NAZISM were obviously stressed in the Nazi editorials. So was NATIONALISM. On the other hand, references to SOCIAL DEMOCRACY went down.

None of this is at all surprising. What is surprising is the large number of symbols which did not significantly change in frequency in 1933, although they did change in their evaluation. Among these were FREEDOM, REVOLUTION, PARLIAMENTARISM, CATHOLIC CHURCH, PEACE, FASCISM, PEOPLE, LEFT, and CRISIS. When the Nazis first took over, they made certain drastic, conscious changes in symbolism, but for the rest they preserved continuity with the past in a way that the Bolsheviks did not.

During their years in power, the Nazis changed their symbolism moderately. The most dramatic change is that which occurred as the war began to go against them. Then their symbolism became more and more extreme, and more and more vituperative. As we have already noted, the variety of symbols decreased. The symbols that persisted were those most suited to anti-other statements rather than pro-self statements. The words whose incidence increased most from 1939-41 to 1942-45 were BOLSHEVISM, DEMOCRACY, and PLUTOCRACY.

V. Summary

We have found that in the Western world there has grown up an institution which we call the "prestige paper." It is a paper in each country read by the elite of that and foreign countries, and expressing a segment of elite opinion. It is always in some way tied to the government, the degree of intimacy being a function of the politization of the particular elite. The prestige paper gives an opportunity for semiofficial expressions of elite opinion and assures widespread dissemination to the elite of policy-relevant information and attitudes.

We documented a number of the assertions just made concerning these papers through biographical data about the editors of the prestige papers. We found, however, that these papers are sufficiently institutionalized that their editorials do not much reflect the personality or the ideosyncracies of any single individual.

We surveyed by content analysis the contents of the editorials of the prestige papers in five major powers. The content analysis consisted of a count of the number of editorials which contained each of several hundred key political symbols. A sample of the editorials since 1890 was studied.

From this content analysis, we found, first of all, that there is heavy concentration on a few key symbols. This finding corresponds to earlier findings in studies of belles lettres and of other nonpolitical forms of communication.

Furthermore, we found that the degree of concentration on a few symbols varies depending on certain political conditions. Using a measurement of symbol variety devised by G. Udny Yule, we found that totalitarianism markedly impoverishes its own political vocabulary and possibly thus weakens its propaganda. We also found that, in wartime, a similar decrease of variety takes place in democratic symbolism, but it is confined to a small segment of the total symbolism. The rest of the body of communications is left more or less unaffected.

We found large differences between papers in the frequency of explicit judgments in the editorials. The London *Times* and the *New York Times* were extremely reticent about making judgments, whereas the French, German, and Russian papers (in that order) were less so. Above all, the totalitarian papers assumed a very unsubtle didactic tone.

Where judgments were extensively made, they could and did vary in the ratio of positive to negative ones. Glorification and vilification are patterns that are not easily related to some one social variable. The totalitarian papers were extreme in whatever they did, but they were not uniform in their balance of judgment. As things became difficult for the Nazis, the *Völkischer Beobachter* took on a vituperative tone. It stressed and condemned the devil symbols. *Izvestia,* on the other hand, has tended more and more to present a rosy, Pollyanna-like picture of the world.

This rosy picture has of course had its dark spots: TROTSKYISM, FASCISM, and IMPERIALISM. These devil symbols were painted in increasingly dark colors, but they were given less and less space in the total picture. In the old days, the Bolsheviks took great pleasure in talking about all the evils and problems in the world, both in Russia and abroad. There were few unequivocally good symbols. Even such symbols as SOCIALISM were both criticized and praised. That is no longer true. Every symbol has its own stereotyped judgment. Each thing mentioned is either a good thing or a bad thing. So the Soviet image of the world is very much like that of the little girl with the curl in the middle of her forehead.

It is usually very very good, but the enemy is horrid. He is the one flaw in an otherwise rosy world.

We measured the degree of stereotyping of judgments of given symbols for each paper. As just noted, that in *Izvestia* in recent years was by far the highest. That in the *Völkischer Beobachter* was also high. In general, there was a close relationship between polarization of political opinions and degree of stereotyping. As sharpening lines have emerged between extreme political camps, the judgments on each side have become more stereotyped.

On the other hand, there were instances of papers so ambivalent and uncertain in their judgments that the uncertainty may well have contributed to the political weakness of the elite whose views the paper shared. Such extreme ambivalence appeared in two cases where the dominant myth was clearly in decay: in Czarist Russia and contemporary France. This finding suggests that it is possible to measure, by the technique used here, the disintegration of a system of values which generally foreshadows the revolutionary overthrow of any elite.

Finally, we tried, with our content analysis, to measure the extent of change in the political values upheld in the editorials. To do this we devised an index of symbolic change based upon chi square. The measurements made had a number of defects, but they may point the way to a method for measuring social change. Symbolic change is the most pervasive aspect of social change; if a stable measure of that can be achieved, it may be possible to quantify discussions of social change.

In this instance, we found the least change in the British editorials, perhaps reflecting the oft-noted conservatism of British character. We found the most change in the Russian press. The French press showed sharp fluctuations, but underlying this, there was a basic continuity and conservatism.

When we looked at the contents of the changes we found that most of them centered around two main trends in the modern world: (1) a shift in the center of attention, in which traditional liberalism is being replaced by proletarian doctrines, and (2) a growing threat of war and a corresponding increase of nationalism and militarism. These trends are noticeable to some extent in the editorials of all the great powers since 1890.

Having thus surveyed the general trends and contents of the prestige-paper editorials, we shall turn in subsequent chapters to a more intensive study of special groups of symbols, the symbols of internationalism and symbols of democracy.

NOTES

1. In order to differentiate in the text between the "prestige papers" of the United States and Great Britain, the latter is referred to as the London *Times* rather than merely *The Times,* its official title.
2. Alex Inkeles, *Public Opinion in Soviet Russia: A Study in Mass Persuasion* (Cambridge: Harvard University Press, 1950), p. 151.
3. Ministères de la Guerre et des Affaires Etrangères, *Repertoire des Journaux et Périodiques Utilisés dans les Bulletins de Presse Etrangère* (Paris: Imp. Courmont, 1918), p. 4. Cf. also Otto Groth, *Die Zeitung: Ein System der Zeitungskunde (Journalistik)* (Mannheim: J. Bensheimer, 1939), II, p. 232.
4. Viscount W. E. B. Camrose, *British Newspapers and Their Controllers* (London: Cassell, 1947), p. 22.
5. Library of Congress, European Affairs Division, *The European Press Today* (Washington, 1949), p. 124.
6. F. Fraser Bond, *Mr. Miller of "The Times": The Story of an Editor* (New York: Charles Scribner's Sons, 1931), pp. 120-22.
7. *New York Times* (July 19, 1922), p. 12.
8. Different grammatical forms of the same word were frequently admitted under the rules of procedure, for example ARBITRATE and ARBITRATION. Homonyms were distinguished, for example, PROTECTION meaning tariffs was counted as such, but not any other meaning of PROTECTION. Under doctrines we included the leading spokesmen (e.g., Marx or the *Daily Worker* could be coded as synonyms for communism).
9. The reader may find a statement of the concepts underlying the RADIR program in a monograph of the Hoover Institute Studies, Harold D. Lasswell's *The World Revolution of Our Time: A Framework for Basic Policy Research.* The list of symbols used was designed to provide indexes of these concepts.
10. Cf. G. Udny Yule, *The Statistical Study of Literary Vocabulary* (Cambridge: The University Press, 1944), p. 21. A number of studies have indicated that nouns play the largest role in giving individuality to bodies of communications.
11. This fact is a central argument of the advocates of Basic English.
12. From Inga Wilhelmsen Allwood, Mark Perlberg, and Martin S. Allwood, "The Vocabulary of Romantic Poetry in England and the Popular American Song Hit," in Martin S. Allwood, ed., *Hobart Mass Communication Studies,* 1949-50 (Geneva, New York: Hobart College, 1950), p. 54. The data on spoken English are drawn from Norman R. French, Charles W. Carter, Jr., and Walter Koenig, Jr., "The Words and Sounds of Telephone Conversations," *The Bell System Technical Journal,* IX (1930), 290-324. The data on written English are drawn from Godfrey Dewey, *Relative Frequency of English Speech Sounds* (Cambridge: Harvard University Press, 1923).
13. Most past studies of word frequencies have been made for purposes not requiring the separation of homonyms. The construction of spelling lists, the improvement of shorthand symbols, or the improvement of acoustical devices does not require differentiation of meaning. Except for studies of poetry, such as Josephine Miles, *Pathetic Fallacy in the Nineteenth Century* (Berkeley: University of California Press, 1942) and *Wordsworth and the Vocabulary of Emotion* (Berkeley: University of California Press, 1942), or studies of authorship, such as G. Udny Yule, *Statistical Study,* the problems so far tackled have avoided meaning. PEOPLE, the 159th word, appeared 78 times in 53 of the 500 phone conversations analyzed. STATE, the 629th word, was used 7 times in 6 conversations. PEOPLE constitutes about one-tenth of one percent of telephone

14. The study of telephone conversations concentrated on phones in a business district. But even were the sample more heavily weighted with home phones or evening calls this conclusion would be unaffected.

15. It should be noted that the heavy incidence of war-relevant symbols is partly due to the date of the study. Also, it should be noted that except for ALLIES and FREEDOM the figures include all grammatical forms of the word. The two exceptions are more clearly political in the form listed than in some other forms. Thus FREE is more apt to refer to price than politics. To ALLY is apt to be used of private individuals. For these two symbols the figures were drawn from tables in Dewey's book in which forms of the same root were not combined. The other figures are drawn from tables combining grammatical forms of the same root.

    In citing rank, where several terms occur with identical frequency, the word we are interested in is assumed to have the highest rank in that group.

    The Dewey list contains a few homonyms in which the political sense which we counted is clearly the rare one. Figures drawn from a table which does not distinguish homonyms would be meaningless for LEFT, RIGHT, and TRUST. The frequency of these is undoubtedly due to their nonpolitical meaning.

16. In this respect our findings confirm the theoretical analysis of G. Udny Yule. He concluded that the statistical characteristics of the distribution of a selected list of words would be the same as that for a total list. Cf. Yule, *Statistical Study,* pp. 25 ff., 97 ff., 183 ff. This has important implications for the statistics of content analysis. It means that the same measures may be applied to total word counts or to selected lists, no matter how rare the words of which they consist. Given an adequate sample, even the rarest words will fall into the same kind of Poisson distribution.

17. Harold D. Lasswell, Nathan Leites, et al., *Language of Politics* (New York: George W. Stewart, 1949), p. 28.

18. Yule, *Statistical Study.*

19. Inkeles, *Public Opinion in Soviet Russia,* p. 172.

20. Quoted in ibid., p. 39.

21. Ibid., p. 166.

22. Ibid., p. 171.

23. Yule, *Statistical Study,* p. 284.

24. A rejected hypothesis: it seemed plausible to the author that the degree of concentration on judgments would be greater than the degree of concentration of attention. A great many words are used in casual or incidental fashion, but it seemed probable that only a few key symbols of a controversial or highly emotionalized character would be singled out for extensive judgment. Like many plausible beliefs, however, this proved untrue. The distribution of judged symbols tended to follow rather closely the distribution of all symbols, the German papers providing an exception. Below are the K values for the five whole samples, both for all symbols and for judged symbols separately.

Country	K for All Symbols	K for Judged Symbols
United States	328	332
Great Britain	299	282
France	189	228
Germany	235	411
Russia	261	280

Less precise inspection of individual periods reveals much the same picture. The high concentration of judgments in the German press is due to a very high concentration in the *Völkischer Beobachter*. From the time the Nazis took power until the Second World War, for example, K for all symbols was 509, but for judged symbols it was 857. In other words the Nazis did what we wrongly thought all the editorials would do. They concentrated their judgments on a few key symbols, symbols like NAZISM and BOLSHEVISM. In this instance what was true of the Nazi press appears to be uniquely Nazi, not a trait of controlled editorials. The same pattern was not found in the Soviet nor in wartime editorials.

25. This criterion gave us between seven and thirty-four characterizable symbols for different periods with the median being sixteen or seventeen.

26. Ties were included. In case of ties, equal frequencies of judgments were entered for each direction. On the use here of pooled data see Chapter One. It would obviously have been better from a statistical point of view to have used some kind of mean, but it would have been unfeasible with the data at hand.

27. The following solution was worked out by M. A. Girshick who gave invaluable help on several phases of this paper.

28. Since 74 percent of judgments were negative this is not as great a departure from what would exist in an unstereotyped model as the previous French subsample, but, as we shall see below, this test begins to be irrelevant when symbols tend all to be judged in the same direction. In any case, with a mean frequency of judgments per symbol of 37, this 5 percent deviation is probably significant.

29. The appropriate number of degrees of freedom would be the number of words.

30. Cf. Paul F. Lazarsfeld and Allen H. Barton, "Qualitative Measurement in the Social Sciences: Classification, Typologies, and Indices," in Daniel Lerner and Harold D. Lasswell, eds., *The Policy Sciences: Recent Developments in Scope and Method* (Stanford, Calif.: Stanford University Press, 1951).

31. To be slightly more accurate: the mean or median is apt to be bigger in the system here being used depending on whether or not the extreme cases are so extreme that the frequency of the terms that change most is below five in either period.

32. The entirely new words such as BOLSHEVISM are, of course, left out of this computation.

CHAPTER THREE
SYMBOLS OF DEMOCRACY*

I. Problem and Method

The Problem

This chapter is an attempt to measure by the technique of content analysis trends in the ideology of democracy. It is an attempt to measure how the popularity of the symbol has changed and how its meaning has changed.

Within the lifetime of our older contemporaries there has taken place an ideological revolution of the first magnitude. DEMOCRACY has become a key symbol of political controversy. In the struggle between Russia and the West, as in domestic struggles between left and right, a battle cry of each side is DEMOCRACY. Conservatives desire to protect DEMOCRACY from encroachments by the welfare state. Radicals wish to complete "merely political" with industrial and social DEMOCRACY. Democracy has become a goal value to which nearly all currents in the stream of civilized thought claim to adhere. It is to modern political controversies what God and the Church were to medieval thought, i.e., an end by which all programs are justified.

The heyday of the symbol DEMOCRACY has been a short one. A century ago democracy was a favored symbol for small extremist plebeian groups only. But since 1870 this term, once so disturbing and revolutionary in flavor, has become respectable and comfortable.[1] Critics now attack DEMOCRACY as passé. For eighty years the term has been the accepted property of both defenders and attackers of the status quo. In this time span it has already become banal, say critics, and has lost its power to stir men's souls. They say that, thanks to the torrential streams of public communications and the rapid social changes in modern society, DEMOCRACY has lived the life course of a key symbol in a period that five hundred or a thousand years ago would have sufficed merely to introduce

*I. Pool, Hoover Institute Studies, Series C: Symbols, No. 4 (Stanford, California: Stanford University Press, January 1952). Abridged and reprinted with permission.

the term. They argue that there has already been a reaction against it. DEMOCRACY, say the critics, is no longer an effective battle cry. If World War I was a war to make the world safe for democracy, World War II was merely a war against fascism—a war in which even those on democracy's side no longer had a glowing faith in the old symbol, and those on the other side openly made fun of the "plutodemocracies." The modern world, according to these critics, is reacting against the futility of parliamentarism and the scepticism implied by civil liberty. Not only in countries which have gone totalitarian but also in those that have not, we hear the stupidity and inactivity of congresses and parliaments ridiculed and the leadership of a strong executive preferred. We also hear that people need a faith to live by; that a society which tolerates men who undermine it cannot survive; that the notion that truth will win in the free market of ideas was a shallow nineteenth-century myth.[2] Is it true that democracy is on the defensive and the popularity of the symbol is declining?

A study of deference to the symbol DEMOCRACY itself may test the assertion that the popularity of the word is declining. It will not, however, tell us whether the popularity of the democratic ideology is going up or down, for a symbol can be appropriated by those who reject the contents implied. Huey Long once made the famous prediction that fascism would come to the United States but it would be called DEMOCRACY. If we wish to make a study of the status of democratic ideology, we should, therefore, take account of trends not only in the symbol DEMOCRACY itself, but also in other symbols which refer to the contents of the democratic ideal. In its broadest sense, DEMOCRACY in this study is defined as the sharing of power. Some of the key aspects of the sharing of power which have played a prominent part in the historical development of democracy include equality (both material and before the law); guaranties of freedom of speech, press, and assembly; guaranties of trial by a jury of one's peers; women's suffrage; abolition of property qualifications; parliamentary supremacy; constitutionalism, etc. If we classify the main elements in the modern Western conception of democracy we come up with three main constellations of ideas, namely: representative government, freedom, and an orientation to the people. These we shall take to be the content of the democratic goal. We shall, in the following discussion, examine not only trends in the use of the symbol DEMOCRACY itself, but also trends in symbols referring to these three elements of democracy.

The four items we shall study (the symbol DEMOCRACY itself and the three elements of democracy) need not follow parallel trends. Has the libertarian element in the democratic ideology increased or decreased? Has concern with the principle of representative government increased or decreased? Have the contents of democratic beliefs been abandoned by writers who continue to use the term? If so, who has done this? Some writers argue that democracy, far from implying a substantive equality, is actually its antithesis, since if men by nature unequal are set on the same starting line and given freedom to go as far as they can as fast as they can, some will go very far and others will scarcely move. Other writers argue that for this very reason democracy requires limitations on individual freedom to prevent the growth of gross inequality.

There is thus a tension between belief in freedom and the adoption of a pro-mass anti-elite orientation. It is hardly appropriate here to consider the philosophical question of whether this tension is a truly irreconcilable contradiction or merely an apparent paradox. This question has been debated at length in various places, including a recent UNESCO symposium on the meaning of the concept of democracy.[3] Here we shall not attempt further to debate the true implications of democracy but shall attempt rather to measure by content analysis the stress given to different aspects of it in different countries and at different times during the past half-century. Here we shall attempt only to observe with new precision the balance and interplay between belief in freedom and adoption of a pro-mass orientation. Here we are concerned with the fact that the paradox between them has bedeviled democratic thought, and that different self-styled democrats have seized one horn or another of the dilemma. We are concerned with investigating whether the democratic ideology has been reinterpreted to stress or repress any of its original elements.

The Method

We limit our problem to the democratic ideology as it has been formally enunciated rather than as it has been practiced, because the method of this study is content analysis. If the Russians were to praise freedom of assembly hundreds of times in a certain body of texts, this would not prove that they had freedom of assembly. It would prove only that they considered freedom of assembly an important thing for which to claim credit. To establish whether they practiced it or not would require use of other techniques, such as interviewing persons who tried to engage in antigovernment activities in Russia. Nonetheless, it is worth our while to examine what the regime says about freedom of assembly, even though that tells us nothing about the facts.

The formulas that people recite are an important part of their behavior and are worthy of study. What things people feel it proper to say are one important part of the pattern of their culture. It is sometimes especially important when it contradicts their behavior. It is not a trivial matter that Americans, from childhood on, hear that all men are created equal. The tension between this ingrained belief and the actual treatment of the Negro is, as Myrdal has pointed out, one of the most important determinants of American behavior. A description of American race relations would therefore be grossly misleading if it claimed to be complete but actually presented only the practices while disregarding their symbolic accompaniments. Such a partial description (e.g., a report on what types of restaurants serve Negroes or a statistical tabulation of the frequency of lynchings) might indeed be very useful if it claimed to be only what it was and not a total picture. In the same way, this content analysis of what has been said about democracy over the years would be utterly misleading if it were presented as a picture of trends in democracy itself. We nevertheless hope and claim that it is useful as a modest attempt to record changes in what has been said about democracy.

It is one of the striking characteristics of discussions of the history of ideas that quite contradictory theses continue to exist side by side for long periods of time. We read on the one hand that this is the age of science, and on the other that there is a reaction against the scientific rationalism of the nineteenth century. We read on the one hand that Americans are individualistic and self-reliant and on the other hand that they are joiners and afraid to be different from the crowd. These apparently contradictory theses may perhaps be reconcilable, but to reconcile them requires a precision in the observation of symbolic behavior which ordinary impressionistic reading has not easily attained. The impressionistic reader tends to apply whichever of the two hypotheses suits the data at hand, forgetting about the other for the moment. If he is studying Hitlerism or existentialism, he thinks of the reaction to rationalism; if he is studying the TVA, he thinks of our scientific tendencies. He does not ask the precise conditions under which each hypothesis operates. Similarly, the behavior of an American, either when he joins the Ku Klux Klan or when he objects to being put into a uniform because he wants to wear what he pleases, seems natural and typical enough if we pick the appropriate generalization and forget about the opposite one.

In the same way the results of this study may seem obvious and common sense at first glance. One must bear in mind, however, that the opposite conclusions would seem equally obvious and fit common sense. If we find increasing attention in the Russian press to the symbol DEMOCRACY, the casual reader may easily say, "This is obvious. Everyone knows that the Russians have reinterpreted 'democracy' to give it their own peculiar twist and made it into a key slogan." On the other hand, if we find a decrease in attention to "DEMOCRACY," the casual reader may equally well say, "This is obvious. Everyone knows that the Russian regime is dictatorial."

The candid reader may wish to test just how obvious the results are by quizzing himself in advance on some of the key results. We therefore summarize here some of the key questions which we have attempted to answer in what follows but without now giving the results.

1. Has attention to the term DEMOCRACY increased or decreased or stood still over the past fifty years? During the past fifteen years? How has this trend differed from country to country?

2. In each of the five countries did the two World Wars result in increased attention to DEMOCRACY, or did the external threat result in reduced attention to such ideological symbols?

3. How do the papers we studied rank in attention to the symbol DEMOCRACY; to the democratic ideology as a whole; to representative government; to the people; to freedom? How do their relative positions today compare with those fifty years ago?

4. Has DEMOCRACY become a more sacred word over the years, i.e., has the proportion of favorable judgments increased? Have the components of the democratic ideology shared in any trends of favor of the term, or have those trends been independent of one another? Did the Bolsheviks express approval or disapproval of DEMOCRACY, of freedom, of the masses?

5. For any given volume of discussion of the general subject matter of democracy, in which countries will the term itself appear most; in which least? Is this a function of the greater or lesser emphasis on theory or dogma as against concrete issues in the political traditions of the country? Are there trends in this respect? Is there a fad of the word DEMOCRACY? If so, where and when?

6. How do the different papers judge the people? How did they rank in attitude before World War I? What changes have there been in attitude since? Does a mass orientation go together with concern for freedom or are they unrelated?

7. Are symbols of representative government more widely used where the practice of representative government *is,* or where it is *not,* part of the political traditions of the people?

8. Under conditions of totalitarian dictatorship, are such symbols as FREEDOM and LIBERTY frequent or are they avoided? What about discussion of dictatorship itself? Can any general rules be given? What changes and differences have there been?

II. The Word "Democracy"[4]

Attention

World summary. It is indeed true that over the past sixty years DEMOCRACY has become one of the key terms of political controversy. Before World War I, only about one out of every thirty-five editorials in our sample used the word at all. In the period since World War II, it appears in every seventh editorial. To put it differently, before World War I the symbol DEMOCRACY accounted for 1.5 percent of the occurrences of the 210 counted ideological symbols. Since World War II DEMOCRACY has accounted for over 4 percent of the symbol occurrences. The rise has been most marked around the two wars.

During World War I the word appeared in about every twentieth editorial and accounted for 2 percent of the symbol occurrences. The trend throughout the war was upward, but really great attention to DEMOCRACY appeared only in the last two years. It will be recalled that Wilson's Fourteen Points were enunciated on December 20, 1916, the czar abdicated on March 15, 1917, and America entered the war on April 6, 1917. It was only with these events that the war came to be discussed extensively in terms of DEMOCRACY. This is reflected in the percentage of the editorials using the symbol year by year:

1914	2 percent
1915	2
1916	4
1917	7
1918	12

This awakened concern with DEMOCRACY did not wane greatly after the war. Of course, there was a drop from the 1918 peak, and a slight, perhaps not significant, slacking off in attention in the late 1920s and early 1930s. But viewing the trends more broadly, one can say that in the postwar years until 1936 there was a fairly steady plateau of attention to DEMOCRACY at a level stimulated during the war. Roughly, every seventeenth editorial referred to DEMOCRACY.

The gathering clouds of World War II produced the next worldwide spurt in attention to DEMOCRACY. The significance of the rise of Hitler had become clear to all with eyes to see. Even the Communist International, which in 1933 had found nothing to choose between fascism and "social fascism" (i.e., social democracy), had, at the Seventh World Congress in 1935, reversed its line and come out for a "People's Front" to fight for DEMOCRACY against fascism. With the adoption of this new line, *Izvestia* came to be full of the word DEMOCRACY.

The symbolism of the People's Front, however, was not limited to the Communist press. It permeated liberal thought in all countries. The prestige papers being analyzed here are not generally liberal papers. By their nature, they usually represent vested interests and the status quo. Nevertheless, the interjection by leftists of the slogan "DEMOCRACY versus Fascism" into the political scene was reflected in these papers, too. It was reflected in part because these papers were discussing news which was not of their making and was sometimes made by those who sought to popularize the word DEMOCRACY. It was also reflected in part because most of these papers stood for DEMOCRACY as they conceived it and therefore could not yield the slogan by default to a rival political tendency. Furthermore, even if there had been no People's Front line, the nature of the conflict between the Nazis and the world would have caused considerable discussion of DEMOCRACY; although without the propaganda impact of the Popular Front movement, other ways of talking about the dichotomy (e.g., "FREEDOM versus tyranny," or "REPUBLICANISM versus autocracy") might have been more widely chosen than the actually dominant formula of "DEMOCRACY versus Fascism." As things really worked out, attention to DEMOCRACY doubled from the 1930-35 level to the 1935-38 level. The proportion of symbol occurrences formed by this term rose to 3 percent, and the proportion of editorials using the word went up to about one in every nine.

It will be recalled that the current rate of references to DEMOCRACY is about one reference in every seven editorials, so it is clear that only a small increase has occurred in the years since 1939. As a matter of fact, this increase in attention occurred not during the war years themselves, but with the end of the war. Words like FASCISM and NAZISM, but not DEMOCRACY, show a sharp rise in the combat years themselves. As has already been mentioned, World War II was popularized more in the name of the struggle against fascism than in the name of a struggle for DEMOCRACY. If, however, we view the whole war crisis from 1936 to 1946, we do find, as we did in World War I, a sharp increase in attention to DEMOCRACY.

The fact that two World Wars seemed to play the crucial role in making DEMOCRACY one of the central goal values of the modern world raises interesting problems. Before Pearl Harbor, pacifists and isolationists often asserted that democracy would not survive another war. The First World War, they told us, which had been fought to make the world safe for democracy, brought only fascism; and a second World War, even if won by the democracies, would make the whole world Fascist. Whatever the future may hold, it is clear in retrospect that the gloom of these Cassandras was premature, at least so far as democratic practices are concerned. So far as the symbols go, it is interesting to note that DEMOCRACY seems to be more popular than it has ever been before.

The popularity of the symbol DEMOCRACY, however, does not in itself secure the practice. The consequences of the First and Second World Wars could conceivably destroy democracy (to say nothing of what a third World War might do). These wars have so acerbated tensions and reduced security that only a blind man would dismiss the possibility of totalitarianism. Yet we must recognize that these conflicts have at the same time popularized the symbol DEMOCRACY. This fact suggests the possibility that, in the modern world, war and the danger of war, whatever they may do to the material conditions of democracy, may tend in some ways to fortify the democratic ideology.[5] For one thing, modern war so strains the resources of the nations involved that extensive effort by all becomes extremely important. The masses can demand their price for making this effort. The price may be a wider sharing of power. This more equitable sharing of power under the pressure of war is illustrated by the British income tax or the American Fair Employment Practices Commission. For another thing, the presence of an external enemy turns most people away from the quest for particularistic goals to goals that may at least be symbolized as representing the commonweal. This was well illustrated by the powerful appeal of the symbol of UNITY against fascism in the People's Front and similar movements. These movements tended to seek more and more comprehensive membership and goals that were increasingly national in scope. Such common goals need not be democratic, but democracy is one model specimen of the species.

In short, we find that concern with DEMOCRACY has increased in the modern world. We find, further, that this increase has been most marked during international conflicts. We suggest that the widespread diffusion of the modern democratic ideology is partly an outcome of those very crisis conditions which threaten its existence. Even preliminary verification, however, requires that we look beyond the global trends and consider national variations.

National trends in detail. Indeed, only the separate national statistics have any scientific validity, since there is no rational weighting for adding five national series together to get a global sample. To put it more simply: suppose the *New York Times* and *Le Temps* show opposite tendencies. To get a global picture should we simply average these two on the implicit assumption of the sovereign equality of states? Whatever its political uses, obviously, this assumption is irrelevant to objective research. Should we deliberately weight them in some other way? If so, how? No simple principle suggests itself. Should we then, in default, count, as we did above, each editorial as one, disregarding the fact that the *New York Times* has more editorials than *Le Temps?* None of these solutions is satisfactory. Clearly, we must look at the national series separately rather than try to infer a single world trend. We cited the combined figures above to present in simple form trends that are so clear and uniform throughout that a combined statement is a convenient shorthand way of saying what we otherwise would have to say more than once. We reported the results above in rough figures, since the numbers themselves have no precise significance. Let us, therefore, turn now to the individual national results. The precise ranking in use of the word DEMOCRACY is shown in Table 1. For the entire period since 1890, total attention to DEMOCRACY is greatest in the German papers.

One might suspect that this surprising fact is due to an artifact. It will be recalled that the series of German papers began in 1910. Since DEMOCRACY is an increasingly used symbol, the absence of the first two decades of the series might raise the average use of the term. Actually, however, if

Table 1
Attention to Democracy

	Percentage of Editorials Mentioning DEMOCRACY	DEMOCRACY as Percentage of Counted General Symbols*
United States	4.6	2.9
Great Britain	4.7	2.2
Russia	5.8	1.2
France	9.5	2.2
Germany	14.0	4.1

*It will be recalled that by the term "general symbols" we mean the listed symbols other than country names.

we compare the five countries only for the period since World War I the results remain virtually unchanged. The rank orders in the two columns are unaffected, and Germany's lead remains virtually the same.

The reasons for the extensive German use of the symbol DEMOCRACY become apparent when we turn to Table 2, which plots the trends in its use. Extensive German attention to DEMOCRACY began in 1918. From then through 1929 it remained consistently high. Indeed, during these postwar years the German prestige papers widely led all others in references to DEMOCRACY. Defeat had forced democracy on Germany. She was in the throes of trying to establish a new democratic government. As in the last few years, democracy was a new and vital issue, and therefore concern with the symbol DEMOCRACY was natural enough.

The subsequent failure of this democratic regime and the rise of government by decree and of the danger of fascism resulted thereafter in a rapid decline of attention to DEMOCRACY in the *Frankfurter Zeitung*. The danger of Nazism was extensively discussed, but the issue was not then being posed as DEMOCRACY versus fascism. DEMOCRACY had lost its position as a key symbol.

Hitler, however, brought that symbol back in a new way—as an object of attack. The *Völkischer Beobachter,* during the Nazi regime again ranked high in attention to DEMOCRACY.

Particularly in the latter half of World War II the Nazis ranted about the pluto-DEMOCRACIES. Later we shall find that all "devil" words became common when the fortunes of war turned against Germany. DEMOCRACY was one of these words. Thus, DEMOCRACY was an important symbol in the German press in two periods: after World War I under the new democratic Weimar regime, and during World War II when Hitler attacked it.

Over the years, other changes have taken place in the use of the term DEMOCRACY in different countries. The most striking change is in Rus-

Table 2
Attention to Democracy by Time Periods

			(a) Percentage of Editorials in Which Symbol Appears					
	Pre-World War I	World War I	1920s	Early 1930s	Late 1930s	World War II Phase 1	World War II Phase 2	Post-World War II
United States	2.1	3.8	2.8	2.9	4.9	9.9	8.1	13.0
Great Britain	3.4	7.5	4.2	4.0	7.2	10.1	4.6	7.0
Russia	.4	6.4	9.1	5.3	32.0	16.7	7.2	23.7
France	5.7	5.0	9.3	11.1	13.6	22.5	8.0	24.8
Germany	3.8	3.2	23.1	6.7	11.3	13.6	24.0	...

			(b) Percentage of General Symbols Which It Constitutes					
United States	2.1	2.0	1.6	2.2	3.6	4.7	4.0	6.1
Great Britain	1.7	3.4	2.1	2.1	2.9	3.3	1.8	2.7
Russia	.0	1.5	1.2	.7	3.4	1.8	.8	2.5
France	1.9	1.5	1.8	2.0	1.9	3.5	2.3	5.1
Germany	2.1	2.7	4.9	1.4	3.6	4.4	7.0	...

sian attention to DEMOCRACY, *Novoe Vremia,* the Russian prestige paper under the Czarist regime, paid negligible attention to that symbol. Indeed, it appeared only four times in 1,066 editorials. In the year 1917, however, it suddenly appeared in almost a third of the *Novoe Vremia* editorials, and it has remained an important symbol most of the time since. From 1918 to 1935 *Izvestia's* use of the term was moderate. The symbol appeared in fewer editorials than in Germany and France, but in more editorials than in the United States and Britain. From 1935 to 1938, the People's Front period, DEMOCRACY again appeared in almost one-third of the *Izvestia* editorials, or more than twice as frequently as in any other country. Then attention began to fall off. During the years of the Stalin-Hitler pact, attention to DEMOCRACY fell off by half. Still, one in six editorials referred to DEMOCRACY (more than in any other paper but *Le Temps*). But with Russia's actual participation in the war, attention to DEMOCRACY almost disappeared. Just 3 percent of the editorials referred to it from 1941 through 1944. The war that had originally been prepared for as a war of DEMOCRACY against fascism had now become the FATHERLAND War. Toward the end of the war, however, attention to DEMOCRACY picked up again. One-fifth of the editorials since 1945 refer to it, more than in any other paper except *Le Monde.* Since World War II, especially in 1948-49, attention picked up as Russia found herself allied with the so-called People's DEMOCRACIES. For the whole period of the Bolshevik regime DEMOCRACY appeared in 10.7 percent of the *Izvestia* editorials as compared with a fraction of one percent in *Novoe*

Vremia under the czars. Thus *Izvestia* moved from negligible attention to DEMOCRACY to moderate attention.

The same Russian trend appears if we review the data for the symbol DEMOCRACY as a percent of all counted symbols. We find moderate use after 1917, with a sharp temporary spurt in 1936-38. The relationship between *Izvestia* and other papers, however, appears very different when we thus change the base for computing percentages. The Soviet editorials were four or five times as rich in ideological symbols of all sorts as the *New York Times* or the London *Times*.[6] That was true, however, not only of DEMOCRACY, but of ideological symbols in general. Thus, when we compare DEMOCRACY with the total symbol flow, it does not appear preeminent in *Izvestia* even in the spurt in 1936-38. From 1918 through 1935 the symbol DEMOCRACY accounted for about one percent of the occurrences of counted symbols in *Izvestia,* which was less than the percentage for any other prestige paper. In fact, 1 percent is but half of the figure for the next lowest paper. After 1939 the figure for Russia is again lower than for any other country. During the war, DEMOCRACY was again but half as important a component of the total political symbol flow as in any other country, and since the war, although considerably more frequent, it is still only half as prominent in the total symbol flow as in France or the United States. From 1936 through 1938, however, DEMOCRACY was almost as prominent in *Izvestia*'s symbol flow as in any other paper. It formed about 3.5 percent of the counted symbols in the *New York Times,* in the *Völkischer Beobachter,* and in *Izvestia,* although it was in considerably less of the total editorials in the other two papers. Thus, whether we consider the proportion of editorials mentioning DEMOCRACY (in which *Izvestia* ranks high) or the proportion of all counted symbols which it forms (in which *Izvestia* ranks low), we still find that the symbol DEMOCRACY was suddenly picked up in 1936, worked for all it was worth during the years when Russia was seeking an alliance with the democracies, and then dropped when Russia reversed her world orientation.

The French, British, and American papers have been more constant in their treatment of DEMOCRACY, although showing some sharp changes during wars. The relative smoothness of trends in France, Britain, and the United States is characteristic of free presses. We shall find that a most distinctive feature of the controlled papers is the sharp fluctuations and reversals in their content patterns. As a result of following a line, totalitarian symbolism tends to be more uniform in any one period than democratic symbolism, but to fluctuate more from period to period. Democratic symbolism, though more varied at any one time, changes less sharply over time.

Nonetheless, some clear-cut trends may be discerned in the free papers.

In the *New York Times* attention to DEMOCRACY has risen notably since the New Deal and especially since World War II. In France, also, there has been a notable recent increase in attention to DEMOCRACY. DEMOCRACY was emphasized in the early phase of World War II, although under Vichy attention to it dropped off drastically.

In the London *Times* the upward trend has not been so pronounced. There was a spurt in British attention to DEMOCRACY in World War I. Attention since has generally not gone beyond the level then attained. Attention to DEMOCRACY in the London *Times* (and to a lesser extent in the *New York Times*) remains low, especially if judged by the number of editorials in which the term appears. The French papers are so much richer in ideological symbols that the symbol DEMOCRACY, although appearing far more often in the French than in the English papers, is not a more important part of the total symbol flow. By either standard, however, British attention to DEMOCRACY remains low. Perhaps this is due to the monarchy and the popularity of its symbolism. In any case, it is worthy of note that this finding of de-emphasis on the symbol DEMOCRACY in the London *Times* corresponds to British public opinion poll findings. In 1947, people in the United States, France, Sweden, Norway, Holland, Canada, and Great Britain were asked whether they considered their country a democracy. The "yes" answers ranged from 95 percent in Sweden and 88 percent in the United States, down to 65 percent in France, 57 percent in Canada, and only 50 percent in Great Britain.[7]

We noted above the relationship between war tensions and attention to DEMOCRACY. During or immediately after World War I, clear-cut increases in attention to DEMOCRACY took place in Britain, Germany, and Russia. In the crisis years of the late 1930s when Nazism threatened the democracies, attention to DEMOCRACY went up in the United States, Germany, and Russia, and during the war itself also in Britain and France.

For the recent years, since the war, we have no German sample. The press in the other countries seems to be continuing the pattern set in the previous decades. In the United States and France attention to DEMOCRACY is higher than ever. In Russia it is high, but less high than in the 1930s. In Britain the term DEMOCRACY has not yet acquired the same hold as elsewhere.

In leaving these data on attention to DEMOCRACY, it would be well to point out some of their limitations. One is naturally tempted to interpret any increase in attention to DEMOCRACY as indicating increasingly democratic attitudes. This is obviously fallacious. It disregards the possibilities of distorting the word and of discrepancies between words and practices. Also it disregards the judgments made. At least one spurt in attention to DEMOCRACY in the above data can be accounted for by attacks upon it. Nazi vitriol regarding the "plutodemocracies" resulted in more than twice as many editorials using this term during the latter years of the war as in any of the papers from the wartime United Nations. At best one may guess that an increase in attention to DEMOCRACY may indicate an increasing concern *with* democracy, not necessarily an increasing concern *for* it.

A superficial glance at the above data might lead one to think that attention to DEMOCRACY is an inverse function of the practice of democracy. That is probably not so, but it would not be altogether astonishing. Democracy is such an important and universal value of men in the modern world that those who are not true to it might find it necessary to protest their loyalty too much. This may indeed be an important factor in the increased Russian use of the term DEMOCRACY, but for the data in general it is not true to say that the increases in attention to DEMOCRACY were correlated regularly with decreasing democracy. German usage, for example, jumped most when Germany entered her most democratic period, the Weimar regime.

What the above speculations do suggest is that concern with the problem of democracy may take several different forms. It may be the concern of the partisan who wishes to popularize it, or of the partisan who wishes to damn it. It may be the concern of those who think it is in danger, or of those who think it is the surging wave of the future. It may be the concern of those who are indifferent toward it for its own sake, but who think it a convenient symbol to use because their audience responds to it. Among these different types of concern our data so far do not help us distinguish. All that we can say is that, spurred by two World Wars, in one way or another, DEMOCRACY has become a central object of political concern in the modern world. To carry our study further we must introduce some additional refinements—specifically, an examination of the judgments made of the word DEMOCRACY.

Judgment

Throughout the period studied—that is, since 1890—DEMOCRACY has been a positively charged term. In the more than eleven hundred sampled editorials that used the word, over two hundred judged it explicitly. Of these, two-thirds approved it and one-third disapproved it. This balance of judgment has not shown any marked trends on a world-wide scale. The judgments of 1890, taken as a whole, were not strikingly different from those of today.

There are, however, striking differences between papers and countries. In Britain, France, and the United States, when DEMOCRACY was judged, the judgment was almost always favorable. The percentage which favorable judgments form of the total of all judgments (both favorable and unfavorable) is: Britain, 88 percent, France, 85 percent; the United States, 82 percent.

Another formula for expressing bias gives heavy weight to the neutral statements. The alternative index is[8]

$$\frac{\text{favorable} - \text{unfavorable}}{\text{favorable} + \text{unfavorable} + \text{neutral}} \quad \text{or} \quad \frac{\text{favorable} - \text{unfavorable}}{\text{all instances of term}}$$

If the ratio of favorable to unfavorable items is the same in two cases this index will clearly give a higher value to the more value-charged text, i.e., the one with fewer neutral statements. The index used in the previous paragraph we shall represent as $f / f + u$; this second one we shall represent as $f - u/r$. The latter index for the editorials from the three countries is: France, 0.16; Britain, 0.06; the United States, 0.05. The high value of this index for the French papers is due to the fact that 23 percent of all their references to DEMOCRACY contained value judgments, whereas such judgments were found in only 7 percent of the references in the London *Times* and 8 percent of the references in the *New York Times*. This finding, however, has no special bearing on DEMOCRACY, since it is a general characteristic of French newspaper writing to contain many value judgments and a general characteristic of the London *Times* and *New York Times* to contain few.[9] Our first index, $f / f + u$, is, therefore, clearly the more useful one for most intercountry comparisons and reveals the common favorable attitude toward DEMOCRACY in the press of the democracies.

In Russia and Germany the press has been ambivalent toward DEMOCRACY. In the Russian editorials 61 percent of the judgments have been favorable, and in Germany less than half (40 percent). In these two countries even more than in France the press has made explicit its value judgments. In Russia, 46 percent of all references to DEMOCRACY were judged; in Germany, 39 percent. The results for these two countries, however, vary greatly from period to period. In Britain, France, and the United States, DEMOCRACY has been a favorable word to about the same degree from the beginning to the end of our sixty-year period. Not so in Russia and Germany. In *Novoe Vremia* DEMOCRACY was too little discussed for any valid conclusions to be drawn. Most of the references were neutral, and the few favorable and unfavorable ones balanced. With the triumph of Bolshevism DEMOCRACY became a much-used word, but a word whose evaluation has been completely reversed from the years of the Revolution till today. DEMOCRACY started out as a word for condemnation and has become overwhelmingly a word for praise. In the first two years of the Revolution the term was used in 12 percent of the editorials, never favorably: 86 percent of these instances were antagonistic and the rest neutral. From 1920 to 1924 the term was used in 8 percent of the editorials, and, of these, 63 percent were antagonistic and again the rest neutral. Following the end of the Leninist era, the term DEMOCRACY was used in only 6 percent of the editorials from 1925 through 1934, and, among these, favorable and unfavorable judgments were evenly distributed. In other words, as the dictatorship consolidated itself, it no longer openly condemned DEMOCRACY, but it did not talk very much about it. Then in the period of the complete entrenchment of Stalin's dictatorship something very remarkable happened. DEMOCRACY was suddenly picked up for extensive use and became a very favorable symbol. Eighteen percent of the editorials after 1935 contained the term, and 97 percent of the judgments were favorable.

It is clear that the Bolshevik tradition contains both favorable and unfavorable attitudes toward democracy. Marx and Engels talked of the outcome of the revolution both in terms of democracy and of the dictatorship of the proletariat. In Russia the Social Democratic Labor party was the organization from which both Bolsheviks and Mensheviks emerged. While the term "social democratic" had thus once been a positive term, after the first World War Lenin deliberately adopted "Communist" as a substitute for it and attacked the European social democrats. Throughout his life Lenin called himself a "consistent democrat"; at the same time he attacked the incompleteness of the conclusions of the mere "democrats." The dictatorship of the proletariat was described as the "democratic dictatorship of workers and peasants." From these samples the historical ambivalence of the Bolsheviks to democracy is clear. What is interesting in our results, however, is that in the Leninist period the adverse usages of DEMOCRACY predominated in frequency in the public press, while in the even more autocratic Stalinist period the favorable usages came to predominate.

This is a recurrent pattern. In the early Bolshevik writings many of the unpalatable and shocking implications of Bolshevik theory are presented baldly and publicly. In the more recent Bolshevik writings a process of sugarcoating has taken place, so that statements counter to the utopian predispositions of the reader disappear.

The Stalinist press also tends to present a black-and-white picture in which the self can do no wrong and the enemy no right, and in which every attribute is either good or bad with no ambivalence.[10] Thus the party no longer engages in subtle dialectical distinctions by which it claims to be DEMOCRATIC and at the same time in its popular press condemns simple DEMOCRACY or social democracy. These anti-Communist forms of democracy are denied even a vestige of claim to the term. Their partisans are said to be not democrats at all, but ones who merely pretend to be democrats for demagogic purposes. They are "social fascists" or "lackeys of American imperialism." The term DEMOCRAT, or DEMOCRACY, which started out more often unfavorable than favorable, thus became univocally favorable after a cooling-off period in which it was little used. We shall see other instances of this pattern later.

In Germany the changes in editorial judgment of DEMOCRACY are far less subtle. Under Weimar it is a favored term; under the Nazis an unfavored one. Between 1919 and 1929, 83 percent of the judgments were *for* DEMOCRACY. Under the Nazis 100 percent of the judgments were *against.* (For the other periods there are too few judgments to allow any confident statement.) Thus significant changes in judgment of DEMOCRACY occurred in the German and Russian, but not in the other samples studied, which remained uniformly favorable to the symbol DEMOCRACY throughout.

III. Democracy and the Democratic Ideology

Correlations Between Them

We have seen that throughout the Western world there has been a sharp rise in the use of the symbol DEMOCRACY. But what has this meant for the contents of the democratic ideology? Does an increase in references to DEMOCRACY mean that there is also increased concern with its attributes? To investigate this problem we drew up a list of terms referring to the three main components of democracy: representative government, freedom, and a mass orientation. The terms used as an index of representative government were CONSTITUTIONALISM, PARLIAMENTARISM, POPULAR SOVEREIGNTY, and MAJORITY RULE. Among the terms used to measure mass orientation were PEOPLE, MASSES, WORKING CLASS, PROLETARIAT. Among the terms used to measure concern with freedom were, on the one hand, LIBERTY, FREEDOM, particular freedoms or rights, SELF-DETERMINATION, and INDIVIDUALISM, and, sometimes, on the other hand, TYRANNY, DICTATORSHIP, AUTHORITARIANISM, ABSOLUTE MONARCHY, and so on. These three groups combined plus a number of other individual symbols (e.g., CLASSLESS SOCIETY) that did not clearly fit into any one of the three main components of democracy constituted our total index of concern with the democratic ideology. The complete index, which consists of about sixty words (counting major synonyms), is given in Appendix D. With this index we could test whether changes in attention to the term DEMOCRACY were correlated with changes in attention to the whole complex.

The chain of language. We should expect to find some sort of correlation, since words occur in clusters, not at random. A sentence, a paragraph, or an article containing the word "caste" is more likely also to contain the word "India" than is one containing the word "reindeer." As Shannon and Weaver have shown, language is a Markoff chain, that is, a stochastic process in which the probabilities depend on the previous events.[11]

Suppose that in the normal course of events a Frenchman, or an Englishman, or an American were to engage in conversation about democracy. The structure of his ideology is such that in a free flow of his thoughts there would in the long run exist rather definite functional relationships between the frequencies of his use of a number of such words as DEMOCRACY, FREEDOM, and EQUALITY. As he talked more or talked less about the general subject matter of democracy, he would be apt to use more or fewer of these words to an extent which could be expressed in a series of equations.

Needless to say, any one symbol or set of symbols would be only a partial determinant of the frequency of any other. There is an equation for each pair of terms, or each pair of sets of terms. The total flow could perhaps be described by a set of equations equal to the number of pairs of words in the language, although, in practice, better predictions would probably result from equations treating idioms consisting of several words as units. Whatever the unit used, the problem is still one of multiple correlation.

Thus the frequency of the symbol DEMOCRACY is a joint function of several sets of terms. Among these we may list the three components of the democratic ideology listed above: freedom, representative government, and a mass orientation. Depending on the culture and the ideology, the symbol DEMOCRACY will be a different function of each of these, and, as we shall see below, these differences are highly significant. One tradition may define DEMOCRACY as freedom while another defines it in terms of the will of the masses. Such differences may be expressed by different equations.

Democracy and antidemocracy. In similar fashion, DEMOCRACY is a different function of words expressing its presence and of words expressing its absence. The same thought may logically be expressed with either kind of word. One may justify the same step by saying one wishes FREEDOM of the press or by saying one opposes CENSORSHIP. It is for most purposes irrelevant whether a writer chooses to say that he stands for FREEDOM or that he stands against TYRANNY. Similarly, he may defend a more EQUAL distribution of wealth or he may attack the PLUTOCRACY. He may call this "a land of government by the PEOPLE" or "a land where DICTATORSHIP will never be tolerated." Yet in practice the two sets of terms are different functions of still other sets of terms and are therefore not identical functions of the term DEMOCRACY. Thus in the United States the word DICTATORSHIP is very highly correlated with the word DEMOCRACY. The two words form a pair which are commonly contrasted. The term DICTATORSHIP is commonly used to criticize oppressive governments abroad or oppressive officials at home. The word

DICTATORSHIP is seldom used in a context where the word DEMOC-RACY is not also very likely. In Russia, on the other hand, the incidence of these two terms, though correlated, is probably correlated less highly, since DICTATORSHIP also forms part of another common constellation of concepts. The DICTATORSHIP OF THE PROLETARIAT is a phrase that will often occur there in paragraphs about RUSSIA, or about the October REVOLUTION, or about CAPITALISTS, or about law enforcement. In these contexts the probability of the incidence of the term DEMOCRACY is less than in the more limited context in which DIC-TATORSHIP is apt to be used in the United States.

We might say the same thing about the word NAZI. A French, American, or Russian editorial discussing NAZISM would be apt to discuss it as a political principle of an undemocratic kind. An editorial in the *Völkischer Beobachter* might have referred to NAZISM in connection with such subjects as the state of the theater, the spectacle at Nuremberg, or the level of employment, without ever relating it to the general ideological counterposition of dictatorship and democracy.

In general, it seems fair to assume that, except in those situations in which given undemocratic practices usually prevail, words referring to these practices are generally used in a context which evokes thoughts of the contrast between these practices and democratic goal values. This assumption is validated by the fact that the correlations between the incidence of the term DEMOCRACY and the incidence of terms referring to its lack are somewhat higher than the correlations between the incidence of DEMOCRACY and that of other terms referring to its presence. In view of this fact we may feel justified in generally pooling these different groups of terms while recognizing that we are actually dealing with joint functions.[12]

The normal equations of DEMOCRACY. Since the use of any one symbol is a joint function of the use of others, the ideological structure of a given communicator on a given topic may be described by his set of equations relating the key symbols relevant to that topic. His ideological predisposition toward democracy, for instance, may be expressed by his set of equations for the word DEMOCRACY.

Predisposition, however, is one thing. The actual outcome in a concrete situation is another. Chance and stimuli outside of the ideological predisposition also affect the flow of communications.

In the course of a discussion the flow of words is affected, for example, by external events. Arguments by an opponent have to be answered and current events alluded to. Thus, the contemporaneous existence of a colonial war for independence or the presentation by an opponent of arguments based on the discrepancy between the democratic ideal and colonial practice would induce use of the term SELF-DETERMINATION greater than that which would occur in a spontaneous and undirected flow of communication. But if we can identify the normal equations representing the distribution of terms which a speaker is predisposed to emit we are in a better position to analyze the effect of particular events upon the flow of his communications.

On the whole, it appears that we can establish some such normal equations for the term DEMOCRACY. Our data are inadequate to support the kind of multiple correlation between a number of groups of terms with the term DEMOCRACY which the problem ideally calls for. Now that the problem has been identified, future investigations may well be designed to do this. Here, however, we can deal with the relation between the term DEMOCRACY and the entire group of other listed democracy-related terms. Occasionally we may also separate those terms that refer to the presence of democracy from those that refer to its absence. Let us start, however, with the simplest overall correlations.

The correlations between the proportion of editorials using the term DEMOCRACY and the proportion using the constellation of listed terms representing the democratic ideology are as follows: United States, +.64; Great Britain, +.76; France, +.70; Russia, +.67; Germany, +.45. Since we are dealing with such small numbers (seven to nine periods in each case), the significance of any one correlation alone is worthy of but hesitant respect. (Using "t" we find that the chance that there is actually no positive correlation is .09, .03, .05, and .31, respectively.) The five samples, however, confirm one another by their common tendency. They provide strong evidence for the expected positive relationship between incidence of the term DEMOCRACY and incidence of the rest of the correlation. This repeated pattern could hardly be attributed to chance.

Because of this consistency, we feel justified in taking a further important but more speculative step. We may hypothesize equations for the relationship in each sample of editorials, based upon the findings in that sample.

We cannot derive the slope and shape of these normal equations from any theoretical model of the relationship of DEMOCRACY to the constellation of related terms. Except for the above theory which predicts that they will be positively correlated, no theory exists relating the two variables. We must derive the equations from the data. In making predictions, however, nothing obliges us to follow the regressions found in the data if we have reason to suspect peculiarities in some of them.

Specifically, when a single equation fits most periods very well, but one or a few periods depart from it widely, it is more reasonable to take as our hypothesis the equation which ordinarily works rather than the equation which includes the deviant periods. The deviant periods may be treated as exceptions which must be explained in terms of special variables. The best prediction for the future would take into account both the general hypothesis and any such special factors as might come into operation.

Normal equations excluding apparently deviant periods were computed for each country. In the discussion below we shall use these equations as our hypotheses of the relationship between the incidence of the symbol DEMOCRACY and the incidence of related symbols. To indicate why we hypothesize these normal patterns rather than the regression equations which our data yield, we report in Table 3 the correlations for these selected periods. (It is clear that no ordinary interpretation in terms of significance can be given these figures.)[13]

Table 3
Correlations in Normal Periods

Sample	Correlations	Number of Periods
United States	.72	7
Great Britain	.94	7
France	.97	6
Russia	.90	6
Germany	.69	5

In at least three cases we seem to have a rather good basis for formulating a hypothesis. The regression equations, which are derived from the above data and are used as our hypotheses for the normal relationship of the symbol DEMOCRACY to the rest of the sixty relevant listed symbols, are listed below.

$$
\begin{array}{ll}
\text{United States} & y = 1.5 + .18x \\
\text{Great Britain} & y = -0.2 + .13x \\
\text{France} & y = -5.4 + .20x \\
\text{Russia} & y = -1.0 + .04x \\
\text{Germany} & y = 1.8 + .15x \\
\end{array}
$$

y = Frequency of DEMOCRACY
x = Frequency of related words

The interpretation of these equations is quite simple. With one possible exception the curves all nearly cut the origin. This means that normal use of the word DEMOCRACY is the simplest possible function of attention to the subject matter. Except in Russia, the *"b"* values indicate that DEMOCRACY will appear once to every five to eight occurrences of other words from our list of sixty symbols relevant to the subject. In the Russian papers it may be expected once to every twenty-five occurrences of these other words.

Clearly the word DEMOCRACY is far less important in the ideology of the Russian editorialist than in that of the London *Times* or *New York Times* writers. In total use of the term, the Russian writers did not differ much from their English or American colleagues, but that is because their attention to relevant subject matters was so much greater. The Russian editorials were full of discussions of the condition of the MASSES. They were full of demands for FREEDOM and LIBERTY. But these discussions were less often placed in the conceptual framework of DEMOCRACY than they would have been by a Western writer. To the Western writer the word DEMOCRACY means such things as LIBERTY and EQUALITY; he cannot discuss them without frequently introducing the name of the master concept—DEMOCRACY—of which they are a part. The Russian editorial writer generally gives a less exalted place to the term DEMOCRACY. It is for him not an inevitable term in discussions of those things which we consider to be the democratic ideology.

One reason for this is that ideas that are conceptualized in the West as DEMOCRACY are thought of in Russia as belonging in a different ideological category. Discussions of EQUALITY, FREEDOM, the welfare of the MASSES, etc., which in the West are referred back to the key goal value of DEMOCRACY, will, in Russia, be referred back to other values: now presumably to socialism or communism, in Czarist days presumably to the good of the Fatherland or its people.

As a result, the word DEMOCRACY is played down in the Russian press compared with what it would be in discussions of similar subject matter in the Western press. *Izvestia*'s attention to the symbols of the democratic ideology has to be about five times as great as that of the *New York Times* or the London *Times* before we may expect equal use of the word DEMOCRACY itself. There are and have been exceptions to this generalization, which we shall discuss below. For the moment we are concerned only with the general rule. Contrary to widespread opinion, it is clear that in both Czarist and Bolshevist Russia a common ideological predisposition prevailed in the use of the term DEMOCRACY, a predisposition which tended to de-emphasize it.

Although the striking thing about the Russian normal pattern is its uniquely low emphasis on DEMOCRACY, the striking thing about the other papers is the close similarity in their normal equations. The concept of DEMOCRACY may be favored by some and opposed by others, but its meaning is apparently sufficiently clearly established in the West so that the context in which the word is used is fairly similar in samples from several papers in three languages. How much similarity there is may be indicated by pooling the data from the Western subsamples. The correlation coefficient for all thirty-one periods for all four Western powers combined is .69. For the three Western democracies—Britain, France, and the United States—it is .78. The common regression equation for the four Western powers, omitting the same abnormal periods as above, is $y = +.35 + .15x$ $(r = .77)$, and for the three democracies it is $y = -1.00 + .16x$ $(r = .92)$. Clearly, a common usage prevails among these Western papers. There undoubtedly are small differences among the Western usages, but they are too small to be established with the size of samples we are using. Even the British equation, which differs most from the others, may easily differ purely by chance, for a moderate change in one point would eliminate the difference. Thus we cannot assert anything about the various Western equations except that, in contrast to the Russian pattern, they are broadly uniform. In the West the symbol DEMOCRACY has been about four times as frequently used as in the Russian editorials, the context being held constant.

Predispositions and stimuli. In previous studies of ideology it was not possible to hold the context constant in any satisfactory manner. How much a change in prominence of an idea or theme reflected a true ideological change, and how much it reflected a change in circumstances, was pure guesswork. The kind of equations we have developed here reduce the guesswork considerably. We can say how prominent an idea or symbol would normally be, given prevailing topics of interest. Allowing for this, we can then estimate the extent of other and variable forces giving it prominence.

In the case of the symbol DEMOCRACY, roughly half of the variance in the editorials studied was usually attributable to variations in attention to the relevant subject matter rather than to changes in attitude toward the symbol. Any fad or change in attitude toward the symbol would be indicated not by a simple change in its frequency but by deviation from the normal equation. To the extent that there is a correlation, the frequency of the term DEMOCRACY is explained by the context in which it appears. The imperfection of the correlation measures the influence of other forces. In our samples the percentage of variance of the word DEMOCRACY which is attributable to variation in the frequency of related symbols is: *New York Times,* 41 percent; London *Times,* 58 percent; French papers, 49 percent; Russian papers, 45 percent; German papers, 20 percent. While these figures show that there is a decided functional relationship between the word DEMOCRACY and its context, they also clearly show that other forces strongly affect the frequency of use of the word DEMOCRACY. It is to these other forces that we shall now turn.

We can judge when such other forces are demonstrably in operation by use of the chi-square test. In every one of our national samples the departures from the hypothesis were considerably greater than could be accounted for by chance. But of the forty period samples only thirteen had frequencies of the symbol DEMOCRACY which deviated from hypothesis more than might happen by chance five times in one hundred. In these thirteen periods, then, forces were demonstrably in operation which changed the symbolic flow regarding DEMOCRACY from that predictable from the normal predisposition of the paper.

What were these forces? The first and most obvious one to consider would be the possibility of a long-run trend. Has there been a fad of the word DEMOCRACY?

Trends.   There is a widespread belief that the symbol DEMOCRACY has been the subject of an ideological fad. Many writers on intellectual trends assert that the word has recently grown in political popularity. There is only partial justification for this assertion. The true picture is less simple than that which impressionistic observers tend to draw. There has been, as noted above, a marked increase in the use of the term DEMOCRACY during the past fifty years. But as we now see, about half of this increase has been due to increasing attention to the entire subject matter of democracy and dictatorship rather than to a changed treatment of the symbol. Democracy-relevant words of all kinds have increased in incidence. The change is more a change in subject of attention than a fad of a word. The recent use of the word DEMOCRACY is not uniformly greater than it would have been *in the same context* at earlier times in the past half-century.

In the editorials of the *New York Times,* however, we do have evidence of an upward trend in use of the word DEMOCRACY. Of the eight periods into which we have divided the half-century, three deviate significantly from the hypothesis. Of these, one is the first period, that is, through 1913; and another is the last period, that is, since 1946. In the first period, before the First World War, DEMOCRACY appeared only 54 percent as often as expected. In the last period, since the Second World War, it has appeared 119 percent more often than expected. Thus our data naturally divide into three segments: the period before World War I, when the word DEMOCRACY appeared only half as often as normal; the interbellum; and, finally, the period since World War II, when DEMOCRACY appeared twice as often as normal. The interbellum periods conformed closely to the hypothetical expectations except for the three years 1930-32. In those years democracy-related words fell off sharply, although the word DEMOCRACY itself did not. Therefore, DEMOCRACY was 139 percent more common than expected during this particular period. Why the other words of the index fell off is difficult to say. The times were such that one would have expected much reference to the mass-orientation component of democracy. Veterans' marches and movements of the unemployed and farmers figured heavily in the news. Perhaps the *New York Times* editorials used the recipe of confidence to bring back prosperity. Whatever the explanation of this short deviation, however, the general picture remains clear. In the *New York Times* editorials, there was after each World War a marked increase in *relative* attention to the symbol DEMOCRACY.

In no other sample, however, do we find any such obvious trend. In the London *Times* in the pre-World War I period the use of the word DEMOCRACY is less than expected from the frequency of related words. It appears only 75 percent as often as hypothesized. During World War I the word was heavily worked, appearing 112 percent more often than expected. Since then, however, in no period has use of DEMOCRACY deviated from expectation by more than chance would account for. In Britain no general trend is visible, although there was an increase in use of DEMOCRACY at the time of World War I.

In Germany no permanent change is visible. In the *Frankfurter Zeitung* the word DEMOCRACY was extensively used in the early years of the Weimar regime and then used less than normal in the last years of the regime. The *Völkischer Beobachter* used it little at first, but later the attacks on the plutodemocracies brought it back to the typical frequency of use.

In France and Russia the only evidence of a general autonomous trend is an increase in the use of the term DEMOCRACY in the past few years. In *Le Temps,* the only period in which use of the symbol DEMOCRACY departed significantly from expectation was 1936-38. This was a time when the fad of the word DEMOCRACY is supposed to have been in full swing. The defense of DEMOCRACY against fascism was a key political concept of the period. At the same time, however, France was seized by strikes and by the agitation of the Popular Front. As a result, there was a marked increase in attention to LABOR, the MASSES, and the PEOPLE—all terms included in that component of the democratic ideology which we call mass orientation. In other words, special circumstances boosted attention to one part of the democratic ideology without boosting attention to the word DEMOCRACY. Thus, in the most recent prewar years, when the supposed fad of the word DEMOCRACY was at its height, attention to that symbol was only 59 percent of expectation.

During World War II, use of the symbol DEMOCRACY was normal, both before and after the fall of France. Since the war our sample has been drawn from *Le Monde,* and in this sample DEMOCRACY is, indeed, more frequent than in the previous *Le Temps* samples. The word appears 80 percent more often than expected.

The Russian sample we shall examine more intensively below. At the moment we need note only that the periods in which use of the symbol DEMOCRACY varies significantly from expectation are 1936-38, 1939-40, and 1946-49, all recent periods. In all of these DEMOCRACY is more common than hypothesized.

Thus, it is true that if we take the end points of the half-century which

DEMOCRACY AND THE DEMOCRATIC IDEOLOGY 173

we are studying, in each sample except the German there is a significant change in the way in which the word DEMOCRACY is used. It is used more now than before, but, except in the United States, the data are characterized rather by constancy over the decades than by a sustained trend, and certainly not by a fad. The change in France—to the extent that it is a genuine change—is a product of the last few years, whereas in the London *Times* no significant increase in use of the term has occurred since World War I. The usual assertion about a fad of the word DEMOCRACY can be sustained only in some qualified ways.

What is usually meant in asserting that there is a fad in the use of the word is that it is used more, not because the context of discussion requires it, but because the use of the symbol has acquired an aura of its own. We find that the use of the term DEMOCRACY has increased, but that much of the increase can be accounted for by greater discussion of relevant subject matters. The unexplained half of the increase, some of which could certainly have arisen from verbal fads, has occurred in varying times and circumstances. In two countries this increase is largely a phenomenon of the last few years, in one it was a phenomenon of World War I, in one it was a fairly steady trend, and in one it did not occur in our sample. Although there is some basis for asserting a fad in the word DE-MOCRACY, we cannot be as dogmatic about it as some authors have been.

A simplified dichotomy, DEMOCRACY versus DICTATORSHIP. Our data lend only limited support to the belief that the word DEMOCRACY has acquired an aura causing it to be used more in any given context than fifty years ago, but a related trend can nonetheless be established. There is a tendency to simplify the dichotomy between DEMOCRACY and its absence. DEMOCRACY is the word apt to be used today to contrast with TYRANNY, DICTATORSHIP, or AUTHORITARIANISM, where fifty years ago FREEDOM, REPUBLICANISM, or CONSTITUTIONAL GOV-ERNMENT might have been used.

The equations just used relate DEMOCRACY to all listed words relevant to either the presence or absence of democracy. Now if we separate those symbols which refer to the presence of democracy from those which refer to its absence, we can compute separate correlations and normal equations just as above. We need not go through the results in detail, for on the whole they do not change the picture. The correlations between symbols referring to democratic practices and DEMOCRACY are of the same order of magnitude as those reported above. Furthermore, in the normal equations the *"a"* values (with one exception) are similar, i.e., close to zero. The *"b"* values are, of course, higher, since our list of index words is now but part of the previous list.

In the American and French samples a chronological trend emerges somewhat more strongly than it did above, now that we look only at the relationship between the word DEMOCRACY and other words referring to democratic practices. In the French sample before World War I, DEMOC-RACY is but 50 percent as frequent as expected, and in the 1920s it is 71 percent as frequent as expected. For the reason noted above, it is only 37 percent as frequent as expected in 1936-38. Otherwise, the various periods conform to expectation. In other words, if we take 1930 as the breaking point, except for the World War I years before and 1936-38 since, use of DEMOCRACY has been more common in the last two decades than in the first three.

In the *New York Times* sample the picture is clearer. The trend is shown in Table 4.

In the British sample, only the pre-World War I period departs from expectation, as it did above, but it does so more than above. In the London *Times* in the quarter-century before World War I, DEMOCRACY is only 54 percent as frequent as predictable from words referring to democratic practices.

Thus we find that the evidence for a trend toward increasing use of DEMOCRACY is stronger when we compare it only with terms of roughly parallel meaning and exclude terms referring to an absence of democracy. In other words, DEMOCRACY is increasingly used where EQUALITY or CONSTITUTIONAL GOVERNMENT, or government by the PEOPLE might have been used by an editorial writer of fifty years ago. At the same time, the increase in its incidence has been no greater than the increase in discussions of the threats of DICTATORSHIP, PLUTOCRACY, and so on. The change has consisted of a simplification of the polarity between democracy, on the one hand, and threats to it, on the other. DEMOC-RACY has replaced some equivalent terms, although it has not become

Table 4

Deviations of Use of DEMOCRACY from Predicted Frequency (percentage of expected)

Pre-World War I	39
World War I	53
1920s	49
1930-32	315
1933-38	109*
1939-41	103*
1942-45	144
1946-49	153

*Not a significant departure.

much more prominent in the total constellation. It has become more a standard formula to counterpose to the dangers that beset it.

The effect of controls on usage. The suggestion of trends in usage may thus explain some, though not all, of the significant departures from hypothesized frequencies of the symbol DEMOCRACY. In the Russian and German samples, another factor which causes deviations is also apparent: deliberate changes of line in a controlled press.

The Russian trend, characteristically, partakes more of a sudden change in directives than of an evolution. The normal relationship between DEMOCRACY and other democratic terms is departed from most in the years from 1936 through 1938, also significantly in the years 1939-40, and again since World War II. In the first of those three periods DEMOCRACY occurred 335 percent more often than expected, a larger deviation than in any other sample. In the other two periods DEMOCRACY occurred 148 and 163 percent more often than expected. The correlation for the rest of the half-century was found to be .90, indicating a rather well defined relationship. The few extreme departures from normal patterns beautifully illustrate the effect of a controlled propaganda line.

During the brief period when the Russian regime, frightened by the rise of Nazism, oriented its foreign policy toward a temporary alliance with the Western democracies, the historical Russian pattern of low attention to DEMOCRACY was abruptly departed from. Then, as noted above, the Communist line proclaimed itself to be the defense of DEMOCRACY versus fascism. DEMOCRACY became the key goal value to which policies were referred both by the Comintern and by the Russian domestic press. As a result, from 1936 through 1938 Russian symbol structure seems to have approximated the Western, in this respect; 32 percent of the editorials mentioned DEMOCRACY. By the Russian equation the expected number would have been 7.5 percent, but by the consolidated Western equation it would have been 29 percent, or close to the actual percentage.

There is a widespread misapprehension that the canonization of the symbol DEMOCRACY which took place in Russia in the middle 1930s became a stable part of the Soviet line. It is true that the judgment of this symbol, once assigned such a high station in the structure of Soviet values, has remained an exclusively positive one. Judgments of it have not recently changed. But its importance in the structure of Soviet symbolism has fluctuated. For a while, attention reverted to a level consistent with Russian ideology from Czarist times on. With the Stalin-Hitler pact and the outbreak of the war in 1939, the reversion to the normal Russian pattern set in. During the two years before Russia's actual involvement in the war, popular recollection of the old line (which, according to the meager evidence that exists, seems to have been fairly popular) was still sufficiently strong to require an explicit affirmation of the consistency of the new line with DEMOCRACY. As a result, for these two years the pattern of attention was halfway between the Western and the Russian patterns. During World War II itself, however, DEMOCRACY was a little-used symbol, and the traditional Russian pattern was closely adhered to.

Since the second World War DEMOCRACY has again become a popular term, but in a new context. Russia has acquired a series of satellites which she calls the People's DEMOCRACIES. Discussion of them and of related matters helped keep attention to DEMOCRACY up even when attention to such of its components as freedom and the masses was low. For the first two years after World War II, attention to DEMOCRACY was not much greater than might be expected. There was no significant departure in frequency of the word DEMOCRACY in 1946-47 from the frequency expected on the basis of normal Russian usage. But in 1948 and 1949, although attention to freedom, to the masses, and to other components of the democratic ideology fell sharply, use of the word DEMOCRACY did not: it was used 356 percent more than expected. For different reasons and in a different context, the frequency pattern of 1936-38 was equaled, and, for the moment, the term DEMOCRACY again received disproportionate attention. *Izvestia* in 1948-49 used the term almost exactly as much as Western editorials would have in the same context. The word DEMOCRACY appeared in 28 percent of the editorials against an unexpected frequency of only 6 percent by the Russian equation but 25 percent by the Western.

To some extent we may say that, in adopting the term DEMOCRACY in the 1930s and again in the last couple of years, the Soviet elite has mimicked Western ideology. It has done so, however, in a heavy-handed fashion. At no period does a Russian paper show attention to DEMOCRACY and the democratic ideology of the same order as found in the West. Obviously, in those periods when the normal Russian equation is conformed to, either attention to the word DEMOCRACY must be much lower, or attention to the entire subject matter must be much greater, than in the Western democracies. However, even in those periods when the term DEMOCRACY was selected as a key symbol and was used according to the Western pattern, the frequencies matched only hypothetical Western values. The balance between DEMOCRACY and related words was the balance one would predict for a situation in which attention to the subject matter was far greater than it ever became in the Western prestige papers. When *Izvestia* chose to use Western symbol patterns, it used them with a repetitiousness and frequency which no editorialist not following a line would have allowed.

These similarities and differences between *Izvestia* and the Western papers raise a number of interesting questions that only further research can answer. We do not know to what extent these equations are characteristic of the ideology dominant in the culture or to what extent they would vary from medium to medium within the culture. The equations would, of course, be different for different media, but how much so? Would the equation for the *New Republic,* for example, closely approximate that for the *New York Times,* with only the contexts differing, or would it be one which places more stress on the word DEMOCRACY in any given context? Whatever the equation, the actual frequencies would certainly be different from those found in the *Times.* Would the pattern perhaps resemble that of *Izvestia* in 1936-38 and 1948-49 in containing much more emphasis on the whole subject matter of democratic values while conforming in general to the same equations as the *New York Times?* Perhaps someday we shall be able in some such way to identify the constants and variables in the flow of symbols in different cultures and ideologies. Then we shall be able to apply significant measures to any relevant body of text and place it ideologically. Now, however, that is not possible.

Like the Russian data, the German data also reveal sharp fluctuations in usage. Both Russia and Germany have felt the shock of drastic revolutionary events more often and more sharply than have the democracies, and this, together with the fact that periodic shifts in the imposed line have forced the communicators to modify the spontaneous flow of their ideas, would lead us to expect a less consistent symbolic pattern in these two countries over the years. To some extent this expectation is confirmed. The correlation between references to DEMOCRACY and references to the rest of the constellation in the German press is only .45. Before and during World War I, the *Deutsche allgemeine Zeitung* editorials conformed fairly closely to the normal German and Western pattern. Since then the symbolic pattern of the German press has fluctuated widely and diversely. With the Weimar regime the word DEMOCRACY, which during World War I had been a slogan of the Allies and of opposition parties, was adopted into elite symbolism. In fact, the word appeared 171 percent more often than expected. This extensive use of the symbol DEMOCRACY continued through 1929.

The subsequent German reaction against this word becomes apparent in the 1930-32 period, although there is no corresponding reaction against discussion of related elements of the democratic complex. On the contrary, discussion of problems relevant to democracy is greater in these years than in any other period in the time span studied. It is only the word DEMOCRACY itself that disappears in the crisis of the early 1930s. Discussion of problems of democracy increased to the point where expected use of the word might have doubled, but actually it fell off by two-thirds. As a result, the frequency of the word DEMOCRACY was only 31 percent of normal.[14]

Under the Nazis, DEMOCRACY was mainly mentioned in scorn. In judgment, Nazi usage reversed the usage elsewhere. In context and frequency it differed, too, although less. From 1933 through 1938, the prewar Nazi years, the symbol DEMOCRACY was played down, though not so much as in 1930-32. It appeared only 58 percent as often as expected from the normal German equation, or 68 percent as often as would be expected in the three Western democratic papers.

With the coming of the war, however, attacks on the plutodemocracies multiplied. Considerations of diplomacy no longer required a subduing of attacks upon them. Until 1941 the democracies, rather than the Bolshe-viks, were the main enemy. Consequently, the incidence of the word DEMOCRACY increased until it again appeared as often as normal and as often as it would have in Western papers.

Actually this is an understatement. We noted above that characteristics of the Nazi situation make the list of symbols which includes antidemo-cratic words a less meaningful correlate of the symbol DEMOCRACY than the list which alludes exclusively to democratic practices. NAZI, FUEHRER, and similar symbols were used with great frequency in con-texts quite unrelated to democracy. Because of this fact, and because they were used to refer to all kinds of political events and activities, it is important to examine the correlation between the incidence of DEMOC-RACY and the incidence of other words referring to democratic practices alone.[15] In our other samples, separating out this group of words does not substantially change the results. Germany, however, went from an authori-tarian regime to a democratic one and then to a totalitarian one. In conse-quence, the balance between words referring to democracy and those referring to its absence is far from stable.

Under the democratic Weimar regime, it will be recalled that the use of the term DEMOCRACY was greater than we should have expected from the total context. It is, on the other hand, no greater than predictable from the context of other words referring to democracy. In other words, what happened under Weimar was a relative decline of use of all words of antidemocratic reference and, correspondingly, a relative increase in inci-dence of all words referring to democracy. The symbol DEMOCRACY alone was not singled out for stress; rather all kinds of democratic prac-tices were.

In the last three years of the Weimar regime, however, we find, as we did above, a great de-emphasis on the word DEMOCRACY while related words increased in frequency. DEMOCRACY appeared only 25 percent as often as the incidence of other words referring to democratic practices would have led us to predict.

After 1933, as we just noted, the use of words alluding to undemocratic practices greatly increased. Consequently, the symbol DEMOCRACY was less frequent than predictable from the incidence of all related words. But if we compare its incidence with that of words referring to democratic practices only, it is no longer significantly less common than predictable. In other words, DEMOCRACY continued to be a fairly stable function of words like EQUALITY, FREEDOM, and the PEOPLE.

This continued to be so until the latter half of World War II. Then, when the fortunes of war turned against the Nazis, they responded by vituperation.[16] As we shall repeatedly note, all the devil symbols became very common in the last years of the war. DEMOCRACY, being one of these, then appeared more often than the context of related words would lead us to predict—60 percent more often, in fact.[17] Such sharp changes, we see, are typical of a controlled press.

Attention to the Democratic Ideology

In the first part of this discussion, we examined fluctuations in attention to the symbol DEMOCRACY. Just now we have seen how these fluctuations could be in part, though not completely, explained by fluctuations in attention to the general area of interest which might be described as the democratic ideology. Let us now examine the amount of attention to that ideology.

Trends.   Much of what we might wish to say has already been incidentally dealt with in the last section. We noted, for instance, a decided increase in discussion of topics related to democracy. This conclusion, however, is oversimple. The trend assumes a somewhat new complexion when we examine the data further. In the previous chapter we noted an increasing total of symbols counted. In other words, not only democracy, but all the goal values in terms of which our symbol list was constructed have acquired growing attention in the past half-century. Our list measures the rise of certain contemporary political attitudes. If we wish to estimate whether democracy has assumed increasing importance relative to the other goal values studied, we must use figures presenting the proportion which symbols on this list form of all counted symbols, not figures of their frequency per editorial.

Furthermore, it is desirable here to separate symbols referring to democracy from those referring to its lack. When we do this we reach the following conclusions:

1. Symbols referring to democratic practices form no larger part—indeed a somewhat smaller part—of the political symbol flow surveyed than they did before World War I.

2. Symbols referring to antidemocratic practices form a considerably larger part of the political symbol flow than they did earlier. The increase came in the 1930s along with awareness of totalitarianism as a major factor in the world scene.

3. Symbols referring to democratic practices and, of course, even more to antidemocratic practices have increased considerably in frequency per editorial as have most of the symbols studied by the RADIR Project.

The evidence for these conclusions is given in Table 5 and Figure 1.

Some of these data are also portrayed in Figures 2 and 3, which show somewhat more vividly the difference in conclusions we come to in using different indexes and different bases. Thus, for example, the frequency of any symbol per editorial is, of course, affected by the general richness in symbols of the paper, that is, by its dogmatic or ideological tone. The Russian, German, and French papers are prone to use key symbols of all kinds far more than the *New York Times* or the London *Times*. The absolute ranking in attention to democracy portrayed in Figure 3 is thus a function of general symbolic richness of the medium as well as of specific trends in democratic symbolism.

Furthermore, the trends are different. When we tabulate only the symbols referring to democratic practices and take them as a percentage of all symbols, it appears that attention to democracy has been fairly constant—even declining in much of our sample. On the other hand, attention per editorial to democracy and dictatorship together has been generally increasing. Both sets of curves, however, indicate increasing concern with democracy since the rise of the totalitarian challenge in the 1930's.

In the West, where democracy had won its major battles for acceptance in the nineteenth century and the first years of the twentieth, it was a declining issue until the challenge of totalitarianism arose after World War I. In France the Republic came to be accepted; in England franchise and reform were won; in the United States the age of reform seemed over. In all these countries other values were stressed until fascism became a serious threat in the 1930s (see Figure 2).

Democracy came to form a larger proportion of the total symbol flow in Russia at just the time when other values were superseding it in interest elsewhere. As we can see in Figure 2, from the outbreak of World War I until about 1935, Russian symbols referring to democratic practices comprised a large and steady proportion of the total symbol flow. Since then that proportion has fallen off. Of course, in the last fifteen years discussion of FASCISM increased. The recent decline is not so marked, therefore, for the list of symbols referring to both democracy and its absence, but even that list forms a smaller portion of the total symbol flow than it did during World War I or during the early years of the Bolshevik regime.

That democracy and its lack suddenly became a topic of major attention in the last years of the Czarist regime is very significant. On the whole, the trends noted seem to be sensitive indicators of events in the real world. When democracy is really at issue—either challenging the status quo or

Table 5
Attention to Democracy

(a) Symbols Referring to Democratic Practices as Percentage of Counted Symbols

	Pre-World War I	World War I	1920s	Early 1930s	Late 1930s	World War II Phase 1	World War II Phase 2	Post-World War II	All periods
United States	22.2	14.2	13.0	7.2	14.7	16.4	11.5	14.6	14.8
Great Britain	14.3	11.2	10.8	9.2	10.0	13.2	11.0	11.7	12.0
France	16.3	12.2	10.1	8.8	10.9	9.5	12.3	12.7	11.7
Germany	15.8	6.0	11.1	12.1	10.1	7.6	9.7	....	10.5
Russia	15.0	21.3	21.2	21.4	15.0	14.0	16.5	18.4	18.6

(b) Symbols Referring to Both Democratic and Antidemocratic Practices as Percentage of Counted Symbols

	Pre-World War I	World War I	1920s	Early 1930s	Late 1930s	World War II Phase 1	World War II Phase 2	Post-World War II	All periods
United States	29.9	18.9	15.6	11.2	23.9	29.3	22.2	19.1	21.0
Great Britain	16.6	11.6	12.8	15.3	18.1	25.0	18.9	14.4	16.1
France	19.8	14.2	13.2	16.9	19.1	20.1	17.1	19.1	16.6
Germany	21.1	10.6	16.2	26.4	36.5	30.1	31.8	....	24.0
Russia	19.5	26.4	25.3	24.5	20.3	18.3	23.8	23.6	23.2

(c) Percentage of Editorials Using any Symbol Referring to Democratic or Antidemocratic Practices

	Pre-World War I	World War I	1920s	Early 1930s	Late 1930s	World War II Phase 1	World War II Phase 2	Post-World War II	All periods
United States	29.8	36.4	28.2	15.0	32.4	61.0	44.7	40.9	33.2
Great Britain	32.6	25.5	25.7	28.5	45.6	75.8	48.9	39.7	34.6
France	60.9	47.3	67.8	92.4	139.1	131.0	60.2	93.7	73.3
Germany	37.7	12.9	76.1	128.8	115.8	92.6	109.3	....	82.8
Russia	43.4	110.0	198.6	177.4	189.3	175.0	206.4	219.8	116.2

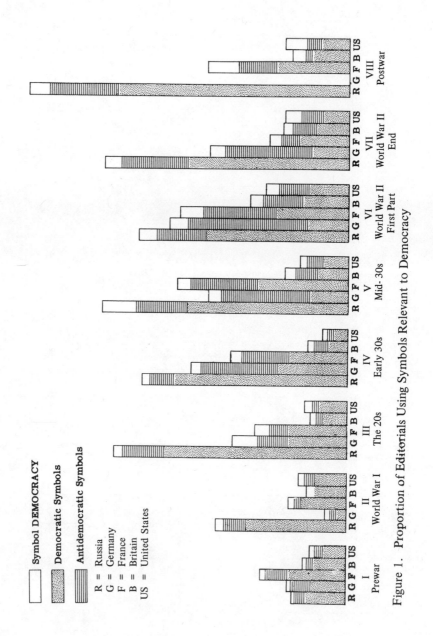

Figure 1. Proportion of Editorials Using Symbols Relevant to Democracy

DEMOCRACY AND THE DEMOCRATIC IDEOLOGY

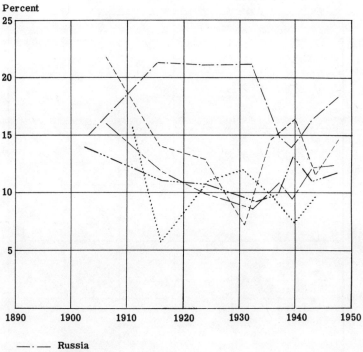

Figure 2. Symbols Referring to Democratic Practices as Percentage of All Symbols

SYMBOLS OF DEMOCRACY

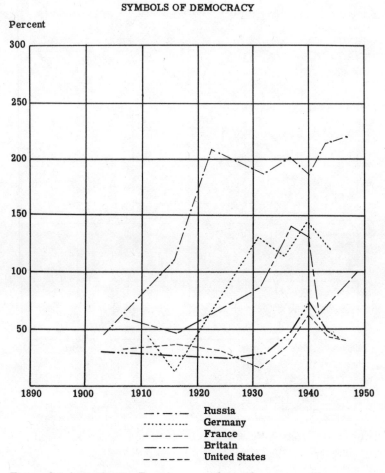

Figure 3. Attention to Democracy and Antidemocracy (Frequency of Symbols per Editorial)

being challenged—the share of symbols relevant to it in the total flow seems to rise.

The balance between democracy and antidemocracy. When we compare papers as to their emphasis on symbols referring to democracy and those referring to its lack, we find that in *Izvestia* and the *New York Times* symbols of democratic practices made up a larger proportion than they did in the other papers. In the *Völkischer Beobachter* symbols of antidemocratic practices formed a larger proportion than in other papers. The division between these two sets of symbols by country is given in Table 6.

The high German attention to antidemocratic practices is largely, but not exclusively, a consequence of Nazism. Before 1930, 67 percent of the symbols relevant to democracy were symbols which referred to its presence rather than its absence. Since then, only 32 percent of the symbols have been of this character.

The Russian press, although often like the German press in its symbolism, is in these respects quite different. The Russian press led far and away in attention to symbols designating democracy and paid relatively little attention to symbols designating its lack. Attacks on fascism from 1936 to the end of World War II somewhat increased the attention paid to absence of democracy; they were then 28 percent of the symbols relevant to democracy as against 19 percent for the whole period of the study. For the rest there is relatively little change over the years. Russian autocracy, unlike German autocracy, has been a fairly constant phenomenon. We find, therefore, a stable relationship between terms designating democracy and the terms designating its opposite.

The tendency of Russian dictatorship to refer to itself by openly antidemocratic symbols less often than German is not surprising if we bear in mind the democratic pretensions of Communist ideology. Growing, as it did, in the womb of social democracy, it never as fully verbalized a rejection of Western democratic symbols as did Nazi ideology. The sharpness of the Soviet rejection of democracy is sheathed in a soft web of democratic terminology. This feature of Soviet communications has been summed up

Table 6
Symbols Referring to Democratic and Antidemocratic Practices

	Democratic practices	Antidemocratic practices
Germany	44 percent	56 percent
United States	70	30
France	70	30
Great Britain	75	25
Russia	80	20

by Trotsky in citing the old Russian proverb, "One does not talk of the rope in the house of the hanged." We shall have occasion to note a number of further instances of this in Russian behavior.

Judgments of the Democratic Ideology

General comparisons. Turning from the attention given the democratic ideology to the judgments made of it, we find increasingly favorable treatment of these symbols everywhere except in Germany. Of the roughly ten thousand instances of these symbols in editorials in our sample, about one-fourth were judged, and of this quarter just over one-third were judged adverse to democracy and just under two-thirds favorable. The percentages of judgments which were favorable to democracy (i.e., pro those symbols designating democratic conditions and anti those designating undemocratic ones) are given in Table 7 for the five sets of papers.

Except for the deviant figure for the German editorials these summary figures show a fairly uniform tone of approval of the main concepts in the democratic ideology.

In all the countries except Russia this tone corresponds fairly closely to the tone adopted toward the word DEMOCRACY itself. The German press was unfavorable by the same percentage to both the word and the whole complex. The French, British, and American papers were, as one might expect, more favorable to the symbol itself than to some of its aspects, giving favorable judgments to the term in some 80-odd percent of the cases and to the concept in some 60-odd percent. The Russian press, however, was more favorable (by ten percentage points) to the components of the concept than to the term itself, indicating—as suggested above—that the Russian press subsumes under other general value terms many of the ideals which we subsume under the heading of DEMOCRACY.

Trends in the Western democracies. These intercountry comparisons are, however, somewhat misleading, since in all countries there have been great changes between time periods. It will be recalled that in the French, British, and American editorials the symbol DEMOCRACY has been a favorable symbol by about the same overwhelming percentage all through the half-century. Not so the associated concepts. In these countries there has

Table 7
Percentage of Favorable Judgments of Democracy

Great Britain	69
France	68
Russia	65
United States	63
Germany	40

been a shift from a predominantly adverse judgment of those things which we now consider to be the components of democracy to a strongly favorable one. Before World War I, although already committed to the word DEMOCRACY, the conservative prestige papers were more often unfavorable than favorable to the things to which the word refers. If we take just the terms designating democratic practices and not the terms designating undemocratic ones, we find that the favorable judgments were but a small minority before the First World War.

Before World War I, as Table 8 indicates, these papers were not kindly toward democratic practices; at the same time, they were even less kindly toward dictatorial ones. Between three-quarters and four-fifths of the judgments of antidemocratic practices were adverse of prodemocratic. As a result, the total bias against democracy before the First World War is not very marked. The prodemocratic percentage of judgments both of symbols designating democratic conditions and of those designating the opposite is given in Table 9.

Table 8
Percentage of Favorable Judgments of Democratic Practices Through 1913

United States	28
France	39
Great Britain	40

Table 9
Percentage of Favorable Judgments of Democracy Through 1913

United States	45
France	45
Great Britain	50

Even these figures, however, are in rather striking contrast to the judgments of the word DEMOCRACY itself and also in contrast to more recent figures.

By now—that is since World War II—the judgments have become largely favorable to democracy. The percentages of judgments favorable to democracy may be seen in Table 10.

This change in point of view, like the general increase in attention to DEMOCRACY, can be related to events around the two World Wars. At no time since the beginning of World War I, except for the Vichy period in France, has the total index been adverse to democracy. A sharp reversal in bias took place during World War I and has persisted with fluctuations.

Table 10
Percentage of Favorable Judgments of Democracy Since World War II

	Terms Designating Democratic Practices	Full List of Terms
United States	88	92
France	50	65
Great Britain	62	75

Table 11 shows the percentage of judgments favorable to democracy during the first World War.

Table 11
Percentage of Favorable Judgments of Democracy, World War I

United States	55
France	92
Great Britain	71

Ever since World War I the balance of judgments in the prestige papers in these three countries has been favorable to democracy. Furthermore, the emotional charge attached to these words in Britain and the United States appears to have increased since the second World War.

We use the formula $f - u/r$, to measure intensity of feeling, since it is a function not only of direction of judgment but of number of judgments. We find that, because the extent of judgment has recently increased, the general tone of the editorials has become more partisan on democracy even though the balance of favorable to unfavorable judgments has not substantially changed. The French editorials, which are generally more biased, have shown a high degree of democratic partisanship ever since World War I but recently have lost some of their fervor for democracy. The British and American editorials, however, have shown extensive partisanship only since World War II (see Table 12).

Table 12
Bias Index for Symbols Related to Democracy

	Pre-World War I	World War I	Interwar	World War II	Post-World War II
United States	−.03	.02	.01	.17	.17
France	−.21	.40	.16	.26*	.10
Great Britain	0.00	.04	.03	.14	.06

*Vichy period omitted.

Russian trends.   The trends in the Russian papers have been in some ways rather similar and in some ways strikingly different from those noted in the three Western countries. In *Izvestia* we find, as we did when discussing the term DEMOCRACY, a recent reversal of the symbolic pattern that prevailed in the 1920s and a heavy-handed elimination of ambivalence of judgment.

Under the czars, the Russian pattern of judgments was not unlike that noted in the democracies, although it was slightly more favorable to democracy. (Divergence between symbols and practice is not a Soviet invention.) Forty-four percent of the judgments of the terms designating democratic conditions were favorable, and 52 percent of the judgments of terms on the entire list were favorable to democracy. (Even in Russia three-fourths of the editorial judgments of undemocratic conditions were adverse to them, i.e., prodemocratic.)

In *Novoe Vremia,* unlike the Western papers, the effect of the first World War was to make the burden of the editorials less prodemocratic. During the war only 44 percent of the judgments favored democracy. The Bolshevik Revolution did not change this. From 1918 through 1928 only 45 percent of *Izvestia* judgments of terms relevant to democracy were favorable. Here again, as with the symbol DEMOCRACY itself, we find that the strong democratic elements in the early Communist tradition were overbalanced in the public press by the antidemocratic elements. This becomes even clearer if we look only at the judgments of terms designating democratic conditions. There were, naturally, many adverse judgments of the PLUTOCRACY, or capitalist TYRANNY, or other such symbols designating undemocratic conditions, but if we eliminate these judgments, we find an even lower proportion of judgments favoring democracy. In fact, between 1918 and 1928 only 33 percent of the judgments of terms designating democratic practices were favorable.

At this point the Stalin dictatorship consolidated its power and all criticism of democracy ceased. Formerly, two-thirds of the judgments were adverse to democracy, but from 1929 until the war, 99 percent of the judgments were favorable to it. At the same time, attacks on symbols designating the opposite of democracy continued, so that if we combine these and take the broader index of all terms on the list, we again find overwhelming judgments in favor of democracy. Specifically, 97 percent of all judgments from 1929 to the war were prodemocratic.

During the same period in which judgments were becoming so absolutely one-sided, the proportion of judgments was increasing, as the press acquired a more propagandistic and partisan tone. This can be indicated by reverting to our index of bias (in which the base is all uses of the symbols in question rather than just judged ones: $f - u/r$). The striking increase in bias is revealed in Table 13. Even neutral uses of these canonized symbols seem to be disappearing before the favorable ones.

Table 13
Bias Toward Democracy: Russia

Pre-World War I	.02
World War I	−.05
1918-28	−.04
1929 to World War II	.20
World War II	.47
Post-World War II	.42

German trends. Only the German papers remained explicitly adverse to the components of democracy—and, because of the Nazis, they were increasingly adverse. In the period before World War I there were only a couple of judgments of democracy altogether, revealing no net bias. During the war, favorable judgments of democracy increased, and though still few, they were uncontradicted by any unfavorable judgments. During the Weimar regime the judgments of democracy were, of course, strongly favorable. Eighty-nine percent of all judgments of democracy were favorable to it, and likewise 88 percent of the judgments of just those terms designating democratic conditions were favorable to democracy.[18]

Under the Nazis, however, the situation was reversed. Only 19 percent of the judgments were favorable to democracy, but the figure is misleading, since it includes judgments of such terms as NAZISM. More relevant is the fact that, of the terms designating democratic practices only, 53 percent were favorable, a figure just barely below that for France for that period and above the figures for the Western democracies before World War I. In other words, the components of democracy, although handled less favorably by the Nazis than by their contemporary rivals, were not openly attacked. These values were too deeply rooted in the Western consensus to be freely attacked. The undemocratic tenor of the Nazi editorials arose from praise of undemocratic conditions rather than from attacks on democratic ones. Furthermore, the coolness of the Nazis to values involved in the democratic ideology also appears in the high proportion of democratic symbols which were neutrally used, i.e., with no explicit judgment at all. Such treatment indicates that these symbols evoke little effect from the Nazi editorialist. Under Weimar the index of bias $(f - u/r)$ for the terms designating democratic conditions was .10, which was higher than for any other country at that time. Under the Nazis it was only .01, which is lower than for any other country at that time. Needless to say, the bias was far greater regarding the entire list of symbols relevant to democracy, which included those designating the Nazi regime itself and some of its favored practices. Here the bias under Weimar was .16 in favor of democracy, and under the Nazis −.34 (i.e., against democracy). But, in this case the former figures are the more significant ones. They indicate that the Nazis, rather than attacking the components of democracy all out or adopting them for their own slogans (as did the Soviets), treated them rather coldly, with a large proportion of neutral references and with the judgments fairly evenly balanced.

IV. The Components of the Democratic Ideology

Three main components of democratic thought may be distinguished in our results. The goal-value democracy involves, first, the sharing of power through the constitutional procedures of representative government. Second, it involves an orientation to the masses of the people. Third, it involves freedom for the individual to exercise his own powers. Each of these elements has played some part in every democratic theory, although their roles have varied. Their roles have also varied in the popularized type of political theory found in the editorial columns of newspapers.

Representative Government

Representative government, for example, is a declining political symbol. Throughout this half-century, it has been the least discussed of the three constituents of democracy we are considering. Enumerated symbols referring to it have appeared in only about one editorial out of fifty. Yet it was more discussed before the recent crisis of democracy than it has been in the last few years.

The extent of discussion of representative government is by no means a function of the acceptance of it in the prevailing ideology. On the contrary, discussion of it appears where it is not part of the consensus. Discussion of it has been greatest in the German papers and next greatest in the French. It has been least in Great Britain. Here, as so often, we find that mere attention to a word (or, for that matter, favorable judgments of it) by no means indicates the strength of the ideological element to which the word refers. Concern with it may indicate only controversy about it. In England, where the constitution has been almost unquestioned, symbols such as CONSTITUTIONAL GOVERNMENT, MAJORITY RULE, and PARLIAMENTARISM have appeared in only 0.5 percent of the editorials. They exceeded one percent only in the 1930-35 period of crisis which led to the abnormal MacDonald national government. They have been only 0.1 percent since the outbreak of World War II. Precisely because these symbols were so noncontroversial they were also almost always neutral.

The favorable judgment of them by the British public shows up in the absence of content judgments in the London *Times* editorials.

In the United States, also, representative government is part of the consensus, and again it is referred to in less than one percent of the *New York Times* editorials. Once more the greatest frequency of discussion of it is in a period of constitutional controversy, such as the New Deal. The Supreme Court controversy and executive ascendency contributed to some comment. From 1935 until 1940 the symbol CONSTITUTIONAL GOVERNMENT appeared in about 2.3 percent of the editorials. Since then, any of these symbols have appeared in but 0.3 percent of the editorials. Judgments of representative government are more prevalent in the *New York Times* than in the London *Times*. Seventy-eight percent of the judgments are favorable and the net bias index is .16.

That Russia also ranks very low in attention to representative government indicates that infrequent use of these symbols is not always a sign of their acceptance into the prevailing consensus. They may equally well be outside the realm of controversy because they are unthinkable or taboo. Actually 1.5 percent of the Russian editorials used these symbols, but every one of these uses was before 1920. Under the czars, CONSTITUTIONAL GOVERNMENT and PARLIAMENTARISM appeared occasionally in the editorials, especially during World War I. During the war these terms appeared in 4 percent of the editorials. POPULAR SOVEREIGNTY and MAJORITY RULE each appeared a couple of times after the October Revolution, but since 1920 there has been no discussion of such subjects at all. The handful of references to representative government between the Revolution and 1920 were all judged favorably. On the other hand, all judgments before the Revolution (with one exception) were unfavorable. The bias index then was −.33. These symbols were obviously not popular ones with *Novoe Vremia*. *Izvestia,* its successor, as representative of the official Russian point of view, favored the technique of silence over that of controversy.

In France, constitutional controversy has raged vigorously and openly. This is reflected in the fact that 5 percent of the editorials allude to these symbols. This percentage, however, has undergone a fairly steady decline from 7 percent before World War I to 1 percent after World War II. In the interwar period attention ran at about 4 percent, except in the years from 1930 through 1935 when it ran at about 6 percent. This trend is part of the gradual decline of domestic "political" issues (secularism, monarchism, etc.) in French politics and their replacement by economic and foreign ones. Although attention to representative government has declined, there has been no tendency for the valuation of these symbols to change; on the contrary, they are all judged very favorably. Eighty-nine percent of the judgments of representative government were favorable, and the index of bias is .22.

In German editorials, too, high attention to representative government has been a function of constitutional controversies. The high German attention to these symbols is concentrated in the interbellum period. During this period 15 percent of the editorials used these symbols as against 2 percent before and 1 percent after. Within the interwar period, use of these symbols declined between the Weimar and Nazi regimes. From the end of World War I through 1929, of all editorials, 18 percent referred to representative government; from 1930 through 1932, the figure was 17 percent; and from 1933 through 1938, it was 9 percent. Furthermore, the direction of judgment changed under the Nazis. Under the kaiser 75 percent of the judgments had been favorable to representative government, and under Weimar 89 percent. Under the Nazis, however, all judgments were unfavorable. Furthermore, judgments in the Nazi *Völkischer Beobachter* were extensive, being made in 44 percent of the editorials in which these terms occurred as against 15 percent under Weimar. In other words, to the Nazis these were very heavily charged negative symbols.

It should be noted, however, that one symbol overwhelmingly predominated during the Nazi period, namely, PARLIAMENTARISM. That was the great bogey in this group of terms. CONSTITUTIONAL GOVERNMENT, ordinarily the most-used term in this group of symbols and one used fairly extensively until 1931, almost disappeared under the Nazis. This symbol they chose to ignore, not to attack—an interesting parallel to the fact that the Weimar constitution was never repealed but remained technically in force throughout the Nazi regime.

Mass Orientation

Even though representative government may be a declining political slogan, appeals to the masses have shown a significant increase in most countries. Also, the judgments made of the masses have become somewhat more favorable. This element of democracy was the one that in the nineteenth century aroused most fear in the critics of the new order. They counterposed "democracy" (meaning equality or mass rule) to "freedom" for the individual. Tocqueville, Cooper, Carlyle, and even John Stuart Mill feared the pressure toward conformity and mediocrity which an egalitarian mass of intemperate ignoramuses might exert. They warned that democracy might subordinate intelligence and originality to the fulsome adulation of the common man. Whether the gloomy forebodings of these prophets have been fulfilled, content analysis cannot judge. It is nonetheless interesting and relevant to see what has happened to symbols of the masses, and also to symbols of freedom, in the public press. We find it to some extent true that fear and contempt for the masses is no longer expressed as frequently in elite publications as it was in the past, and that adulation is more frequent. This is especially true in Russia, a country in which democracy has been defined to exclude the individualistic elements of Western democracy and to require the subordination of the citizen to the state. The relationship of these trends to the prophecies of nineteenth-century liberals is, however, not so simple as might appear at first glance. We must defer final conclusions on these points until we come to the symbols of freedom.

Attention. Mass symbols appeared considerably more often than symbols of representative government. Their incidence in the editorials read is shown in Table 15.

The Russian papers clearly lead in use of mass symbols. The *New York Times,* though it uses them only in a very moderate proportion of its editorials, actually gives them a larger role in its symbol output than most

Table 14
Mass Orientation

	Percentage of Editorials Using a Mass Symbol	Mass Symbols as Percentage of All Symbols
Russia	81	16.1
France	26	5.9
Germany	20	5.7
United States	15	9.5
Great Britain	15	6.8

Table 15
Attention to Mass Symbols: *New York Times*

	Percentage of Editorials Using a Mass Symbol	Mass Symbols as Percentage of All Symbols
1900-1913	16	16.1
1914-18	18	9.5
1919-28	19	10.3
1929-32	8	6.0
1933-38	10	7.6
1939-41	18	8.6
1942-45	8	4.0
1946-49	13	6.2

of the other papers. Mass symbols in the *New York Times,* however, have been a constant or declining subject of attention and thus a declining portion of the *New York Times's* symbol flow.

The low attention to mass symbols from 1929 through 1932 and under the New Deal is particularly striking. As noted above, these were the years of the movements of farmers, veterans, and the unemployed; of the formation of the CIO and the quadrupling of union membership. The explanation seems to be that the mass symbols are predominantly negative symbols in this elite paper. The *New York Times* has, however, been affected by the spread of democratic attitudes in the past fifty years. Its present class bias is less than it formerly was. But it has not, in these few short years, swung from extensive carping at the masses to extensive glorification. That kind of change, which occurred in *Izvestia,* is proceeding more gradually in the *New York Times.* Its criticisms of mass symbols have declined, but it also uses them less than before. Whether in the future they will continue to be fairly colorless symbols in the *New York Times,* or whether they will be picked up eventually as positive symbols, time alone can tell. In any case, we see reflected in the trend of the *New York Times* a gradual form of the plebeian revolution of our times, which in Russia took a more drastic form.

The Russian use of mass symbols increased, of course, with the Revolution, but large Russian attention to the masses is not just a postrevolutionary development. In the first place, the large increase in Russian mass references becomes very moderate when we allow for the general increase in length and dogmatic turgidity of the editorials. Key symbols have become so numerous in the Russian editorials that most kinds of counted key symbols, regardless of content, show a sharp increase. We can put the symbols of mass orientation in perspective by reviewing the proportion which such symbols are of all symbols (see Table 16).

But even when the mass orientation of the Russian editorials is thus deflated, we still find Russian use of these symbols to be greater than elsewhere, and we still find that this emphasis is not just a post-Bolshevik phenomenon. We compare in Table 17 the incidence of mass symbols in the different samples for periods before the Revolution and for the latest period.

Russian use of mass symbols reached a peak as a result of the Revolution, but it shows some signs of slacking off despite a temporary spurt at the end of World War II. Mass symbols were particularly common in the years that followed the Revolution and roughly up to 1935. In the latter 1930s and especially the period of the Stalin-Hitler pact, mass references declined. The second World War revived again the waning attention of the Soviet elites to their masses. This revived attention lasted through 1947. In

Table 16
Russian Attention to Mass Symbols

	Percentage of Editorials Using a Mass Symbol*	Mass Symbols as Percentage of All Symbols
1892-1904	19	9.8
1905-13	33	11.2
1914-17	66	15.9
1918-28	156	19.8
1929-35	143	19.8
1936-38	135	14.4
1939-40	119	12.5
1941-45	125	14.4
1946-49	147	15.8

*Since the percentages for different symbols were added together, the index can exceed 100 percent.

Table 17
Attention to Mass Symbols

	Before World War I	During World War I	Since World War II
(a) Percentage of Editorials Using a Mass Symbol			
Russia	23	66	147
France	23	14	41
Germany	17	2	. . .
United States	16	18	13
Great Britain	15	17	19
(b) Mass Symbols as Percentage of All Symbols			
Russia	10.3	15.9	15.8
France	7.6	4.3	8.4
Germany	9.5	2.0	. . .
United States	16.2	9.5	6.2
Great Britain	7.6	7.7	7.3

fact, in 1946-47 mass symbols reached an incidence of 180 percent of the editorials and 17.6 percent of the symbols used. In the following two years, however, the incidence of mass symbols was only 111 percent of the editorials or 13.4 percent of the symbols. Apparently the Soviets are continuing to shift away from the mass orientation of the revolutionary years, back toward a level which, in relation to the total symbol flow, is not far from that of the editorials in *Novoe Vremia*. But even those, it must be recalled, devoted extraordinary attention to the masses.

It may perhaps be objected that an index containing such class terms as MASSES, LABOR, WORKING CLASS, and PROLETARIAT could be expected to behave much differently in Russia from the way it will act in a "capitalist" country and, therefore, that this is not a satisfactory index of mass orientation. The inclusion of such specifically laboring-class terms among the others of AGRARIAN or general reference undoubtedly accentuates the differences, but the same results may be seen if we use the inclusive word PEOPLE alone. Table 18 reveals this clearly.

It is clear that the Russian mass orientation is not simply a product of the proletarian orientation of Communist theory. It is a phenomenon that in a much milder fashion antedates the Bolshevik regime and one that applies to all mass terms, whether of restricted working-class reference or not. It is no accident that one of the most appealing symbols to Russians toward the end of the nineteenth century was Narodnik. This name meant specifically "of the people," and the followers of the movement often went to live in the villages in order to associate with the peasants. Deference to *vox populi* and fear of being estranged and isolated from the mass of people around has had a profound effect on the official Soviet form of "democratic" ideology.

Judgments. This same phenomenon appears, too, if we look at judgments of the masses. Before World War I they were anything but favorable. It is perhaps not surprising that at this period LABOR and the WORKING CLASS were damned seven times in the Western democracies for every once they were praised, and that PEOPLE—a favorable term—was far less often judged. It is indeed in line with expectations that prewar judgments of the masses in elite papers are negative. What is surprising is that the least adverse judgments were in *Novoe Vremia*. The percentage of favorable judgments in each country before World War I was as shown by Table 19.

As in the case of attention, the Russian divergence from the Western pattern has become more striking as a result of Bolshevism. The London *Times* and the *New York Times* have yielded to the growing strength of

Table 18
Uses of the Symbol PEOPLE

	Before World War I		World War I		Since World War II	
	No.	Percentage	No.	Percentage	No.	Percentage
Russia	13	6.0	39	9.3	59	6.4
France	5	1.5	3	.9	23	4.7
Germany	2	1.1	0	0	...	...
United States	8	7.9	11	5.5	4	1.9
Great Britain	4	2.0	7	3.0	4	1.4

Table 19
Percentage of Favorable Judgments of the Masses through 1913

Russia	44
France	8
United States	12
Great Britain	18
Germany (Insufficient cases)	

mass movements, not by reversing their judgments, but simply by refraining from judgment. In no period since the first World War has either of these two papers had enough judgments to enable us to compute a ratio. If we take the entire period since World War I as a whole, however, we find that British judgments were favorable in only 31 percent of the cases and American in only 17 percent of the cases. In the French press, where judgments are more frequent, we can spell out the trend in greater detail. Favorable judgments went from the prewar level of 8 percent up to 19 percent between World War I and 1935. In the strike period of 1936 to 1938 they dropped temporarily to 10 percent, but they went up again to 38 percent with World War II, and finally up to 41 percent in the postwar period. French judgments have thus over the years come to be as favorable as were judgments in the Russian press before World War I.

During this time in which the Western papers were gradually becoming less strongly antagonistic to the masses, the Russian press was becoming strongly favorable. This was, however, not an unvaried trend. The immediate result of the Revolution was to reduce the favorable judgments of the masses. As in the case of the symbol DEMOCRACY itself, the Bolshevik tradition contains contradictory tendencies in its orientation to the masses. Just as it claims to be a DEMOCRATIC movement, so it claims to be a PROLETARIAN movement, a WORKING-CLASS movement, a PEOPLE'S movement, a MASS movement. All these words are, therefore, in part positive. On the other hand, ever since Lenin developed his organizational theory in *What Is to Be Done,* the Bolsheviks have counterposed their leadership role to the apathy and conservatism of the undirected masses. *What Is to Be Done* stresses throughout the incapacity of the masses to lead themselves to socialism. This concept of the backwardness of the masses has been summed up in a metaphor popularized extensively by Stalin. Subservience to the masses and underestimation of the leadership role of the party is called *Khvostism,* which means "tailism."

This ambivalence of Bolshevik theory toward the masses makes the balance between favorable and unfavorable judgments a particularly significant index. We find here, as we did with the symbol DEMOCRACY, that in the early years of the regime the public press did not hesitate to criticize bluntly and frankly ideas and groups close to it and identified with it.

Nothing was sacrosanct, and criticism was approved as the road to clarity. Under Stalin, however, this kind of sophisticated ambivalence has disappeared from the public press. Each symbol has its own automatic and almost irreversible judgment. If communism is a MASS movement and a WORKING-CLASS movement, then these terms must always be positive. New words must be found for the enemy. Since the movement is in favor of the peasants, oppositionist views can no longer be attributed to stupid or backward "peasants" (as they could have been in Lenin's day) but rather to kulaks; the word "peasant" must be saved for positive uses. Similarly, the modern Soviet press does not talk of the "backwardness" of the American WORKING CLASS or PEOPLE as it would once have done. The American WORKING CLASS or PEOPLE are almost by definition those who belong to Left Wing unions or vote for Progressive party candidates. The rest of the population consists of imperialists and tools of Wall Street.

Thus we find that the proportion of favorable judgments of the masses, which had been 44 percent under the czars before World War I and 39 percent during the war, actually fell to 29 percent in the initial period of the Bolshevik regime, that is, through 1925. But from then until World War II, the percentage of judgments of the masses which were favorable was exactly 100 percent. For some reason there was a dip at that point to 87 percent, perhaps an expression of the desperate demand for mass sacrifice in resistance to the Nazis; but after the war the figure goes back to 97 percent.

These figures on the percentage of judgments for and against the masses may give a somewhat misleading impression of the suddenness of the change between the Leninist and Stalinist lines. They might be taken to indicate that a complete about-face occurred in one year between two diametrically opposed ways of talking. Compared with what may prove to be a parallel but century-long shift in the *New York Times*, it was sudden. Still, it took more than one year. There were hints of the impending change and hesitancies in making it, which took the form not of judgments but of absence of them. That is to say, between the period when negative judgments predominated and the period when positive judgments prevailed, there was a three-year period in which few judgments were made. Adverse judgments, it is true, disappeared overnight in 1926, but the general tone of bias seems to shift more gradually, as a result of the restrictions on judgments from 1926 through 1929. The trend of gradual increase in bias toward the mass symbols (as contrasted to a one-time sudden reversal) may be seen clearly represented in Figure 4.

The trend toward adulation of the masses revealed in Figure 4 is a striking one. From 1918 to 1947 there was a secular trend of decreasing criticism and increasing adulation of the masses. The thirty years divide

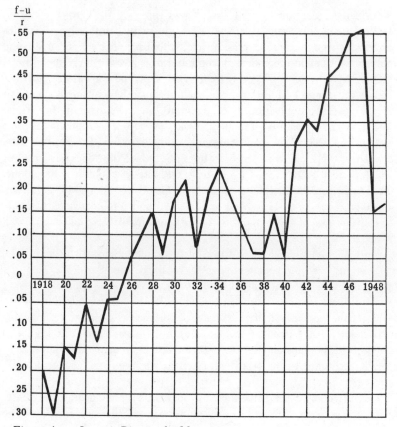

Figure 4.   *Izvestia* Bias to the Masses

into four rather well defined periods: 1918-25, 1926-40, 1941-47, 1948-49. In the first of these periods judgments were quite frequent. Thirty-seven percent of all editorials through 1925 which mentioned the masses judged them. The proportion of these judgments which was favorable gradually increased until 1925, although it never hit 50 percent; i.e., the balance of judgments remained adverse to the masses. Then from 1926 on there was a new line. The masses, as we have already seen, were from then on always judged favorably, but judgments were few at first. From 1926 through 1940 only 13 percent of references to the masses involved judgment, but in 1941 judgments suddenly increased again, and continued to increase. Of course, only by an increasing frequency of judgments could there be any rise in the index, since judgments had been 100 percent favorable since 1926. Thus from 1926 on the index reflects not a change in the balance of judgments but a change in the frequency of them. In the period from 1941 through 1947, a total of 47 percent of the references to the masses were judged.

Before going on to consider what has happened in the last several years, let us survey the first three periods into which the data fall. These three periods reveal a pattern repeated over and over in the Soviet editorials: the reversal of the sentimentalization which was attached to key terms at the time when the Bolsheviks first took over.

If we survey the first three periods—a period of adverse (but decreasingly adverse) judgments, a period of infrequent but universally favorable judgment, and a period of frequent and favorable judgment—with certain hypotheses in mind, we can begin to explain the overall trend revealed in Figure 4. We may formulate three relevant hypotheses about fluctuations in the frequency of judgments:

1. *In a period of changing judgment, judgments will be reduced.* (Because of the natural human disinclination to admit a change of viewpoint, a writer or speaker is apt to avoid judgments during the initial period after a change of line.)
2. *Other things being constant, the more extremist the viewpoint of a body of communications the larger the number of judgments that it will contain.* (For Communist propaganda the corollary of this may be that there will be more judgment in Left periods than in Right periods.)[19]
3. *Other things being constant, the more critical a communicator deems a situation, the greater the number of judgments he will express.*

The first of these hypotheses is confirmed by the changes in judgments of the masses which we are here discussing and numerous similar changes to be noted later. A suggestive parallel is the frequent increase in "Don't know" replies to pollers when the public is about to shift from one judgment to another. The second and third hypotheses are confirmed, at least in part, in the previous chapter.

Now if we look at our results more closely and with these hypotheses in mind, we find some explanations for our data. It will be recalled that, from 1918 to 1925, judgments were running at 37 percent. In 1926 and 1927, after the line had been changed, judgments of the masses were made in only 7 percent of the editorials using these symbols. This conforms to the first hypothesis that judgments are less frequent while their direction is being reversed. It also fits in with the other two hypotheses, since this was in fact a right-wing period, and also the period at which the expectation of proximate world Communist revolution had finally been fully dissipated in the minds of the Soviet leadership. Before 1925 the Soviet elite contemplated an imminent world cataclysm. From then until World War II they recognized that a stabilization had taken place with the world divided between communist and capitalist segments which were bound to live side by side in an uneasy *modus vivendi* for some time to come. Since no final crisis seemed to impend, the pattern of low judgment continued until sharply broken in reaction to the shock of Hitler's invading armies.

During the period of relatively infrequent judgments from 1926 to 1940, however, there were fluctuations in judgments. In 1928 a left-wing period set in, from which the Communists did not emerge until 1935, after the rise of Hitler. Then came a swing to the Right, signalized on the international scene by the Seventh World Congress of the Conmtern in 1935. In the subsequent period, judgments dropped off. This rightward movement of the Communist line during the middle and late 1930s accounts for the break in the otherwise regular trend of increasing approval of the masses. Since all judgments of the masses had for some time been favorable, a decreasing frequency of judgments in this period, 1936-38, in which the Communist line took a less extremist turn, helps account for the fall in the bias index that appears in Figure 4.

By 1941 Soviet judgments of the masses had been uniformly favorable for fifteen years, although they had varied in frequency. A new "Bolshevik tradition" had been established, and its divergence from the older, more critical, one was no longer likely to disturb Soviet writers or readers. At this point, therefore, judgments of the masses could become numerous without raising suspicions of a change in line, so long as they continued to be in the now established direction. The established line was merely being accentuated. Judgments had been relatively infrequent when the change of direction first took place; they were very infrequent in 1926-29 and only moderately frequent thereafter. By 1941, however, there was no longer any doctrinaire obstacle to utilizing a positive mass orientation to the full.

World War II created the situation in which it became expedient to stress an appeal to the masses. Favorable judgments of the masses became very frequent. The heroism and sacrifice of the PEOPLE and the WORKERS became a major theme and one to which much affect was attached. Furthermore, this was a period of crisis in which judgments of all kinds doubled as *Izvestia* assumed a more frenetic tone.

In the postwar period this tone, as measured by the frequency of judgments, has somewhat subsided. Of all general symbols, 63 percent were judged during World War II, 66 percent in 1946-47, and 40 percent in 1948-49. Of mass symbols, 42 percent were judged during the war, 56 percent in 1946-47 and 16 percent in 1948-49. Clearly, the sharp decline in judgments of mass symbols cannot be accounted for solely by the general subsidence of judgments.

More to the point is a decline in mass orientation which we noted above in discussing the attention figures. It is perhaps to be expected that a dictatorship, even one growing out of a mass movement, will gradually become more concerned with elite maneuvers and less with mass feelings. If so, we may predict that the reversal of trend noted in the past several years may begin a long-range development. Until recently, Russian attention to the masses stayed very high while praise constantly increased. In the past few years both attention and praise have dropped off. In both these respects the editorials resumed a trend suggested in the middle and latter 1930s but interrupted by World War II. The trend is now sufficiently clear to suggest a tentative prognosis of continued loss of concern with the masses.

Up to now, in commenting on judgments made of the masses, we have omitted the German data. Unfortunately, the frequency of judgments in our German sample is insufficient to make any comparison of periods possible. We can report judgments in the German press only for the entire span of our study. On this basis we can compare all five sets of papers (see Table 20).

Our inability to report fuller German results is particularly unfortunate since the German press, in one respect at least, clearly had a pattern very similar to that in Stalinist Russia and unlike that anywhere else: When the

Table 20
Judgments of the Masses

	Percentage of Judgments Favorable	Bias Index
Germany	80	.05
Russia	55	.32
Great Britain	24	−.04
France	19	−.14
United States	15	−.07

masses were judged they were praised. The proportion of German editorials which cast judgment, however, was so low that the bias index was
much lower than in Russia. Unfortunately the sparse data make it impossible to identify the variables in the German picture that might explain
both the pattern and its parallelism with the Stalinist one.

Particular symbols. Though German judgment trends cannot be more
fully explored, German attention trends prove quite revealing. In Imperial
Germany 7 percent of the editorials referred to the masses (17 percent
before World War I and 2 percent during it). In Weimar Germany 26
percent of the editorials referred to the masses, and in Nazi Germany 20
percent of the editorials did. This is interesting in contradicting the usual
assumption that Nazi demagogy like the Communist, involved a great
stress on the mass. In this respect the Nazi symbolism lay between that of
prewar Imperial Germany and that of Weimar. The term VOLK which is
included in our list of mass-oriented terms, did indeed have a fad in the
years of the Nazi regime. It appeared in 17 percent of the editorials from
1933 through 1945, as contrasted to less than one percent under the
kaiser, and 8 percent under Weimar. This rise in the use of the term VOLK
was offset, however, by the complete disappearance of such terms as
WORKING CLASS or LABOR from our sample during the Nazi regime. In
short, although we find no heavy emphasis on symbols of mass orientation
under the Nazi regime, we do find an interesting interplay among them by
which all class terms disappeared and were replaced by the comprehensive
term VOLK.

Similar shifts among the terms composing the index of mass orientation
appear in the London *Times* during wartime. Each war resulted in an
increased use of the encompassing term PEOPLE and a decreased use of
segmental or class terms referring to the *demos.* Table 21 makes this clear.
This expression of national unity in wartime may seem rather natural and
not surprising. Perhaps it is; but if so, it is noteworthy that in no other
country did the pressures toward wartime unity take the form of discussing the whole people more and its parts less.

Table 21
Percentage of Mass Terms in London *Times*

	PEOPLE	Other Mass Terms
Pre-World War I	4	11
World War I	7	10
1919-29	3	14
1930 to World War II	1	10
World War II	6	6
Post-World War II	4	15

Another interesting change in the symbolism of the London *Times* has been the abandonment of the term the MASSES. In the period before World War I, this term was used in 3.5 percent of the editorials. Since then it has appeared in only 0.6 percent of the editorials, and in no period has it appeared in more than 1.5 percent. This term in English has a contemptuous connotation, and its disappearance corresponds to the above-noted tendency of the British press increasingly to avoid judgments of the masses. The critical tone of the period before 1914 has been replaced by an objective and neutral one.

In England there has been no clear trend in references to labor—references to the Labour party were counted separately—although there has been an increase since World War II. Neither has there been any trend of increasing attention to labor in the United States. Contrary to our expectations, the highest attention to this symbol was in the 1920s, not under the New Deal or recently. The percentage of *New York Times* editorials using this symbol in certain key periods was as follows: pre-World War I, 3.4 percent; 1919-29, 9.0 percent; 1933-38, 5.2 percent; 1939-41, 7.3 percent; post-World War II, 3.8 percent.

In France there seems to be some tendency for the comprehensive term PEOPLE to supplant the class terms such as MASSES, LABOR, and PROLETARIAT; up to 1939 the latter exceeded the former by more than two to one. Since then, the term PEOPLE has exceeded the other terms. This is not a mere wartime phenomenon, since there was a high degree of uniformity in the ratio in every period before 1939 including World War I; there is similarity also between the World War II period and postwar period (not including Vichy). In the 1936-38 period there was a tremendous increase in references to LABOR and the MASSES, as a result, undoubtedly, of the strike waves, but this was accompanied by a corresponding increase in attention to the PEOPLE.[20] It might be added that this big increase in mass symbols, because of the strike wave and popular-front government, accounts for the fact that this period failed to conform to the correlations noted above between attention to DEMOCRACY and attention to its components. These political events produced a spate of mass references that, by the nature of the subject matter, were not accompanied by references to the symbol DEMOCRACY.

Now having surveyed the mass orientation of the papers in our sample[21] and having found in them a shift toward greater attention to the masses and more approbation of them—a shift which was particularly strong in Russia, but present also to some extent elsewhere—let us inquire whether this has been at the expense of the liberal symbols of freedom. Is Tocqueville's hypothesis supported by our data? We cannot judge the effects of a mass orientation in *practice,* but it is nevertheless suggestive to see whether the *symbols* displace each other or converge.

Freedom

Freedom and mass orientations.   By now the reader should be accustomed to the fact that stress on a given type of symbol and stress on the corresponding practice do not necessarily go together. Symbols of representative government, it will be recalled, appeared most often where the practice was least secure. Symbols of mass orientation showed no such regular pattern, but were often high under regimes in which the masses were denied all power. It therefore comes not as a platitude, but rather as somewhat of a surprise, that in one respect at least there is a clear correlation between symbolic emphasis on the different components of democracy and practice. Specifically, the relative emphasis on the libertarian aspects of democracy as against mass orientation corresponds to what one would infer from knowing the differences in the ideological bases of democracy in the different countries. The tension between the ideal of mass egalitarianism and the ideal of liberty shows up in a markedly different emphasis on the symbols of these two. The ratio of symbols of freedom to symbols of mass orientation in the five countries included in our sample is given in Table 22.

Table 22
Ratio of Symbols of Freedom to Symbols of Mass Orientation

France	.80
Great Britain	.72
United States	.52
Germany	.36
Russia	.18

Furthermore, if we separate the totalitarian regimes from their predecessors, we find that, under the Nazis, symbols of freedom were only 26 percent as frequent as mass symbols, and that under the Soviet regime, symbols of freedom were only 14 percent as frequent as mass symbols. In the democracies, on the other hand, the rise of the totalitarian menace resulted in an increased emphasis on symbols of freedom. Where the Anglo-American liberal tradition of democracy prevailed rather than the less libertarian Continental tradition of democracy, the reaction to the fascist threat took the form of a much greater attention to symbols of liberty rather than to mass symbols. In Great Britain since 1939 the libertarian symbols have been 116 percent as frequent as the mass symbols and in the United States 127 percent as frequent. (In France—in the same period, the Vichy interlude excluded—contradictory and antiliberal pressures have been at work, and hence the libertarian symbols were but 58 percent as frequent as the mass ones.) Thus the totalitarian threat to liberal democracy has resulted in a polarization of the conflicting ideologies. Each side increasingly stresses a different component of the democratic tradition while claiming the tradition as its own. Despite a tendency on each side to assimilate all the attractive elements of the democratic ideology, totalitarian demagogy has placed relative stress on mass orientation and the democratic response on defense of freedom.

It is significant that the three main elements of democracy which we are examining seem to be uncorrelated. Despite their intimate philosophical relationship in the body of democratic doctrine, discussion of each in the mass media of our sample seems to vary quite independently from discussion of the others. Indeed, it is this fact that has made possible the widely diverging presentations of the democratic ideology in different countries. Nonetheless, there are certain common features which should not be overlooked.

Attention. Specifically, the rise of Nazism was a world-shaking phenomenon that was bound to be reflected in the symbol flow in all countries. This may be seen if we look at the sample figures of attention to freedom, disregarding the balance between that and attention to any other component of democracy.

For the entire half-century, editorial attention to the libertarian components of democracy was as shown in Table 23.

Freedom played about the same role in the symbol flow of the editorials from the three democracies. The French editorials, however, contained more libertarian symbols per editorial because they were much richer in symbols in general. The Russian and German papers devoted less of their symbol flow to freedom, but the absolute attention depended on the editorial structure.

In trend, as well as in the overall level of attention, the three democratic states show a common pattern in the use of libertarian symbols. In all three states they became a smaller part of the symbol flow after World War I but became more important again with the rise of Hitler. The trend is revealed in Table 24.

In Germany the proportion of the symbol flow which libertarian symbols formed declined under the Nazis. In the last three years of the Weimar regime, when the Nazis threatened, these symbols rose from 2 to 2.7 percent of the symbol flow. When the Nazis took over, it fell to 1.6 percent

In Russia the early response of the dictatorship to these symbols was not dissimilar to that in Germany, but later there was a striking change. Before World War I, 3.9 percent of the symbols used were libertarian. During the war itself, in Russia as in the other Allied countries, the use of these symbols increased; it went up to 4.5 percent. After World War I, during the initial years of the Bolshevik regime (until 1928), the use of these symbols dropped as it did in Germany when the Nazis took over. Libertar-

Table 23
Symbols of Freedom

	Percentage of Editorials Using a Libertarian Symbol	Libertarian Symbols as Percentage of All General Symbols
France	21	4.7
Russia	15	2.9
Great Britain	11	4.9
United States	8	4.9
Germany	7	2.0

ian symbols represented only 1.4 percent of the total. Then, as the regime became increasingly totalitarian, these symbols of freedom virtually disappeared. From 1929 through 1938 only 0.3 percent of the editorials mentioned any symbols such as FREEDOM, SELF-DETERMINATION, and INDIVIDUALISM. World War II, however, brought a significant change in Soviet symbolism. Libertarian symbols again became important. A plausible explanation could be that freedom was not being advocated in reference to national liberation from the invader rather than personal liberation from authority. But this explanation is at best a partial one, since the trend of increased attention to freedom set in before the invasion (1938-39, to be exact), dropped off during the start of the invasion, and continued even more strongly for a while after it. In 1939-40, these symbols were used by 13 percent of editorials; in 1941-42, by 2 percent; in 1943-45, by 29 percent; in 1946-47, by 32 percent; and then in 1948-49, by 15 percent. The proportion of the symbol flow thus formed was: 1939-40, 1.3 percent; 1941-45, 2.1 percent; 1946-47, 3.1 percent; 1948-49, 1.8 percent. That this revival of libertarian symbols was not just the reflection of discussions of national liberation is conclusively shown by the fact that some of the symbols that picked up most notably, e.g., RIGHT TO VOTE, are purely domestic. For these data, therefore, other explanations are needed. The fact that symbols of freedom are now used whereas they were used scarcely at all from 1929 through 1938 may be explained in part because the regime, now fully entrenched, no longer avoids a symbolism that earlier in the consolidation of totalitarianism would have stimulated dangerous thoughts. In the 1930's totalitarian practices aroused soul searching and anxiety even among the Soviet elite. A libertarian symbolism would have reinforced such critical tendencies. At that time, therefore, it was necessary to avoid symbols which would arouse such *petit bourgeois* qualms, although now such symbols can be partly assimilated.

Symbols of tyranny. So far we have drawn these conclusions on the basis of a list of terms designating freedom only. If we use also a list referring to

Table 24
Libertarian Symbols as Percentage of All General Symbols

	Pre-World War I	World War I	1920s	Early 1930s	Later 1930s	World War II		Post-World War II
						Phase 1	Phase 2	
United States	5.4	3.9	2.4	2.2	5.9	7.2	7.4	8.4
Great Britain	6.5	3.3	2.4	3.5	4.0	8.3	6.7	4.4
France	6.4	7.1	1.8	3.7	3.6	4.8	4.2	3.9

Table 25
Percentage of Editorials Using Given Symbols: Germany

	Pre-World War I	World War I	Weimar to 1929	1930-1932	Nazis to 1938	World War II
Symbols designating freedom	9	2	9	13	7	3
Symbols designating tyranny	2	1	14	51	80	54
Total	11	3	23	64	87	57

the opposite of freedom, i.e., a list including FASCISM, NAZISM, TYR-ANNY, etc., the results are substantially the same with a couple of exceptions. The obvious exception—and the one that caused us to prefer the above index for our comparisons—is in the trend in Germany. Here the situation is as shown in Table 25.

Obviously, the tremendous increase in symbols of tyranny after 1930 is simply due to references to the Nazis, and these in the German press had no necessary relation to discussions of freedom. When the Nazi dictatorship began, symbols referring to it increased still more, while symbols of freedom tended to disappear.

Under the Soviet dictatorship, too, the temporary disappearance of references to freedom by no means meant the simultaneous disappearance of references to oppression. The latter can be localized or specified in a way that the former cannot. Thus reference to *Czarist* or *Capitalist* oppression does not clearly invite unwanted thoughts on Soviet practice in the way in which a reference to freedom does, regardless of how qualified. The good is one; evils are many. Consequently, there is nothing particularly ludicrous in a sinner's complaining about abuses by others that hurt him; that happens every day. But it does provoke thoughts on hypocrisy to see him preaching virtue. The Russian figures on the percent of editorials using these types of symbols are as shown in Table 26.

As Table 26 indicates, the greatest use of the symbols of tyranny is during the period of the Fascist menace. The same is true for the French, British, and American papers. In the prestige papers in all these countries, references to tyranny run well below references to freedom until discussions of the Nazis set in. In France the libertarian terms outnumber the others by three to one, in Britain and the United States by more. In the late 1930s and 1940s, the references to tyranny increase (although in Britain less so). Since no other conclusions appear from studying the latter it seems hardly worth while to follow out this list. The list of terms designating freedom is clearly the more significant one and we return to it.

Judgments. The balance of judgments of freedom in all papers at all periods is strongly favorable except in Russia before the 1930s. Table 27 gives the percentage of favorable judgments. Freedom has been increasingly approved during the half-century. In Table 28 may be found the percentage of favorable judgments in each country before World War I.

From the end of World War I until Pearl Harbor, *New York Times* editorials practically never judged freedom. In the last few years, however, it has become a moderately charged concept. It was judged 12 percent of the time during the war and 26 percent since. It is invariably judged favorably.

In the London *Times,* judgments have also been few, but not so few as to prevent computation of a balance; 90 percent of judgments of freedom have been favorable since 1914.

Table 26
Percentage of Editorials Using Given Symbols: Russia

	Pre-World War I	World War I	1918-1928	1929-1935	1935-1938	1939-1940	Post-World War II	World War II
Symbols designating freedom	9	19	11	2	3	13	18	24
Symbols designating tyranny	4	4	7	17	46	42	58	31
Total	13	23	18	19	49	55	76	55

Judgments in *Le Temps* remained overwhelmingly favorable (92 percent) until Vichy, when favorableness of judgment to freedom dropped to 63 percent. For some reason, after liberation the percentage of favorable judgments in the French editorials continued lower than before (69 percent), a decline paralleling that in attention.

Only in the Russian papers do we find a considerable variation in judgments of freedom. As in judgments of the word DEMOCRACY and in judgments of the masses, we find that in the early years of the Bolshevik regime the symbolism was less liberal than under the czars, and we find that under Stalin a completely stereotyped symbolism has set in. Before World War I, under the czars, freedom was a less positive symbol than elsewhere; during the war, only 33 percent of the judgments of freedom were favorable. To the early Bolsheviks, freedom, like the masses and DEMOCRACY, was an ambivalent concept of which the public press stressed the unpopular side. (Forty-four percent of the 1918-28 judgments favored freedom.) Later, as we have seen, use of these terms virtually disappeared until 1939. When they reappeared, they reappeared as unambiguously positive terms. All *Izvestia* judgments of the libertarian terms after 1929 were favorable. Furthermore, they became very highly charged terms. Since 1939, some 63 percent of the editorials using these terms have judged them. Thus symbols of freedom have become, in Russia as elsewhere, highly positive terms, even though they are less stressed relative to the masses than in the countries where liberal traditions prevail.

Table 27
Percentage of Favorable Judgments of Freedom

Germany	100
United States	89
France	87
Great Britain	74
Russia	66

Table 28
Percentage of Favorable Judgments of Freedom through 1913

United States	76
France	74
Great Britain	59
Russia	55

V. Summary and Conclusions

We have surveyed the terminology of democracy in some detail. We have analyzed the editorials of the past fifty years with what may seem undue refinement. What conclusions of broad social relevance has this effort provided?

Broadly speaking, we have noted an increasing concern with the notion of democracy. It is obvious that the democratic goal has acquired a grip on modern thought. It is well known that DEMOCRACY has entered the consensus to which lip service is generally given. What we can add is some refinement on when, how, and in what respects.

Today the judgments expressed about democracy are strongly favorable, irrespective of the practice in a given country. The word DEMOCRACY itself was approved all through the last half-century in the British, French, and American editorials. The word is now always approved in the Russian editorials, too, although in the early days of the Bolshevik regime it was more often condemned than approved. Only the Nazis openly and consistently attacked DEMOCRACY as an evil, and even they avoided sharp attacks on the contents of the democratic ideology, although using the word DEMOCRACY as a devil symbol.

The contents of the democratic ideology—representative government, freedom, and orientation toward the masses—are now also discussed with deference, but that has not always been so. Before World War I, although tyranny was disapproved by the Western elite, so were many key democratic concepts, particularly the symbols of the masses. Until thirty-five years ago the editors of prestige papers openly expressed disapproval of the MASSES and other democratic symbols. Since then their attitude has changed. Today, both in the democracies and in Russia, the various components of the democratic ideology, as well as the word DEMOCRACY itself, are positively charged or are neutral notions. DEMOCRACY, which was once a somewhat radical doctrine, has become the official doctrine of modern states.

In Russia the swing has been most extreme. That fact, however, reflects not only an attitude toward democracy but also some general characteristics of the Soviet press. In the first place, any controlled press is prone to sharp changes of line. In the second place, as we saw in the previous chapter, Soviet editorial judgments are very one-sided and overwhelmingly favorable. The Soviet editorials present a Pollyanna-like picture of the world, using a few devil symbols and many symbols which are judged favorably 100 percent of the time. Some democratic symbols are prominent among these.

In the early years of the Soviet regime, judgments were neither so one-sided nor so favorable. The tone of the Soviet press then was largely critical. DEMOCRACY, the PEOPLE, and numerous other relevant symbols have since shared a characteristic pattern of judgment change. First the judgments in *Izvestia* were ambivalent, though more often critical than not. Then use of the term declined, and judgment declined even more. Finally, the term began to reappear, and so did judgments, but this time the judgments were all favorable. Thus, between the Leninist and Stalinist periods, there transpired a reversal of tone. The now totally controlled press acquired an overrigid and unrealistic formula. Thus the trend toward increasing approval of democracy, noted everywhere except in Nazi Germany, was carried to a point of caricature in *Izvestia*.

While judgments of democracy have thus been growing favorable, has concern with it also been rising? The answer to this question is less simple than it seems. At first glance the answer is an unequivocal "yes." The word DEMOCRACY and related words appear in many more editorials than they did fifty years ago. But that is true not only of democratic symbols but of all types of symbols counted. In other words, the whole range of goal values which the RADIR program studied—democracy, safety, fraternity, and abundance—plays a larger role in the editorial focus of attention today than it did a half-century ago. What, then, is the position of democracy relative to competing goals?

The word DEMOCRACY itself is a larger part of the total symbol flow than half a century ago, but the constellation of words which refer to the various things which we consider to constitute a democracy is not. Indeed, the symbols referring to democratic practices form a somewhat smaller part of the editorial symbol flow than they did before World War I. At the same time, symbols referring to antidemocratic practices form a larger part of the total flow than they did earlier, the increase having come with the rise of totalitarianism in the 1930s. In recent years it is not FREEDOM and the PEOPLE on which attention has focused but DICTATORSHIP and FASCISM. Taking the two groups together, there is no uniform change.

This result does not fully substantiate the common notion that democracy has acquired the center of the stage in modern politics. It is often said that now it is the fashion to justify all policies in terms of DEMOCRACY. That is true. But then, the same thing may be said about peace, and security, and economic welfare. All these subjects have gained in attention.

Democracy has not superseded the others. Nor has it, as others contend, been superseded; for any given context it is discussed neither much more nor much less than fifty years ago. The contexts, however, have changed.

This is best seen by relating the symbol DEMOCRACY to the symbols which refer to related practices. We found that equations could be computed for each country relating these two variables. This shows that the context, as contrasted to external factors, was a major determinant of attention to DEMOCRACY. Specifically, nearly half the variation in attention to DEMOCRACY could be explained by variations in the topics under discussion. The residual variation hypothetically could be partly a result of a growing tendency to refer specific values back to the more general value of DEMOCRACY. Such an autonomous fad of the symbol DEMOCRACY could be demonstrated for the *New York Times,* but—to our surprise— prevailed only partially elsewhere.

The tendency to relate other (generally more specific) symbols to the general symbol DEMOCRACY is fairly uniform in each subsample except the Russian. In all four Western subsamples, the words on the specific list which we used as an index of attention to democracy occurred five to eight times for each instance of the word DEMOCRACY itself. In the Russian subsample they occurred twenty-five times for each use of DEMOCRACY. The symbol DEMOCRACY is thus normally played down in the Russian press.

The similarity of the word constellations in the four Western states may be taken to mean that, whatever the attitude toward it, there is a substantial core of uniformity in the meaning of the word DEMOCRACY in these subsamples. In Russia the conception is completely different, many subjects being subsumed under such other values as SOCIALISM, which, in the West, would be referred back to DEMOCRACY.

The difference in conceptions of democracy becomes clear when we look separately at each of the main components of the democratic ideology. Since Tocqueville, the dilemma of democracy has often been seen as a conflict between the goals of mass rule and freedom. These two elements have been stressed differently in the Eastern and Western theories of democracy. The ratio of symbols of freedom to symbols of mass orientation was highest in those papers in which the tradition of classical liberalism was strongest—*Le Temps,* the London *Times,* and the *New York Times.* It was lowest in *Izvestia,* in which mass symbols dominated. With time, however, all the papers assumed a more positive orientation toward the masses. The highly critical tone which prevailed everywhere before World War I has given way either to praise or to neutrality, and attention to mass symbols has been growing.

A third component of the democratic ideology is the system of representative government. Symbols referring to the practices of representative government are less frequently found than those referring to other aspects of democracy and are growing even rarer. This does not necessarily indicate weakness in this element of democratic thought. On the contrary, representative government seems to be the sort of practice that is discussed mainly when it is under attack and is taken for granted otherwise. Some symbolic indices seem to be positively correlated with the practices to which they refer, i.e., what is done is what is talked about; some seem to be negatively correlated, and some not correlated at all. Some (and representative government seems to be one of these) are correlated with controversy about the subject rather than the practice of it.

One instance of the variety of possible responses in similar situations is the difference between the Nazi and Soviet press in attention to antidemocratic practices. In the Nazi press, references to antidemocratic practices predominate over the symbols of democracy. In *Izvestia* the reverse is true. The other papers stand between these two extreme examples. The Nazis, in other words, used a symbolism corresponding to their totalitarian practice while the Soviets veil their practice with democratic words. The Soviet press gives lip service to the democratic element in their Communist tradition.

This was most true in the years 1936-38 when Russia was following a policy of rapprochement with the democracies. The extreme swing in Soviet symbolism about democracy well illustrates the extremism that is characteristic of a controlled press. Orders went out to stress DEMOCRACY, and immediately this symbol was used far more than in any other subsample, although previously the Russian press had de-emphasized it During World War II the symbol was dropped as a key symbol, but since then it has been picked up again in reference to the satellite peoples' democracies.

The spurt in use of the symbol DEMOCRACY in the 1930s, though most marked in Russia, was not an exclusively Russian phenomenon. We have noted that, in general, it is easy to overestimate the fad of this symbol, but it is true that there has been some tendency to simplify the terminology by which the polarity of autocracy and free government is referred to. Whereas fifty years ago the word chosen to counterpose to autocracy might have been REPUBLICANISM, FREEDOM, or POPULAR GOVERNMENT; the formula today is most often DEMOCRACY versus DICTATORSHIP. Thus, perhaps in part as a result of the Russian decision to popularize this slogan, DEMOCRACY has tended to replace some closely equivalent words.

These, in brief, are the central conclusions of our study of symbols of democracy. Some of the results are what one might have expected. Indeed, if that were not so, one might well question the validity of the method used. More often, however, the results, though reasonable, might not have been fully predicted in advance. Often, alternative results have equal prima facie plausibility. To show this, we started out with a series of questions to be answered. It would be well here to summarize the answers.

1. *Has attention to the term DEMOCRACY increased or decreased or stood still over the past fifty years? During the past fifteen years? How has this trend differed from country to country?*

Attention to the term DEMOCRACY has increased greatly over the past fifty years everywhere (although not always by much more than many related ideas). In the *New York Times* and the French papers it is used more now than in the late 1930s, but in *Izvestia* and the London *Times* it is not (cf. Table 2).

2. *In each of the five countries did the two World Wars result in increased attention to DEMOCRACY, or did the external threat result in reduced attention to such ideological symbols?*

Both wars in their net effect tended to increase attention to DEMOCRACY, but that increase was not necessarily related to actual combat. In the latter years of World War I, thanks to Wilson's use of it, the symbol was popularized in the Allied countries. In France, however, the purely national danger was used to justify the war more than was ideology. In Germany DEMOCRACY became part of elite symbolism only after defeat.

In World War II the big spurt in attention to DEMOCRACY came before the outbreak of fighting. The rise of the Nazi menace resulted in increased use of this symbol in the late 1930s and thereafter. The effect of the actual outbreak of fighting was varied, but again one may generalize that when the physical danger became sufficiently acute ideological arguments were used less; otherwise, often more (cf. Table 2).

3. *How do the papers we studied rank in attention to the symbol DEMOCRACY; to the democratic ideology as a whole; to representative government; to the people; to freedom? How do their relative positions today compare with those fifty years ago?*

The precise ranking depends, of course, on the index selected—whether the percentage of editorials using the symbol or the percentage of symbols which it forms (cf. Table 1, Table 14, and Table 23 for full data). In general, however, we may say that the German papers ranked highest in use of the symbol DEMOCRACY, this being a result of the tendency of the German editorials to use highly general and abstract symbols. The German and French editorials ranked highest in attention to representative government, the Russian in attention to the masses, and the French in attention to liberty. The German papers ranked lowest in attention to liberty.

4. *Has DEMOCRACY become a more sacred word over the years, i.e., has the proportion of favorable judgments increased? Have the components of the democratic ideology shared in any trends of favor of the term,*

or have those trends been independent of one another? Did the Bolsheviks express approval or disapproval of DEMOCRACY, of FREEDOM, of the MASSES?

DEMOCRACY has become a sacred word in Russia, where it was often criticized before 1929. In the Western democracies it was a sacred word throughout the past half-century. At the turn of the century it was, and it is now, virtually always judged favorably. In Germany, on the other hand, this word, which had been approved under Weimar, became a term of abuse under the Nazis.

Representative government, like DEMOCRACY, has been generally approved all along except in Czarist Russia. Freedom has been increasingly approved over the last half-century, but a recent decline in approval of symbols of freedom in *Le Monde* should be noted. The masses have been increasingly approved as noted below in more detail under Question 6.

The Bolsheviks in the Leninist years were very critical in their approach and tended to be ambivalent even to symbols ordinarily identified with them; DEMOCRACY, the masses, and symbols of freedom were all criticized more often than praised. But in the Stalinist period these symbols have all become univocally positive.

5. *For any given volume of discussion of the general subject matter of democracy, in which countries will the term itself appear most; in which least? Is this a function of the greater or lesser emphasis on theory or dogma as against concrete issues in the political traditions of the country? Are there trends in this respect? Is there a fad of the word DEMOCRACY? If so, where and when?*

In any given context the word DEMOCRACY will be used about equally in any of the papers except the Russian, where it will normally be used less. In the *New York Times* there has been a trend toward increasing use of the word in any given context, and in France there may be some such trend. In general, however, there is not an obvious fad except in so far as there is a growing tendency to substitute the word DEMOCRACY for such alternative words as FREE GOVERNMENT in referring to the opposite of AUTOCRACY or DICTATORSHIP.

6. *How do the different papers judge the people? How did they rank in attitude before World War I? What changes have there been in attitude since? Does a mass orientation go together with concern for freedom or are they unrelated?*

The masses were strongly disapproved before World War I except in Russia where the predominance of disapproval was small. Since then the French papers have gradually become less hostile; the London *Times* and the *New York Times* have stopped judging; and the Russian papers since 1928 have become very favorable to the masses.

7. *Are symbols of representative government more widely used where the practice of representative government is, or where it is not, part of the political traditions of the people?*

Symbols of representative government are used where the practice is under dispute, not where it is an accepted part of the traditions.

8. *Under conditions of totalitarian dictatorship, are such symbols as FREEDOM and LIBERTY frequent or are they avoided? What about discussion of dictatorship itself? Can any general rules be given? What changes and differences have there been?*

Symbols of freedom are not necessarily avoided by a totalitarian regime. On the whole, however, they do seem to be less used. The general principle seems to be avoidance of such symbols, as of all subjects which might arouse dangerous thoughts. But under appropriate conditions a dictatorship, too, can stress the theme of freedom as have the Russians in the last decade. Reference to dictatorship also can vary greatly. The Russian editorials avoided reference to their own dictatorial conduct; the Germans did not.

These answers to the questions we started out with do not seem startling, but in each case they could have been reversed—or at least varied—and remained plausible. Usually the answers are less categoric than the questions. They thus illustrate that facts are often more pedantic than scholars.

The scholar can hope to extract a new simplification from the complexity of the facts only after he has become aware of complexities far greater than those he originally realized existed. One such simplification we may have achieved above in establishing functional relationships between the frequency of one symbol, DEMOCRACY, and other symbols in the context of which it appears. Such equations make it possible to make empirical and quantitative studies of meaning. With the aid of these equations it became possible to gain some insight into differences between the Soviet usage of the term—with its low relative emphasis on DEMOCRACY, its stress on the mass components of it, and its tendency to subsume under such headings as SOCIALISM concepts which, in the West, would be related to DEMOCRACY—and the Western libertarian usage. With the aid of these equations we also were able to measure the way in which events and totalitarian controls produced sharp short-run deviations from established predispositions.

NOTES

1. Cf. Arthur Rosenberg, *Democracy and Socialism: A Contribution to the Political History of the Past 150 years*, trans. George Rosen (New York: A. A. Knopf, 1939).
2. For a good example of this type of critique of democracy cf. E. H. Carr, *Conditions of the Peace* (London: Macmillan & Company, Ltd., 1942).
3. Richard P. McKeon and Stein Rokkan, eds., *Democracy in a World of Tensions* (Chicago: University of Chicago Press, 1951). This book represents the results of UNESCO's Philosophical Inquiry into Current Ideological Conflicts.
4. Included in these results are also the forms DEMOCRAT and DEMOCRATIC, but not party names.
5. Although we refer here to the modern world, the same phenomenon was understood by classical analysts of politics. They saw that the Roman Republic was gradually democratized, with the biggest steps being taken in wars when the plebs could make concessions a condition of support. At the same time, the Republic died and the Empire succeeded largely as a result of militarism and conquest. The same contradictory pressures appeared then as in the modern world.
6. Cf. Table 4 in Chapter 2.
7. *Public Opinion Quarterly*, XI, No. 2 (1947), 282 ff.
8. Adapted from the Janis-Fadner coefficient of imbalance, in Harold D. Lasswell, Nathan Leites, *et al., Language of Politics* (New York: George W. Stewart, 1949), chapter viii.
9. Cf. Table 14 in Chapter 2.
10. Cf. Figure 2 in Chapter 2.
11. Claude E. Shannon and Warren Weaver, *The Mathematical Theory of Communication* (Urbana, Ill.: University of Illinois Press, 1949).
12. As we shall see below, it is only for the German data that the two groups of terms are sufficiently uncorrelated so that it makes a difference to our conclusions which index we use.
13. It is important to emphasize that we are correlating the frequency of these terms per editorial. The absolute frequencies, being a function of sample size, are obviously correlated. Any two words, say DEMOCRACY and "raincoat," will both appear more often in a large sample and less often in a small one. To avoid spurious correlation we must record their incidence per standard base.
14. The uses of the terms are too few during 1930-32 to permit reliable indices of judgment to be computed. For what it is worth, however, we might note that the proportion of judgments declined by half in this transitional period. In other words, between extensive use as a plus word and extensive use as a minus word there was a period of slight use as a neutral word.
15. One interesting fact regarding the German sample emerges when we examine the normal equation relating DEMOCRACY to other words referring to its presence. It will be recalled that the normal German equation relating DEMOCRACY to all relevant words was much like that for the *New York Times* or London *Times*. Not so the German equation relating DEMOCRACY to other democratic words only. We find in Germany a pattern in which editorial discussion of democracy will involve more use of the general symbol DEMOCRACY and relatively less use of equivalent, usually narrower, terms than in other countries. In any given context of equivalent terms DEMOCRACY will be about twice as common in the German editorials as in the London *Times*. (The *New York Times* is intermediate but generally closer to the British balance.) The meaning

of this finding is that the German editorials are at a more abstract ideological level than the others. They stressed vague master symbols rather than more concrete ones.

16. It is interesting to compare this finding with that of the only other reported study in the field, Ernst Kris, Hans Speier, et al., *German Radio Propaganda* (New York: Oxford University Press, 1944). In this investigation the authors studied Nazi wartime domestic transmission through the spring of 1943. On the surface they seem to contradict our results. They said (p. 121), "While in the initial stages [of the war] negative attributes of the enemy are more often stressed than the positive attributes of the self, after three and a half years of fighting the distribution of attention is reversed." Also (p. 62): "Earlier in the war, the newscaster flooded it [the newscast] with invective—though he has sobered up considerably since the winter crisis of 1941-42."

Actually, however, the apparent contradition is easily resolved if we look at the periodization of the data. We divided the war into two periods, the breaking point being January 1, 1942. We found less self-praise and much more anti-other invective in the second period. Kris and Speier did not find this as late as the end of the first year and a half of our second period. But in our results it was most marked in 1944-45, not in 1942-43. Kris and Speier reach a similar conclusion in an addendum (p. 124): "Our quantitative studies do not extend beyond the spring of 1943. It is our impression that our findings on the development of the relative stress on self and enemy do not hold true for the most recent period of defeat."

17. The trend here noted, using data only for symbols referring to democratic practices, and the trend noted above for the relation of DEMOCRACY and all related words are actually more consistent than the significant results above reported indicate. From 1933 through 1938 DEMOCRACY was low, though not significantly, relative to words referring to democratic practices, but considerably lower relative to antidemocratic symbols and, therefore, significantly low relative to the whole list.

In 1939 through 1941 it became high (but not significantly), relative to other words referring to democracy. (This was due to wartime attacks on the "pluto-democracies.") But it was still low relative to antidemocratic words. (This was due to the heavy use of self-references by the Nazis.) As a result, DEMOCRACY was used just as predicted from the total list.

Then from 1942 through 1945 the attacks on the "plutodemocracies" intensified. DEMOCRACY was, therefore, significantly more common than predicted from the other democratic symbols. It was, however, still low relative to antidemocratic words because the Nazis naturally still talked about themselves, though less than before. In those last years, relative to the total list, DEMOCRACY was more common than expected, though not significantly so.

18. It will be recalled that when we discussed the symbol DEMOCRACY it was necessary to distinguish the situation under Weimar as before and after 1929. We noted, however, that there was no change then in attention to the constellation of democratic symbols. There is no change in their evaluation either. No significant difference appears in the judgments.

19. Cf. N. C. Leites, "The Third International on its Changes of Policy," in Lasswell, Leites, et al., *The Language of Politics*, pp. 299 ff., for a discussion of Communist lines. Cf. also N. C. Leites and I. Pool, "The Response of Communist Propaganda to Frustration," ibid., pp. 345 ff. and 356 ff., for a discussion of Comintern "mass orientation" in Left and Right periods. The results of that study to some extent contradict those of the present one. It concluded: "In

general, there is greater attention to the masses in Right periods." It should be noted, however, that what is true of Comintern propaganda is not necessarily always true of Soviet domestic propaganda, although obviously they have much in common.

20. *Front Populaire* was not included under this symbol.

21. The Soviet shifts from term to term within this constellation are discussed in the next chapter, *Symbols of Internationalism,* since they depended primarily on shifts in orientation toward the world proletariat versus the Russian people.

CHAPTER FOUR
SYMBOLS OF INTERNATIONALISM*

I. Problems and Method

In centuries past, deliberation on war and peace was generally the peculiar province of the ruler. Before the democratic era, the right of the public to an opinion on state policy was not recognized on any topic; but even after the rise of public opinion on domestic affairs, foreign policy was long a closed sphere. As Hans Speier has shown, only during the last century has public opinion claimed the right to be heard on matters of dealings between states.[1]

Today all statesmen, no matter how dictatorial, recognize the power and claims of public opinion—at least to the extent of devoting considerable effort to influencing them on a world scale. The Voice of America, the Iron Curtain, the Cominform is each in its way a tribute to the relevance of public opinion to national security in this twentieth, most violent, of centuries. If public opinion is indeed an important factor in the making or destroying of a peaceful world community, it would be useful to measure its trends in the major powers. To do this on a small scale is the purpose of this chapter.

Public opinion, however, is not a unit. In every country there are the opinions of the "ins" and the opinions of the "outs", of the great and of the small, of those who control mass media of communication, and of those who control only their own voices. The segment of opinion we are studying in this book is that of the elite.

The prestige papers have represented, more or less unofficially, the government point of view, especially on foreign policy. To some extent this has been true for domestic policy, too. The lead editorial in *Le Temps* or the London *Times* (not to mention *Izvestia* or the *Völkischer Beobachter*) is often nothing more than a government feeler or unofficial expression of policy, even when dealing with domestic matters.

On domestic matters, however, these papers may sometimes differ with

*I. Pool, Hoover Institute Studies, Series C: Symbols, No. 3 (Stanford, California, Stanford University Press, August 1951). Abridged and reprinted with permission.

the official policy. The *New York Times* has never been a New Deal paper, and, similarly, other prestige papers have sometimes not gone along with "left-wing" policies of some of their governments. This kind of politics, however, usually stops at the water's edge. The prestige papers and the foreign offices of their countries have generally seen eye to eye and have had very good working relations.[2] The international symbols in these papers, therefore, are probably a reasonably accurate index of the policies of states towards each other.

The dynamic balance in the attitudes of states towards each other is in constant change over the years. One nation grows more hostile to another and as a consequence each draws closer to potential allies. Some of the allies fall out among themselves and again a repositioning takes place among the entire group. Like a giant mobile, a constant but not random shifting takes place among the components.

It would be very useful to measure this process, and one way of doing this is to count the favorable and unfavorable judgments made by each major actor about the others. Such an index reveals the congealing and dissolution of blocs among the powers. It also shows the growth of hostility, as war approaches, and the gradual restoration of "normalcy" at its end.

The analogy of a mobile and the assumption of a constant interaction of the attitudes of the great powers imply that, despite the conflict among them, this is in some sense one world. In a world of slow communication or slight interaction, one part might change its public opinion about another with little reciprocal effect on the public opinion of the second toward the first. This can happen even today between the less influential members of the world community. The racial attitude of some South American country towards Chinese may provoke no counterhostility in China. The extent of travel, trade, journalistic communication, and official contact between them may be so slight as to permit quite independent courses of attitude change.

For the major powers, however, this luxury of irresponsibility no longer prevails. Changes in attitude and in military posture in any one power are known and responded to in the next morning's newspapers in all the major powers. It is in such interaction that the world is becoming one, no matter how divided politically. To the extent that this has already become one world, there might be expected to be: (a) a high degree of reciprocity in the hostility or friendship between any two powers, (b) a high correlation between changes in hostility and friendship, and (c) quick response of one power to another. The extent of this mutuality of attitude is something we can try to measure in this content analysis of the elite press.

We have now indicated two measures we can make. First, we can measure the hostility and friendship of a given power towards others, and second, we can determine the extent to which these attitudes are reciprocal and affect each other.

Attitudes by nations towards each other are one important component of public opinion that affects the possibility of a peaceful world community. There are other attitudes that are equally relevant. The values people cherish affect the policies they will support. The extent to which violence is enjoyed or feared, and the extent to which security is demanded influence prospects of peace and war. So does the strength of the myth of the nation or of the countermyth of some supranational brotherhood. To measure the hold of such values we have included in our symbol list a number of symbols referring to the institutions, ideologies, and culture patterns involved in international relations.

Attitudes are ordinarily thought of as being directional—for or against. But of almost equal importance with the attitudes expressed toward foreign nations and toward the mechanism of international relations is the total amount of attention to these. American isolationism, for example, was not so much an attitude of hostility towards the outside world as it was an attitude of purposeful indifference. Therefore, our measurements of newspaper opinions relevant to international attitudes take account not only of degrees of friendship and hostility, but also of the extent to which the newspapers in the major powers thought it necessary and expedient to express views and inform their readers on other than domestic matters.

Our index of attention to international relations consists of the sum total of the frequencies of all the symbols designating foreign states. In this connection, however, the special rules used in counting country names should be here mentioned. We were interested in the symbol UNITED STATES, for example, not as a geographic object, but as a nation-state. For our purposes UNITED STATES meant not only a stretch of land but also a government. Among the synonyms, therefore, which the readers coded as appearance of symbol UNITED STATES were not only AMERICA (where it meant the United States and not the continent) or UNCLE SAM, but also the government referred to by the names of its members. Thus if the *Völkischer Beobachter* said "Roosevelt is a meddler in trying to make peace in Europe," this was recorded as UNITED STATES (minus). We thus excluded names of human beings from our symbol list and treated names of national and party leaders as symbols of their function. According to these rules, ROOSEVELT was not automatically and in all cases listed as UNITED STATES. Statements about his campaigns for the presidency or other similar activities as a party leader were recorded as statements about the DEMOCRATIC PARTY. In interpreting the results that follow, these rules should be kept in mind, though they are less important than one might think since most editorials dealing with a government mention the country name at some point, and under our rules each symbol was counted only once per editorial.

II. Patterns of Hostility and Friendship

Long-Run Patterns

"The probability of war," says Quincy Wright, "is a function of the distances between states and of the policies which they pursue."[3] By distance, Dr. Wright means not simply geographic mileage, but rather distance in its metaphorical sense, as used, for example, by sociologists who talk of "social distance." The relevant types of distance which determine the relationships of states, Wright classifies under eight headings: (1) technological, (2) strategic, (3) intellectual, (4) legal, (5) social, (6) political, (7) psychic, and (8) war-expectancy distance. The first two of these are a constant object of study by general staffs. Aircraft ranges and speeds, shipping problems, etc., all affect the technological and strategic distances between any two states. Legal and political distance are a constant object of study by ministries of foreign affairs. Psychic distance—the one we are here concerned with—is also of great interest to statesmen and policy makers, but it has probably been less well measured than most of the others.

Students of international relations have made a few attempts to find ways of measuring the degree of friendliness and hostility among states. In the past they have been estimated in a rough way by journalists, diplomats, and scholars; and more recently the development of polling on an international scale has provided occasional accurate measurements of these attitudes. Many studies have been made by sociologists of national prejudices (usually of college students) by means of attitude scales. Occasionally content analysis has been used. In one notable series of content analysis studies, opinions concerning particular foreign states were copied from newspapers and then distributed on an eleven-point scale.[4] In that way trends in press hostility were plotted.

An outstanding study of psychic distance among states is that by Frank L. Klingberg,[5] based upon questionnaires sent to experts on international relations. On the basis of their estimates, he computed the psychic distance of the United States, Britain, France, Germany, Russia, and Japan from each other at various dates between 1937 and 1941.

The present study differs from most of these previous ones in providing an unusually long perspective. Since we have examined newspapers for half a century or more, it is possible to take a rather broad view of the more or less stable elements of the modern balance of power. Over this period the attitude of each newspaper studied reflected fairly faithfully the general level of security, and of indulgences enjoyed by its own nation in the world scene.

Great Britain, until recently, enjoyed the most influential role in world politics and was an example of a secure power. Correspondingly, the London *Times* expressed least hostility towards the other nations of the world. The United States in the first part of this half century was also secure, though its power position was limited because it tended to isolate itself from the rest of the world. Now it has supplanted Britain in the top power and security position. The *New York Times* ranked next in friendliness to the outside world. The French had a far less secure position than Britain or America; on the other hand, they suffered fewer deprivations over the bulk of the half century than did the Russians or the Germans. The presses in these three countries rank in corresponding order. In the papers read from each country, the percentage of judgments of foreign countries which were favorable is as follows:

Great Britain	49
United States	40
France	36
Russia	23
Germany	22

These figures seem to be easily explained by some kind of frustration-aggression or insecurity-aggression hypothesis. Two other explanatory hypotheses can be fairly easily disposed of. The evidence does not support the hunch that these differences in judgment of the outside world reflect differences in journalistic conventions regarding politeness. That this hypothesis fails to explain the data is shown by comparing judgments of foreign countries with judgments of all other symbols. The latter range only between 39 percent and 47 percent favorable, a smaller range than that noted above and with the countries in quite a different rank order.[6] Furthermore, this hypothesis would not explain the changes in the judgments which took place over time. These changes are, however, compatible with changes in degree of security or frustration as we shall see below.

Another plausible but unsubstantial hypothesis would explain the extensive British approval of the outside world as approval of the Empire and Commonwealth. Colonies are, of course, neither strictly the self, nor strictly non-self. It is hard to place them in an appropriate psychic relationship to the press of the mother country. Like human children, depending on how they behave, they may be very strongly identified with the parent, or fairly strongly rejected. Since about one quarter of the outside world was in this peculiar relationship to Britain, it might be suspected that Britain's imperial position might explain her being most favorable to the outside world.

This explanation, however, does not suffice. If we subtract a country's own colonies from "the outside world" we still find the same relationship prevailing. It is true that the British positive judgments are reduced from 49 to 44 percent. At the same time, the positive judgments of each of the other three powers with colonies is reduced by just one percentage point. All this leaves the basic relationship unchanged.

It thus seems most probable that the degree of hostility expressed about the external world should be explained as a function of insecurity. Conversely, friendly attitudes towards the outside world are a function of satisfaction with the world as it is.

The particular targets of hostility vary over the years, but certain traditional enmities and friendships have persisted fairly constantly. Table 1 reports the judgments of each of the great powers by the prestige papers of each of the other great powers. These are expressed as the percentage of favorable judgments out of the total favorable and unfavorable.

One of the most remarkable things about the results in this table is the high reciprocity of judgment within each pair of powers. Fifty-seven percent of the French editorial judgments of the UNITED STATES were favorable, and 56 percent of the American editorial judgments of FRANCE were favorable. Seventeen percent of the American judgments of GERMANY were favorable and 18 percent of the German judgments of the UNITED STATES were favorable. With the exception of the two pairs United States-Russia and Great Britain-Russia, all the pairs show about the same sentiments from either side. In each of these two exceptional cases, the difference between the percentage of favorable judgments by one side and by the other is 17. The difference in percentage of favorable judgments of Germany and France by each other is 6. In every other case the difference is at most 3 percentage points.[7]

The significance of the great reciprocity of judgments between paired powers is that it indicates the existence of a greater degree of established interdependence than one would expect. It is not surprising that the rise of

Table 1
Percentage of Favorable Judgments of Major Powers

Judgments of	In the papers of				
	United States	Great Britain	France	Russia	Germany
United States		66	57	38	18
Great Britain	64		63	21	14
France	56	64		29	13
Russia	21	38	31		10
Germany	17	17	7	13	

a Hitler to power in Germany produced both an increase in attacks on the UNITED STATES in the German press and of attacks on GERMANY in the American press. From that, however, it does not follow that the percentage of adverse judgments in the two presses would be the same. Impressionistic common sense might well support the surmise that the Nazi press would be much more vitriolic, and that the less propagandistic press of a democracy would be somewhat more restrained in condemning the enemy. Common sense could also support the contrary surmise that, while war preparations were under way, the controlled Nazi press might be toned down in an attempt to bolster American isolationism, but that an uncontrolled American paper with strongly anti-Nazi attitudes would respond to the actions rather than the verbal silences of the Nazis.

The operation of either of these mechanisms would clearly result in a discrepancy between the percentage of unfavorable judgments in the two papers; so, too, would the mechanism of ignorance or indifference to what the other was saying. In a face-to-face debate in the UN General Assembly, one readily expects that if the American delegate attacks forced labor in Russia, the Russian delegate will answer with some remarks about chain gangs in the United States. In an arena of this sort relatively rarely, and then as a result of deliberate strategy, does a country refrain from handing back tit for tat.

The same is not true, however, for less fully attended-to communications. The tone of Russian statements about America is more a function of the current party line and of international relations than it is of what an Oshkosh newspaper might say in its current editorial on Communism. It also is unlikely that either praise or condemnation of America in some minor Russian paper would arouse response in American journalists or policy-makers.

We are dealing here, however, neither with an isolated story in the Oshkosh Gazette, nor with face-to-face debates at international conferences. We are dealing with a body of communications intermediate between these in world audience attention. What the London *Times* or *New York Times* or *Izvestia* says is followed rather closely by diplomats, and by the appropriate offices in governments and press agencies throughout the world. On the other hand, the editorials in these papers are neither read enough nor sufficiently regarded to be major determinants of reciprocal attitudes. The high degree of reciprocity cannot be explained as a simple process of "trade-lasts" or name calling. (If it could, there would be not only long-term mutuality of attitude but also parallel short-term fluctuation in approval and criticism. We shall examine below to what extent this is so.)

The high degree of reciprocity does, however, reflect a surprising degree of cultural interdependence among at least the Western powers. The prevailing elite attitude in one country somehow gets communicated to the elite in another country and comes to be reciprocated in turn. The general high level of French friendliness towards the United States, coupled with resentments at Uncle Shylock and his excessive power; loud, uncultured, and overrich tourists; and Coca-Cola, closely corresponds to the American friendliness towards France, coupled with disparagement of governmental instability, technical backwardness, nationalism, and wine. International cultural interchange has become so effective that this reciprocity of shared attitudes prevails among all the great powers except perhaps Russia. There may not be a world community of communication, but in this respect, there is certainly a Western one.

Besides its cultural significance, the high degree of reciprocity of judgments by countries of each other also has a rather convenient technical consequence for the simplification of this study. We can use a single figure representing the psychic distance of any two powers instead of having to talk of the hostility of each one toward the other. By simply splitting the small difference between the two judgment indices for each pair we shall have a reasonably accurate measure for all cases except two (the American-Russian and British-Russian relationships). We shall merely keep in mind that the single psychic distance figure to some extent distorts these two. Our psychic distance index is the mean percentage of unfavorable judgments of each member of the pair by the other.

To represent graphically the constellation of attitudes prevailing for the past half century, an attempt was made to construct an illustrative model. There was no a priori reason why this should prove possible. If the relationship of states is capable at all of being represented by a series of points in space, then the psychic distances of any three powers can be represented by a triangle, and any four powers by a three-dimensional figure. Plotting five powers, however, might well require four dimensions. The fact that in this instance the psychic distances of the five powers could be represented in visual space with only minor distortions indicates that mutual attitudes among the five powers are determined by a limited number of major factors, specifically three. For example, the psychic distance between Britain and France and between Britain and Germany are not independent things. They are both largely determined by a single attitude toward the consolidation of power of the European continent. Due to similar kinds of interdependence among the mutual attitudes of the different countries, the five powers form a constellation sufficiently simple to be represented in a three-dimensional model. The model is presented in Figure 1.

This model shows the close affinity of the three allies, France, Britain, and the United States. Sharply at odds with them, and fortunately also with each other, are two "out" nations of the Western community, Germany and Russia. The short periods when these two submerged their

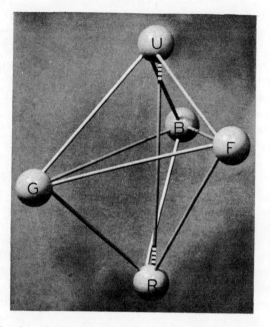

Figure 1. Psychic Distances of Major Powers: Measured by Content
Analysis

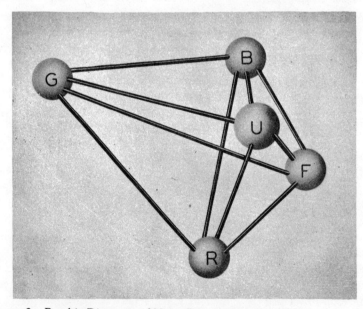

Figure 2. Psychic Distances of Major Powers: Klingberg Study

conflicts and united to challenge the dominant powers have been fraught with danger for the latter, but in the past half century their usual isolation has protected the more cooperative Western democratic powers.

The model also shows that while all three of the secure powers have been hostile to both of the insecure powers, the main target of hostility has differed. The United States has been most hostile to Russia, and less so to Germany. Britain and France have been most hostile to Germany, and only moderately hostile to Russia over the half century as a whole. Nevertheless, Germany and Russia have both been clearly isolated from the group with greatest world influence.

On the face of it, the results of this analysis seem reasonable. They are sufficiently reasonable that one might consider them as yielding support to the validity of quantitative techniques for the study of political communications. Needless to say, many critics have been highly sceptical as to whether counting frequencies of symbols, without intensive intuitive consideration of each statement in its context, is likely to yield any politically or socially relevant results. The results here presented seem, by common sense, to indicate that they do.

Fortunately, however, we can go beyond common sense; the results seem to conform quite closely to results obtained by a previous piece of social science research which used older and more established techniques. This was the study, mentioned above, of Frank L. Klingberg, who set out to investigate the opinions of experts on international affairs as to the relationships of the major states towards each other. The men whose opinions he obtained were versed in the traditional learning of history and political science about diplomacy and strategy. The assumption of Klingberg's study was that their collective judgments would be of considerable merit. He studied the relations of seven powers: our list, plus Italy and Japan. He asked the experts to rank six great powers in order of friendliness to one another. He did this for each of the seven states. Between March 1 and March 14, 1939, he received 193 schedules. From these schedules he constructed a model of the type we have used. It is reproduced in Figure 2, with the points for Japan and Italy removed.[8]

The visual impression of a close similarity between the models is confirmed by a rank order correlation of the distances in the two models. It comes out as +.92.

The similarity between Klingberg's model, based on the opinions of experts, and our model, based on content analysis, confirms, to some extent, the hope that the counting procedures of content analysis can yield valid results about social behavior. Here two entirely different methods have yielded approximately the same picture of the friendliness constellation of the great powers.[9] Only on the relative attitudes of Britain and the United States toward Russia is there a clear difference, and it will be recalled that these two pairs were those on which our results were least reliable.

There is one important difference between Klingberg's results and ours. Klingberg's results were specific for a single period. Ours represents sixty years. The close correspondence, despite this difference, is of great significance in indicating the relative constancy of the international balance for the half-century.

Although there were many short-term fluctuations, the lineup in the two great wars was similar, and also the lineup in March 1939, when Klingberg made his study, corresponded to this typical lineup for the whole period. Klingberg himself seems to stress the importance of the short-term fluctuations. He made similar studies for November 1938, April 1939, June 1940, and June 1941 (though none of these others is based on as adequate a sample as the March 1939 study). The November 1938 and April 1939 studies yielded basically similar results.[10] The June 1940 and June 1941 results were different in a number of important respects, but the first of these periods was dominated by the Russo-German alliance and the second was in the midst of the Vichy regime. These situations, in which Russia and France were closer to Germany and further from Britain and the United States, were certainly only temporary fluctuations around the more usual balance.

Klingberg's emphasis on the short-term fluctuations led him to conclude that:

> Attitudes of states or governments can apparently change very quickly. . . . The rapidity of these shifts in attitudes . . . . suggests that it may be discovered that less importance should be attached to so-called basic factors—as geographical and economic factors, which usually change slowly if at all—than is sometimes supposed.[11]

Our half-century model, however, by placing these short-term fluctuations in context, restores the basic factors to proper emphasis. It becomes clear that we are dealing with a dynamic equilibrium which, due to certain rather fundamental forces, tends constantly to reapproach a single balance but is constantly being forced from that equilibrium by sharp jolts.

In saying this, we do not intend to imply that the same equilibrium which dominated the first half of the century is likely to dominate the second. The past stability of the world power structure in no wise contradicts the predictions of those analysts who claim, for example, that Germany has lost its crucial role as a polarizer of attitudes, and that Britain and France are likely to play quite different roles now that they are no longer, strictly speaking, great powers. No magical immortality is attributed to the model we have constructed. It is intended merely to represent the prevailing pattern that persisted through one important epoch of human history. Knowledge of this pattern provides us with a useful baseline in examining short-run trends that appeared within that period.

Short-Run Changes

We noted above some interesting differences in the extent of xenophobia among the major powers. We found that those relatively satisfied with the world distribution of values tended to be more friendly towards the outside world than those who felt insecure in the status quo. We mentioned that we would find this thesis compatible with the changes in attitude through time compared with the changes in the distribution of world values.

One might suspect, offhand, that wars would be periods in which national self-glorification would be accentuated, and hostility to the outside world increased. This, however, is not necessarily the case. There is in any war much overt hostility toward the enemy, of course, but whether there is an overall growth of antiforeign attitudes depends on the nature of alignments in the war. The last war, for example, broke down American isolationism and resulted in a far greater increase of friendly judgments of allies, in the *New York Times,* than it did of hostile judgments to the enemy. Not the fact of war or conflict, but the satisfaction with one's own position, vis-à-vis the other powers, seems to be the most important determinative factor. If we examine the trend of xenophobia over the past half-century we find that the effects of the first and second World Wars were quite opposite.

Let us start out with the simplest summary time series: the mean proportion of all favorable judgments of the outside world in the five papers we are studying. This trend is as follows:

Pre-World War I	38%
World War I	27
1920s	20
1930s to World War II	21
World War II, phase 1	32
World War II, phase 2	39
Post-World War II	31

In the peaceful years before World War I, judgments of the outside world were relatively friendly. The war reduced these, but it was in the troubled postwar years, when the hopes of reestablishing a stable concert among the great powers diminished, that total hostility to all foreign powers reached its greatest intensity. The Second World War, contrary to the First, made most of the great powers so utterly dependent on allies that there was a temporary marked increase in favorable references to the outside world.

France, Britain, Russia, and the United States all praised each other and also their minor allies.

Since the war, however, there has been a rapid increase of xenophobia. For 1946-49, as a whole, the level of favorable judgments is still fairly high, but insofar as we can describe a trend, it is sharply downwards. Only from the *New York Times* and *Le Monde* do we have enough judgments to separate 1948-49 from the first postwar years, and in each of them the percentage is down at the prewar nadir again.

The average time series curve for the five countries is fairly closely paralleled by the individual curves for the *New York Times,* the London *Times,* and the Russian papers. The nature of these trends may be seen in Figure 3.

The British and American curves are fairly parallel. They reach their nadirs, however, at somewhat different periods. The least American approval of foreign countries comes in the twenties, when the League of Nations had been rejected and the country adopted an explicit isolationist course. The least British approval comes only in the thirties, when Britain found her entire structure of security and empire threatened. There were few developments in the colonies of which she could approve in that troubled decade, and in Europe she approved neither of rising Germany nor, in those appeasement days, of her wartime allies.

The peaks of the British and American curves are also somewhat different. Before World War I, when Britain was the dominant and most satisfied power, she was most favorable to the outside world, over half the judgments being approval. In the World War II peak, the United States was the nation which had become dominant, and the *New York Times* was the paper which expressed most approval of the outside world (63 percent of judgments).

The long-run shift in general satisfaction can be better seen if we convert the series in Figure 3 to index numbers, using the pre-World War I percentage of favorable judgments as the base. We then find that by World War II and the postwar period, the indices of satisfaction were as shown in Table 2.

Table 2
Judgment Index

	Base Figure (=100)	World War II (Index)	Postwar (Index)
United States	.42	138	86
Great Britain	.52	108	69
Russia	.30	97	63
France	.47	79	51
Germany	.20	65	–

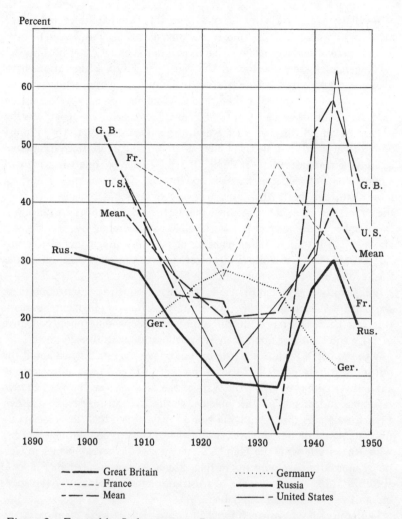

Figure 3. Favorable Judgments as Percentage of Judgments of Outside World (Graphed by Midpoints of Periods)

In other words, over a quarter of a century the United States had gained most or lost least in friendship to the outside world, with Great Britain, Russia, France, and Germany having moved in the direction of hostility.

These figures seem to support the view that national frustrations have tended to make powers more hostile to the outside world, while satisfactions have tended to make them less so. The figures, however, must be used with caution, since a glance at Figure 3 reveals how irregular was the process by which this end result was achieved over the years. Also, it must be borne in mind that an index number ignores the importance of original absolute differences. For example, the difference in rate of growth of xenophobia between the Russian and French press may prove nothing more than that the Russian press was very xenophobic to begin with. Yet, the French trend is not surprising. Before the first World War, France was the number two power in the world diplomatic community, and she was also next to Britain in the percentage of favorable judgments of the outside world. The First World War, however, cost France her position, just as the Second World War has cost Britain hers.

In the thirties, although France's position continued to deteriorate, there was a marked increase in the proportion of favorable judgments. Perhaps this was because France, at this point, was depending upon collective security and therefore upon friendly collaboration with foreign powers.

With the fall of France, the proportion of favorable statements about the outside world dropped. The French press at this period was in no position explicitly to approve either the Axis or the Allies. Since the War, French favorable judgments of the outside world have dropped still further. French weakness throughout the world today is such that she is inevitably discontented with developments everywhere. There is contentment neither with Russia nor with the United States, nor with developments in Germany, nor with developments in Indo-China. In the world arena France is suffering from a general sense of frustration, and consequently the treatment of world news is xenophobic.

The editorials of *Novoe Vremia* in Czarist Russia were far more xenophobic than those in Britain, France, or the United States, but not nearly so much as in the period of revolutionary Russia's isolation from the capitalist world. From the first to the second World Wars, Russian judgments of foreign powers were almost *ipso facto* condemnations. During the war, and since, some meager attention to the Western and satellite allies that Russia had reacquired changed the picture very slightly, but the burden of the press remained overwhelmingly antiforeign.

As a matter of fact, a finer breakdown of the *Izvestia* judgments in the thirties reveals that the change set in, as one might expect, in the middle thirties at the time of the adoption of the People's Front collective security line. Through 1935 only 2 percent of the judgments of the outside world were favorable. From 1936 through 1938, 20 percent were favorable. With the rise of Hitler, the Russians were no longer completely dissatisfied with the status quo. They acquired a vested interest in preserving it against the new challenger.

Only the German papers were as thoroughly xenophobic as the Russian. Insofar as we can tell, they followed quite a different trend from any of the others. (Because there are few judgments in a relatively small sample, the German data on this point is less reliable than that for the other papers.) Despite the fact that Germany's international position declined with her loss of World War I, she nevertheless approached friendly collaboration with the Western powers somewhat more under the Weimar regime than before. (It will be recalled that our German sample begins only in 1910). The resulting decline in the intensive xenophobia expressed in the German editorials is, however, small. The proportion of favorable judgments went from 20 percent before the war to 28 percent in the twenties. It then went to 25 percent from 1930 through 1932 and remained at 25 percent under the Nazi regime until the war. Basically, there is no change until the second World War in which Germany, much more isolated in her struggle than any of the Western allies, vigorously denounced the outside world. Her Axis partners did not materially enter into her symbolic image of the sources of her strength.

All in all, the trend data on attitudes towards the outside world do not lend themselves to any simple one-factor explanation. They do not have any one or two clear-cut correlates. Nevertheless they lend some additional support to, and are compatible with, the hypothesis that editorial aggressiveness towards the outside world is a function of the satisfaction of the state with its position in the world.

Along with the changes in attitudes towards the outside world as a whole, changes were taking place in the attitudes of the major powers towards each other. Our data are insufficiently rich in judgments to enable us to construct reliable models such as the one given above for each of the major periods into which the international history of this past half-century may be divided. This is especially so since after the first World War the *New York Times* and London *Times* adopted an extremely sober editorial tone, with few judgments. Using the long-term model as a base, however, we can trace the major fluctuations and trends. Short-term changes we can consider only for a few times and places. But we can compare the situation before World War I, during World War I, the interbellum up through the early thirties, World War II together with the preceding years of Nazi threats, and the postwar years. During these five periods, the main realignments in Western international relations of the past half-century occurred. Table 3 records the trends in psychic distance for each pair of powers through these periods.

Table 3
Trends in Psychic Distances Among the Major Powers

	Pre-World War I	World War I	1920s & Early 1930s	Late 1930s & World War II	Post-World War II
Britain-France	48	2	46	22	(58)
U.S.-Britain	46	12	X	23	35
U.S.-France	46	23	(51)	(18)	(60)
France-Russia	48	30	94	100	(77)
Britain-Russia	71	44	97	26	(100)
U.S.-Russia	64	57	94	30	(94)
U.S.-Germany*	(63)	(82)	(62)	(99)	X
Britain-Germany	(55)	95	66	99	(100)
France-Germany	(61)	93	91	91	(96)
Russia-Germany	(71)	92	92	95	(93)

X Inadequate data to compute distance.
() Inadequate data to compute distance with reliability.
* All psychic distances to Germany before World War I and since World War II are unreliable, in that they represent only the attitude of the given paper towards Germany, not the reciprocal attitude too. It will be recalled that our German sample stops in 1945. Before World War I the sample was too small to provide any reasonable number of judgments.

Before World War I there were none of the sharp polarities that have since come to mark the relationships of the powers. The most striking development since is the growing intensity of both hostilities and friendships. Since World War I, the powers have been clearly grouped into friends and enemies; before then no such well defined structure existed. This is shown by the range of values of the index of psychic distance. Before the first war, the indices of psychic distance ranged between .46 and .71 or over a total spread of .25. The pairs Britain-France, U.S.-France, U.S.-Britain, and France-Russia were all friendly to about the same moderate extent. Favorable judgments predominated slightly over unfavorable ones. At the opposite extreme, Britain-Russia and Germany-Russia were substantially critical of each other, but not to as extreme a degree as since. In between were the pairs U.S.-Russia, U.S.-Germany, France-Germany, and Britain-Germany. The views of each other expressed by all powers tended to approximate fairly closely an even balance of praise and blame, although there was a small preponderance on the side of negative judgments. Since negative judgments seem to predominate slightly throughout our study (for domestic symbols as well as for international ones), this slight hostility is not revealing. What is significant, in the years prior to World War I, is the relative evenness of attitude of each nation toward each other nation.

Expressed in graphic terms, this means that a model of the relationships of the powers before World War I would differ from the basic model in that it would be a more nearly equilateral figure. No two nations would be as close together as the democracies are in the long-term model, and none would be as distant as Germany and Russia became. At the same time the model, if on the same scale, would be somewhat smaller than the long-term model, and still smaller than the later models, for the total amount of hostility expressed about foreign countries has grown. This change sets in with World War I and continues thereafter.

What happened with the outbreak of World War I might well have been predicted. The allies for the most part drew together in mutual laudation. Russia was to some extent left out of this by the London *Times* and especially by the *New York Times*. Otherwise the polarization between the sides was complete. The psychic distance between Germany and all four other powers became very great, and the psychic distance among the four tended to become small. This polarization in wartime is not surprising. It is important only as a prelude to a change in the subsequent peacetime structure.

The interbellum was marked by a rapid restoration of very nearly the prewar attitudes between the pairs Britain-France, U.S.-France, Britain-Germany, and U.S.-Germany. (There are insufficient judgments to construct an index for U.S.-Britain for this period.)

Two important changes, however, had modified the world situation, increasing the total amount of hostility among the great powers. The first was the Russian revolution. This had made a breach of major proportions between Russia and all four other powers. Her psychic distance from all of them was over .90. This was one major division among the powers. The other new division was that between Germany and France. The peace did not heal this hostility; the sense of insecurity and loss on each side was too great, and provocations continued. As a result, the psychic distance of the French and German papers remained almost at the wartime level. The lines between friends and enemies in this period can be very clearly drawn.

World War II and its prelude further accentuated this polarization. Between psychic distances .18 and .30 will be found the judgments among all the allies. At psychic distances of more than .90 will be found all the other judgments.

It should be pointed out that France and Russia, though on the allied side in certain phases of the war, were, until close to the end, not in at the same time. Consequently, criticism of Russia is found both before the fall of France and under Vichy. The Vichy paper (in the two years for which we read it) did not much affect the other indices, since it used the technique of silence rather than direct contradiction of the more usual French attitudes. Thus it did not praise Germany and condemn Britain and the

United States; it merely refrained from condemnation of Germany and praise of Britain and America. It thus did not much affect the indices. It should also be noted that references to the Free French are included in the references to FRANCE. Hence France continues to show up as an ally. The polar division between the powers, therefore, stands out on the graph despite the actual vicissitudes of the war.

Wide divisions continue into the postwar or cold-war years. Although our graph is not reliable for this period, it points to the conclusion that one would expect: it points toward a continuation of the trend toward an increasingly structured and hostile relationship among the powers. While the close allies, Britain and the United States, are thrown together much more closely than any pair previously in peacetime, Russia and Germany are uniformly rejected. Only France is to any degree in an intermediate position. Furthermore, the total amount of hostility expressed among the great powers has increased markedly. The relationship among the powers has shifted from a fairly even multilateral structure of moderate attitudes toward a structure of polarized blocs.

The nature of these blocs can be seen somewhat better if we examine the deviations from reciprocity in the attitudes of states towards each other. Over the entire period, it will be recalled, these deviations were surprisingly small. The *New York Times* was more hostile to RUSSIA than was the Russian press to the UNITED STATES, and the London *Times* was more friendly to RUSSIA than the Russian press to GREAT BRITAIN. (These discrepancies largely arose in the Czarist epoch.) Also, France was somewhat more hostile to GERMANY than Germany to FRANCE.

For the rest, the attitudes were very close to reciprocal. That, however, does not mean that they were reciprocal at all times. At one point country A might arouse the enmity of country B. For awhile thereafter the hostility of country B to country A would be greater than that of A to B. But if this situation continued long, B, by its resistance to A, would in turn incur the hostility of A. Thus a long-term balance might exist despite short-term imbalances.

This interaction is illustrated by the German and American trends of judgments of each other during the approach of World War II. American antipathy to the behavior of Nazi Germany was moderately but definitely expressed in the *New York Times,* but the German editorials refrained from attacking the United States until the Nazi menace had forced America to break definitely from neutrality, and then, of course, the *Völkischer Beobachter* took a much more vitriolic tone than the staid *New York Times* ever does. The data for hostility as a proportion of all references to the other state are presented in Table 4.

Future studies might profitably investigate these mechanisms more fully than is possible here. Samples could be constructed suitable for estimating

Table 4
German and American Criticisms of Each Other

	New York Times	Völkischer Beobachter
1938	.08	.00
1939	.05	.00
1940	.12	.00
1941	.06	.60
1942	.04	.55
1943	.02	.83
1944	.13	.67
1945	.08	.83

the degree of interaction in different situations by the time lag required to reestablish reciprocity in a new attitude after a change by one party from an old one. The data for this study do not usually permit us to operate with sufficiently short time periods to allow any such estimates. For only a few pairs can we plot extended annual series with any degree of reliability, and these only for the more stable judgment index: favorable minus unfavorable judgments over total uses of symbol.

The two most trustworthy such series are presented below (Figure 4 and Figure 5). They indicate rather clearly that there is a very definite correlation between changes in mutual attitude, but they also show that at any one moment the flow of friendship or hostility may be much stronger in one direction than the other.

The potential reliability of such measurements of deviation from reciprocity is indicated by a comparison of our results with those in Klingberg's pioneering study.[12] Klingberg constructed an index of unpopularity for each of the major powers. He did this by summing up the vectors representing the hostility towards a given power felt by each of the other powers. Thus the index of unpopularity for Great Britain among the group of powers we are studying would be the sum of the scores representing the attitude towards Britain of the United States (1.27), France (1.25), Russia (0.30), and Germany (0.08), or a total of 2.90. He found that in 1938 Britain was the most popular power with the other four great powers, the United States next, followed by France, Russia, and Germany in that order.

Our data yield precisely the same rank order of popularity for the interbellum period. (We cannot give a reliable ranking for a narrower time period.) Germany and to a slightly lesser extent Russia were the targets of extensive criticism in this period—more extensive criticism than the criticism they handed out. Britain and the United States, on the other hand, criticized far more than they were criticized. These characteristics of the

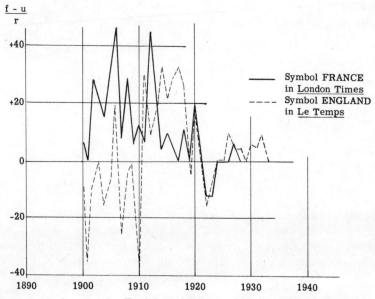

$\dfrac{f - u}{r}$

Symbol FRANCE
in London Times
Symbol ENGLAND
in Le Temps

Figure 4. Judgments by French and British of Each Other (Graphed Year by Year)

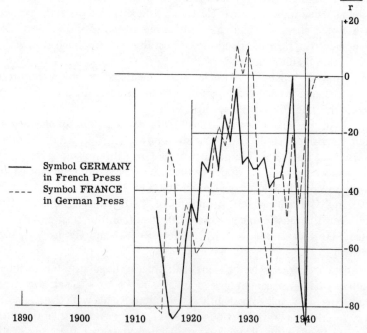

$\dfrac{f - u}{r}$

Symbol GERMANY
in French Press
Symbol FRANCE
in German Press

Figure 5. Judgments by French and Germans of Each Other (Graphed Year by Year)

editorials apparently closely reflect the friendliness of the nations as estimated by experts.

In any popularity contest there may be either general agreement among
the judges or a majority party may outvote a minority party. In the
present case, the judges are the contestants. It is therefore interesting to
note there were no clearly defined parties. Aside from self-estimation, the
powers were pretty well agreed on the ranking of the other powers. As
measured by the deviations from reciprocity, Britain was the most favored
power of each of the other nations, and with few exceptions the others
followed in sequence: United States, France, Russia, Germany. This finding is closely concurred in by the content analysis and by the experts in
Klingberg's study.

The rather technical reasoning on which this conclusion is based may
perhaps be given a graphic explanation. The model shown in Figure 1
connects any two countries by a single line representing their mean mutual
distance. Suppose our model had two arrows of unequal length—instead of
one line—each arrow representing the hostility of one power in the pair
toward the other. The longer arrow would represent greater hostility, the
shorter arrow less hostility. Then the arrow representing criticism by
Britain (London *Times*) would always be longer than the arrow representing criticism of Britain (by all other papers)—since Britain has, in every
case, given more criticism than she has received. For the United States this
would be true of all pairs of arrows except, of course, that connecting
Britain and the United States. And so the progression of popularity would
proceed regularly in the order stated, no matter which nation was making
the judgments.

In the Klingberg and present studies together there are but three exceptions, shown in tabular fashion by Table 5. A plus in the table indicates
that the first-named country in the pair was less disapproved by the second
than was the second by the first. A minus naturally indicates that the first
country received more criticism from the other than it gave. The three
circled pairs (each of course repeated once) deviate from the usual progression of popularity for this period.

The relative popularities indicated in the last few paragraphs were, of
course, only those in a limited time period. Before the first World War,
Britain was at the other end of the scale. She was then the dominant world
power, and target of the jealousy of the rest. She was therefore the criticized member of each pair rather than the other way around.

A number of other similar items of historical interest appear from the
detailed figures. They reveal rather clearly, for example, the pattern of
appeasement before World War II. As shown in Table 3, *Le Temps* remained consistently hostile to Germany after World War I. The density of
attacks declined, as revealed in Figure 5, but there was no return (as in

SYMBOLS OF INTERNATIONALISM

Table 5
Relative "Popularity" of Major Powers

	Klingberg study	Content Analysis
Great Britain–United States	+	+
–France	+	+
–Russia	+	+
–Germany	+	+
United States–Great Britain	–	–
–France	⊖	+
–Russia	+	+
–Germany	+	+
France–Great Britain	–	–
–United States	⊕	–
–Russia	+	⊖
–Germany	+	+
Russia–Great Britain	–	–
–United States	–	–
–France	–	⊕
–Germany	⊖	+
Germany–Great Britain	–	–
–United States	–	–
–France	–	–
–Russia	⊕	–

Britain and the United States) to the mixed judgments of Germany that prevailed before World War I. The closest approach to a rapprochement apparently came in the late twenties, but even before Hitler reached power, the conflict over reparations and worsening internal conditions had produced rather hostile attitudes on both sides.

The rise of Hitler might have been expected to accentuate this tone in both sets of editorials. It did not. The *Völkischer Beobachter* did indeed proceed to attack France with vehemence in 1933 and 1934, when Versailles was still the great issue and the Nazis were still weak. (Attacks on Britain picked up around 1937 and on the United States only around 1941.) But neither the physical threat nor the vituperation of the Nazis produced an overt response in *Le Temps*. Instead of increased criticism of Germany as the threat grew, editorial judgments remained at about the 1929-32 level until 1937 and 1938, when extensive praise of Germany suddenly appeared. In those two years one-third of the judgments were favorable to Germany.

In the London *Times* no favorable judgments of Germany were found during the Hitler years. Unfavorable judgments, however, also vanished from 1935 through 1938. There had been criticisms of Germany in 1932, 1933, and 1934, but from 1935 none again appeared until 1939, when appeasement was finally abandoned.

Only the *New York Times* did not show this appeasement pattern. It had adopted a neutral attitude toward Germany from the end of the War through 1932, but from 1933 on it consistently contained criticism of Germany. Even *Izvestia* adopted a tone of appeasement. The Russian press since 1918 has been continually hostile to all the other powers, as indeed the other powers have been toward Russia. This hostility did not disappear in 1933, but oddly there was no significant increase in it.

In noting this, however, it should be borne in mind that we are examining judgments of GERMANY, not of the symbol FASCISM, which was the standard appellation of the Communists in this period for their German enemy. It is nevertheless significant that there was no increase in attacks upon the German government or nation until the outbreak of World War II. Then finally there was a very marked increase. Also it should be noted that in the period of the Stalin-Hitler pact there were no judgments of GERMANY at all; attacks ceased completely. In the *Völkischer Beobachter*, likewise, all criticism of RUSSIA stopped during the pact, and there was but one random favorable judgment.

Although the prestige papers in France and Britain seemed to be attempting appeasement in their generally moderate treatment of the symbol GERMANY previous to the outbreak of hostilities, nevertheless, a number of changes in editorial content did take place as a result of the Nazi regime. We can here note a drawing together of some of the other powers.

French press treatment of both BRITAIN and RUSSIA illustrates this. As far as editorial tone indicates, France in her friendly relations to Russia has always been in the position of suitor rather than sued. In the prewar years of the current century and during World War I, France was more friendly towards RUSSIA than was any other power. But while in *Novoe Vremia* criticism and praise were fairly evenly balanced, in *Le Temps* praise decidedly predominated. Then with the Russian revolution this relatively friendly treatment came to an end. Each side condemned the other, though *Le Temps* somewhat exceeded *Izvestia* in this respect. The rise of Hitler finally forced some rapprochement and led to the Franco-Soviet Mutual Assistance Pact of 1935. *Le Temps*, however, was too conservative ever to become friendly towards RUSSIA; but from 1932 until the sharp class struggles of 1936 there was little criticism, and in 1934 and 1935 there was even more praise than criticism. (RUSSIA had not been praised in our French sample—barring one solitary symbol—since before the Bolshevik Revolution.) *Izvestia* did not follow suit. In precisely the years of the Franco-Soviet pact, attention to FRANCE almost disappeared from *Izvestia*, and the scattered judgments that occurred were never favorable. The Russians, apparently, did not value their alliance as much as did the French.

The French press modified its attitude towards BRITAIN in the same way as it did toward RUSSIA. Their rapprochement did not fully set in until 1936, but unlike the change in attitude toward RUSSIA, it continued. Before and after World War I and since World War II, France has had a fairly steady attitude of roughly balanced praise and blame of BRITAIN. During both wars this gave way to a most one-sided glorification which probably reflected both France's great dependence on her allies and also the heavy-handed French censorship. In World War II, however, this glorification set in well before hostilities. The percentage of judgments criticizing BRITAIN (in other words, the *Le Temps* component of the psychic distance between them) is presented below for the key periods:

Pre-World War I	58
World War I	3
1920s	51
1930-1935	36
1936-1938	7
1939-1940	0
1945 on	58

Except for wartime alliances, France's hostility to the outside world has been growing. We noted this above, when we saw that with the decline in her security and power, her dissatisfaction with the world increased. This applies to her relations with the great powers too. After 1914 references to GERMANY remained hostile. After 1917 references to RUSSIA normally were hostile. References to the UNITED STATES are now becoming less friendly.[13] The latter, like references to Britain, became very friendly when Germany threatened, but in nonwar years they tended to a common level of moderate friendship. From 1900 to 1913, 43 percent of *Le Temps* judgments of the UNITED STATES were critical, and in the twenties, 41 percent. Since World War II, however, the judgments have been 60 percent critical.

Thus we find that before World War I, France's component of her psychic distance from each of the other powers ranged from .37 (for Russia) to .61 (for Germany); while since World War II, it ranged from .58 (for Britain) to .96 (for Germany). Her mean psychic distance from the other powers increased from about .50 (even praise and criticism) to .73 (a strongly hostile attitude).

Russia likewise has become much more hostile to the other powers. In her case, the big change dates from 1917. Even before World War I the Russian press was more hostile to the other powers than were any of the other papers. (Mean criticisms were 64 percent of judgments, as contrasted with 48 percent in Britain. The United States, then highly isolationist, was second, with a mean of 59 percent adverse judgments of the great powers.)[14] But since the Revolution criticisms have been between 90 and 100 percent of judgments. Only during the war years were there more than sporadic favorable references to any of the other great powers. From 1941 through 1945 BRITAIN and the UNITED STATES were favorably judged in a few and uncontradicted editorials. This stopped abruptly in 1945. In our sample since World War II, there has been but one isolated favorable reference to another power.

This pattern was, of course, closely matched by the treatment of Russia in the papers of the other powers. From the Revolution until World War II, not a single favorable reference to RUSSIA turned up in our sample of *New York Times'* or London *Times'* editorials. Then from the Nazi invasion to 1945, the favorable references were 86 percent in the *New York Times* and 81 percent in the London *Times*. Since then, all London *Times* judgments have been unfavorable, and so have 94 percent of *New York Times* judgments.

Needless to say, the startlingly friendly tone of these papers during the war represented not ordinary friendship, but a leaning over backwards to avoid offense. After all, the function of editorials is criticism. Not even self-judgments are as uniformly favorable as the wartime judgments of Russia. (The proportion of self-judgments which were favorable were: Germany 82 percent, France 78 percent, Britain 65 percent, United States 63 percent, and Russia 49 percent.) Nor are judgments of a country's closest allies apt to be that favorable except in those situations where a sense of dependence leads to voluntary or compulsory censorship against offending.

Thus before World War I, although America's attitude toward France was marked by traditional friendship, only 52 percent of *New York Times'* judgments of FRANCE were favorable. Towards England, American traditional attitudes have been somewhat more ambivalent, although basically friendly. Before World War I, 49 percent of *New York Times'* references to ENGLAND were favorable. Since that time, Franco-American relations have suffered a number of blows, but America has been drawn into an extremely close alliance with Britain, one sufficiently secure not to be threatened by honest discussion. As a result we find that during the second war, 69 percent of *New York Times'* references to BRITAIN have been favorable, and since the war, 64 percent.

It is in the light of these figures that one should judge the significance of the 80 or 90 percent favorable treatment sometimes accorded allies in a war. Such treatment clearly represents a reaction against the dangers of revealing opposite feelings. Such one-sidedness is typical of an overly self-conscious alliance. We find instances of this kind not only in the Allies' treatment of RUSSIA during the last war, but also in their treatment of FRANCE after her fall (*New York Times* 82 percent favorable), and in the relations among most of the Allies in World War I. In the first war, *Le Temps* was 88 percent favorable to the UNITED STATES, and 97 percent to BRITAIN; the London *Times* was 83 percent favorable to the UNITED STATES, and 100 percent to FRANCE; and the *New York Times* was 93 percent favorable to BRITAIN. These figures invite a repetition of the caveat against any oversimple correlation of symbolic indices and underlying attitudes.

III. Patterns of Attention to Foreign Nations

The slant of hostility or friendship expressed in a group of editorials may have significance or not, depending on how much attention is paid to the situation. Occasional friendly remarks in the *New York Times* about Switzerland have less importance than frequent, somewhat more mixed but also friendly, expressions of attitude towards Great Britain—even if the latter are somewhat less uniformly friendly. It is therefore necessary to consider not only the direction of judgment on symbols but also their frequency. This is particularly necessary if we are interested in isolationism. Isolationism need not involve much overt hostility toward the outside world, although there is obviously some implicit hostility involved in cutting oneself off. Instead of overt hostility, isolationism can take the form of simple disregard of and inattention to the outside world.

The amount of attention to the outside world in the editorials in the five subsamples is shown in Figure 6, which graphs references to foreign countries during the past half-century. One obvious pattern stands out in all subsamples: a large increase in attention to foreign affairs during wars. Besides this banal conclusion we may note important trends in several countries. Particularly noteworthy are a tremendous drop in Russian attention to the outside world since 1928, and a marked increase in American attention since 1939.

In addition to these trends, we note an increase in French and German attention to foreign nations. The German increase is for the most part not reliable, since the first point in the series represents only the years 1910 to 1913 and is therefore not comparable with the beginning points of the other series. Nevertheless, the French and German papers, like the *New York Times,* seem to have become increasingly concerned with world affairs. The London *Times* alone has shown no discernible trend in attention. In the interbellum it was less conscious of the outside world than before World War I, but since World War II its attention has picked up again.

The Russian and American series deserve somewhat fuller study. To bring out the drastic change in Russian attitudes, we have summarized the data in Figure 7. From a situation in which the Russian press—both before

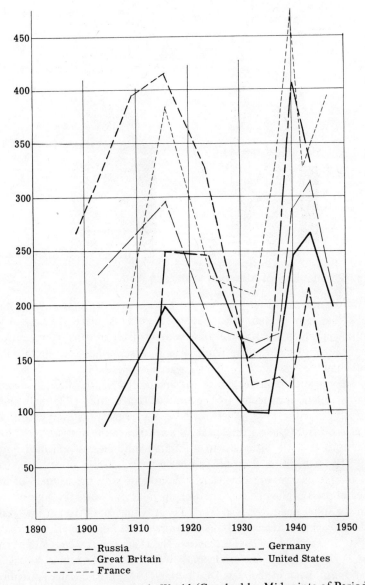

Figure 6. Attention to Outside World (Graphed by Midpoints of Periods)

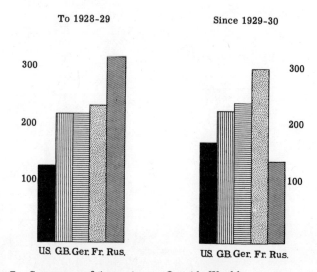

Figure 7. Summary of Attention to Outside World

the Revolution and after—was far more concerned with what happened abroad than any of our other papers, there took place a change to a situation in which the Russian press contains least editorial comment on foreign affairs. Indeed, since World War II, *Izvestia* has been more isolationist than the *New York Times* ever was.[15]

By impressionistic inspection of the annual figures, the Russian change towards isolationism seems to become noticeable after 1925, and more markedly so after 1928. There had been in Russia, as everywhere, an earlier drop from the wartime peak in attention to the outside world; but from 1918 to 1925 attention to most foreign countries remained quite high. Then it began to drop off and has done so sharply since 1928. The date of this change was obviously synchronous with the triumph of the policy of socialism in one country over the policy of world revolution.

On the other hand, the *New York Times,* which until the last few years paid less attention to world affairs than any of the other papers, now ranks roughly in the middle in this respect. The change in the contents of the *New York Times* did not set in until World War II crumbled American isolationism. Even in the New Deal period (1932 through 1938) attention to the outside world was very low. Only in the period beginning in 1939 did a sharp change occur.

During the early years of the war, while both Russia and the United States were still neutral, *Izvestia* cut itself off from the conflict, paying less attention to the outside world than ever before, but the *New York Times* manifested a vigorous interest. Since the War this interest has remained high, as high as during the first World War. America's abandonment of isolationism and her new role of active leadership in world affairs has resulted in attention to the outside world approaching that of the London *Times*. It is, however, still far below the level of attention of *Le Matin*, but then the facts of geography force France to have an anxiety and awareness of what goes on beyond her borders far greater than that of a non-Continental power. The regions to which main editorial attention has been paid by papers in the different countries correspond fairly closely to the regions of greatest diplomatic concern by the governments of those powers. More detailed data are included in Appendix G. A summary of the data is presented in Table 6.

It is obvious that attention by a power to its own region is apt to be low in this table, since we are not including self-references. Thus, attention by all other powers to the Western Hemisphere consists largely of references to the United States. *New York Times'* references to the Western Hemisphere, which include only references to the rest of the hemisphere, are naturally low. The proper item for comparison, in this case, is clearly attention to the Western Hemisphere other than the United States; in this, *New York Times* attention runs highest. In the same way, American attention to Europe, although only one percentage point below that of the Russian papers is probably significantly less than that of any Continental power, since the low figure represents Russian attention to Europe not including Russia. When we keep this point in mind, the data reveal a very high degree of similarity in the general distribution of attention among the five sets of papers.

There are, of course, differences. The *New York Times* devotes much attention to BRITAIN, to Western rather than Eastern Europe, to the Western Hemisphere, and to the Far East. The London *Times* devotes attention to the Empire, and consequently high attention to Africa and the Orient, and low attention to Europe. It is the only paper which does not devote two-thirds to three-quarters of its external attention to Europe. The German papers devoted most attention to her traditional enemies, FRANCE and RUSSIA, and also much attention to Eastern Europe. The low German attention to the non-European world, especially the East, may be partly due to the fact that our German data begin only in 1910, not many years before she lost her colonies. If the series were more nearly like that of the other powers, the percentages might also be more similar. French attention to GERMANY is high, and also to the minor powers of Eastern and Western Europe, and to Africa. Russian attention is concentrated on Eastern Europe and Asia.

Yet despite these differences, a consensus on the major arenas of international politics seems to exist. The rank correlations (rho) between any two sets of papers on the regional distribution of attention range between .76 and .94.

Not only is there a high degree of stability in the world distribution of attention from paper to paper, but also from year to year. There have,

Table 6
Regional Distribution of Geographic Symbols Expressed as Percentage of
All Geographic Symbols in Newspaper (Self-References Excluded)

To	Attention by paper in				
	United States	Great Britain	Germany	France	Russia
Great Britain	17.7		15.4	11.2	9.1
Germany	10.0	9.0		13.4	10.8
France	8.2	8.8	15.3		9.0
W. Europe, other	10.7	12.9	16.2	16.2	9.0
Total (Western Europe)	46.6	30.7	46.9	40.8	37.9
Russia	6.2	5.0	9.1	6.5	
E. Europe, other	9.4	10.3	17.2	17.1	24.7
Total (Eastern Europe)	15.6	15.3	26.3	23.6	24.7
Europe as whole	6.5	6.0	5.5	6.8	6.8
Total (Europe)	68.7	52.0	78.7	71.2	69.4
United States		8.4	6.6	6.4	4.8
W. Hemisphere, other	8.0	4.9	2.6	3.7	2.8
Total (W. Hemisphere)	8.0	13.3	9.2	10.1	7.6
Near and Middle East	3.1	4.7	2.3	3.9	4.8
Far East and Oceania	15.9	15.9	6.3	7.6	15.0
Africa	3.0	8.2	3.1	5.7	3.0
Miscellaneous	0.5	0.2	0.1	0.0	0.0
Super-regional empires as wholes	0.8	5.7	0.3	1.5	0.3
Total	100.0	100.0	100.0	100.0	100.0
Geographic symbols as % of total editorials	146.3	222.0	229.1	254.6	276.6

however, been some significant changes despite the fact that the attention
pattern has been basically stable over the half-century. Attention to the
UNITED STATES, for example, has been growing. In the London *Times,*
instances of the symbol UNITED STATES were 7.2 percent of the
geographic symbols before World War I, between 9 percent and 10 percent
in the interbellum, and 11.2 percent since World War II. The trend since
World War I is steadily upward, except for a notable drop between 1939
and the time of American involvement in the war. This temporary drop is
probably accounted for by the scrupulous avoidance of editorial controversy between interventionists and isolationists. Aside from this temporary
drop in attention to the UNITED STATES, the trend in London *Times*
since the First World War has been upward.

Similarly, in the French papers attention to the UNITED STATES has gone up markedly, having now become greater than attention to any other power. (As shown in the tables in Appendix G, UNITED STATES went up from 4.9 to 12.1 percent of the geographic symbols.)

The Russian press before the Revolution referred very little to the UNITED STATES. The UNITED STATES was less referred to than the Near East or Africa, and it was referred to only a third or half as much as any other major power. After the Revolution, relative attention to the UNITED STATES roughly doubled, but only since World War II has it become really extensive, having almost doubled again.

While attention to the UNITED STATES has been increasing, attention to FRANCE has been declining. In the *New York Times* and the Russian papers, it has gone down by about half over the half-century, and it has shown a similar trend in the British and German papers. The decline, however, has not been continuous. The zenith of attention was generally reached at some point in the vicissitudes of the political conflicts growing out of the first war. German attention to FRANCE reached its maximum in the early years of the Hitler regime, but was high during the conflicts over the Rhineland and reparations, too. Russian attention to FRANCE reached its maximum in the early thirties, in the period of rising Nazism.[16] American attention to FRANCE was highest in the twenties, and went down steadily thereafter.

Attention to GERMANY and to RUSSIA has fluctuated rather widely. Attention to GERMANY has been high generally when she has been a danger. In the period, however, when appeasement was strong, attention to GERMANY remained low in France and England. In this respect, these data on attention confirm trends noted above, based on judgments. In similar fashion, attention to GERMANY by *Izvestia* went down during the period of the pact.

Attention to RUSSIA has recently risen to higher levels than ever before. This is a very recent trend, however. Until World War II the press in the capitalist countries devoted less attention to Bolshevist RUSSIA than it had to Czarist RUSSIA. They found little to say about the new and distasteful regime.

In other parts of the world, the most notable trend has been the decline in attention to Africa. Despite a temporary increase of attention during the African campaigns of World War II, the general trend is quite clear in all countries and probably reflects the decline in importance of the struggles over colonies.

One last set of symbols deserving mention are those that refer to groups of countries in Europe. (Regional symbols would be of interest elsewhere in the world, too, but there are not enough of them to support conclusions.) It is perhaps significant that references to EUROPE as a unit, rather than to particular nation-states, have increased on the whole.

Our symbol list included the three symbols EUROPE, EASTERN EUR-OPE, and WESTERN EUROPE. In the twenties there was a noticeable increase in the use of the symbol EUROPE in all papers except *Izvestia* (in which it came later). This persisted roughly until World War II, since when this symbol has declined. Its place, however, has been taken not by national symbols, but by the two regional symbols EASTERN and WEST-ERN EUROPE. The three symbols together are now used perhaps as much as before. (The figures are given in Table 7.) This general increase in supernational references, with the substitution, since the war, of the two units for the still more general term EUROPE, reflects fairly accurately the trend of events.

IV. Symbols of National Security and Diplomacy

Attention

So far, we have examined the state of international relations at various times by studying the editorial mention of the names of foreign states. Relevant to the same problem is also a large vocabulary of *international political* symbols referring not to the states which are the actors in diplomacy, but to the processes of international relations themselves. The use of such terms as ARMAMENT, DISARMAMENT, ARBITRATION, CONCILIATION, IMPERIALISM, NATIONALISM, IRRIDENTISM, IN-TERVENTION, BALANCE OF POWER, COLONIZATION, MONROE DOCTRINE, MANDATES, NEUTRALS, TARIFFS, VERSAILLES TREATY, LITTLE ENTENTE, SELF-DETERMINATION, WAR, PEACE, etc., in newspaper editorials reveals the orientation of the paper towards world affairs. Just as attention to the world beyond one's frontiers constitutes an index of isolationism, so attention to the processes of war and peace, compromise and conflict, negotiation and defense, constitute an index of concern with one's position in the family of nations.

Full data on attention to these symbols of international politics are given in Appendix F. These data, however, are unduly affected by the brute facts of war and peace. The symbols WAR and PEACE are the most common in the list and occur most during wars. To allow for this, and to see what is significant in the data, we summarize in Table 8 the attention to international relations in peacetime periods.

From this table it is clear that, except in Russia, attention to international politics has risen in the past half-century. This finding provided a key to a number of results in the previous chapter. When we reported the distribution of symbols of democracy, we noted that most of them have become an increasing part of the total symbol flow in *Izvestia*. Such results offhand seem to indicate a greater growth of attention to these values in Russia than the West, but they are largely due to the fact that the foreign

Table 7
Regional European Symbols as Percentage of All Geographic Symbols for Country in Given Period

	Pre-World War I	World War I	1920s	Early 1930s	Middle 1930s	World War II Phase 1	World War II Phase 2	Post-World War II
United States								
E. & W. Europe	.2	.1	.4	1.1	0	.3	.4	4.0
Europe	4.6	4.2	9.0	7.7	8.7	7.0	5.5	5.0
Total	4.8	4.3	9.4	8.8	8.7	7.3	5.9	9.0
Great Britain								
E. & W. Europe	.1	.0	.1	.4	.2	.1	.4	3.4
Europe	5.4	3.4	7.3	7.3	7.8	6.6	5.4	7.1
Total	5.5	3.4	7.4	7.7	8.0	6.7	5.8	10.5
Germany								
E. & W. Europe	0	0	0	0	0	0	0	–
Europe	0	1.6	7.4	8.1	5.1	5.1	5.6	–
Total	0	1.6	7.4	8.1	5.1	5.1	5.6	–
France								
E. & W. Europe	0	0	.2	.3	.3	.4	0	1.9
Europe	6.3	3.2	7.8	12.0	8.3	11.2	5.9	3.9
Total	6.3	3.2	8.0	12.3	8.6	11.6	5.9	5.8
Russia								
E. & W. Europe	.1	0	.1	0	0	0	0	0
Europe	6.9	6.8	5.6	8.8	5.1	13.8	8.5	10.3
Total	7.0	6.8	5.7	8.8	5.1	13.8	8.5	10.3

affairs segment of the symbolic pie has been contracting in Russia while expanding elsewhere. Thus, all domestic subjects have been given more of the total attention in Russia and less elsewhere.

In their broadest aspects, these results clearly parallel the above-noted trend toward or away from isolationism. That is, the broadest trends in attention to world politics parallel those in attention to foreign states. Measured either way, America has recently moved away from isolationism, while Russia has moved toward it. A closer look at the figures, however, reveals that the parallelism is not as clear cut as one might expect. One might assume a priori that the two indices of attention to external rather than domestic relations would be highly correlated, but it turns out that this is not so. The relationship between attention to the outside world and attention to the processes of international relations is complicated.

Our own domestic conflict between isolationists and internationalists has tended to direct our thinking into an oversimplified polarity. We reduce the possible positions to a single scale between these two limits. We define one limit as (a) a lack of interest in, and conversance with, foreign areas, coupled with (b) confidence that one is secure in one's own bailiwick. This

Table 8
International Political Symbols as Percentage of All General Symbols

	Pre-World War I	1920s	Early 1930s	Late 1930s	Post-World War II
France	22	34	28	28	32
Germany	18	39	28	18	–
Great Britain	27	44	41	44	36
United States	24	41	35	33	41
Russia	37	23	14	14	21

confidence is reflected in a lack of sense of urgency in preparing for or resolving international conflicts. We define the other limit as an interest in what goes on abroad, growing out of concern for the relationship of one's state with other states.

In America, therefore, we expect that the man who is interested in war and peace will also want to be informed on world affairs and will read with avidity the foreign cables. The central strategy of almost all the American pressure groups behind international cooperation is to promote interest in, and knowledge of, world affairs. They all work on the assumption that dissemination of information about world affairs can only help international cooperation.

This identification of interest in foreign events with advocacy of a vigorous foreign policy, and the parallel identification of indifference to foreign events with an attitude of withdrawal, can be highly misleading when applied outside of the American scene. This is true, for example, of references to Russian "isolationism." If this term is used as meaning lack of attention to world affairs (which is how we use the term here), it may legitimately be applied. But if it carries the connotations of the whole complex of American isolationism, including restricted foreign aims, it is misleading.

After the last war, there was a great deal of discussion about whether Russia would revert to the "isolationism" which supposedly characterized her foreign policy from 1924 through 1934, or would continue to cooperate with her wartime allies—these being treated as the only two alternatives. In fact, of course, she has done neither. She has reduced her contacts with the outside world as a means toward important and aggressive foreign policy objectives, not as a result of indifference towards them.

The point that is missed, in the oversimplified image of possible international attitudes, is that both the isolationist and internationalist positions popular in this country rest on liberal assumptions that are taken for granted. The isolationist assumption is that of laissez faire, or live and let live. It is assumed that if each looks after his own business, problems will take care of themselves, and no one will resort to violence unless offended.

The internationalist assumption is that good will and reasonableness of men in general will lead to knowledge and truth and will thus promote cooperation for the mutual benefit of all those who participate.

These assumptions, characteristic of nineteenth-century liberalism, are not shared by all ideologies. It is perfectly possible to conceive of a great interest in what goes on in the outside world, coupled with complete cynicism about the ideological abstractions under which this is discussed in diplomacy, and also about the mechanisms of world cooperation. The attitude would be characteristic of some "power politics" points of view. These would describe world events as simply the calculated actions of ENGLAND, FRANCE, RUSSIA, etc., with little said about such principles as FREE TRADE, or MILITARISM, or such objectives as PEACE or PATRIOTISM. Interest in world affairs would, in this combination, go with lack of enunciation of guiding principles. Conversely, it is possible to have a very vigorous foreign policy with clear-cut objectives to which importance is attached, but to care little for information about the outside world. Indeed, for some such foreign policies, lack of knowledge may be a virtue. If the policy demands that the outside world be treated as despicable and as merely a target on which to project domestically determined demands, then ignorance may be prized as a proof of loyalty and a sign of superiority.

The clarification of these points is important as an introduction to the analysis of our data, since it turns out that the relationships between isolationism, as we here use the word, and attention to the traditional substantive topics of international relations are far from simple. In the *New York Times* there is the very close relationship which our analysis of American attitudes would lead one to expect. Whenever isolationism is strong, as in the interbellum, attention is low both to foreign countries and to the mechanisms and subjects of foreign policy. Whenever events have forced this country from isolationism, there is an increase in both the volume of material on foreign states and the volume of material on international relations. The coefficient of correlation between these two indices for the eight basic periods into which we have divided the half-century is .96. The periods are few, but the correlation is so exceptionally high as to be quite clearly significant.

This high correlation between attention to the outside world and attention to international politics, which represents the complete identification of the two elements in the American ideology, is lacking in any of the other papers studied. In the British and French papers there are moderate correlations (.68 and .64 respectively). In the German and Russian papers such correlations are lacking. (The figures are Germany .28, Russia −.07.) It must be recalled, however, that we are dealing here not only with small numbers, but also with time series, and a more valid analysis of the reasons for these data can be made by looking at the trends. In Figure 8 the attention to fifty-six international political symbols is plotted together with attention to foreign geographic symbols.

One thing that stands out clearly for all sets of newspapers except the Russian is that in the interbellum there was a relative increase in the use of those ideological and institutional terms which make it possible to talk of international relations other than as the acts of a series of states. In the 1920s and in the early 1930s faith existed in the meaningfulness of such principles as DISARMAMENT, NATIONALISM, and NONINTER-VENTION, such institutions as the LEAGUE OF NATIONS and the WORLD COURT, and such instrumentalities as the TREATY OF VER-SAILLES or SANCTIONS, to an extent greater than before World War I or after World War II. This statement is based not on the absolute frequency of such symbols, which, like the geographic ones, tended to go up in periods of war and crisis and down in periods of relative tranquility, but on their frequency relative to total attention to the outside world.

In other words, for any given amount of treatment of world affairs, these symbols other than state names were more numerous in this period than before or since. The ratio between these international political terms and the geographic ones was generally at its peak in the twenties or thir-ties. It stood in each case above that for the entire period as shown for each country in Table 9.

The presence of the tendency in the interbellum to use the international political terms in the discussion of international relations largely accounts for the imperfection of the correlations recorded above for England and France. In the cases of Germany and Russia, other factors were also at work. In Germany a great change occurred with the rise of Hitler to power. Editorial references to other powers went up immediately as a result of the Nazis' aggressive campaigns, but references to the ideological or institutional components of diplomatic activity remained small. The Nazis justified their activities at a very elementary ideological level. Beyond the names of the actors, it took little vocabulary other than that of everyday life to describe the world as the Nazis saw it. They were satisfied to shout "Benes ist ein Lügner" rather than engage in disquisi-tions on the principles and practices of international relations.

Indeed, if we look at the symbols used from the list of 56 nongeographic ones relevant to international relations we find that the relatively few uses of these terms were concentrated on a very small number of different symbols. Of the 56 symbols on the list, only 16 appeared in our sample of the *Völkischer Beobachter* and of these, 8 accounted for almost 90 per-cent of the *Völkischer Beobacher* references (Table 10).

The Nazi flow of communications thus reflected that elementary kind of power politics analysis to which we alluded above. The Nazi editorials revealed an intense awareness of the outside world, but not coupled with

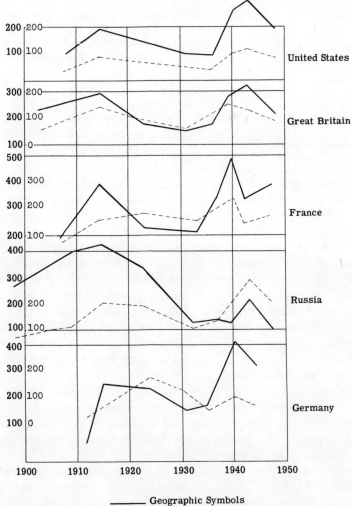

Figure 8. Attention to International Affairs (Graphed by Midpoints of Periods)

Table 9

Ratio of National Security and Diplomatic Symbols to Foreign Geographic Symbols

	1920s	Early 1930s	Entire Half-Century
United States	.51	.47	.43
Great Britain	.49	.47	.39
Germany	.76	.90	.47
France	.78	.73	.54

any sense of it as an institutionalized community. Although they had little interest in the instrumentalities and doctrines of diplomatic activity, they showed no impulse toward withdrawal. Consciousness of the external enemies was too acute for that.

In some ways the recent Soviet press has been at the opposite extreme; in some ways it is much like that of the Nazis. It also is very impoverished in the variety of symbols by which it deals with world affairs. And it likewise has shown quite different attention trends toward the countries of the outside world and toward the international relations of the Soviet state. But while the Nazi press tended to replace international political symbols by simple state names, the Soviet press has more and more stressed ideology regarding foreign policy at the same time as it has sharply reduced its attention to the outside world.

Let us consider first the relationship of these two indices. A glance at Figure 8 will reveal that the lack of correlation in the two Russian series is not due to short-run, random fluctuations, but to differences in trend. With one exception, the slope of the lines between any two successive periods is the same for each index. Clearly, then, there is some correlation between the two series. *Izvestia* does respond to changing world conditions by parallel increases or decreases of attention both to foreign states and to the other symbols of international relations. In fact, the correlation of changes from period to period between the two indices is .89 (or, omitting 1939-40, .98). The reason no correlation appears over the long run is the difference in trend.

The difference between the two trends is very significant and deserves close scrutiny. What is the meaning of the fact that the Russian press, which before 1928 discussed the outside world more than any other, has since stopped talking about what goes on in foreign countries, but at the same time has increasingly discussed matters of relevance to foreign policy? The most plausible explanation for this strange phenomenon would be that the editorial writers were giving expression to an inflexible

Table 10
International Political Symbols in *Völkischer Beobachter*

Symbol	Percentage of Instances of All Symbols on List of International Political Symbols	Cumulative Percentage
WAR	31	31
PEACE	15	46
TREATY OF VERSAILLES	13	59
LEAGUE OF NATIONS	8	66
IMPERIALISM	7	73
ARMAMENTS	6	79
AXIS	5	84
FATHERLAND	5	89
NATIONALISM	3	92
ENTENTE	3	95

nationalism. We suggested above that this kind of symbol pattern might appear where a number of specific conditions existed. These include:

1. Considerable anxiety about, and concern with, the position of one's state vis-à-vis the outside world. (This is an important difference from American isolationism.)

2. The predominance of domestic motives for concern with foreign policy. (The real facts abroad are therefore less important than domestic needs or dogmas in determining external attitudes; facts may even be embarrassing.)

3. Hostility to the outside world which takes the form of labelling international attention as wicked and disloyal.

Where such conditions exist, a state is apt to adopt chauvinistic policy and to talk much about national grandeur or national dangers, but little about what really goes on abroad.

The applicability of this explanation to the Russian press can be confirmed by examining the international political terms which predominate and also by examining the dates of the changes. *Izvestia*, like the *Völkischer Beobachter*, has labored a very small number of key symbols. Seven terms from our list of 56 account for 90 percent of the instances of use in the past decade, and 11 terms account for 95 percent of the cases. These terms are indicated in Table 11.

It is perfectly clear that these terms are predominantly oriented towards the power and might of the nation itself. They are terms that are relevant to foreign policy, but they are not primarily terms useful for talking about diplomatic and similar international dealings. The distinctive feature of the

Table 11
International Political Symbols Appearing in *Izvestia* Since 1939

Symbol	Percent of Instances of All Symbols on List	Cumulative Percentage
FATHERLAND-		
MOTHERLAND	29	29
WAR	26	54
PATRIOTISM	15	69
PEACE	7	76
IMPERIALISM	7	83
MILITARY		
OCCUPATION	5	88
ARMAMENTS	3	90
COLONIZATION	2	92
ALLIES	2	93
CRISIS (international)	1	94
NEUTRALS	1	95

list is the prominence of the symbols FATHERLAND-MOTHERLAND and PATRIOTISM. (FATHERLAND-MOTHERLAND were not distinguished, but were treated as a single symbol.)

These terms are so different from typical diplomatic terminology that one suspects that they appear at least as often in editorials that are domestic in their avowed subject matter as in editorials explicitly on foreign policy. We have no count on this point, but an impressionistic review of current Soviet press items confirmed this suspicion.

It is this type of content material which has come to predominate in the Soviet press in recent years and which accounts for the nationalistic trend noted above. The symbols of old-fashioned militaristic patriotism have been revived, while symbols useful for talking about the outside world have rapidly decreased in number. This trend has been a fairly steady one.

The graph in Figure 8 reveals that the trend toward decreasing attention to the outside world relative to symbols of international politics has been continuous, at least since World War I. The drastic changes in this direction, however, come in two jumps: one after 1928, when the full-fledged Stalinist policy of "socialism in one country" and building up of Russian might came into effect, and the other after 1939, with the Stalin-Hitler pact. It is in the latter period that the specifically nationalistic terms which predominate in the above list came into widespread use.

To illustrate the change in Russian ideology from internationalism to nationalism a number of the key terms in *Izvestia* have been plotted year by year in Figure 9. The first two graphs simply document what has been said above. They reveal the decline in interest in organizations for international cooperation and the growth in the use of the terms FATHER-

LAND and PATRIOTISM. It is noteworthy that only in 1945, at the time of the creation of the United Nations, did it receive any noticeable amount of attention in the *Izvestia* editorials. Despite the leading role of Russia in it, the U.N. has received far less Russian attention than did the League of Nations. The attention of *Izvestia* readers has not been focussed on this central agency for international cooperation.

The term FATHERLAND-MOTHERLAND was apparently resuscitated from the limbo of Czarist terminology in 1934. From then on its use increased steadily until about 1939, since when it has appeared in about two-thirds of the *Izvestia* editorials. PATRIOTISM was revived a little later. Its first extensive use was in 1938, and since then its use has increased steadily until now it appears in about half the editorials. It should also be noted that judgments of it have been reversed since the early years of the Bolshevik regime. It was judged once favorably in 1919, but unfavorably 6 times up to 1925. Then it was not judged again until 1941 except for 1 favorable judgment in 1939. With the war, however, it became a very strongly positive term. It was judged adversely once in 1941 and once in 1943, but has been judged favorably 49 times since 1941.

Even in *Novoe Vremia* there had been no such unambivalent endorsement of PATRIOTISM. It was judged adversely 14 times to 12 favorable judgments before 1918. In this respect the Russian prerevolutionary paper was unique. In many respects it was the least blatantly nationalistic of any. We have already noted that it paid most attention to the outside world. Also it was most self-critical. The symbol RUSSIA was judged favorably in only 40 percent of the judgments in *Novoe Vremia*. This compares with judgments in the other countries of themselves ranging between 63 and 76 percent favorable at that time and between 63 and 82 percent favorable in general.[17] Since then, needless to say, the judgments of RUSSIA have been reversed. From then through 1938, 76 percent of the judgments of the U.S.S.R. were favorable, and since then 91 percent have been favorable.

It thus seems clear that the ultrachauvinistic content of *Izvestia* for the past ten years does not represent a reversion to prerevolutionary patterns. The thesis that there has been such a reversion in the content of Russian foreign policy undoubtedly has merit, but it is an oversimplification of the situation to assume that Russian aggressiveness today is nothing more than the imperialism of the czars. On the contrary, in many respects the internationalism and self-deprecation of the early years of the Bolshevik regime were a more genuine continuation of some elements of Russian ideology than the violent nationalist reaction which has come since. Nowhere in our sample of the press in the past half-century, except in Nazi Germany, has there been such a one-sidedly nationalistic treatment of the news as in Bolshevik Russia since the late thirties.

The shift is apparent not only if we look at those terms usually used to

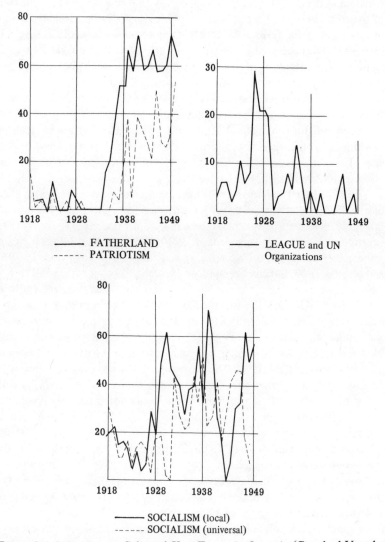

- FATHERLAND
----- PATRIOTISM

- LEAGUE and UN
Organizations

- SOCIALISM (local)
----- SOCIALISM (universal)

Figure 9. Attention to Selected Key Terms in *Izvestia* (Graphed Year by Year)

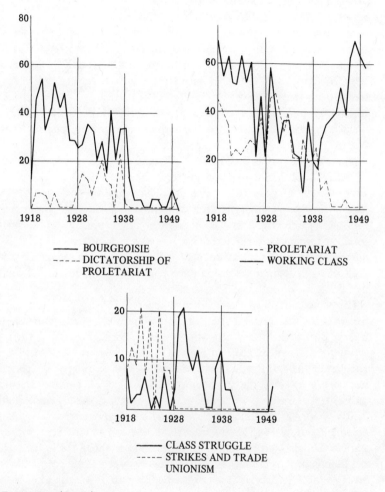

Figure 9.   (Cont.)

describe the world scene, but also if we examine the peculiarly Marxian, or more accurately Communist, terminology which the Russians used for this purpose for many years. The world is no longer described as a struggle between the BOURGEOISIE and PROLETARIANS, but as a struggle between FATHERLAND and IMPERIALISTS. In this process many class terms have been disappearing as nationalist terms have been increasing. Among the class terms that have gone by the boards are PROLETARIAT (about 1938), CLASS STRUGGLE (about 1941), STRIKES and TRADE UNIONISM (about 1928). It is interesting to note that when *Izvestia* found it no longer opportune to refer to STRIKES or TRADE UNIONS it apparently picked up the more general term CLASS STRUGGLE as a temporary substitute. That, too, was then discarded by the time of World War II.

While such terms as PROLETARIAT have been dropped, it is true that WORKING CLASS has not been. This fact, nevertheless, illustrates the same pattern of growing nationalism. The symbol WORKING CLASS as used in *Izvestia* generally has domestic reference, but the synonym PRO-LETARIAT refers to this class as exploited by capitalists. It is, therefore, used for foreign rather than for contemporary Soviet workers. During the middle 1930s both terms were played down in favor of the term PEOPLE. This was a deliberate gesture in the attempt to form a common front with middle-class elements against fascism.

The same growth of nationalism is apparent if we look at the graph in Figure 9 for the term SOCIALISM as a domestic and as a universal term. Except during the war years, when the ideological character of the regime was played down in favor of eternal Russia, the term SOCIALISM as an appelation for the Russian system continues to be extensively used, as it has been ever since the thirties. World SOCIALISM, however, has in the past three years been discarded as an important Soviet symbol. Until recently SOCIALISM as a universal conception appeared in roughly four editorials out of ten; it now appears in one out of ten. Thus we see not only in the selection of traditional diplomatic symbols, but in the selection of Communist symbols, as well, a tendency to play down the world struggle for Socialism, in favor of the building up of Russia.

It would be easy to explain some of these phenomena simply as consequences of the Second World War. That explanation is undoubtedly partly correct. A rapid culmination of nationalist trends in symbolism can usually be dated somewhere between 1939 and 1941. That explanation, however, fails to take account of the fact that in none of the respects here mentioned has there been a reversion to prewar patterns, even by 1949. The chauvinist character of *Izvestia* has apparently become permanent. Also it should be noted that the most important changes—the revival of PATRIOTISM and FATHERLAND, the decline of class terms, etc.—had all set in by the middle 1930s. The revival of Russian nationalism was certainly a response to external as well as internal dangers, but it was not simply a consequence of the experience of the war. The die had been cast before that.

Variety of Symbols

We listed above the most common counted symbols relevant to international relations from the editorials of the *Völkischer Beobachter* and from *Izvestia* in the past decade. It would be well to compare these with similar lists from the London *Times*, the *New York Times*, and the French prestige papers.[18] (See Table 12.)

The American and British lists are strikingly similar. Except for a transposition of the symbol CRISIS, the first eight items on the two lists are the same and in the same order. Insofar as choice of vocabulary reflects the concepts in terms of which the world is viewed, it is apparent that the London *Times* and *New York Times* were in agreement in their analysis of the world situation in the past decade.

The differences which separate the remaining papers stand out rather clearly if we look at the leading terms. WAR and PEACE were in every case high among these and so may be disregarded. The remaining top terms in the *Völkischer Beobachter* were all terms of abuse for external enemies. TREATY OF VERSAILLES, LEAGUE OF NATIONS, and IMPERIALISM (which together made up more than one quarter of the instances of relevant terms) were all "devil" terms. Vilification was clearly the predominant pattern in the Nazi treatment of world affairs.

Izvestia went in much more for self-glorification. Aside from WAR and PEACE, the only words in the first three quartiles were FATHERLAND and PATRIOTISM. Between them they accounted for over 40 percent of the instances of symbols on the list. It is true that the favorite Russian term of vilification in this period is not included on the list of international relations terms. It is FASCISM. Were it included, however, it would still rank somewhat below PATRIOTISM in frequency, although it would displace PEACE from the top three quartiles. It is interesting, and probably quite contrary to popular impressions, that the symbol PEACE is only about half as important in the recent Russian vocabulary of international relations as in that of any other powers.

In all three democracies a distinctive feature of the top three quartiles of symbol use is the emphasis on the UNITED NATIONS and ALLIES. This reflects both in war and peace a much more positive and less nationalistic international orientation than that of the totalitarian powers. Bolstering the conclusion is the large number of diplomatic terms in the tails of the distributions for the three democracies. Such terms as SELF-DETERMINATION, DISARMAMENT, ARBITRATION, CONCILIATION,

Table 12
International Political Symbols Appearing Since 1939

Symbol	Percent of Instances of Symbol on List	Cumulative Percentage
French Papers		
1. WAR	23	23
2. PEACE	14	37
3. UNITED NATIONS	7	44
4. MILITARY OCCUPATION	5	49
5. FATHERLAND	5	54
6. ALLIES	5	58
7. NEUTRALS	5	63
8. AXIS	4	67
9. IMPERIALISM	4	71
10. CRISIS (International)	3	74
11. INTERVENTION	3	77
12. PATRIOTISM	3	79
13. ARMAMENTS	3	81
14. BLOCKADE	3	84
15. CONCILIATION	2	86
16. DISARMAMENTS	2	87
17. NATIONALISM	1	89
18. RAPPROCHEMENT	1	90
19. MILITARISM	1	92
20. PAN-SLAVISM	1	93
21. ATOMIC POWER	1	94
22. MEDIATION	1	94
23. ARBITRATION	1	95
London *Times*		
1. WAR	39	39
2. PEACE	14	53
3. UNITED NATIONS	9	61
4. ARMAMENTS	5	66
5. ALLIES	5	71
6. AXIS	4	75
7. NEUTRALS	3	78
8. CRISIS (International)	3	81

INTERNATIONALISM, etc., may not be individually numerous in any paper, but they are quite significantly present in the democratic papers and, to all intents and purposes, absent from the totalitarian ones.

Judgment

Up to now we have considered only attention to the symbols referring to international relations. Also important is how they are judged. We would like to know to what extent the editorials in any paper at any time lined themselves up in favor of a peaceful world community and to what extent against it. We can do this by looking at the judgments. On the one side

Table 12 (cont.)

Symbol	Percent of Instances of Symbol on List	Cumulative Percentage
9. PATRIOTISM	2	83
10. NATIONALISM	2	85
11. SELF-DETERMINATION	2	87
12. LEAGUE OF NATIONS	1	88
13. BLOCKADE	1	90
14. DISARMAMENT	1	91
15. ISOLATIONISM	1	92
16. INTERNATIONALISM	1	93
17. CONCILIATION	1	94
18. IMPERIALISM	1	94
19. ARBITRATION	1	95
20. TARIFFS (or INTERVENTION or PAN-AMERICAN all equally frequent)	–	95
New York Times		
1. WAR	37	37
2. PEACE	14	51
3. UNITED NATIONS	9	60
4. ARMAMENTS	9	69
5. ALLIES	7	76
6. CRISIS (International)	3	79
7. AXIS	3	82
8. NEUTRALS	2	84
9. ISOLATIONISM	2	86
10. ATOMIC POWER	2	87
11. IMPERIALISM	1	88
12. LEAGUE OF NATIONS	1	90
13. BLOCKADE	1	91
14. DISARMAMENT	1	92
15. NATIONALISM	1	92
16. PATRIOTISM	1	93
17. SELF-DETERMINATION	1	94
18. MILITARISM	1	95

there are identifications with all humanity; on the other, with one's own nationality against the outsiders. On the one side there are expressions favorable to harmony and friendship; on the other, expressions favorable to power, force, and domination. We shall call such expressions of attitudes, judgments for or against a world community.

Not all symbols referring to international relations can be classified on one side or the other of this polarity. A judgment in favor of the MONROE DOCTRINE or the TREATY OF VERSAILLES may occur in an editorial of either nationalist or internationalist tendency. To advocate SANCTIONS, or a BLOCKADE, or a policy of BALANCE OF POWER, may, depending on time and circumstance, be to advocate war and aggression, or to advocate cooperative international action to prevent war. Such symbols have a variable relation to the basic value of world community. It is therefore not very useful for us to tabulate judgments of them.

Some terms, however, are so unambiguously related to the ideal of a world community that, by selecting them from the total list of international symbols, we can construct an index of attitudes toward this value. To be for NATIONALISM, for example, may be a good or bad thing at a given time or place; but whether good or bad, every judgment in favor of NATIONALISM is in some sense a judgment against a broader loyalty. In the same way, advocacy of PEACE, of international organizations, or of DISARMAMENT, whether desirable or undesirable at any given time, is in some sense advocacy of world harmony. With such symbols (not quite half the total list of international symbols, but somewhat over half in frequency of use) we have constructed an index of world community.

The dominant conclusion to which an examination of this index leads is that there is in the modern world a great degree of consensus in the lip service given the ideal of world community. In all the newspapers and at most times the general tenor has been distinctly favorable to this value. The percentages of judgments favorable to world community during the entire half-century are as follows:

United States	70
Germany	69
France	67
Great Britain	64
Russia	62

Opposition to this ideal appears mostly in wartime. In wartime editorials one is apt to find pleas for patriotism and pleas against the desire for peace. Even in these editorials, however, judgments in favor of world community have exceeded those against it, except in France in World War I and Russia in World War II, but the index value has generally been lower than in peacetime. Since the wartime situation is a somewhat special one it might be well to present the world community index omitting the years 1914-18 and 1939-45. If this is done, the percentage of judgments favorable to world community in each country becomes as follows:

United States	84
Germany	71
France	71
Great Britain	67
Russia	67

No general trend stands out clearly from the data, but on the whole it seems that the interbellum editorials were more favorable to world community than either those before World War I or those since World War II. This is fairly clear in France, where the percentage of judgments favorable to world community before World War I was 60, between the wars 75, and since the last war 65.

In the London *Times* it is a little less clear. Before World War I, 70 percent of the judgments of world community were favorable. From 1918 through 1935, 75 percent of these judgments were favorable. In 1936, however, the drive for armaments and preparedness set in, so if we include the last three prewar years, only 64 percent of the judgments in the interbellum were for world community. It would seem reasonable, however, to include these last peacetime years with the war years that followed, in which case the suspected trend would stand up. Since World War II, 64 percent of the London *Times* judgments have been for world community.

In the *New York Times* we have a situation somewhat like that in the London *Times*. In the pre-World War I years, 88 percent of the judgments were favorable to world community. Then in the 1920s and early 1930s, 97 percent of the judgments were the same way. If, however, we add the last few years before 1939, only 86 percent of the interbellum judgments remain favorable to world community. In any case, since the Second World War the percentage is down to 77.

It is in *Izvestia* that the trend away from the ideal of world community is most notable. In *Novoe Vremia*, before 1918, 62 percent of the judgments were in favor of world community; then after the Bolsheviks came to power the figure went up to 80 percent, second only to that in the United States. Since World War II, however, *Izvestia* has been, as noted, highly nationalistic. Only 43 percent of the judgments of world community have been favorable. Except for the immediately prewar armament drives in Britain and the United States, this is the only instance of a peacetime period in which the bulk of the judgments have gone against world community. In these other two instances this was due entirely to editorial demands for armaments and preparedness. Only in the last few years in Russia have we had an explicit reversal of the usual ideological identification with humanity rather than with the nation state.

International Organizations

International organizations were discussed to the extent shown in Table 13 and Figure 10.

Such discussion became extensive only after World War I. Before then, international organizations were mentioned in 1 percent of the editorials in Russia, 0.7 percent in France, and less elsewhere. In the 1920s the picture changed. *Le Temps,* supporting a French foreign policy based largely on collective security, mentioned these organizations in 15.6 per-

Table 13
Attention to International Organizations

	Percentage of Editorials Mentioning Organizations	Organizations as Percentage of Counted General Symbols
France	9.9	2.2
Germany	7.8	2.3
Great Britain	5.7	2.7
United States	5.5	3.5
Russia	3.2	0.6

cent of the editorials. Under Weimar, the German papers were close in attention (although with a different attitude), 14.7 percent of the editorials mentioning international organizations. The *New York Times*, thanks to the debate over the League, discussed them in 9.5 percent of the editorials in the twenties; *Izvestia*, in 8.2 percent; and the London *Times*, in 6.9 percent.

In the thirties, as international tension grew, the French and British press gave increasing attention to the League and related bodies. *Izvestia* and the *Völkischer Beobachter*, under their nationalistic totalitarian regimes, and the *New York Times*, now that the affiliation controversy had been settled in favor of isolation, withdrew attention from the world organizations. The situation continued until the outbreak of World War II, when everyone lost interest in the League.

Since then the UN has taken the League's place in the French, American, and British papers, indeed to an extent greater than ever before. But while the *New York Times* has abandoned isolationism in this respect, *Izvestia* has become almost oblivious to the existence of the UN.

In judgments, the *New York Times*, which was in favor of the League as well as of the UN, has been the most uniformly favorable. There were no unfavorable judgments of any international organization in our sample of that paper. The judgments that did occur were concentrated in (a) the period of the League affiliation controversy and (b) the period since the conception of the UN.

The French and British papers were favorable to the international organizations in 72 percent of their judgments. That, however, is a misleading statement, since the unfavorable judgments were concentrated on the UN. Among the few London *Times* judgments in the interbellum, all are favorable, and in *Le Temps*, 95 percent are. Since World War II only 60 percent of the London *Times* judgments have been favorable, and only 14 percent in *Le Monde*. The role of the organized world community has apparently

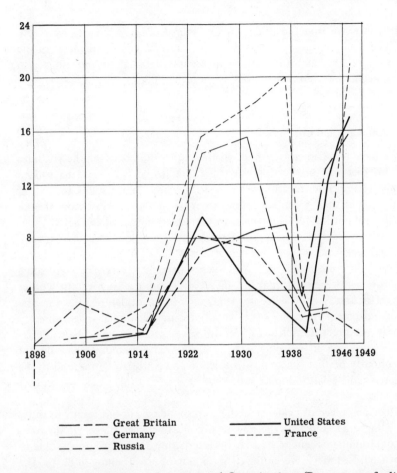

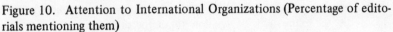

Figure 10. Attention to International Organizations (Percentage of editorials mentioning them)

grown in importance in the eyes of these papers, but their satisfaction with it has declined as their own influence has also declined.

The dominance of Britain and France in international organizations may be at an end, but their power position remains better than that of Russia or Germany before World War II. The latter countries found themselves for the most part at odds with, and hostile to, the international organizations. Under Weimar, only 40 percent of the German judgments were favorable, and under Hitler, none were. *Izvestia's* judgments before the last war were only 8 percent favorable. Even when Russia joined the League this was not reflected in favorable treatment of it, any more than Russia's membership in the U.N. is reflected in *Izvestia's* treatment of it.

In short, we find that judgments of international organizations largely parallel, and seem to be affected by, the same factors as judgments of the external world, and that attention to international organizations also parallels isolationism as measured by our other indices.

V. Summary and Conclusions

We have found there is a high positive correlation between the attitudes on international affairs expressed in the editorials which we have been studying and other measures of the relationships among states. In a word, editorials in the "prestige papers" seem to be a good expression of elite public opinion on foreign affairs. In part this is a special characteristic of the subject matter. These newspapers have traditionally acted as semi-official spokesmen of their foreign offices. Material from a different source or on a different topic might yield very different results. There are some situations in which the more the lip service given to a practice, the weaker it is. (Cf. the symbols of representative government described in the previous chapter.) There are other situations in which what is said directly reveals the practice. A fruitful task for social research would be to determine when one or the other relationship is likely to hold. Here we do not simply assume that the trends revealed in the editorials correspond to the trends in the relationship of states; we have some evidence, however, that they do.

One such piece of evidence is the correspondence of our results to those of Klingberg's studies of the psychic distances between states. On the basis of questionnaires sent to experts on international relations he was able to construct a model representing their opinion of how friendly or hostile the states were to each other. In our study we made a similar model based upon editorial expressions of opinion about the different states. The two models lead to substantially the same conclusions. The validity of content analysis as a method for measuring political attitudes, at least in this type of situation, is substantially supported by the closeness of our results to those of Klingberg's earlier experiment.

Further support to the validity of results based on the analysis of these editorials is given by the correspondence between our results and well-known trends in international relations. The trend of America away from isolationism is clearly revealed in the attention given by the *New York Times* to foreign countries and world organizations. The regional distribution of attention to the different continents and major powers corresponds closely to the known distribution of spheres of influence and diplomatic activity. The practice of appeasing the Nazis by France and

Britain, and in 1939-40 by Russia, shows up in the editorial treatment of Germany by the papers of those powers. All in all, these correspondences seem to establish the possibility of using content analysis data on editorial judgments to measure the psychic distances of powers, and data on editorial attention to measure political attention.

Even so, one cannot simply categorize the data as proving the growth or decline of unity in the world community. The world is a community or not in a good many different ways. Among the different factors are the degree of interaction, the degree of consensus on common ideals, the degree of organized unity, the degree of mutual attention, and the degree of mutual friendship. In interaction this world certainly has become one. The whole world has become responsive to events everywhere, or, more accurately, to events in the same main centers of policy formation.

Although there are differences, the basic regional distribution of attention in all five papers is substantially the same. For all of them in the past half-century Europe has clearly been the center of the world. And the rank correlation of attention to this and other areas among all papers is quite high. Furthermore, the attitudes in any one of the great powers are strongly reflected in all of the others.

There is, for example, a remarkable degree of reciprocity in the attitudes of states toward each other. This reciprocity is not necessarily immediate, but in the long run if elite editorial opinion in state A is hostile to state B, then elite opinion in state B will become hostile to state A to almost exactly the same degree. Since this process takes time, the attitudes of each state toward the other may at no moment be exactly alike, but over the years they seem to approach a common reciprocal attitude. Somehow in this interdependent world the attitudes of the elite in one state come to be known and returned by the elite of other states.

In the ideals to which lip service is given there is also much unity in the modern world. The ideal of a world community has generally predominated in the editorials, no matter now narrowly nationalistic the practices defended. This was probably most fully so in the interbellum years. Both in judgments of world community and in attention to international political symbols, these years represent the high tide of idealistic internationalism. Cynicism and particularism may now be on the increase. In Russia, at least, this is certainly true. In Russia since World War II, editorial judgments made the first clear-cut break from the cosmopolitan symbolism that has prevailed everywhere else in the West up to now. In its place has come a highly nationalistic set of values.

Some of the same tendencies are visible if we look more closely at the symbols of international organizations and at international political symbols. Attention to international organizations set in after the first

World War and has increased since. Like attention to foreign states, it has most markedly increased in the *New York Times,* which, since the end of the controversy over joining the League, had reflected American isolationism by giving relatively little attention to these instrumentalities. While America has been abandoning isolationism, Russia has been adopting it, and in her recent symbol flow devotes very little attention to international organizations. But except for *Izvestia,* the trend toward increased attention to international organizations seems general.

Other types of international political terminology may be showing somewhat less vitality than the titles of the international organizations. Except in *Izvestia,* the greatest emphasis on those symbols which are commonly used for talking about the instrumentalities and principles of international relations seems to have been in the period between the world wars. The use of such terms, rather than simply the names of countries and organizations, gave an ideological bent to the discussions. The sharpening of conflicts and the growth of a certain cynicism may partly account for the recent decline in these terms. It is obviously possible for a highly ideological terminology to be very nationalistic, as has been the case with *Izvestia* recently. This, however, has not been the situation in the other papers. In the other papers the decline in the use of international political symbols probably reflects a loss of faith in the general ideological symbols, in terms of which international actions in the past have been justified, and a loss of faith in the significance and efficacy of the institutions and mechanisms through which diplomatic relations have been conducted.

The declining use of certain symbols relevant to world affairs is not due to any general loss of interest in the outside world. Aside from *Izvestia,* which has been turning towards isolationism, the amount of attention to world affairs has been growing, again indicating world interdependence in some respects. Until the Second World War, the *New York Times* editorial attention to the outside world was less than that of any other prestige paper, but now it ranks somewhere in the middle. *Izvestia* now is the paper which gives least attention to the outside world although it used to give most. The change set in with the Stalin regime and its policy of "socialism in one country." Elsewhere, the general trend seems to be towards increasing interaction as measured by attention to what goes on abroad.

While the world community may be increasingly tightly knit as far as interaction is concerned, it is certainly not becoming more unified in attitude. On the contrary, hostility is growing, and lines are becoming more sharply polarized between friends and enemies.

In the long-term model of state relations for the past half-century we find that three states have been rather friendly: France, Britain, and the United States. The other two powers we have studied have been at odds not only with these three, but with each other. Germany and Russia have been the isolates of the world community.

This situation, however, while fairly stable in broad outline, has been evolving. Before the First World War there was no such clear-cut lineup. There was both less total hostility and also a more even distribution of hostility and friendship. Germany and Russia were not the subjects of as much hostility, and consequently the other three powers were not drawn as closely together.

In the interbellum Britain and the United States tended to return to their prewar positions regarding Germany and France, but France remained extremely hostile to Germany, and all became extremely hostile to Bolshevik Russia. Since World War II, this process of polarization has been completed. England and the United States have drawn very close together, with France a little further away, while Germany and Russia are both completely rejected. All this time, the total amount of hostility expressed has been increasing.

Hostility to the outside world, as measured by our data, seems to be very much a function of insecurity. Those nations which have at any given moment dominated the world scene have generally said little that was adverse to the other powers in the prestige papers. The insecure or unsatisfied powers, on the other hand, have generally had editorials full of hostile judgments of foreign states. This shows by a comparison of the papers in the different powers and perhaps also by a comparison of trends. As a power has declined in world position, the editorials coming from it tended to become more critical of the outside world. This can be seen in the French and British press. The same process can be seen in reverse in the *New York Times*. All through our sample Germany and Russia, the most dissatisfied powers, have had the most vituperative press.

The same frustration-aggression mechanism is operative regarding international organizations. The British and French papers have become far more critical of the U.N. than they were of the League, which they dominated. Here, as elsewhere, we see the evidences of a world of nations more and more forced into contact with each other, but less united in attitude. Among the democracies, the changes of attitude have been mixed. In some ways the democracies have drawn closer together in the face of outside threats. In war, when faced by the Nazi and Soviet threats, they have tended to become more friendly. In recent years one of the most common refrains of editorials in these three states has become the power and friendship of their allies. At the same time, the burden of the Soviet press has become nationalistic self-glorification. The older class terminology has given way to a purely national one. FATHERLAND and PATRIOTISM have become the two key terms. The total picture is that of an increasingly bipolar world.

NOTES

1. Hans Speier, "Historical Development of Public Opinion," *American Journal of Sociology* LV (1950): 4.
2. During the period covered by this study three exceptions might be noted, i.e., three situations in which the foreign policy of the prestige paper differed somewhat from that of the foreign office:

   a. The *New York Times* has been consistently internationalist, and thus at times at odds with administration policy. The *New York Times* was for the League of Nations, for low tariffs, and lukewarm on neutrality legislation. In holding these views it was probably close to the private views of most State Department career men and Secretaries of State, but sometimes opposed to official administration policy.

   b. The London *Times,* under Geoffrey Dawson, was strongly pro-imperialist. In this respect its policy was not different from that of the government, but the views of *The Times* were more consistent and more intense.

   c. *Le Monde* has recently become a "neutralist" organ, but this does not seriously affect our results, since the clash between the pro-American orientation of the French government and the "neutralist" views of *Le Monde* dates largely since 1949, when our sample terminated.

3. Quincy Wright, *A Study of War* (Chicago: University of Chicago Press, 1942), vol. II, p. 1240.
4. James T. Russell and Quincy Wright, "National Attitudes in the Far Eastern Controversy," *American Political Science Review,* XXVII (1933), 550-76; Quincy Wright and C. J. Nelson, "American Attitudes toward Japan and China, 1937-1938," *Public Opinion Quarterly* III (1939), 46-62; Wright, *Study of War,* Appendix XLI, pp. 1466-76. This last and Appendix XL summarize the work of Wright and his students in the field of psychic distance, which is probably the most valuable work to date on this subject.
5. Frank L. Klingberg, "Studies in the Measurement of the Relations Among Sovereign States," *Psychometrika* VI (1941): 335-52; Wright, *Study of War,* Appendix XL, pp. 1466-71.
6. Russia 47%, Great Britain 43%, United States 39%, France 39%, Germany 38%.
7. Adjustments due to the different starting dates of the different newspaper series have no affect on either the mean or median deviations from reciprocity. We shall therefore avoid the difficulties of modifying our series for each pair. Such adjustments would lower the Russo-American and Russo-German discrepancies, and would raise the Franco-Russian one, thus giving more support to the statement we make below that in the periods of friendly Franco-Soviet relations, France has tended to be the suitor.
8. Klingberg, "Studies in Measurement," p. 349.
9. Experts, of course, base their judgments in part on an impressionistic feeling of what the newspapers say. They also take account, however, of what other sources say, and what states do. In part, then, this test of validity indicates that counting and non-counting approaches to newspapers yield similar results, and in part it indicates that prestige newspaper contents parallel other indices of hostility.
10. The November 1938 model is reproduced in Wright, *Study of War,* p. 1471.
11. Klingberg, "Studies in Measurement," p. 351.
12. Klingberg, thesis, pp. 63 f.

13. Since the conclusion of our study, *Le Monde* has adopted an avowed "neutralist" line. It is worthy of note that this was foreshadowed in our postwar data.

14. Germany is not included in this comparison. Cf. note to Table 3.

15. It has been suggested that one reason for this fact is that the Russian press is more specialized than the press elsewhere. *Izvestia* is the government paper, *Pravda* the party paper, and *Trud* the trade union paper. Each paper attends to the appropriate subject matter. This is true, and *Krokodil*, for example, contains many references to the United States while *Izvestia* editorials do not. The government paper, however, has traditionally been the place where much attention was paid to foreign policy. In the twenties *Izvestia* was the main organ for foreign policy material. The striking thing is the change in this source.

16. The contradiction between this statement and the one above, to the effect that attention to France disappeared in the years of the Franco-Soviet Pact, is apparent rather than real. In the first place, a break occurred in 1935. That was the year in which attention to France almost disappeared. In the earlier thirties it had been considerable. In the second place, the two indices are computed on different bases. The present figures are concerned with the regional distribution of geographic symbols. The present figure is thus the proportion which FRANCE constitutes of all geographic symbols. The previous figures represent the proportion of editorials referring to a given symbol. We noted above a growing isolationism in Stalinist Russia. Thus in the thirties all references to foreign states declined drastically. But until 1935, those to FRANCE, while declining, declined more slowly than the others. The French *proportion* thus reached its peak at that time although the *actual number* of references to France was going down.

17.

Judgments of Self (Percentage Favorable)

	Pre-1918	Whole Sample
Germany	76	82
France	70	78
Great Britain	63	65
United States	64	63
Russia	40	49

18. For the present comparison, we are using 1939-49 where possible. Our French sample, however, has no 1943 or 1944 papers, and the latest period on which we have German data is the Nazi period, 1933-45. All these periods involve some war years and some nonwar years, but the proportions differ.

Except for the French subsample, the K values for symbols of international politics are all quite similar (United States 1790, Great Britain 1860, Russia 1800, Germany [a longer sample] 1500, France 950). The French press is most varied in these symbols as in all. The above K values are all high, but then we are dealing with a war decade and with the group of symbols central to it. The results are therefore what we would expect. We are concerned not with the index of symbolic variety as such, but with the type of symbols used.

APPENDICES

APPENDIX A
SYMBOL LIST FOR THE NEWSPAPER STUDY

Countries

Africa
Afghanistan
Albania
Alsace-Lorraine
Andorra
Arabia
Argentina
Armenia
Asia (symbol)
Asia (residual)
Australia
Austria-Hungary
Austria

Baltic Provinces
Balkans
Bolivia
Bosnia
Brazil
Bulgaria
Burma

Canada
Central America
China
China—Communists
China—Nationalists
China
Colombia
Costa Rica
Crete
Cuba
Czechoslovakia

Dardanelles
Denmark
Dominican Republic

Ecuador
Egypt
Estonia

Ethiopia
Finland
Fiume

Greece
Guatemala

Haiti
Honduras
Hungary
Herzegovina

India
Iran (Persia)
Iraq (Mesopotamia)
Ireland
Israel (also Jews in Palestine)

Japan

Latvia
Liberia

Macedonia
Manchuria
Mexico
Mongolia
Montenegro

Newfoundland
New Zealand
Nicaragua
Norway

Palestine
Arabs in Palestine
Panama
Paraguay
Peru
Poland

Rumania
Saudi Arabia, Yemen

Serbia
Siam
Sweden
Switzerland
Syria, Lebanon
Tangier
Transjordan
Turkey
Young Turks
Tibet
Trieste

Antarctic
Arctic

North America
South America
Europe
Near East, Middle East
Far East, Orient, East

Siberia

Union of South Africa

U.S.S.R.
White Russians
Uruguay
Venezuela
West Indies
West
Yugoslavia

Bering Straits (Sea)
Chinese Turkistan
Danube, Danubian Confederacy
Danzig
Eastern Europe
Greenland
Iceland
Korea
Lithuania
Luxembourg
Dalmatia
Galicia
Pan American Union
Scandinavian Union

Countries with Colonies

British Isles
British Commonwealth (Canada, Australia, N. Zealand, Union of So. Africa, India, Pakistan)
British Empire (symbol)
British possessions in Africa (symbol and residual)
Bechuanaland Protectorate
Southwest Africa
Kenya
Tanganyika
Nigeria
Anglo-Egyptian Sudan
British Somaliland
Suez Canal
British possessions in Latin America (symbol and residual)
British possessions in the Pacific

British possessions in the Mediterranean
British possessions in China
Malay States and Singapore
Sarawak
British New Guinea
Ceylon
Burma

Belgium
Belgian Congo

France
French Empire (symbol)
French Union (symbol)
French Africa (symbol and residual)
Algeria

Morocco
Tunisia
Fr. West Africa
Fr. Equatorial Africa
Madagascar
French possessions in the Pacific
  (symbol and residual)
New Caledonia
French possessions in the Caribbean
  (symbol and residual)
French possessions in other parts of
  America (symbol and residual)
French Indo-China
French possessions in China

Spain
Franco Spain
Republican Spain
Spanish Morocco

Holland
Netherlands Indies (symbol and re-
  sidual)
Netherlands Empire
Borneo
Sumatra
New Guinea

Portugal
Portuguese Empire (symbol and residual)

Angola
Mozambique

Italy
Italian Empire (symbol and re-
  sidual)
Italian East Africa
Italian Somaliland
Libya
Eritrea

Germany
German Empire (symbol and re-
  sidual)
German Africa (symbol)
Kamerun
German Southwest Africa
German East Africa
German possessions in China

United States
U.S. possessions in the Pacific
  (symbol and residual)
Hawaii
Philippines
Alaska
Canal Zone
U.S. possessions in the Caribbean
  (symbol and residual)
Puerto Rico

International Organizations

Instruction to readers: under respective symbols, place committees,
conferences, officers of organizations.

League of Nations
Mandates, mandate system
International Tribunal—The Hague

International Labor Organization
United Nations
United States of Europe
Treaty of Versailles

Washington Conference (1922)
Second International
Third International

Minorities

The symbols apply to the terms only in a minority role.

National minority (ities)

Arabs

Asiatics (Chinese, Japanese, others)

Boers

Croats

Czechs

Danes

Dutch

Finns

French

Germans

Hungarians (Magyars)

Italians

Irish

Poles

Rumanians

Russians

Scandinavians (Norwegians, Swedes)

Serbs

Slovenes

Slavs

religious minority (ies)

racial minority (ies)

Catholics (Irish Catholics in Ireland, Catholic parties)

Christians

Hindus (Gandhi)

Moslems

Jews

anti-Semitism

Negroes

Protestants (Reformation)

racial prejudice

Ideological Terminology

democracy

freedom

equality

individualism

majority rule

liberty

popular sovereignty

fraternity

bill of rights

free speech

free press

free religion

right of assembly

right of contract

right of movement

right to choice of occupation

censorship

race superiority

civil rights

franchise

free trade

free enterprise (private enterprise)

private property

people

plebiscite

self-determination, self-government

protectionism, tariff

free election (right to vote)

proletariat

masses

classless society, destruction of classes

class struggle

bourgeois democracy

dictatorship of the proletariat
interest slavery
usurer
plutocracy, (Wall St., the 60, 200, etc., families)
working class, labor
dictatorship of labor
state ownership (state monopoly)
bourgeois liberalism

authoritarian
totalitarian
police state
tyrannical state
military (garrison) state
centralization, centralized government
dictatorship

social democracy (also Social Democrats as a political party)
the family
progress
the comfortable life

social fascism
the leader
Positive Christianity
Aryan

Center
Right
Left
reactionary
Conservatives (e.g., British Conservative party)
Radical
Moderate
reform
Liberal
balance of power
isolation, isolationism
Drive to the East (Drang nach Osten)
the Eastern Question
occupation (military)
Labour party
Progressive

Doctrines

Instruction to readers: list under appropriate symbol the leaders, parties, publications associated with it, e.g., communism universal—under this put Marx, and all terms associated with universal Communist movement. Communist party—Thorez, *L'Humanité,* La Terr, the French Communist party, and all other occasions when communism has a definitely local association.

agrarianism (ian)
communism (ist) (universal) (also anti-Communism)
communism (ist) (*local*)
bolshevism (ist)
Marxism
Reds
Soviets

functionalism
corporationism

classical liberalism (also just liberalism)
constitutionalism
nationalism, Nationalist(s)
jingoism
nazism
socialism (universal)
socialism *(local)*
syndicalism, unionism, (trade unions, etc.)

pacifism, antimilitarism
militarism

imperialism
colonization

fascism

dialectical materialism
collectivism
anarchism (nihilism)
Catholic Church
pope, vatican
Christianity
clericalism
anticlericalism

masonic, free masonry
zionism

monarchical absolutism
monarchy (constitutional
   monarchy)

parliamentarism
scepticism
atheism
agnosticism
pessimism
idealism
activism
positivism
pragmatism

capitalism(ist)
trusts, cartels

pan-Slavism
Monroe Doctrine

particularism
paternalism
humanism
irredentism

internationalism

Security Symbols

war, demand for war
peace, demand for peace
crisis (internal—that is, in country
   where paper is published)
crisis (external—outside country
   where paper is published even if
   internal in another country)
revolution
counter revolution
terrorism
civil war (insurrection also)
resistance (against violence or
   domination only, not for such
   things as "His Majesty's Opposition exhibits some resistance to
   Mr. Blank's proposal")
survival
armaments, mobilization (military
   only)
disarmament

arbitration
conciliation
mediation
evolution
intervention
nonintervention
security
insecurity
strike(s)
blockade
sanctions (economic and military)
government use of violence (this
   symbol represents forcible action
   taken by the government against
   some group domestically, as
   against strikers—you may not find
   these exact words used and the
   term is to convey an idea not to
   be taken absolutely literally. Does
   not refer to violence outside
   country.)

Miscellaneous

Sentimental Slogans
patriotism
our country
Fatherland
Land of the Free (Liberty)
Land of our Fathers

Foreign Terms
(ideologically significant terms used
   by one country and adopted by
   another)
fuehrer
dirigisme
etatisme
Cesarisme
laissez faire
Pax Britannica
casus belli
rapprochement
status quo
chauvinism
Kultur (refers to German usually)
Mittel Europa
Kontinental Europa
coup d'etat

porto franco (open port)

Others
State (the State e.g. as contrasted
   to private enterprise, etc., not
   "the foreign States. . . .")
leadership
order
discipline
authority
blood (meaning race)
folk
soul
faith
universality
revelation
spirit (spiritual forces)
religion
Allies
Entente
Axis
Triple Alliance
neutrals, neutrality
Central Powers
Little Entente

APPENDIX B
AMOUNT OF CHANGE IN MAJOR SYMBOLS*

I. Russia

A. Change Between Successive Periods and Successive Peacetime Periods

1. 1892-1904 and 1905-1913 (Novoe Vremia)			2. 1892-1913 to 1914-1917 (Novoe Vremia)		
	Chi Square	Change Index		Chi Square	Change Index
War	18.0	56	War	196.1	1,147
People	18.0	263	People	93.4	546
Peace	2.3	7	Peace	6.6	38
State†			Fatherland	31.6	185
Reform	1.6	5	Conservatives	.5	2
Revolution	33.4	104	Allies	507.4	2,967
Conservatives	6.0	18	Socialism	11.5	68
Nationalism	32.0	100	Monarchy	37.6	220
Fatherland	.6	2	Crisis	.0	0
Armaments	60.8	189	Freedom and Liberty	48.6	284
Crisis	.0	0	Triple Alliance	.2	1
Socialism	1.2	4	Patriotism	9.7	57
Triple Alliance	2.1	6	Labor	5.8	34
Patriotism	2.0	6	Entente‡		
Labor	1.0	3	Catholics‡		
Order	37.6	118	Neutrals†		
Liberals	1.2	4	Liberals	.0	0
Pan-Slavism	85.5	266	Masses	16.3	95
Catholics	.0	0	Jews‡		
Freedom and Liberty	14.7	46	Democracy†		
Monarchy	2.5	8	Revolution	.6	4
Total	387.1	1,205	Capitalism	3.9	23
			Nationalism	.2	1
Mean 60 Median 13			Pan-Germanism	51.1	299
			Radicals‡		
			State‡		
			Armaments	.1	1
			Total	1,021.2	5,972
			Mean 299 Median 202		

*Unless otherwise indicated the twenty most common words are listed. (Italic)

†Word used less than 5 times in earlier period; i.e., a "new" word. This word is skipped in enumerating the twenty used for the mean index, but not in enumerating the twenty for the median index. (Not Italic)

‡Word used less than 5 times in later period; i.e., a word that has disappeared. This word is skipped in enumerating the twenty used for the mean index, but not in enumerating the twenty for the median index. (Not Italic)

I. Russia

A. Change Between Successive Periods and Successive Peacetime Periods (Cont.)

3. 1914-1917 to 1918-1928 *(Novoe Vremia, Izvestia)*			4. 1892-1913 to 1918-1928 *(Novoe Vremia, Izvestia)*		
	Chi Square	Change Index		Chi Square	Change Index
War	121.2	275	*War*	55.8	127
Soviet†			Soviet†		
People	26.8	61	*Peace*	.2	0
Working Class	986.1	2,241	*Working Class*	2,013.6	4,576
Peace	10.1	23	*People*	65.8	149
Bourgeoisie†			Bourgeoisie†		
Fatherland	60.8	138	*Reform*	10.4	24
Revolution	789.8	1,795	*Revolution*	1,056.5	2,401
Allies	24.1	55	*Fatherland*	67.9	154
Masses	571.8	1,300	*Masses*	2,193.7	4,986
Monarchy	.3	1	*Conservatives*	2.3	5
Imperialism†			*Imperialism*	5,730.5	13,024
Freedom and Liberty	36.4	83	*Socialism*	394.6	897
Proletariat	975.7	2,218	Proletariat†		
Socialism	112.2	255	*Crisis*	1.3	3
Communism	540.0	1,227	Communism†		
Patriotism	26.0	60	Triple Alliance‡		
Capitalism	440.2	1,000	*Capitalism*	972.8	2,211
Entente	11.1	25	*Patriotism*	4.1	9
Bolshevism†			Bolshevism†		
Democracy	5.2	12	Red†		
Crisis	1.2	3	Counterrevolution†		
Trade Unions	20.8	47	*Monarchy*	117.1	266
Conservatives	.2	0	Entente†		
Total	4,760.4	10,819	*Reactionary*	332.5	756
			Democracy†		
Mean 541 Median 638			*State*	30.0	68
			Allies	280.6	638
			Catholics	13.3	30
			Intervention†		
			League of Nations†		
			Trade Unions	105.4	240
			Total	13,447.8	30,564
			Mean 1,528 Median 2,306		

I. Russia

A. Change Between Successive Periods and Successive Peacetime Periods (Cont.)

5. 1918-1928 to 1929-1935 *(Izvestia)*			6. 1929-1935 to 1936-1938 *(Izvestia)*		
	Chi Square	Change Index		Chi Square	Change Index
Soviet	.0	0	Socialism	18.6	248
Socialism	97.4	468	Soviet	34.3	457
Working Class	32.7	157	Collectivism	7.9	105
Collectivism	917.2	4,410	Bolshevism	21.5	287
Bourgeoisie	10.2	49	People	9.5	127
Bolshevism	55.7	268	Capitalism	3.2	43
Revolution	8.3	40	Masses	.2	2
People	18.9	91	Revolution	3.7	50
Masses	.0	0	Proletariat	4.7	63
Proletariat	1.3	6	Fatherland	84.5	1,126
Imperialism	25.5	122	Working Class	4.7	63
Capitalism	2.3	11	Fascism	63.3	843
Communism	.2	1	Communism	40.6	541
Armaments	119.1	572	Democracy	106.8	1,425
War	10.4	50	Bourgeoisie	.0	0
Crisis	13.1	63	Red	31.6	421
Red	13.2	64	War	.3	4
Class Enemy	107.4	516	Trotskyism	66.7	889
Counterrevolution	16.1	77	Imperialism	.1	1
Dictatorship of Proletariat	33.3	160	Discipline	4.2	56
Total			Total	506.4	6,753

Mean 338   Median 116

Mean 356   Median 70

I. Russia

A. Change Between Successive Periods and Successive Peacetime Periods (Cont.)

7. 1936-1938 to 1939-40 *(Izvestia)*	Chi Square	Change Index	8. 1939-1940 to 1941-1945 *(Izvestia)*	Chi Square	Change Index
Soviet	.3	6	Communism	7.3	58
Socialism	8.3	173	Soviet	.7	5
Bolshevism	11.3	236	Fatherland	.0	0
Communism	12.5	260	War	120.7	966
People	.0	0	People	.9	7
Fatherland	16.4	342	Red	15.8	126
Capitalism	.4	8	Collectivism	1.3	10
Collectivism	2.3	49	Bolshevism	.9	7
Revolution	.3	7	Capitalism	57.6	461
Red	8.2	171	Fascism	96.5	772
Masses	3.4	70	Revolution	13.9	111
War	2.8	59	Working Class	20.6	165
Fascism	7.6	158	Imperialism	14.4	115
Imperialism	2.2	47	State†		
Democracy	5.2	108	Discipline	19.3	155
Discipline	10.3	215	Patriotism	13.9	112
Bourgeoise	9.2	192	Masses	7.0	56
Working Class	.1	1	Military Occupation†		
Proletariat	1.0	21	Peace	.3	2
Patriotism	7.5	156	Freedom and Liberty	.2	2
Total	109.5	2,279	Family†		
			Democracy	8.1	65
Mean 114 Median 89			Spirit†		
			Allies†		
			Monarchy†		
			Marxism†		
			Equality†		
			Armaments	11.2	90
			Total	410.8	3,285
			Mean 164 Median 113		

I. Russia

A. Change Between Successive Periods and Successive Peacetime Periods (Concl.)

9. 1941-1945 to 1946-1949 *(Izvestia)*	Chi Square	Change Index
Soviet	.0	0
Socialism	16.5	171
War	55.2	575
Fatherland	.1	1
People	.4	4
Working Class	22.2	231
Red	16.0	167
Bolshevism	7.0	72
Collectivism	.7	7
Communism	121.8	1,269
Fascism	23.7	247
Patriotism	.0	0
State	8.1	85
Masses	38.8	404
Military Occupation‡		
Revolution	3.6	38
Peace	.3	4
Democracy	35.5	370
Imperialism	.2	2
Freedom and Liberty	1.9	20
Discipline	.6	6
Total	352.7	3,673

Mean 184   Median 79

10. 1936-1938 to 1946-1949 *(Izvestia)* §	Chi Square	Change Index
Soviet	.0	0
Socialism	13.9	145
Bolshevism	1.2	12
Fatherland	38.0	395
Communism	2.7	29
Working Class	101.9	1,061
People	.2	2
Collectivism	17.0	176
Capitalism	46.7	487
War	31.5	328
Revolution	6.2	65
Patriotism	77.2	804
Masses	.2	2
Progress†		
Fascism	6.8	70
State†		
Democracy	3.6	38
Freedom and Liberty†		
Bourgeoisie §		
Peace	1.5	16
Imperialism	1.7	17
Security†		
Fraternity†		
Monarchy†		
Leadership†		
Franchise†		
Discipline	2.0	21
Red	18 6	194
Total	370.7	3,862

Mean 203   Median 160

§Only 19 symbols were sufficiently frequent in this period.

I. Russia

B. Cumulative Changes Since Before World War I

	1. 1892-1913 to 1918-1928 (Novoe Vremia, Izvestia) See Table A-4 above		2. 1892-1913 to 1929-1935 (Novoe Vremia, Izvestia)	
	Chi Square	Change Index		Chi Square	Change Index

	Chi Square	Change Index		Chi Square	Change Index
War	24.4	117	Liberals‡		
Socialism	1,023.7	4,922	Jews‡		
Peace	5.9	29	Nationalism‡		
Soviet†			Radicals‡		
People	125.6	604	*State*	1.2	6
Collectivism†			*Right*	22.6	109
Reform	8.8	42	Freedom‡		
Bolshevism†			*Order*	.0	0
Fatherland	.0	0	Catholic Church‡		
Masses	1,003.0	4,822	*Left*	.2	1
Conservatives‡			Democracy†		
Proletariat†			Social Fascism†		
Crisis	22.5	108	*Social Democracy*	50.8	244
Capitalism	645.0	3,101	Family†		
Triple Alliance‡			Pan-Slavism‡		
Working Class	325.7	1,566	Moderates‡		
Patriotism‡			Moslems‡		
Communism†			Spirit‡		
Catholics‡			Colonization‡		
Revolution	246.7	1,186	Christians‡		
Bourgeoisie†			Strikes‡		
Imperialism	673.4	3,238	Anarchism‡		
Class Enemy†			Pope, equality‡		
Dictatorship of Proletariat†			Christianity‡		
Armaments	32.3	155	Center, Security‡		
Class Struggle†			Constitutionalism‡		
Classless Society†			Clericalism‡		
Fascism†			Protestants‡		
Red†			Chauvinism‡		
League of Nations†			Anti-Semitism‡		
Counterrevolution‡			Race Superiority‡		
Discipline	55.5	267	*Militarism*	3.1	15
			Total	4,270.1	20,532

Mean 1,027   Median 4,872

I. Russia

B. Cumulative Changes Since Before World War I (Concl.)

	3. 1892-1913 to 1936-1938 (Novoe Vremia, Izvestia)§		4. 1892-1913 to 1946-1949 (Novoe Vremia, Izvestia)	
	Chi Square	Change Index	Chi Square	Change Index
War	1.7	22	60.3	628
Soviet†				
Peace	1.2	16	.0	0
Socialism	770.5	10,273	678.3	7,066
People	124.6	1,661	174.6	1,818
Bolshevism† / Fatherland			509.7	5,310
Reform‡ / Reform†				
Communism† / *Working Class*			656.0	6,833
Fatherland / Conservatives‡	92.8	1,237		
Capitalism / Bolshevism†	404.5	5,394		
Conservatives‡ / *Crisis*			.0	0
Revolution / Communism‡	183.3	2,444		
Crisis‡ / Triple Alliance‡				
Masses / Collectivism‡	314.5	4,193		
Triple Alliance‡ / *Patriotism*			160.4	1,671
Fascism† / *Masses*			350.2	3,648
Patriotism / Progress†	1.9	26		
Collectivism† / Catholics‡				
Working Class / *State*	39.0	519	116.2	1,210
Democracy† / *Revolution*			91.1	949
Bourgeoisie† / Liberals, Jews‡				
Red† / *Monarchy*			1.9	20
Proletariat† / Nationalism‡				
Trotskyism† / Radicals‡				
Imperialism / Armaments‡	284.6	3,794		
Discipline / *Freedom*	88.3	1,178	40.6	423
Catholics‡ / *Democracy*			450.2	4,690
Liberals, Jews‡ / Fascism†				
Monarchy‡ / *Imperialism*			184.9	1,926
Nationalism‡ / Order‡				
Radicals, State‡ / *Capitalism*			11.9	124
Armaments / *Security*	6.8	91	25.5	266
Order / Fraternity, Leadership†	12.9	172		
Total / Franchise†	2,326.5	31,020		
Discipline			36.9	384
Mean 2,216 Median ∞ / Catholic Church, Left‡				
Family			5.4	56
Colonization			5.2	54
Total			3,559.2	37,076

§ Only 14 symbols were sufficiently frequent in this period.

Mean 1,854   Median 6,950

I. Russia

C. Cumulative Changes Since Early Days of Soviet Regime

1.1918-1928 to 1929-1935
(Izvestia)—see Table A-5
above

2. 1918-1928 to 1936-1938
(Izvestia)

3. 1918-1928 to 1946-1949
(Izvestia)

	Chi Square	Change Index		Chi Square	Change Index
Soviet	33.4	446	*Soviet*	44.7	466
Socialism	110.7	1,476	*Socialism*	81.4	848
Working Class	30.1	401	*Working Class*	4.3	45
Bolshevism	104.0	1,386	*Fatherland*	1,027.2	10,699
Bourgeoisie	3.3	44	Bourgeoisie‡		
Communism	44.6	595	*Bolshevism*	105.2	1,096
Revolution	.0	3	*Revolution*	6.0	62
People	36.3	484	*People*	52.9	551
Masses	.3	3	*Masses*	1.0	10
Capitalism	7.8	104	*Communism*	34.1	355
Imperialism	7.7	103	*Imperialism*	17.7	184
Fatherland	20.6	275	*Collectivism*	493.8	5,144
Proletariat	2.4	32	Proletariat‡		
Fascism	692.1	9,227	*War*	11.9	124
War	2.1	28	*Capitalism*	18.4	192
Collectivism	134.6	1,795	*Patriotism*	298.7	3,111
Red	3.0	40	*Red*	9.0	94
Democracy	47.6	635	Progress†		
Counterrevolution	286.8	3,824	Counterrevolution‡		
Trotskyism†			*State*	31.0	322
Discipline	14.9	198	*Peace*	.1	1
Total	1,582.2	21,099	*Monarchy*	4.5	47
			Democracy	22.2	231
Mean 1,055 Median 424			Entente‡		
			Reactionary‡		
			Allies‡		
			Crisis	.3	3
			Total	2,264.2	23,585

Mean 1,179   Median 410

II. France

A. Change Between Successive Periods and Successive Peacetime Periods

	1. 1900-1913 to 1914-1918 *(Le Temps)*		2. 1914-1918 to 1919-1929 *(Le Temps)*		
	Chi Square	Change Index		Chi Square	Change Index
Socialism	293.2	776	Socialism	.0	0
Allies†			War	303.0	332
War	7.2	19	Allies	70.4	77
Neutrals	1,183.2	3,130	Peace	125.1	137
State	9.6	25	Neutrals	203.3	223
Freedom and Liberty		67	State	227.5	249
Left	25.2	5	Freedom and Liberty	37.8	41
Peace	1.9	5	Left	578.6	634
Revolution	1.9	2	Revolution	40.5	44
Patriotism	2.1	5	Communism†		
Reform	16.6	44	Patriotism	6.4	7
Fatherland	26.7	71	Crisis	107.6	118
Crisis	.4	1	Fatherland	1.9	2
Entente	230.4	610	League of Nations	696.3	764
Trade Unions	18.0	48	Entente	21.2	23
Central Powers†			Security	122.9	135
Working Class	5.3	14	Central Powers‡		
State Ownership	36.9	98	Versailles Treaty†		
Strikes	1.5	4	Militarism	9.1	10
Democracy	.3	1	Democracy	35.2	39
Militarism	22.1	58	Working Class	65.7	72
Security	.3	1	State Ownership	12.5	14
Total	1,883.6	4,984	Bolshevism	110.9	122
			Total	2,775.9	3,043

Mean 249　　Median 35

Mean 152　　Median 126

II. France

A. Change Between Successive Periods and Successive Peacetime Periods (Cont.)

3. 1900-1913 to 1919-1929 *(Le Temps)*	Chi Square	Change Index	4. 1919-1929 to 1930-1935 *(Le Temps)*	Chi Square	Change Index
Socialism	26.0	28	Socialism	3.5	8
War	111.0	122	Crisis	54.4	118
State	47.8	52	War	31.7	69
Peace	206.3	226	State	2.8	6
Left	66.9	73	Peace	.7	1
Communism	1,349.8	1,480	Left	.9	2
Revolution	19.9	22	Communism	9.2	20
Allies†			Security	36.5	79
Reform	1.2	1	Allies	79.0	172
Crisis	78.2	86	League of Nations	1.9	4
Freedom and Liberty	.1		Revolution	.1	0
League of Nations†			Order	31.4	68
Trade Unions	3.4	4	Versailles Treaty	6.9	15
Security	158.6	174	Nazism†		
Patriotism	.4	0	Democracy	1.7	4
Versailles Treaty†			Disarmament	3.2	7
Working Class	6.5	7	Working Class	4.1	9
Democracy	22.5	25	Reform	.1	0
Strikes	2.3	3	Bolshevism	16.1	35
Bolshevism†			Dictatorship	18.9	41
Disarmament	1,150.1	1,261	Marxism	48.7	106
Right	33.5	37	Total	352.1	764
People	14.0	15			
Order	32.6	36	Mean 38 Median 12		
Total	3,330.9	3,652			

Mean 183   Median 63

II. France

A. Change Between Successive Periods and Successive Peacetime Periods (Cont.)

5. 1930-1935 to 1936-1938 (Le Temps)	Chi Square	Change Index	6. 1936-1938 to 1939-1940 (Le Temps)	Chi Square	Change Index
Crisis	.1	0	Left	21.6	304
Left	33.9	201	War	37.1	522
Socialism	.1	0	Peace	.3	4
Peace	26.7	158	Nazism	19.3	272
State	5.9	35	Crisis	5.0	71
War	12.4	73	Soviet	20.4	287
Security	.0	0	Socialism	8.0	113
Revolution	12.3	73	Communism	.0	0
League of Nations	.5	3	Revolution	9.1	128
Order	17.8	105	Security	.3	4
Communism	15.9	94	Order	10.2	144
Marxism	12.2	72	Resistance†		
Nazism	.7	4	League of Nations‡		
Trade Unions	32.6	193	Democracy	4.8	68
Democracy	1.1	6	Marxism‡		
Freedom and Liberty	9.5	56	Neutrals	10.3	145
Disarmament	9.0	53	Trade Unions‡		
Authority	9.5	56	Freedom and Liberty	1.4	19
Reform	2.6	15	State	2.3	32
Intervention	43.3	256	Fascism	.1	1
Total	245.9	1,453	Bolshevism	9.9	140
			Authority‡		
Mean 73 Median 56			Intervention‡		
			Reform	1.0	15
			Working Class‡		
			Civil War, Masses‡		
			Strikes‡		
			Conciliation‡		
			Patriotism	.1	1
			Evolution‡		
			Rapprochement‡		
			People	4.1	58
			Total	165.3	2,328
			Mean 116 Median 136		

II. France

A. Change Between Successive Periods and Successive Peacetime Periods (Cont.)

7. 1939-1940 to 1941-1942 *(Le Temps)*§			8. 1941-1942 to 1945-1949 *(Le Temps, Le Monde)*†		
	Chi Square	Change Index		Chi Square	Change Index
War	18.3	208	*War*	.2	1
State	13.4	153	*Communism*	229.2	1,033
Peace	20.6	235	*State*	.2	1
Axis	13.5	153	*Democracy*	85.8	386
Nazism‡			*Peace*	1.2	5
Security	4.1	46	*People*	39.3	177
Soviet	12.3	140	*Axis*	34.4	155
Fatherland†			*Soviet*	23.6	106
Communism	14.2	161	*Security*	.2	1
Reform	.4	4	U.N.†		
Resistance‡			*Fatherland*	29.1	131
People	1.1	16	Socialism†		
Democracy	10.7	122	*Reform*	2.2	10
Neutrals	5.0	57	Military Occupation†		
Freedom and Liberty‡			*People*	39.3	177
Crisis	3.8	43	Allies†		
Fascism‡			*Neutrals*	15.4	69
Authority†			Freedom and Liberty†		
Left‡			*Crisis*	4.6	21
Revolution	.4	4	*Revolution*	.1	0
Imperialism‡			*Working Class*	.2	1
Bolshevism‡			Order†		
Socialism‡			Syndicalism†		
Red	2.7	31	*Spirit*	.2	1
Working Class†			Total	505.3	2,275
Intervention†					
Spirit†			Mean 134 Median 109		
Patriotism	.9	10			
Armaments‡			†Only 17 symbols were sufficiently frequent in this period.		
Blockade‡					
Total	121.3	1,384			

Mean 92   Median 153

§Only 15 symbols were sufficiently frequent in this period.

II. France

A. Change Between Successive Periods and Successive Peacetime Periods (Concl.)

B. Cumulative Changes Since Before World War I

1. 1900-1913 to 1910-1928 *(Le Temps)*--see Table A-3
2. 1900-1913 to 1929-1935 *(Le Temps)*

9. 1936-1938 to 1945-1949 *(Le Temps, Le Monde)*

	Chi Square	Change Index		Chi Square	Change Index
Left	103.2	465	*Socialism*	2.5	5
War	6.9	31	*Crisis*	265.3	577
Peace	30.7	138	*War*	.2	0
Communism	10.9	49	*State*	48.3	105
Crisis	62.3	281	*Left*	51.5	112
Democracy	23.6	106	*Peace*	81.2	176
Socialism	16.8	76	*Revolution*	13.1	28
People	73.0	329	*Security*	367.5	799
Revolution	33.4	150	*Reform*	.3	1
Soviet	22.0	99	League of Nations†		
Order	37.0	167	*Freedom and Liberty*	.0	0
U.N.†			*Order*	139.6	304
Security	8.0	36	*Trade Unions*	3.2	7
State	1.8	8	*Communism*	302.5	658
League of Nations‡			*Patriotism*	.2	0
Military Occupation†			Nazism†		
Marxism	31.1	140	*Working Class*	.2	5
Allies†			*Democracy*	25.0	54
Trade Unions	14.1	63	*Strikes*	10.5	23
Freedom and Liberty	5.0	23	*Disarmament*	973.8	2,116
Working Class	3.7	17	*Dictatorship*	282.1	613
Nazism	17.1	77	Marxism†		
Reform	4.6	21	*Nationalism*	20.0	43
Spirit†			Total	2,586.8	5,626
Imperialism†					
Fatherland	.6	3	Mean 281 Median 80		
Total	505.8	2,279			

Mean 114   Median 139

II. France

B. Cumulative Changes Since Before World War I (Concl.)

3. 1900-1913 to 1936-1938 (Le Temps)	Chi Square	Change Index	4. 1900-1949 to 1946-1949 (Le Temps, Le Monde)	Chi Square	Change Index
Socialism	1.5	9	Socialism	8.6	39
Left	144.2	853	War	58.6	264
War	12.9	76	State	7.4	33
Peace	163.2	965	Communism	1,134.9	5,112
State	1.2	7	Left	4.8	22
Crisis	106.8	632	Democracy	150.8	679
Revolution	40.2	238	Revolution	.9	4
Order	225.7	1,335	People	165.2	744
Reform	1.5	9	Reform	1.5	7
Communism	416.1	2,462	Soviet†		
Freedom and Liberty	8.9	52	Peace	29.0	131
Security	145.6	861	U.N.†		
Trade Unions	14.3	85	Freedom and Liberty	.3	1
League of Nations†			Security	59.3	267
Patriotism	1.8	11	Crisis	2.4	11
Marxism†			Military Occupation†		
Working Class	7.3	43	Trade Unions	.6	3
Nazism†			Allies†		
Strikes	2.9	17	Patriotism	6.0	27
Authority	61.9	367	Working Class	.4	2
Intervention	174.7	1,034	Order	8.8	40
Democracy	19.8	117	Spirit†		
Fascism†			Imperialism	10.8	48
Civil War	205.1	1,214	Fatherland	4.9	22
			Radicals	.6	3
Total	1,755.4	10,387	Total	1,655.7	7,459

Mean 519   Median 302

Mean 373   Median 85

III. Great Britain *(The Times)*

A. Changes Between Successive Periods and Successive Peacetime Periods

1. 1890-1913 to 1914-1918	Chi Square	Change Index	2. 1914-1918 to 1919-1929	Chi Square	Change Index
War	377.7	1,131	War	389.9	370
Allies†			Peace	1.3	1
Reform‡			Allies	.3	0
Peace	3.9	12	Labor Party	10.1	10
Liberals	22.7	68	Patriotism	54.1	51
Patriotism	11.4	34	Bolshevism	67.6	64
State	15.5	46	Democracy	16.6	16
Democracy	17.4	52	Labor	6.7	6
Radicals‡			People	23.9	23
People	6.4	19	League of Nations†		
Freedom	2.7	8	Militarism	37.4	35
Militarism	38.4	115	Trade Unions	3.0	3
Conservative	1.8	5	Armaments	15.6	15
Armaments	34.3	103	Communism†		
Revolution	3.0	9	Socialism	.1	0
Labor Party	36.5	109	State	36.0	34
Progress‡			Freedom	10.2	10
Labor	2.0	6	Strikes	11.1	11
Socialism	.5	11	Entente	8.7	8
Trade Unions	1.8	5	Revolution	4.8	5
Entente†			Versailles Treaty†		
Strikes	.1	0	Conservatives	.1	0
Tariffs‡			Disarmament†		
Masses‡			Soviets†		
Monarchy‡			Liberals	.1	0
Catholics‡					
Security	.5	1	Total	697.5	662
Anarchism‡					
Resistance‡			Mean 33 Median 13		
Order‡					
Free Trade‡					
Arbitration‡					
Moslems‡					
Franchise‡					
Crisis	.8	2			
Nationalism	2.2	7			
Total	579.4	1,733			

Mean 87   Median 49

III. Great Britain

A. Changes Between Successive Periods and Successive Peacetime Periods (Cont.)

3. 1890-1913 to 1919-1929   4. 1919-1929 to 1930-1935

	Chi Square	Change Index		Chi Square	Change Index
War	39.7	38	*War*	3.1	5
Peace	22.9	22	*Peace*	22.3	37
Reform	123.0	117	Allies‡		
Allies†			*Socialism*	25.4	42
Liberals	69.5	66	*Labor Party*	.1	0
Labor Party	280.0	266	*League of Nations*	1.6	3
State	13.4	13	Bolshevism‡		
Bolshevism†			*Conservative*	5.3	9
Radicals	70.2	67	*Labor*	6.2	10
Labor	30.7	29	*Armaments*	17.9	30
Freedom	29.2	28	*Trade Unions*	5.2	9
League of Nations†			*State*	.0	0
Conservative	4.7	4	*Communism*	1.3	2
Trade Unions	31.7	30	*Security*	6.1	10
Revolution	1.9	2	*Strikes*	16.5	27
Communism†			*Revolution*	.2	0
Progress	43.9	42	*Versailles Treaty*	8.6	14
Strikes	15.4	15	*Disarmament*	.5	1
Socialism	.7	1	*Democracy*	.1	0
Versailles Treaty†			Nazism†		
Democracy	2.1	2	*Soviets*	6.2	10
Disarmament	129.4	123	*Liberals*	.5	1
Soviets†			*Tariffs*	37.9	63
Security	.3	0	Total	164.9	273
People	3.1	3			
Armaments	8.1	8	Mean 14 Median 10		
Total	919.8	876			

Mean 44   Median 40

III. Great Britain

A. Changes Between Successive Periods and Successive Peacetime Periods (Cont.)

	5. 1930-1935 to 1936-1938		6. 1936-1938 to 1939-1940	
	Chi Square	Change Index	Chi Square	Change Index
War	2.5	8		
Peace	24.7	81		
Socialism	3.3	11		
Armaments	70.9	233		
Labor Party	3.8	12		
League of Nations	.4	1		
Conservative	4.6	15		
Labor	9.5	31		
State	.5	2		
Democracy	8.5	28		
Security	1.3	4		
Dictatorship	10.7	35		
Communism	.0	0		
Internationalism	10.2	33		
Revolution	2.4	8		
Freedom	11.7	38		
Disarmament	2.6	8		
Civil War	72.8	239		
Nazism	.4	1		
Fascism	8.7	28		

	Chi Square	Change Index
War	121.1	585
Freedom	94.2	456
Armaments	1.2	6
Peace	.6	3
League of Nations	7.7	37
Nazism	158.1	764
Labor	3.5	17
Democracy	2.7	13
Security	1.5	7
Neutrals	21.8	106
Socialism‡		
Allies†		
Dictatorship	4.5	22
State	3.2	15
Internationalism	2.8	14
People†		
Civil War	.1	1
Soviets	.2	1
Labor Party	.1	0
Axis†		
Fascism	.7	3
Resistance†		
Fuehrer†		
Revolution	.5	2
Crisis	.5	2
Trade Unions	.1	9

Total (5): 249.4   816

Mean 41   Median 14

Total (6): 425.2   2,054

Mean 103   Median 19

III. Great Britain

A. Changes Between Successive Periods and Successive Peacetime Periods (Cont.)

7. 1939-1940 to 1941-1945	Chi Square	Change Index	8. 1941-1945 to 1946-1949	Chi Square	Change Index
War	1.1	2	War	92.6	224
Peace	.5	1	Peace	.2	0
Freedom	14.8	30	Freedom	24.5	59
U.N.†			U.N.	1.6	4
Nazism	25.7	51	Nazism	29.7	72
Security	.2	0	Patriotism	270.6	655
Armaments	66.5	133	Security	.1	0
Axis	13.8	37	Soviet	17.3	42
Democracy	17.0	34	Axis‡		
Resistance	25.2	50	Labor	124.3	301
Neutrals	19.8	39	Resistance	23.1	56
Progress†			Democracy	5.6	13
Allies	3.4	7	Progress	.6	1
People	.1	0	Labor Party	26.9	65
State	10.1	20	Allies	11.1	27
Soviet	.6	1	Trade Unions	28.6	69
Labor Party	8.5	17	People	4.6	11
Crisis	1.6	3	Socialism	46.3	112
Axis	.4	1	Armaments	2.0	5
Fascism	1.0	2	State Ownership†		
Tyranny	2.0	4	Crisis	.0	0
Spirit†			Conservatives	5.2	13
Reform†			Total	714.9	1,729
Christianity†					
Order†			Mean 87 Median 58		
Conservatives†					
Nationalism†					
Trade Unions	.9	2			
Total	212.3	424			

Mean 21   Median 19

III. Great Britain

A. Changes Between Successive Periods and Successive Peacetime Periods (Concl.)

9. 1936-1938 to 1946-1949

	Chi Square	Change Index
War	26.0	63
Peace	.8	2
Armaments	51.1	124
U.N.†		
League of Nations	28.0	68
Patriotism	112.0	271
Labor	.2	1
Communism	74.3	180
Democracy	.0	0
Soviet	33.2	80
Security	3.1	8
Labor Party	1.7	4
Socialism	.6	1
Trade Unions	10.0	24
Dictatorship‡		
Progress†		
Internationalism‡		
State Ownership†		
Freedom and Liberty	.0	0
Crisis	6.3	15
Conservatives	.9	2
Civil War	6.6	16
Revolution	3.6	9
Fascism‡		
State	.8	2
Nationalism	1.4	3
Total	360.7	873

Mean 44   Median 65

B. Cumulative Changes Since Before World War I

1. 1890-1913 to 1919-1929 (see Table A-3 above)
2. 1890-1913 to 1930-1935

	Chi Square	Change Index
War	7.4	12
Peace	3.3	5
Reform‡		
Socialism	34.7	57
Liberals	34.9	58
Labor Party	178.5	295
State	8.3	14
League of Nations†		
Radicals‡		
Conservative	.1	0
Freedom	18.9	31
Armaments	145.2	240
Revolution	2.1	3
Security	8.7	14
Progress‡		
Communism†		
People	10.8	18
Labor	.7	1
Patriotism	3.3	5
Disarmament	103.2	170
Tariffs	.2	0
Democracy	.6	1
Masses‡		
Monarchy	3.4	6
Trade Unions	.1	0
Nazism†		
Nationalism	10.0	16
Total	574.5	946

Mean 47   Median 44

III. Great Britain

B. Cumulative Changes Since Before World War I (Concl.)

	3. 1890-1913 to 1936-1938		4. 1890-1913 to 1946-1949	
	Chi Square	Change Index	Chi Square	Change Index
War	13.5	44	*War*	105.4	255
Peace	10.3	34	*Peace*	23.0	56
Reform‡			*Reform*	32.0	78
Armaments	438.6	1,438	U.N.†		
Liberals	208.2	682	*Liberals*	30.8	74
League of Nations†			*Patriotism*	97.5	236
State	6.6	22	*State*	13.3	32
Labor	15.6	51	Communism†		
Radicals‡			Radicals‡		
Democracy	13.8	45	Soviet†		
Freedom	1.1	4	*Freedom*	1.8	4
Security	12.7	42	*Security*	44.9	109
Conservative	3.9	13	*Conservative*	2.5	6
Socialism	2.6	9	*Labor*	27.6	67
Revolution	5.7	19	*Revolution*	2.2	5
Dictatorship†			*Democracy*	16.9	41
Progress‡			*Progress*	.0	0
Internationalism†			*Labor Party*	68.3	165
People‡			*Socialism*	1.0	2
Civil War	46.6	153	*Trade Unions*	10.7	26
Patriotism	.1	0	State Ownership†		
Labor Party	25.8	85	*Crisis*	19.1	46
Tariffs	1.3	4	*People*	.1	0
Fascism†			*Nationalism*	12.4	30
Communism†			*Strikes*	.5	1
Conciliation	41.6	136	Total	509.8	1,233
Masses‡					
Monarchy‡			Mean 62 Median 71		
Trade Unions	.0	0			
Catholics‡					
Strikes	.1	0			
Soviet†					
Neutrals	9.2	30			
Total	857.3	2,811			

Mean 14   Median 102

IV. The United States

A. Changes Between Successive Periods and Successive Peacetime Periods

1. 1900-1913 to 1914-1918	Chi Square	Change Index	2. 1914-1918 to 1919-1929	Chi Square	Change Index
War	247.3	127	People	7.2	10
Republicans	31.7	16	War	1,186.1	1,647
Peace	21.7	11	Republicans	4.4	6
Democrats	5.5	3	Peace	258.3	359
People	81.9	42	Democrats	5.2	7
Labor	80.4	41	Allies†		
League of Nations†			Tariffs	9.1	13
Allies	68.8	35	Neutrals	477.9	664
Trade Unions	26.7	14	Reform	6.4	9
Neutrals	117.7	60	Armaments	339.2	471
Communism†			Trade Unions	6.0	8
Armaments	20.0	10	Freedom and Liberty	22.0	31
Socialism	1.3	1	Trusts	2.0	3
Freedom and Liberty	38.1	20	Labor	4.0	6
Disarmament†			Strikes	6.8	9
Revolution	4.6	2	Revolution	21.9	30
Strikes	1.3	1	Progress	4.7	6
Democracy	4.7	2	Democracy	9.5	13
Versailles Treaty†			Conservatives	.1	0
Bolshevism	31.2	16	Socialism	7.2	10
Soviets†			Progressives	53.4	74
Labor Party†			Total	2,431.3	3,376
Tariffs	7.7	4			
Nationalism†			Mean 17 Median 10		
International Tribunal†					
Patriotism†					
Capitalism	3.8	2			
Conservatives	.3	0			
Constitutionalism	13.6	7			
Total	808.3	414			

Mean 21   Median 18

IV. The United States

A. Changes Between Successive Periods and Successive Peacetime Periods (Cont.)

3. 1900-1913 to 1919-1929

	Chi Square	Change Index
People	35.0	18
War	631.7	324
Republicans	94.8	49
Democrats	41.1	21
Tariffs	50.0	26
Peace	290.2	149
Reform‡		
Labor	191.7	98
Trade Unions	.0	0
League of Nations†		
Trusts	61.5	32
Communism†		
Strikes	10.1	5
Socialism	35.0	18
Freedom and Liberty	1.2	1
Disarmament	480.6	247
Progress	33.2	17
Allies†		
Democracy	4.9	3
Versailles Treaty†		
Revolution	19.0	10
Bolshevism†		
Armaments	264.9	136
Soviets†		
Labor Party	214.9	110
Nationalism	146.9	75
International Tribunal	177.5	91
Total	2,784.0	1,430

Mean 71   Median 40

4. 1919-1929 to 1930-1935

	Chi Square	Change Index
War	19.9	36
Republicans	3.2	6
Democrats	11.6	21
Tariffs	8.5	16
Peace	4.2	8
League of Nations	8.7	16
Labor	19.1	35
Communism	.7	1
Trade Unions	16.4	30
Democracy	.0	0
People	1.2	2
Conservatives	5.3	10
Socialism	10.2	19
Soviets	.1	0
Disarmament	10.2	19
Revolution	.7	1
Strikes†		
Nationalism	.2	0
Allies	11.1	20
Labor Party	.0	0
Versailles Treaty	7.9	14
Total	139.2	254

Mean 13   Median 9

IV. The United States

A. Changes Between Successive Periods and Successive Peacetime Periods (Cont.)

	5. 1930-1932 to 1933-1938			6. 1933-1938 to 1939-1941	
	Chi Square	Change Index		Chi Square	Change Index
Republicans	44.4	50	*War*	280.7	588
War	.0	0	*Armaments*	285.5	599
Democrats	12.0	13	*Democrats*	18.9	40
Peace	.1	0	*Nazism*	142.9	299
Tariffs	22.9	26	*Republicans*	14.4	30
Armaments	44.4	50	*Peace*	19.7	41
League of Nations	5.0	6	*Labor*	4.2	9
Labor	6.3	7	*Democracy*	25.0	52
Communism	.1	0	*Communism*	1.8	4
Democracy	12.3	14	*Freedom and Liberty*	72.2	151
People	2.0	2	*Dictatorship*	2.0	4
Nazism	30.1	34	*People*	26.2	55
Conservatives	6.7	7	League of Nations‡		
Freedom and Liberty	8.6	10	*Neutrals*	.1	0
Soviets	4.3	5	Internationalism‡		
Dictatorship	5.7	6	*Soviets*	46.0	97
Revolution	4.7	5	Nationalism‡		
Internationalism	.3	0	*Crisis*	10.0	21
Nationalism	.0	0	*Trade Unions*	5.4	11
Crisis	.4	0	Allies†		
Total	210.3	235	Socialism†		
			Strikes	.3	1
Mean 11 Median 6			*Fascism*	6.7	14
			Security	17.9	37
			Isolationism	7.8	16
			Total	987.4	2,069
			Mean 104 Median 54		

IV. The United States

A. Changes Between Successive Periods and Successive Peacetime Periods (Cont.)

	7. 1939-1941 to 1942-1945		8. 1942-1945 to 1946-1949		
	Chi Square	Change Index		Chi Square	Change Index
War	46.6	76	*War*	167.2	271
Peace	3.8	6	*Peace*	7.5	12
Armaments	161.7	263	*Nazism*	52.6	85
Nazism	1.2	2	*U.N.*	8.8	14
Democracy	2.1	3	*Allies*	57.2	93
Allies	160.1	260	*Democracy*	19.5	32
Freedom and Liberty	.1	0	*Freedom and Liberty*	.0	0
U.N.†			*Communism*	391.7	636
Labor	31.2	51	*Axis*	28.8	47
Axis†			*Soviets*	128.9	209
People	15.6	25	Resistance‡		
Resistance†			*Armaments*	88.2	143
Neutrals‡			*Trade Unions*	.0	0
Trade Unions	.0	0	*Strikes*	121.2	197
Soviets	15.9	26	*Security*	3.1	5
Security	.5	1	*Republicans*	44.7	72
Crisis	3.1	5	*Jews*	.3	0
Jews†			*Labor*	49.6	80
Dictatorship	16.2	26	*Crisis*	.5	1
Progress†			*People*	8.8	14
Fascism	2.9	5	*Progress*	.1	0
Republicans	3.7	6	Total	1,178.7	1,911
Tyranny	33.4	54			
Democrats	8.9	15	Mean 96 Median 60		
Spirit†					
Revolution	2.8	5			
Communism	3.7	6			
Total	513.4	835			

Mean 42   Median 26

IV. The United States

A. Changes Between Successive Periods and Successive Peacetime Periods (Concl.)			B. Cumulative Changes Since Before World War I		
			1. 1900-1913 to 1919-1929 (see Table A-3 above) 2. 1900-1913 to 1930-1932		
9. 1933-1938 to 1946-1949					
	Chi Square	Change Index		Chi Square	Change Index
War	90.9	148	People	15.7	29
Peace	100.8	164	Republicans	55.8	102
Democrats	30.8	50	Democrats	57.2	105
U.N.†			War	32.8	60
Republicans	5.2	8	Tariffs	3.7	7
Democracy	86.0	140	Peace	29.4	54
Armaments	.3	1	Reform‡		
Communism	83.5	136	League of Nations†		
Labor	.2	0	Trade Unions	16.5	30
Freedom and Liberty	79.4	129	Communism†		
Nazism	1.1	2	Trusts‡		
Soviets	163.3	265	Labor	.2	0
Dictatorship	5.6	9	Strikes‡		
Strikes	57.9	94	Democracy	1.9	3
League of Nations	3.0	5	Freedom and Liberty	1.4	3
Security	85.0	138	Conservatives	5.6	10
People	6.6	11	Progress†		
Trade Unions	9.3	15	Soviets†		
Internationalism‡			Socialism	1.6	3
Atomic Power†			Revolution	1.6	3
Crisis	3.8	6	Liberals	.7	1
Nationalism	2.1	3	Nationalism	55.7	102
Allies†			Labor Party	55.7	102
Progress‡			Free Trade	.3	1
Jews	7.4	12	Plutocracy‡		
Total	822.1	1,336	Arbitration‡		
			Franchise‡		
Mean 67 Median 111			Anarchism‡		
			Crisis	7.8	14
			Negroes‡		
			Free Enterprise‡		
			Monroe Doctrine‡		
			Orders‡		
			Progressives	2.3	4
			Internationalism†		
			Armaments	28.2	52
			Total	374.0	685
			Mean 34 Median 57		

IV. The United States

B. Cumulative Changes since Before World War I (Concl.)

	3. 1900-1913 to 1933-1938		4. 1900-1913 to 1946-1949	
	Chi Square	Change Index	Chi Square	Change Index
People	36.2	40	*People* 12.3	20
War	57.6	64	*War* 364.7	592
Republicans	.1	0	*Republicans* 4.2	6
Democrats	22.1	25	*Peace* 411.6	668
Tariffs	41.5	46	*Democrats* 9.0	15
Peace	42.3	47	U.N.†	
Reform‡			Tariffs‡	
Armaments	407.7	455	*Democracy* 53.1	86
Trade Unions	14.5	16	Reform‡	
Labor	9.7	11	Communism†	
Trusts	28.2	32	*Trade Unions* 1.3	2
Democracy	34.4	38	*Freedom and Liberty* 108.7	177
Strikes	2.8	3	*Trusts* 17.9	29
Communism†			Soviets†	
Freedom and Liberty	.8	1	*Labor* 4.3	7
Nazism†			*Armaments* 344.7	560
Progress‡			*Progress* .2	0
Dictatorship†			*Strikes* 23.5	38
Socialism	.1	0	*Socialism* 1.1	2
League of Nations†			*Security* 161.9	263
Revolution	.9	1	Nazism†	
Internationalism†			Atomic Power†	
Nationalism	87.8	98	*Crisis* 48.3	78
Crisis	20.7	23	Allies†	
Negroes‡			Jews†	
Free enterprise‡			Imperialism†	
Monroe Doctrine‡			*Revolution* .0	0
Order	.4	0	Civil Rights†	
Fascism†			*Disarmament* 27.0	44
Soviets†			Liberals, Free Trade‡	
Radicals	20.9	23	Plutocracy‡	
State	20.9	23	Arbitration‡	
			Franchise, Anarchism‡	
Total	849.6	946	*Negroes* .0	0
			Free Enterprise .3	0
Mean 47 Median 43			Total 1,594.2	2,587
			Mean 129 Median 131	

V. Germany

	1. 1919-1929 to 1930-1932 (Frankfurter Zeitung)			2. 1930-1932 to 1933-1938 (Frankfurter Zeitung, Völkischer Beobachter)	
	Chi Square	Change Index		Chi Square	Change Index
War	4.5	50	Nazism	41.3	233
Nazism	160.8	787	Fuehrer	82.7	467
Democracy	13.7	152	State‡		
State	29.1	323	Bolshevism	18.3	103
Peace	.5	5	War	6.7	38
Nationalism	.0	0	People	3.3	19
Versailles Treaty	3.5	39	Nationalism	32.6	184
Social Democracy	.1	1	Jews†		
Entente	.3	4	Social Democracy	20.6	116
Socialism	.6	7	Communism†		
Allies‡			Peace	2.2	13
League of Nations	.1	1	Marxism	11.1	63
Militarism‡			Socialism	7.8	44
Revolution	.4	5	Democracy	6.1	34
Left	1.7	19	League of Nations	6.6	37
Center	.2	2	Revolution	.0	0
Reactionary‡			Center‡		
Conservatives	10.7	119	Classical Liberalism†		
Right‡			Conservatives‡		
People	1.5	16	Parliamentarism	.9	5
Parliamentarism	.0	0	Versailles Treaty	4.8	27
Bolshevism	.0	0	Catholic Church	.1	1
Constitutionalism	.3	4	Freedom and Liberty	.1	1
Dictatorship	.5	6	Dictatorship‡		
Total	228.6	2,540	Radicals‡		
			Left	3.6	20
Mean 127 Median 29			Fascism	2.6	15
			Crisis	3.6	20
			Total	255.2	1,440
			Mean 72 Median 110		

V. Germany (Cont.)

3. 1919-1929 to 1933-1938
(Frankfurter Zeitung, Völkischer Beobachter)

	Chi Square	Change Index
War	27.7	156
Nazism	1,153.1	6,515
Democracy	13.9	78
Fuehrer	288.3	1,629
Peace	5.7	32
Bolshevism	14.8	84
Nationalism	31.4	177
People	15.1	86
Versailles Treaty	19.0	107
Jews†		
Social Democracy	18.1	102
Communism†		
Entente‡		
Marxism†		
Allies‡		
Revolution	.5	3
Militarism‡		
Classical Liberalism	13.8	78
Left	11.5	65
Parliamentarism	.8	5
League of Nations	63.0	356
Socialism	3.8	21
Reactionary‡		
Center‡		
Right‡		
State‡		
Constitutionalism‡		
Dictatorship‡		
Working Class‡		
Capitalism	2.2	13
Catholic Church	3.5	20
Fatherland	3.2	18
Radicals‡		
Freedom and Liberty	.7	4
Total	1,690.3	9,549

Mean 478   Median 132

4. 1933-1938 to 1939-1941
(Völkischer Beobachter)[§]

	Chi Square	Change Index
Nazism	14.1	174
War	35.1	433
Fuehrer	3.5	43
People	5.8	72
Bolshevism	2.5	31
Jews	5.2	64
Communism	.3	3
Versailles Treaty	25.0	308
Peace	.1	2
Democracy	.4	5
Marxism	1.2	15
Armaments	20.3	250
Revolution	.4	5
Axis†		
Classical Liberalism‡		
Capitalism	2.5	31
Parliamentarism‡		
Plutocracy†		
League of Nations‡		
Imperialism	1.0	13
Total	117.4	1,449

Mean 97   Median 68

§Only 15 symbols were sufficiently frequent in this period.

V. Germany (Concl.)

5. 1939-1941 to 1942-1945
(Völkischer Beobachter) [§]

	Chi Square	Change Index
War	6.6	89
Bolshevism	140.2	1,869
Nazism	2.7	36
Jews	.5	7
People	1.6	21
Plutocracy	30.1	401
Fuehrer	.6	8
Democracy	69.4	925
Versailles Treaty	3.3	44
Communism	1.0	13
Peace	2.5	34
Revolution	.4	5
Armaments‡		
Capitalism	.4	5
Axis‡		
Imperialism	.4	6
Total	259.8	3,463

Mean 247   Median 66

[§] Only 14 symbols were sufficiently frequent in this period.

APPENDIX C
EDITORS OF THE PRESTIGE PAPERS

This memorandum is designed to help shed some light on a significant modern institution whose institutional character has as yet received little recognition: the prestige paper. The RADIR content analyses assume that the prestige paper editorials represent a stable index of elite attitudes, and not just the idiosyncracies of some editor. To validate this assumption we decided to look into the personnel of these papers.

If such papers as the *New York Times, Izvestia,* or the London *Times* are indeed institutions which function to express the views of significant segments of the elite and to disseminate to the elite at home and abroad information and judgments needed by them to function as an elite in a great society, then we would expect certain consequences concerning the recruitment of the editors. We would expect them to derive from the same social circles as members of the elite. We would expect them to have shared the education and other attitude-forming experiences of members of the elite. We would expect their careers to parallel at various points the careers of elite members in that culture. We would expect them to maintain personal contact through clubs, marriages, etc., with members of the elite. We would expect them to maintain close contact with the representatives of the state power. Finally, we would expect them to acquire, in their role of elite-allied intellectuals, considerable prestige and honor. To test these hypotheses is the purpose of this paper.

It is based on too small a sample to claim much reliability. It would be well worth someone's time to extend this study to include publishers, managing or deputy editors, and editors of nonprestige papers. Still, the results based on our small sample of 31 persons are fairly striking, and since this sample almost exhausts the universe of recent editors in chief of prestige papers in the five main powers, it is worth reporting.[*]

---

*Methodological note: Two sources of inaccuracy in this paper ought to be noted here. (a) Time spans are usually computed not from exact dates but from years alone. Thus in our sources a man may be said to have been in military service 1917-18. This could theoretically be two days or two years. In this paper it would be recorded as one year. (b) The other problem is how to interpret lack of information. We have tried to be careful not to interpret nonreporting as nonexistence of a trait unless the evidence is fairly strong. Thus failure to mention scholarships and academic honors does not prove that a man was a mediocre student. In the absence of explicit information on that point we cannot know whether the man's record was average or the sources incomplete.

The sample consists of the following persons:

	Dates as Editor in Chief	Number
United States		
New York Times		
Charles R. Miller	1883-1922	
Rollo Ogden	1922-37	
John H. Finley	1937-38	
Charles Merz	1938-	4
Britain		
London *Times*		
Thomas Chenery	1877-84	
George Earle Buckle	1884-1912	
Geoffrey Dawson	1912-19, 1923-41	
Henry Wickham Steed	1919-22	
Robert M. Barrington Ward	1941-48	
William Francis Casey	1948-	6
France		
Le Temps		
Adrien Hebrard	1867-1914	
Emile Adrien Hebrard	1915-25	
Adrien Hebrard	1925-29	
Louis-Mill	1929-31	
Jacques Chastenet	1931-42	
Emile Mireaux	1931-42	
Le Monde		
Hubert Beuve Mery	1945-	7
Germany		
Norddeutsche allgemeine Zeitung		
Otto Runge	1902-17	
Fritz Reineck	1918- ? (out by 1922)	
Frankfurter Zeitung		
Heinrich Simon	1914-33 or 1934	
Völkischer Beobachter		
Alfred Rosenberg	1921-38	
Wilhelm Weiss	1938-45	5

	Dates as Editor in Chief	Number
Russia		
Novoe Vremia		
Alexis S. Suvorin	1876-1912	
Mikhail A. Suvorin	1912-16	
Boris Suvorin	1916-17	
*Izvestia**		
Iurii M. Steklov	1917-25	
Ivan I. Stepanov-Skvortsov	1925-28	
Maksmilian A. Savelev	1929-30	
Gerald I. Krumin	1930-31	
I. M. Gronsky	1931-34	
Nikolai I. Bukharin	1934-37	9

The two most striking characteristics of this group are their high intellectual attainments (see Table 1) and their close ties with government and the elite. All but one of the editors had a college education. Outside of Russia all of them obtained degrees and only four did not go on to graduate work. Only two of those who went on into graduate work did not attain a degree. While the large majority had graduate education, still they generally stopped short of the Ph.D. The sample of non-Russian editors contains two Ph.D.'s (both German) and three LL.D's (all French), a considerable segment, but clearly a minority.

The Russian pattern here, as on many other points, is different. (About the formal education of the *Novoe Vremia* editors we know nothing, although they were educated men, judging by their professions: one teacher, two playwrights.) The Bolshevik editors all had some higher education, but typically their schooling was interrupted by revolutionary activities. Of the five on whom we have information, one got a degree from a teacher's training institute and one got a Ph.D. The other three attended universities but never got degrees. Thus the Russian editors, like the others, were educated men although they lacked the usual credentials.

Not only did the editors receive a lot of education, they also did well in what they had. In most cases we have no data on their academic careers other than degrees and fields of specialization. But where the biographical data is full enough, it tends to show a high level of attainment (see

*Since 1937 *Izvestia* has had an editorial board and the editor in chief is not revealed. But see the addendum at the end of this appendix.

Table 2). In seven cases the editors won honors or scholarships in school. In two cases they made rather ordinary records. One editor got an ordinary B.A., and one, although described as a brilliant student, avoided an honorific record by misconduct. He was expelled once from high school and once from college. But the academic record of these two men reflected the presence of competing and academically unrecognized interests rather than lack of capacity. This is abundantly shown by their later scholarly attainments. The former became a self-taught orientalist with scholarly translations from Arabic and Hebrew, and an Oxford professorship to his credit. The latter became an amateur classicist and linguist of no mean proportions. The seven men whose academic abilities were recognized by their universities received among them one Phi Beta Kappa, four "firsts" at Oxford, and five scholarships, as well as a poetry prize.

The intellectual interests of these men continued throughout their careers. Only six editors published no books, on one editor there was no information, and the other twenty-four published about 117 books among them (Table 3). Of these seventy-five books dealt with politics and economics and another nineteen with history. These were the fields in which these men specialized as newspaper editors; but they also wrote twenty-three books in other fields, including two books about literature, a novel and a number of plays; three volumes of philosophy, three on classics or orientalia; one book of art criticism, two books on military matters, and two on journalism.

These editors also held twenty-one memberships in learned, cultural, or artistic societies. Perhaps one explanation for their extensive participation in intellectual activities and also of their selection of a symbol-manipulating profession was their early exposure to a similar environment. Many of the editors came from families engaged in symbol-manipulating activities (Table 4). In almost half the cases we do not know the occupation of the editor's father, but of the other seventeen fathers twelve were in symbol-manipulating occupations. Three were clergymen; one a solicitor; one a Senator; one a printer and author; and five were editors or publishers. The last were all in family newspapers where the sons went on in the business. In these five cases an economic as well as an intellectual influence was operating. But that still leaves seven editors from symbol-rich environments unconnected with the newspaper to which they succeeded, as against two sons of businessmen and two sons of farmers and one son of a clerk.

We know the family background of nine of the wives of the editors. Of these, four had symbol-manipulating fathers: one professor, one clergyman, one clergyman-professor, and one novelist. All of these wives married editors from similar backgrounds.

From the results so far it seems quite clear that we are dealing with a group that has been deeply imbued with the intellectual content of the

Table 1
Level of Education Attained

Country	High School	Higher Ed. (no degree)	Undergrad. Degree	Grad. Study	Don't Know	Total
U.S.	0	0	2	2	0	4
Britain	0	0	1	5	0	6
France	0	0	1	4	2	7
Germany	1	0	0	3	1	5
Russia	0	3	1	1	3	9
Total	1	3	5	15	6	31

Table 2
Scholastic Record

Country	Honors or Prizes	Ordinary Record	Don't Know	Total
U.S.	3	1	0	4
Britain	4	1	1	6
France	0	0	7	7
Germany	0	0	5	5
Russia	0	0	9	9
Total	7	2	22	31

Table 3
Authorship of Books

Country	Number of Editors		
	No Books	Don't Know	Books
U.S.	1	0	3
Britain	1	0	5
France	3	0	4
Germany	1	0	4
Russia	0	1	8
Total	6	1	24

culture of which they are a part. These men are far from being ivory tower intellectuals, however. They are primarily executives. While all of them wrote scores to thousands of editorials, editorial writing was not their main job. At least it had ceased being that by the time they reached the status of editor in chief. The editorial or "leader" writer is generally an important member of the staff, but subordinate to the editor in chief. The

Table 3
Authorship of Books (Continued)

Country	Pol. and Econ.	History	Military	Journalism	Philosophy	Literature	Novels Plays	Art	Orientalia Classics	Total by Country
U.S.	11	1	0	0	0	0	1	0	0	13
Britain	19	2	0	0	0	0	4	0	2	27
France	6	7	0	0	1	1	0	0	1	16
Germany	17	1	2	0	2	0	0	1	0	23
Russia	22	8	0	2	0	0	6	0	0	38
Total	75	19	2	2	3	1	11	1	3	117

Number of Books

Table 4
Father's Occupation

Country	Clergy	Teacher	Prnt'g Publish'g	Law and Pol.	Total Symbol Manip'g	Business	Farming	Clerical	Don't Know	Total by Country
U.S.	1	0	0	0	1	1	0	0	2	4
Britain	2	0	0	1	3	1	0	0	2	6
France	0	0	2	1	3	0	0	0	4	7
Germany	0	0	2	0	2	0	1	0	2	5
Russia	0	1	2	0	3	0	1	1	4	9
Total	3	1	6	2	12	2	2	1	14	31

Table 5
Editors in Government Service

Country	Elec- tive Posts	Full-Time Civilian Jobs	Temp. or Part-Time Jobs	Military Service	Total in Govt. Service	Total Not in Govt. Service	Don't Know
U.S.	0	1	2	1	2	2	0
Britain	0	2	2	1	4	2	0
France	3	3	1	2	5	0	2
Germany	2	2	2	1	3	1	1
Russia	4	4	1	0	4	0	5
Total	9	12	8	5	18	5	8

editor in chief may set the paper's editorial policy, but he leaves most of the writing to others and devotes himself primarily to administration. Yet the qualities of an "intellectual" seem essential to fill this job effectively.

Besides intellectual attainments, the other striking characteristic of the careers of the editors was deep immersion in governmental activities. Only five of the editors were never engaged in governmental service (six, if one excludes military service). Only four of the non-Russian editors were what might be called professional civil servants at some point in their career, and one was a professional soldier. But eight of them at some time held full-time government jobs, five held elective offices, seven held temporary or part-time posts of sufficient importance to be reported in the biographies, and five had military service (Table 5).

The Bolshevik editors present a special problem in this connection. By the nature of the Soviet system they were all necessarily public employees, but all on whom we have information also held full-time jobs that would rate as a public office under a capitalist system. One was a commissar, one a member of the Politburo—the highest position there is other than Stalin's—and all those in public office held elective as well as appointive positions.

The full-time government jobs accounted for more than half of the non-journalistic part of the careers of the editors (Table 6). (The Russians are excluded from the tabulation.) Many of the editors, at some point in their careers, had jobs in fields other than journalism. Specifically, the eighteen editors on whom we have this information spent, in total, 470 years in the field of journalism. Against this the seventeen editors on whom we have information spent a total of 197 years in other fields. Thus the average editor spent about 11 years of his life in other occupations. Of this time, just over half went to the government; 102 of the 197 years devoted to nonjournalistic occupations were spent in government employ. (Seventeen of these years are military service. This does not include time spent in

Table 6
Time Distribution of Careers

A. Duration in Years of Journalistic Career

Country	Number of Men Included	Duration Previous Editors	Incumbent	Total	Mean
U.S.	4	121	33	154	38.5
Britain	6	115	37	152	25.3
France	5	88	9	97	19.4
Germany	3	67	0	67	22.3
All papers	18	391	79	470	26.1
				Median	29.0

B. Duration in Years of Nonjournalistic Career[*]

Country	Number of Men Included	Duration Total with Govt.	Mean with Govt.	Total Private	Mean Private	Total	Mean
U.S.	4	20	5.0	18	4.5	38	9.5
Britain	6	39	6.5	19	3.2	58	9.7
France	4	21	5.2	42†	10.5	63	15.7
Germany	3	22	7.3	16	5.3	38	12.7
All papers	17	102	6.0	95	5.6	197	11.6
Median			6.0		5.0		11.0

*Part-time jobs not included.
†One man accounts for 31 of these years.

compulsory military training on which we have no data. Nor did we intend to include time spent below the officer level. This, however, turned out to be no problem. All of the five men with military service were officers. One, a professional officer, spent 7 years in the German army coming out a captain. The others included two majors and two lieutenants. One of the majors was attached to the general staff.)

The careers of Geoffrey Dawson and of H. Wickham Steed illustrate the intertwining of public and private careers in Britain. Dawson took the civil service examination for the administrative class upon completion of his work at Oxford. He started with the Post Office but soon transferred to the Colonial Office where he served from 1898 to 1901. Viscount Milner then asked for his services as private secretary on his mission to South Africa to help overcome the consequences of the Boer War. He held this post until 1905. At this point he gave up his intended career in the civil service to accept a position as editor of the *Johannesburg Star*. He did this not for personal reasons but rather as a service to the Empire. He was placed in the job as a means towards winning South Africa more closely to the Empire, the purpose for which he had come to South Africa in the first place. When five years later he returned to England, he joined the London *Times*. Throughout his quarter-century career in the *Times* he continued to follow a strongly imperialist line. Thus we see in Dawson's career one of the ways in which the prestige newspapers have been tied in with government policy. A man with a personal background and close connections in government service, himself went in as editor of the paper and continued to work for the same goals in that position as he had when he was an official.

Wickham Steed's career followed a somewhat different sequence. He started as a correspondent and worked up to editor in chief in 1919. Before reaching that position, however, he filled an important government wartime job. During the first war he directed propaganda to the enemy in central Europe and headed a special mission to Italy. Wickham Steed lost his editorship when Northcliffe died and Astor took over the *Times* in 1922. Most of his career then was spent in private endeavors, but from 1937 to 1947 he served as a broadcaster in the overseas service of the BBC. For the second time in his career Wickham Steed was serving as an official exponent of the government's point of view, to which the London *Times* has always been at least respectful.

John H. Finley, *New York Times* editor in 1937-38, is the only editor of this paper with a somewhat similar career. Charles Merz, the present editor, served with the American Commission to Negotiate the Peace in Paris in 1918-19, but only Finley has had a major career as a public servant. His career differs significantly from those of his British counterparts in that very little of it was connected with Washington. Before joining the *New York Times,* Finley was President of the College of the City of New York from 1903 to 1913 and Commissioner of Education of the State of New York from 1913 to 1921. He was also a member of a railroad arbitration board, 1913-14; chairman of the New York State Commission for the Blind, 1913; member of the New York State Constitutional Convention Commission, 1914-15; New York State Regents representative on the American Educational Mission to France, 1917; a member of the American Army Educational Commission in France, 1918; and chief of the Red Cross in the Near East, 1918-19. This is a fabulously active public career, yet it is noteworthy how little of it involved national positions. The highly pluralistic character of American society has prevented the kind of close integration of the editorial elite with the governmental elite which we find in the other major powers. There has never been a tendency for the *New York Times* editor to be a "government man," the way the editors of other prestige papers often are.

In France the editor of a prestige paper is less apt to have a career as a civil servant than as an elective official. None of the British or American editors have run for office as have the French, German, and Russian ones. A London *Times* or *New York Times* editor would probably feel that that kind of partisanship was incompatible with the objectivity his position calls for. Yet three of the editors of *Le Temps* have been members of parliament. Adrien Hebrard ran for the Chamber of Deputies in 1871 and lost; was elected Senator in 1879 and was reelected in 1888. He lost in 1897. All of these campaigns were while he was editor. Louis-Mill was a deputy from 1902 to 1906, many years before he became editor. Emile Mireaux was a Senator from 1936 to 1940, during which years he was also editor of *Le Temps*. Hebrard and Louis-Mill also served in departmental and local councils.

These men also held a number of nonelective governmental positions. Hebrard was a member of the Commission on Public Buildings and National Palaces, the Superior Council of Fine Arts, and the Superior Council on Historical Monuments. Mireaux was Minister of Education in Petain's cabinet for a few months in 1940.

As we would expect, the closest connections between the editors and the state other than that under communism are found in the Nazi press. Before the Nazi period the situation in Germany was not unlike that in the other European powers. One of the editors of the *Norddeutsche allgemeine Zeitung*, for example, had been a parliamentary secretary before getting into journalism (Fritz Reineck). The two editors of the *Völkischer Beobachter*, however, have been politicians at least as much as journalists. Alfred Rosenberg, one of the leading Nazis, and the leading Nazi "philosopher," was a member of the Nazi party before Hitler. Both he and Wilhelm Weiss participated in the Munich beerhall putsch. Rosenberg was elected to the Reichstag in 1930. He went on diplomatic missions to London in 1931 and London and Rome in 1932-33. In 1933 he became director of the foreign office of the Nazi Party. He also held the title of the Fuehrer's Deputy for the Ideological Education of the Nazi Movement and from 1940 Supervisor of Party Wartime Youth Education. In 1941 he was elevated to ministerial status as Reichsminister for Occupied Eastern Territories. For his war crimes in that post he died on the gallows in 1946.

By 1938 his political activities were taking so much time that he moved upstairs from active editorship of the *Völkischer Beobachter*. He became advisory editor and Wilhelm Weiss assumed the editorship. Weiss had been a professional army officer from 1911. (He is the only editor in our sample who had no higher education.) With the demobilization of the German army, he became involved in the *Freikorps* and in ultranationalist activities. As a fighter rather than an intellectual, he became an S.A. group leader. Yet, somehow, he got into journalism and succeeded at it. He edited a number of papers starting in 1919 and was with the *Völkischer Beobachter* from 1927. Though active in politics throughout this period, his first strictly governmental position since his demobilization from the army came in 1933 when he entered the Reichstag. He also became a member of the praesidium of the Reich Press Chamber. He had been leader of the Party Press Union since 1932.

The editors of *Izvestia* are like Rosenberg, in that journalism is for them an adjunct of party politics. On the other hand, the Frenchmen, although they went far enough in party politics to run for office, were journalists first and politicians by avocation. The Bolsheviks and Rosenberg were politicians first and journalists as a party assignment. Of the five *Izvestia* editors on whom we have information, all joined the revolutionary movement at an early age under the Czars—two at fifteen, one at seventeen, one at nineteen, and one at the advanced age of twenty-one. Only one has no records of prerevolutionary arrests or exiles in his biography. Three were sent to Siberia and two went into exile abroad. Three achieved seats on the Central Committee of the Communist Party, one was a member of the Central Control Commission and one a member of the Politburo.

The prestige papers fall into three gradations in respect to their relations with the state. There are the official organs, the semiofficial organs, and the independent papers. These three gradations are well reflected in the careers of the editors. The editors of *Izvestia* and the *Völkischer Beobachter*, official propaganda organs, are politicians at least as much as they are editors. The editors of the London *Times* and *Le Temps*, semiofficial organs, have had careers that have brought them into close liaison with the men of state. The editors of the *New York Times*, a more independent paper, have had careers further removed from those of central government officials. In these respects the editors of each paper reflect the structure of the elite in their country. The road to an elite position in a totalitarian state is through politics and the party. In France or Britain the elite is not that highly governmentalized, but still there have been close family, social, and political ties between the elites of the state and of the economy. In the United States this is least so. The dominant economic elite has until recently tended to look with scorn upon "the bureaucrats" and have had little to do with them. Access to the American elite has been through channels of private enterprise.

That the careers of the editors parallel those for other elite positions can be seen if we look not only at their relationship to government but at other aspects of their social and economic background. Naturally enough, few of the non-Bolshevik editors were ever poor. The salaries that go with the job of editor in chief of a great newspaper were sufficient to assure that in their later lives they were at least moderately well off. But the lives of many of the editors reveal signs of wealth beyond this level (Table 7). This is a point on which the biographies are notoriously diffident. Figures

Table 7
Wealth

Country	Wealthy or Well-to-do					No Indica-tion More Than Salary	Inconclu-sive Signs of Wealth	No In-forma-tion	To-tal
	By Birth	By Mar-riage	Self-Made	Source Un-known	To-tal				
U.S.	0	0	1	0	1	2	1	0	4
Britain	1	*	0	1	2	3	1	0	6
France	3	1	1	1	6	1	0	0	7
Germany	2	*	0	0	2	2	0	1	5
Russia	2	0	1	0	3	6†	0	0	9
Total	8	1	3	2	14	14	2	1	31

*One by both birth and marriage.
†All *Izvestia* editors.

are never stated, and one must go by incidental signs such as ownership of estates, occupation of parents, etc. In eight of the non-Bolshevik biographies there is no indication of wealth beyond the man's salary. This, of course, does not prove that it did not exist, but there are none of the usual signs. In two more cases some signs exist, but they are too ambiguous to justify a conclusion that the man was wealthy. In fourteen cases there are definite indications of wealth. Only three of these seem to be self-made wealth. In all three cases the editor was part owner of the paper which he built up to the status of the great paper that it has become. In these cases the exertions of the editor redounded to his benefit as a capitalist, too. For the most part, however, the career of editor of a prestige paper is not one to make a man wealthy. In two cases we cannot tell where the wealth comes from. But the fact that a goodly proportion of the editors were men of means seems to be accounted for by the families from which they came. Eight of the editors seemed to come from wealthy families. Only two clearly came from families of average income, and these were sons of farmers.

Of the fourteen men who were apparently fairly rich or well-to-do, six were editors of *Le Temps*. Our content analysis of the prestige papers has revealed *Le Temps* to be the most conservative on economic questions and the most violently antisocialistic (excepting the *Völkischer Beobachter*). It is probably no accident that the editors of *Le Temps* are most class conscious and most plutocratic in background. Probably also, it is a reflection of the relatively low social mobility in French economic life that *Le Temps* has this oligarchic character. If we exclude *Le Temps,* there is little indication of much concentration of direct editorial control in the hands of men of wealth, whatever may be the means of indirect control.

On the other hand, there does seem to be a distinct class bias in the selection of editors of the London *Times*. It is not an oligarchic bias, nor is it a bias toward an aristocracy of title. It is rather a bias favoring an aristocracy defined by education and so well described as "the cousin-hood." Out of the last 73 years three Oxford men have presided over the *Times* for 60 years. (There was one Cambridge man and one from Trinity College, Dublin. One studied abroad.) Eton has given two of the six editors; two other "great" public schools, two others. These four among them have presided over the *Times* for 67 of the 73 years, and a fifth editor who attended a minor public school brings the total for public-school men to 71 of the 73 years. One's grandmother was a titled Lady, and another married the daughter of a titled Lord. Another was the cousin of a Lord. The last was one of five brothers, all of whom were in *Who's Who* and the father of whom was in the *Dictionary of National Biography*. Another of the editors, one of the three without titled connections, had an uncle and a father-in-law in the *Dictionary of National Biography*. Only one of the editors, the incumbent, seems to have no claim to entrance into the charmed circle, whether by birth, education, or marriage. This may be a mistaken conclusion due to the fact that the biographical materials on living Britishers are far more reticent than those on dead. (The *Times* gave the incumbent, Casey, six lines when he was appointed.) Casey's lack of signs of status may, on the other hand, be a fact reflecting the breakdown of British class lines. Casey has spent most of his early life outside England, having been born in South Africa and educated in Dublin. In any case, it should be noted that this appointment was regarded as a surprising one and a makeshift one. The new editor was 63 at the time of his appointment (1948) and both *Time* and *Newsweek* stated openly that Lord Astor was deferring a more permanent appointment until it became clearer what the political future of Britain was to be.

No data exist which would enable us to say easily and with accuracy what the chances of a British baby are to achieve some of the standard signs of membership in the upper class: an Eton and Oxford or equivalent education; family connections with the aristocracy or with the most respected segments of the middle class. Whatever the probability, it is clearly small. It is infinitesimal compared with the frequency of such signs among the London *Times* editors. Four of these editors each had more than one such sign of status and only one had none.

Only among the editors of the *New York Times* do we find little evidence of class rigidity. One was the son of a farmer, one was the son of a minister, and two others fail to mention their father's occupation. One was born in Hanover Center, N.H., one in Sand Lake, N.Y., one in Grand Ridge, Ill., and one in Sandusky, Ohio. While all of them went to college, one worked on a farm and in a printing plant in the course of his educational years, and another worked his way through college, at least in part. Only one followed the well-to-do pattern of college education. He went to Yale where he joined Zeta Psi and Wolf's Head. On the whole, these men seem to represent Main Street in their origins rather than Park Avenue, the street where some of them lived in their later life. While two of them do claim colonial ancestry, they nevertheless seem to show the relative class mobility in American life.

In each country, the social background of the editors reflects fairly faithfully the characteristics of the social structure.[*] Their lives are much like the lives of cabinet members from that country. In England we find the dominance of social class and education; in France, the dominance of politics, the law, and education; in America, the dominance of Main Street. In Germany we find sharply distinct patterns in Imperial Germany, Weimar, and the Third Reich, though the frequencies from each are too small for any general conclusion. We might, nevertheless, note that the imperial editor on whom we have data seems to have had bureaucratic training and a partially aristocratic background. The Weimar editor was a liberal intellectual from a business family. The Nazis were middle class with broken careers. One was a professional officer and the other a refugee *Auslandsdeutscher*. As in each of the countries, the editors seem to be a part of the elite and share its characteristics. The papers they edit may be considered elite papers not only because they are bought by the elite, and because they are under pressure from the state, but also because the men who create them move in elite circles in their own lives. They have those traits which make them socially acceptable as part of the elite and which tend to make them share elite attitudes.

In addition to the main points so far noted (the high intellectual attainments of the editors and their close ties with government and the elite), we may also note a few other points about the lives and careers of the editors. The position of editor of a prestige paper is only a moderately secure one. The nontotalitarian editors live to a fairly normal age, the mean age at death being 71.2 and the median 73. They generally die in bed.

The same is not true of the totalitarian editors. Two were executed, at least two purged, and one has disappeared. The two Nazis met hard ends. Rosenberg was one of the Nuremberg trial defendants and was hanged. Weiss has never been found; whether he is now dead or living somewhere

---

*No conclusions can be drawn about Russia. The three editors of *Novoe Vremia* all belong to a single family: father and two sons. They, therefore, provide no basis for statistical generalization. The father was the son of a peasant and started his career in the direst of poverty. His two sons, however, benefited from his self-made wealth. The biographies of the Bolshevik editors give us no information on such matters. The two who mention family backgrounds include one son of a teacher and one son of a clerk. Certainly none of the Bolsheviks became wealthy, and we do not know how most of them started.

under a false identity we cannot know. It seems clear, however, that these violent ends are a function of totalitarianism, not of the profession.

Of the *Izvestia* editors, only one ended his days an honored man. Stepanov Skvortsov died in office in 1928 and was buried in the Kremlin wall after nation-wide tributes. (The fact that he was a Stalinist intellectual who died conveniently at a time when Stalin was busy destroying the prestige of Trotsky, Zinoviev, Bukharin, etc., may have had something to do with this striking honor. Skvortsov was a member of the first Council of Peoples Commissars, had translated *Das Kapital* into Russian, and had belonged to the revolutionary movement since 1891.) The other editors all disappeared from the public eye in the middle 1930s, at the time of the great purge. Only three of the five, however, can be identified as having been purged. On the other two we have no information. Bukharin was the leading defendant in one of the great show trials and was hung. Gronsky and Steklow were deported to Siberia and have disappeared from view.

The pretotalitarian editors who have survived to see totalitarianism take over have generally gone into exile. This happened to two of the editors of *Novoe Vremia,* both of whom continued to publish abroad—one in Paris and one in Belgrade. The editor of the *Frankfurter Zeitung* also became a refugee. One former editor of the *Norddeutsche allgemeine Zeitung,* however, managed to continue a journalistic career under the Nazis.

In democratic eras the dangers of the profession are still considerable, although not fatal. The editor of a prestige paper is in the limelight and is inevitably responsible for the line of the paper. With political changes many editors have lost their jobs. The terminations of the careers of the editors of the prestige papers are indicated in Table 8.

The number of retirements is significantly small. The bulk of the editors either were separated from their jobs or died with their boots on. The age to which a few of them continued seems to indicate a fascination in the

Table 8
Termination of Career

Country	Died in Office Ages	No.	Separated from Job	Retired	Incumbents	Total
U.S.	73,81	2	0	1	1	4
Britain	57,57	2	3*	1*	1	6
France	80,DK,67	3	2	1	1	7
Germany	0	0	5	0	0	5
Russia	78,58	2	7	0	0	9
Total		9	17	3*	3	31

*One editor was removed then returned to the job after four years. Later he retired. He is, therefore, counted in both columns. Consequently, the rows do not add.

job and a driving energy which is found in few fields of endeavor. Those who were separated from their jobs generally lost them for reasons of changing policy.

The three discharges from the London *Times* all grew out of the changes of ownership from the Walter family to Lord Northcliffe and then to Lord Astor. Northcliffe tried to change the character of the paper somewhat and make it more of a mass paper. He let Buckle go four years after he took over and then let Dawson go when Dawson resisted the speed and extent of the changes he desired. When Astor took over, Wickham Steed was let go and Dawson brought back.

The two editors of *Le Temps* whose jobs were terminated were the coeditors under Vichy. Their jobs came to an end when *Le Temps* was closed up by the Vichy regime in November 1942. Both of these men retained their reputations through the vicissitudes of the times. One served in the Free French forces. Yet, they have apparently been effectively debarred from continuing their normal careers. They have both taken up book writing, a career that does not require them to find employment.

The turmoil of German life for the past half-century is illustrated by the fact that none of the German editors was able to continue to a normal termination of his editorship. The two editors of the *Norddeutsche allemeine Zeitung* were casualties of the collapse of the imperial regime. The editor of the *Frankfurter Zeitung* was a Jew and became a refugee from Hitler. The ends of the two Nazi editors we have already noted. Rosenberg, however, had already left the job of editor in chief in 1938 for higher political positions. His was the only case of a voluntary separation for promotion to a better job.

None of the Russian editors retired. One *Novoe Vremia* and one *Izvestia* editor died in office. The rest were removed. One *Novoe Vremia* editor lost his job by financial incompetence; one, by the Revolution. *Izvestia* editors were removed rather freely and were moved by the Party from paper to paper. For example, three *Izvestia* editors also at some time held the same position on *Pravda*. Even more striking is the job switch that occurred in 1930. M. A. Savelev had been editor of *Izvestia;* and G. I. Krumin, of *Economic Life*. In 1930 they traded jobs. Since the Party moved editors around that freely, the rate of removal is not a good index of insecurity. The fact that all of the editors ended up demoted to very minor roles, if not purged, does demonstrate real insecurity.

The later careers of the editors who lost their jobs is of some interest. We separate the Russians from the others because of the difference in turnover. Of the seven Russians on whom we have information, six became editors of other papers or magazines. One became an encyclopaedia editor and one got a government job supervising higher education. Only one held no later positions, since he went on trial at once.

Of the non-Russians, three became writers; two became cabinet ministers (Rosenberg and one of the last editors of the *Le Temps* who joined the Vichy cabinet). Two became editors of other papers or magazines. Two became professors, one of history and one of political science. One became a foundation executive. One became a refugee with independent means. The later careers of two, including Wilhelm Weiss, are clouded in obscurity. The later careers of the eight men on whom we have data include eleven types of jobs, since some did more than one thing.

Since job stability and career lines were so different in Russia from elsewhere, it would be well to keep separate the two sets of figures. Elsewhere the mean term of an editor in chief (not including the incumbents) was 14.7 years, and the median term 11 years. Most of the editors also served in subordinate positions on the papers which they later edited. They were associated during most of their working lives with that prestige paper. Some of them also were in such "upstairs" positions as chairman of the board or advisory editor. The mean length of association with the paper was 23.6 years; and the median length, 24 years (Table 9). Thus only about one-half the average editor's time with the prestige papers was in the top editorial job. Five of these men never worked for any other paper. Eight worked for one other, and only three for three or more others. This is a rather small number for such a proverbially itinerant profession as journalism (Table 10).

If we restrict our attention to only those other jobs which served as apprenticeship for the top editorial position, we find that the mean apprenticeship on the prestige paper itself was 7.7 years; and the median, 6.5 years. The mean apprenticeship on other newspapers or magazines was 3.7 years; and the median, 2 years (Table 11).

This is a surprisingly short journalistic apprenticeship. Its brevity is in part accounted for by a tendency to admit young men into the job of editor in chief and in part by a tendency to recruit from other professions.

Table 9
Length of Association with Prestige Paper

Country	Years	Previous Editors Mean	Previous Editors Number of Men	Incumbent Years
U.S.	47,17,17	27.0	3	19
Britain	25,32,26,27,22	26.4	5	37
France	53,26,11,11	25.3	4	5
Germany	15,2,28,24,18	17.4	5	
All Four Countries		23.6	17	
Median		24.0		

Table 10
Mean Number of Other Papers Worked On (Includes Magazines and Press Services)

U.S.	2.7
Britain	0.5
France	0.8*
Germany	2.0
Russia	4.3†

*Two men not included because of lack of data.
†For *Izvestia* editors the figure is 5.4—for *Novoe Vremia* editors it is only 1.0.

Table 11
Journalistic Apprenticeship

| Country | Mean Duration in Years | | | Number Having No Apprenticeship | |
	Apprenticeship on other Papers	Apprenticeship on Prestige Papers	Number of Men	On other Papers	On Prestige Papers
U.S.	9.0	8.3	4	0	0
Britain	2.2	19.0	6	4	0
France	3.0	1.2	5	2	4
Germany	2.0	3.8	5	3	3
All Four Countries	3.7	7.7	20	9	7
Median	2.0	6.5			

The mean age at appointment was 44.3; the median age, 44; and six editors in chief entered their jobs under 35.

In Russia the mean term as editor in chief was only 6.7 years instead of 14.7 years, and the median was 3 years instead of 11. Unlike the other editors, none of the *Izvestia* editors moved up to the top post from an apprenticeship on the same paper. Apprenticeship on other papers is hard to estimate because work on revolutionary papers is not a regular job.

Regular journalistic apprenticeship (mostly after 1917) ranged from 3 to 14 years for *Izvestia* editors, with the mean being about halfway between. This is about the same amount of apprenticeship found elsewhere, and *Izvestia* editors were but little older. Their mean age at appointment was 45.7 instead of 44.3, and their median age 46 instead of 44 (Table 12).

We have already mentioned from time to time some of the nonjournalistic jobs that the editors held. All but three of them had some profession other than journalism. By profession we here mean both more and less than a job. A job held for a short time we do not consider to be a

Table 12
Age at Appointment as Editor in Chief of Prestige Paper

Country	Number of Men	Ages	Mean
U.S.	4	34,66,64,45	50.2
Britain	6	51,29,37,48,49,63	46.2
France	5	33,65,38,46,43	45.0
Germany	5	38,29,34,28,46	35.0
Russia	7	42,52,44,55,45,36,46	45.7
All papers	27		44.7
Median			45.0

Table 13
Nonjournalistic Profession

Country	Law	Govt. Civil Service	Pro- fessors, Teachers	Social Work Foundations	Social Research
U.S.	0	1	1	1	0
Britain	4	1	2	1	0
France	4	1	0	0	2
Germany	0	1	1	0	0
Russia	0	1	2	0	0
Total	8	5	6	2	2

Country	Min- istry	Au- thor	Draft- ing	Poli- tics	None	Don't Know
U.S.	1	0	0	0	2	0
Britain	0	2	0	0	0	0
France	0	2	0	0	0	2
Germany	0	0	1	0	1	1
Russia	0	1	0	6*	0	2
Total	1	5	1	6	3	5

*All the Bolsheviks.

profession. On the other hand, being admitted to the bar we consider to constitute belonging to the profession of law even if the individual never practiced. Considering professions in this way we find among the editors eight lawyers, five civil servants, five professors, and a number of other professions. The prominence of the lawyer-journalist in France has often been noted. It is somewhat surprising to find it in Britain as often as we do.

The list of professions in Table 13 covers the editors' lifetimes. What we are now concerned with, however, is experience before entering journalism. Fields of study are summarized in Table 14. This table covers the twenty-six men who had a higher education, although on four of them we have not the relevant information. The remaining twenty-two studied many more than twenty-two subjects since many of them switched from one field to another. A typical sequence is classics at Oxford followed by reading for the bar at Lincoln's Inn.

Fourteen of the editors had worked at some other field before entering journalism. Among the *New York Times* editors, one had worked briefly on a farm and in a print shop; one had been a clergyman; and one had been a university president, social worker, and civil servant. Among the London *Times* editors, one had been a civil servant and one a playwright. Among the French editors, two had practiced law; one had been in the diplomatic service; and two had been engaged in social and economic research and propaganda. Among the German editors, one had been a parliamentary secretary; one, a teacher; and one, an army officer. One Russian editor had been a teacher and writer. All the Bolsheviks had been primarily professional revolutionists, whatever incidental jobs they may have held. (On five men we have no information about prejournalistic jobs.) Three of the French editors swung directly into the post of editor in chief from a successful career in another field. All the others, about whom we know, however, had to serve a journalistic apprenticeship.

Another type of experience which probably all of them had was foreign travel. We know of the travels of twenty. Regarding the eleven other men we have no information. This may indicate that some of these men travelled less than average, but in most cases the problem is simply lack of good sources. Seven of these men are French or German; it seems unlikely that any of them never crossed the borders of their countries. The four Russians may indeed never have been abroad. A number of the editors were very extensively travelled men. One had been a foreign correspondent for 17 years, and five others had been foreign correspondents for shorter periods. *Fourteen* (including four of the foreign correspondents), *had lived a significant portion of their lives abroad.* Three had been born abroad. In addition to those already described, two others can be called widely-travelled on the basis of many shorter trips taken.

Another qualification for the post of editor in chief was gregariousness. Though intellectuals, they were also activists and mixers. Most of the non-Russians belonged to many organizations. Just how many organizations they belonged to we cannot know since they are never all listed. Still, it is useful to note the number of organizations listed in the biographical sources. The eighteen men for whom we have this information list membership in 61 organizations. These are primarily clubs and learned or cultural societies. (See Table 15.)

Table 14
Field of Study

Country	Law	Social Science	History	Philo-sophy	Letters
U.S.	0	1	0	0	0
Britain	4	1	0	0	1
France	4	0	1	0	2
Germany	0	1	0	1	0
Russia	1	3	2	0	2
Total	9	6	3	1	5

Country	Divinity	Arts	Mathe-matics	Drafting	Don't Know
U.S.	1	0	0	0	1
Britain	0	0	1	0	0
France	0	0	0	0	2
Germany	0	1	0	1	1
Russia	0	0	0	0	0
Total	1	1	1	1	4

Table 15
Memberships

Country	Number of Men	Learned Societies Social Sciences	Learned Societies Humanities	Prof-essional	Clubs	College Fraternities
U.S.	4	0	4	0	9	3
Britain	6	0	3*	0	9*	1
France	4	5	1	1	1	0
Germany	4	1	0	5	0	0
Total	18	6	8	6	19	4

Country	Public Service, Trustees, etc.	Political	Charity	Religious	None	Total
U.S.	6	1	2	0	0	24
Britain	3	0	0	0	0	16
France	1	1	0	0	0	8
Germany	0	4	0	0	0	10
Total	10	6	2	0	0	61

*Four London *Times* editors belonged to the Athenaeum. This is listed here under Clubs. It could alternatively be put under Humanities.

The Russian biographies do not mention the nonpolitical organizations these men belonged to, with one exception. (Bukharin belonged to two learned societies.) Indeed, the Bolsheviks were so political that they may have belonged to no other organizations.

We have not listed in the above memberships affiliations with political parties. The six political groups referred to are such associations as The League for Proportional Representation. Party affiliation (we seldom know if it is membership) is known for nine of the non-Russian editors whose party affiliations are not stated. Perhaps one would be justified in surmising that they are always the same as those of the paper; while probably true, there would be no research gain in assuming that. The *Izvestia* editors were, of course, all Bolsheviks.

The job of editor in chief of a prestige newspaper is a powerful and honorific one, but it is not a conspicuous one. Probably not one New Yorker or one Londoner in a thousand could name the editor of the *New York Times* or London *Times*. We could go further and make the same guess of ignorance even for the readers of the paper, since the editor's name does not appear in the masthead. On the whole, the editors of the prestige papers have prided themselves on their anonymity. There have been, of course, exceptions such as Alfred Rosenberg, but most of them have shunned the limelight. Some have even avoided submitting biographical data to *Who's Who*'s and directories. Strange as it may seem, three of the editors appear in none of the standard biographical dictionaries, and others who have submitted data have skipped many of the honorific and important aspects of their lives.

Still, in elite circles where the channels of power influence are known, these men are recognized and honored. Most of these men have been the recipients of significant honors. One, Adrien Hebrard, the great editor of *Le Temps*, deliberately avoided honors as likely to compromise the objectivity or reputation for objectivity of the paper. For the same reason George Earle Buckle declined a baronetcy. But despite these exceptions, medals, orders, and honorary degrees have come in large numbers to the editors (Table 16). Again we cannot know how many such honors are unlisted, but thirteen men report 81 such honors.* This figure, however, is somewhat misleading since one man, John H. Finley, collected 45 of them. A better indication of the frequency of reported honors is the median number of four. In view of the anonymity which these men cultivated, four honorary degrees or orders of knighthood is a significant token of respect.

---

*The Bolsheviks gave no honors in the early days and our data stops with 1937. We therefore omit the Russians here. It should be recalled, however, that one editor was buried in the Kremlin wall.

Table 16
Honors Received

| Country | Number of Men | | Number of Honors |
	None	Some	
U.S.	0	4	55
Britain	0	4	14
France	1	3	7
Germany	0	2	5
Total	1	13	81

Conclusions: The above results seem abundantly to confirm the belief that the prestige paper has become an institution of considerable importance in the social structure of Western powers. We started with a number of hypotheses about the careers and backgrounds of editors who might be effective spokesmen for and to an elite audience. All these hypotheses have been confirmed in our sample.

The editors do derive from the same social circles as the elite. In countries with established aristocracies they are often related to them by birth or marriage. In most countries the editors have come from families of wealth. However, where revolutions have brought in plebeian elites, the editors have also been plebeian.

The editors have partaken of the education and other early attitude-forming experiences of the elite. In most cases they are extraordinarily well educated men, having gone far in the most prestigeful of established educational institutions. There are, however, exceptions in those countries where the elite is by origin a plebeian revolutionary one. For instance, the characteristic early experience of the Soviet editors, as of the Soviet elite, was arrest and exile.

The editors do parallel in their careers the careers of elite members in their country. There are some striking parallelisms between the typical careers of the editors and the careers found in the comparative cabinet studies of the RADIR Project to be typical for cabinet members. The editors in Soviet Russia, like the Politburo members, are, above all, Bolshevik politicians. In Nazi Germany they are marginal men of broken careers. In France they are apt to be lawyer-journalists with experience in elective office. In Britain they are often members of the "cousinhood" from Eton and Oxford.

The editors do maintain close connections with the government. The papers fall into three groups: official, semiofficial, and independent. The editors of all had extensive careers in politics or public office, but the extent of their political involvement was a function of the relationship of the paper to the state. The editors of the official papers were politicians first and journalists second, while at the other extreme, the editors of the semi-independent *New York Times* were least involved in public jobs. The editors of the *New York Times,* alone among the prestige papers, seem to be primarily journalistic technicians. They are newspapermen who have made good as newspapermen, and their social background matters little. They are in their field the counterpart of the independent private businessman who stands or falls by his occupational skill and who has little use for or connection with organs of power; such a man is the ideal model for the American elite.

The editors do acquire considerable prestige and many honors. In all respects, then, the editors conform to those patterns of life which we would predict for the heads of one of the key institutions in the social structure. They fit into the type of pattern we would predict for the heads of national churches or the heads of governments. They provide evidence in their careers for our assumption that the prestige paper has become the same kind of central social institution. The social structure of such institutions tends to reflect, each in its own way, the social structure of the society as a whole. For example, if the prestige paper is indeed a central institution, then the dependence or independence of the paper on the state is apt to be a function of the degree of organic connection of the economic with the political elite in the society as a whole. Thus, when we find the elite of a microcosm so closely corresponding to what we would expect from our knowledge of the elite of the macrocosm, we are justified in treating the prestige paper as the same type of central institution as the dominant church, the army, or the school system.

Addendum to Appendix C

While this study was in press an item appeared in the *New York Times* which, together with a couple of other pieces of information, enables us to partly fill the gap in the list of *Izvestia* editors. The *Times* reported on October 12, 1951 that L. F. Ilichev, "former editor in chief of *Izvestia*" had become editor of *Pravda.*

No formal announcement has been made of the change but Mr. Ilichev's name recently appeared in a list of Soviet notables that gave his title as "chief editor" of the newspaper *Pravda. . . .*

Little is known about Mr. Ilichev. He was appointed editor in chief of *Izvestia* in 1944, but has not occupied that post recently. An individual named Gubin was indicated as *Izvestia's* editor some months ago.

We may surmise that Gubin is K. A. Gubin, who in 1948 and 1949 was listed as editor of *Moskovski Bolshevik,* organ of the Moscow Soviet and Moscow Committee of the Communist Party. Ilichev replaced L. K. Roginsky on December 2, 1944. When Roginsky took office is not known.

The few facts which we have on these three additional editors in no case contradict, in fact in each case confirm, conclusions drawn above. We noted that the Soviet editors, unlike the others, were treated as a part of a general press corps and were moved around by the Party from paper to paper. Seven out of nine had been removed from their jobs. The figure is now nine out of twelve.

These removals were not always demotions. Ilichev's promotion to *Pravda* makes him the fourth man to have been chief editor of both of these papers.

We noted above that the mean term of *Izvestia* editors in chief was less than half as long as that of the editors of the other prestige papers, specifically 6.7 years. Ilichev's term was seven years. Roginsky's, if he served the full time between Bukharin and Ilichev, would have been the same, but it is probable that it was actually somewhat shorter.

We noted that the *Izvestia* editors were in general professional journalists, although they were professional politicians first. All we know about the journalistic backgrounds of these three men is that, as noted, Gubin had been editor of another paper first, and Ilichev is described in *World Biography* (New York, 1948) by the phrase "Engaged in journalistic work many years." (No further information is given about him.) These two seem to fit the category of professional journalist. On the political side Ilichev seems to fit, too. To quote the *Times* again:

In recent postwar years, Mr. Ilichev has been on the editorial board of *Bolshevik,* the theoretical organ of the Soviet Communist party, and his name has been second on the list of editors. His name has been printed there directly following the editor's and even preceding that of P. N. Pospelov, one of the top Soviet theoreticians.

Needless to say these *Izvestia* editors more than fit the pattern of anonymity noted above for the editors in general. Indeed their passion for anonymity makes the staid editors of the *Times* of London seem like exhibitionists. The meagre information available and our dependence on such indicators as rank order in lists of names testifies to that. Here, however, we are not dealing merely with the reticence of individuals, but with the Soviet security phobia and pattern of secrecy about all types of information.

APPENDIX D
DEMOCRACY-RELEVANT SYMBOLS

Freedom
Liberty
Free elections
Right to vote
Suffrage Franchise
Civil rights
Freedom of speech
Freedom of press
Freedom of assembly
Freedom of religion
Bill of Rights
Freedom of movement
Freedom of choice of occupation
    (right to work)
Totalitarian
Authoritarian
Military state
Police state
Tyranny
Tyranny of majority
Syndicalism
Labor unions
Agrarianism
Masses
Labor
Working class
Proletariat
People
Constitutionalism
Parliamentarism

Popular sovereignty
Majority rule
Dictatorship
Absolute monarchy
Caesarisme
Censorship
Government use of force
Centralization
Leader
Leadership
Etatisme
Corporation state
Feudalism
Trusts
Usurer
Plutocracy
Authority
Clericalism
Discipline
Fascism
Nazism
Aryan
Blood
States rights
Self-Determination
Equality
Individualism
Anticlericalism
Classless society

APPENDIX E
INTERNATIONAL POLITICAL SYMBOLS

Allies
Arbitration
Armaments
Atomic Energy
Axis
Balance of Power
Blockade
Casus Belli
Central Powers
Chauvinism
Colonization
Conciliation
Crisis External
Disarmament
Drang nach Osten
Eastern Question
Entente
Fatherland
Free Trade
Imperialism
International Court
I.L.O.
Internationalism
Intervention
Irredentism
Isolationism
Jingoism
Kontinental-Europa

League of Nations
Little Entente
Mandates
Mediation
Militarism
Military Occupation
Mittel Europa
Monroe Doctrine
Nationalism
Neutrals
Non-Intervention
Pan-Americanism
Pan-Germanism
Pan-Slavism
Patriotism
Pax-Britanica
Pacifism
Peace
Rapprochement
Sanctions
Self-determination
Tariffs
Triple Alliance
United Nations
United States of Europe
Versailles Treaty
Washington Conference
War

APPENDIX F
SYMBOLS OF INTERNATIONAL POLITICS

1. Percentage of Editorials in Which a Symbol Appeared

	Pre-World War I	World War I	1920s	Early 1930s	Late 1930s	World War II Phase 1	World War II Phase 2	Post-World War II	All Periods
France	69	150	175	152	208	225	139	156	137
Germany	32	66	185	136	57	105	65	- - -	108
Great Britain	53	140	89	77	111	149	130	93	86
United States	23	87	75	47	45	102	107	87	63
Russia	80	198	184	102	128	200	251	198	131

2. As Percentage of All General Symbols.

	Pre-World War I	World War I	1920s	Early 1930s	Late 1930s	World War II Phase 1	World War II Phase 2	Post-World War II	All Periods
France	22	45	34	28	28	35	39	32	31
Germany	18	54	39	28	18	34	19	- -	31
Great Britain	27	64	44	41	44	49	50	36	40
United States	24	49	41	35	33	49	53	41	40
Russia	35	47	23	14	14	21	29	21	26

APPENDIX G
PERCENTAGE OF ALL GEOGRAPHIC SYMBOLS OTHER THAN SELF-REFERENCES

Sample	France	Germany	Great Britain	Italy	Spain	Scandin-avia	W. Europe Total	Russia	Balkans	Baltic States
France										
2 1900-1913	---	11.3	10.7	5.0	2.3	1.6	35.7	6.8	8.3	---
3 1914-1918	---	17.9	8.6	4.8	0.8	2.6	43.3	6.6	15.1	0.4
4 1919-1929	---	15.8	13.4	7.3	1.0	1.2	43.9	6.8	5.1	1.2
5 1930-1935	---	15.1	13.3	4.0	1.2	1.0	44.7	3.9	3.4	0.6
6 1936-1938	---	10.0	11.2	9.8	5.5	1.2	47.2	4.5	5.5	0.5
7 1939-1940	---	10.3	9.1	4.6	1.2	9.1	39.2	7.3	6.1	4.3
8 1941-1942	---	9.7	9.0	5.2	0.7	2.1	28.8	4.9	8.0	0.1
9 1945-1949	---	7.6	10.8	2.7	0.5	.9	36.4	9.6	7.3	0.1
All periods	---	13.4	11.2	5.5	1.9	1.8	40.8	6.5	7.7	0.6
Germany										
2 1910-1913	---	---	6.7	---	---	0.7	33.3	13.3	---	---
3 1914-1918	15.0	---	20.7	4.1	1.0	3.8	50.6	10.5	4.8	0.6
4 1919-1929	18.1	---	13.2	6.7	1.6	0.5	47.4	7.0	4.7	2.6
5 1930-1932	17.8	---	11.1	8.9	2.2	2.2	45.2	7.4	3.0	0.7
6 1933-1938	20.2	---	13.0	8.2	2.7	1.4	49.0	12.3	3.1	1.0
7 1939-1941	11.4	---	16.8	6.3	1.8	3.9	47.7	7.8	5.7	---
8 1942-1945	7.6	---	18.1	6.0	2.0	2.0	39.0	11.2	4.4	---
All periods	15.3	---	15.4	6.5	1.8	2.1	46.9	9.1	4.5	1.1

GEOGRAPHIC SYMBOLS (Cont.)

Sample	France	Germany	Great Britain	Italy	Spain	Scandin-avia	W. Europe Total	Russia	Balkans	Baltic States
Great Britain										
2 1890-1913	8.4	7.3	---	2.3	1.2	1.1	28.0	5.2	4.6	---
3 1914-1918	11.4	15.2	---	3.9	0.6	1.5	41.6	7.4	8.5	0.4
4 1919-1929	10.8	7.5	---	4.0	1.1	1.5	30.7	4.7	3.6	1.2
5 1930-1935	11.2	15.1	---	5.0	1.7	2.2	29.8	2.6	2.4	0.6
6 1936-1938	10.8	9.1	---	5.9	6.3	3.6	41.2	3.4	1.5	---
7 1939-1940	10.5	12.6	---	5.1	3.5	4.6	40.0	2.2	4.2	0.8
8 1941-1945	6.6	11.4	---	4.5	0.6	2.1	28.4	6.0	5.2	0.4
9 1946-1949	5.9	7.3	---	2.0	0.4	1.3	24.0	6.3	3.7	---
All periods	8.8	9.0	---	3.5	1.4	1.7	30.7	5.0	4.5	0.4
United States										
2 1900-1913	8.7	8.5	18.0	2.5	2.0	2.0	44.7	7.0	1.7	0.2
3 1914-1918	8.8	14.5	11.1	2.5	0.6	2.5	44.1	4.9	6.1	0.1
4 1919-1929	11.4	8.3	16.9	3.9	1.1	1.5	46.8	5.4	3.8	1.0
5 1930-1932	9.6	9.6	19.5	3.1	1.1	2.8	49.4	4.4	1.8	---
6 1933-1938	7.7	11.0	17.5	5.7	4.4	1.7	50.5	4.7	2.5	0.2
7 1939-1941	6.4	12.3	19.1	4.0	0.8	5.4	51.6	5.0	4.2	1.7
8 1942-1945	5.5	10.9	22.7	3.6	0.6	1.8	47.7	6.4	2.8	0.5
9 1946-1949	4.3	6.9	17.4	2.6	0.7	1.2	41.3	10.7	6.8	0.5
All periods	8.2	10.0	17.7	3.4	1.3	2.2	46.6	6.2	3.7	0.6
Russia										
1 1892-1904	10.9	10.1	10.2	3.9	1.0	1.4	40.4	---	7.2	1.4
2 1905-1913	5.8	7.2	7.2	3.5	0.8	1.4	27.4	---	19.1	1.0
3 1914-1917	6.8	15.7	6.6	2.5	0.1	4.5	41.6	---	13.3	2.5
4 1918-1928	11.6	8.6	10.9	3.5	0.3	2.8	39.3	---	3.9	6.7

Russia (cont.)

Sample	Austria-Hungary	Other E. Eur.	"Europe"	Europe Total	Near and Mid. East	Africa	China	Japan	Other Far East	Miscellaneous
5 1929-1935	13.0	12.3	12.6	42.9	2.7	0.8	1.1	---	1.1	4.2
6 1936-1938	5.1	11.2	10.2	42.9	0.8	7.1	---	---	1.0	---
7 1939-1940	3.4	8.5	6.8	30.5	1.7	1.7	8.5	---	8.5	10.2
8 1941-1945	3.3	26.3	5.2	46.3	2.2	---	5.2	---	5.2	8.9
9 1946-1949	4.7	23.3	5.8	36.0	1.2	---	1.2	---	4.7	4.7
All periods	9.0	10.8	9.1	37.9	3.5	0.7	2.3	---	9.1	3.2

GEOGRAPHIC SYMBOLS (Cont.)

Sample	Austria-Hungary	Other E. Eur.	"Europe"	Europe Total	Near and Mid. East	Africa	China	Japan	Other Far East	Miscellaneous
France										
2 1900-1913	5.4	0.9	6.3	63.4	5.5	10.1	2.0	2.3	7.1	0.1
3 1914-1918	9.3	4.2	3.2	82.1	4.6	2.5	0.3	0.5	2.3	0.1
4 1919-1929	2.4	5.3	7.8	72.4	4.2	5.0	0.8	1.4	3.9	0.0
5 1930-1935	4.3	4.3	12.0	73.3	0.5	6.2	1.0	1.4	4.1	0.0
6 1936-1938	4.1	7.8	8.3	77.9	1.4	6.4	2.1	2.8	2.9	0.0
7 1939-1940	4.0	11.1	11.2	83.3	2.0	1.5	0.9	0.9	2.2	0.0
8 1941-1942	1.0	0.7	5.9	49.4	5.2	4.9	1.7	6.3	9.7	0.0
9 1943-1949	1.6	4.1	3.9	63.0	14.8	3.5	1.5	1.8	6.6	0.0
All periods	4.6	4.2	6.8	71.1	3.9	5.7	1.2	1.7	4.7	0.0

GEOGRAPHIC SYMBOLS (Cont.)

Sample	Austria-Hungary	Other E. Eur.	"Europe"	Europe Total	Near and Mid. East	Africa	China	Japan	Other Far East	Miscellaneous
Germany										
2 1910-1913	6.7	26.7	0.0	80.0	0.0	6.7	---	---	---	0.0
3 1914-1918	4.8	3.5	1.6	76.4	2.5	6.7	0.6	1.6	2.6	0.0
4 1919-1929	4.4	8.2	7.4	81.7	2.6	1.5	1.6	1.0	2.0	0.0
5 1930-1932	4.4	2.2	8.1	71.1	0.7	3.7	2.2	2.2	3.0	0.0
6 1933-1938	5.1	8.2	5.1	83.9	0.7	2.7	1.7	2.7	4.6	0.0
7 1939-1941	2.7	12.0	5.1	91.1	2.7	2.7	0.3	2.4	4.2	0.0
8 1942-1945	1.6	6.5	5.6	68.3	2.4	3.2	0.8	4.4	3.2	0.8
All periods	3.9	7.6	5.5	78.7	2.3	3.1	1.2	2.1	3.0	0.1
Great Britain										
2 1890-1913	3.5	1.0	5.4	47.6	4.0	10.8	2.6	2.2	13.1	0.2
3 1914-1918	6.1	3.0	3.4	70.5	5.8	3.2	0.5	1.0	5.8	0.1
4 1919-1929	2.0	3.5	7.3	53.0	5.4	6.2	3.1	2.0	10.2	0.0
5 1930-1935	2.5	2.6	7.3	47.9	3.0	8.0	2.4	2.2	12.5	0.0
6 1936-1938	2.7	3.6	7.8	60.2	5.1	3.6	2.1	2.8	6.7	0.4
7 1939-1940	0.8	6.2	6.6	60.9	3.5	7.5	1.0	1.3	8.9	0.5
8 1941-1945	1.5	3.6	5.4	50.4	3.4	10.0	1.5	3.9	12.6	0.2
9 1946-1949	1.8	3.8	7.1	46.8	9.5	5.8	2.2	1.5	13.9	0.2
All periods	2.8	2.7	6.0	52.0	4.7	8.2	2.2	2.2	11.4	0.2

United States

2 1900-1913	2.0	0.8	4.6	61.0	2.3	4.1	4.0	6.5	7.5	0.4
3 1914-1918	4.1	2.0	4.2	65.6	2.4	1.8	0.6	14.6	3.3	0.0
4 1919-1929	2.3	4.3	9.0	72.5	4.1	2.3	3.5	3.7	5.2	0.6
5 1930-1932	1.1	2.2	7.7	66.7	2.8	1.5	4.2	2.2	7.2	2.0
6 1933-1938	2.5	2.2	8.7	71.2	2.3	2.7	3.5	3.3	5.5	0.5
7 1939-1941	1.0	4.8	7.0	75.3	2.0	4.1	2.6	3.1	5.9	1.4
8 1942-1945	1.1	3.4	5.5	67.3	2.0	4.9	3.6	7.0	11.4	0.1
9 1946-1949	2.1	3.2	5.0	69.5	5.7	1.2	3.6	3.3	11.0	0.3
All periods	2.1	3.0	6.5	68.7	3.1	3.0	3.1	5.7	7.1	0.5

Russia

1 1892-1904	8.2	2.3	6.3	65.8	4.3	4.3	4.0	2.6	11.6	0.0
2 1905-1913	10.3	3.3	7.7	68.8	9.1	3.0	2.0	3.9	8.2	0.0
3 1914-1917	11.7	3.9	6.8	79.8	4.5	2.3	0.8	1.8	3.9	0.0
4 1918-1928	3.0	10.2	5.6	68.8	3.9	1.9	2.6	4.3	7.7	0.0
5 1929-1935	1.9	6.5	8.8	65.4	0.0	0.7	4.2	5.4	7.6	0.0
6 1936-1938	3.1	1.0	5.1	53.1	5.1	8.2	0.9	10.2	15.4	0.0
7 1939-1940	1.7	10.2	13.6	74.7	5.1	3.4	3.4	1.7	5.1	0.0
8 1941-1945	3.0	9.3	8.5	81.1	0.4	1.1	0.4	1.1	7.0	0.0
9 1946-1949	5.8	7.0	10.5	68.6	0.0	1.2	1.2	4.7	5.7	0.0
All periods	7.2	5.2	6.8	69.3	4.8	3.0	2.8	3.2	9.0	0.0

GEOGRAPHIC SYMBOLS (Concl.)

Sample	Empires as Wholes British	French	United States	Latin America	Other W. Hemis.	W. Hemis. Total	GRAND TOTAL	No. of editorials in which a symbol appears
France								
2 1900-1913	0.8	0.7	4.9	2.5	0.6	8.0	100.0	1,917
3 1914-1918	0.4	0.1	5.1	1.4	0.6	7.1	100.0	1,455
4 1919-1929	0.9	0.5	7.2	1.3	2.4	10.9	100.0	2,043
5 1930-1935	1.4	1.2	7.3	1.5	2.1	10.9	100.0	961
6 1936-1938	1.0	0.5	2.3	0.5	2.2	5.0	100.0	580
7 1939-1940	0.3	1.2	4.0	1.5	2.1	7.6	100.0	329
8 1941-1942	0.3	3.8	8.0	9.0	1.7	18.7	100.0	288
9 1945-1949	0.6	0.2	12.1	2.4	3.5	18.0	100.0	881
All periods	0.8	0.7	6.4	1.9	1.8	10.1	100.0	8,454
Germany								
2 1910-1913	—	—	6.7	0.7	5.9	13.3	100.0	15
3 1914-1918	—	—	4.8	3.8	1.0	9.6	100.0	314
4 1919-1929	—	—	7.7	1.6	0.3	9.6	100.0	612
5 1930-1932	2.3	—	11.9	3.0	0.0	14.8	100.0	135
6 1933-1938	—	—	1.4	1.0	0.3	2.7	100.0	292
7 1939-1941	0.9	—	2.1	2.4	1.2	5.7	100.0	333
8 1942-1945	—	—	15.3	1.2	0.4	16.9	100.0	249
All periods	0.3	—	6.6	2.1	0.5	9.2	100.0	1,950
Great Britain								
2 1890-1913	6.5	0.2	7.2	2.0	3.6	12.8	100.0	4,274
3 1914-1918	3.4	—	6.6	0.6	2.5	9.7	100.0	986

Great Britain (cont.)								
4 1919-1929	6.7	--	9.1	1.9	2.4	13.4	100.0	1,894
5 1930-1935	7.0	0.2	9.3	4.1	3.4	16.8	100.0	996
6 1936-1938	4.7	--	9.9	2.5	2.0	14.4	100.0	527
7 1939-1940	5.1	0.2	5.7	2.2	3.2	11.1	100.0	593
8 1941-1945	3.6	0.3	10.0	1.3	2.8	14.1	100.0	1,580
9 1946-1949	4.6	0.1	11.2	1.5	2.7	15.4	100.0	891
All periods	5.6	0.2	8.4	2.0	2.9	13.3	100.0	11,741
United States								
2 1900-1913	0.5	--	--	8.1	5.6	13.7	100.0	1,869
3 1914-1918	0.1	0.1	--	8.7	2.8	11.5	100.0	1,355
4 1919-1929	0.9	--	--	4.8	2.4	7.2	100.0	2,840
5 1930-1932	2.4	--	--	6.4	4.6	11.0	100.0	544
6 1933-1938	1.0	--	--	5.7	4.3	10.0	100.0	888
7 1939-1941	1.1	--	--	2.7	1.8	4.5	100.0	1,158
8 1942-1945	0.4	0.1	--	1.3	1.9	3.2	100.0	1,633
9 1946-1949	0.7	0.1	--	2.8	1.8	4.6	100.0	1,219
All periods	0.8	0.0	--	5.0	3.0	8.0	100.0	11,506
Russia								
1 1892-1904	0.2	--	3.4	1.6	2.2	7.2	100.0	1,969
2 1905-1913	--	--	3.1	0.9	1.0	5.0	100.0	1,269
3 1914-1917	--	--	3.5	0.9	2.5	6.9	100.0	709
4 1918-1928	0.6	0.1	6.5	0.6	1.6	8.7	100.0	1,444
5 1929-1935	1.1	--	13.0	0.4	2.3	15.7	100.0	261
6 1936-1938	1.0	--	6.1	--	0.0	6.1	100.0	98
7 1939-1940	--	--	6.8	--	0.0	6.8	100.0	58
8 1941-1945	--	--	5.9	--	3.0	8.9	100.0	270
9 1946-1949	--	--	11.6	--	7.0	18.6	100.0	87
All periods	0.3	0.0	4.8	0.9	1.9	7.6	100.0	6,165

INDEX